Marty Appel

CASEY STENGEL

Marty Appel was the youngest public relations director in baseball history when George Steinbrenner elevated him to the New York Yankees post in 1973. He worked for the team for ten seasons, beginning in 1968, and followed it by producing its games on WPIX television. He is the author of twenty-three books, including the *New York Times* bestsellers *Munson: The Life and Death of a Yankee Captain* and *Pinstripe Empire: The New York Yankees from Before the Babe to After the Boss*. He resides in New York City with his wife, Lourdes, and has two grown children, Brian and Deborah.

www.appelpr.com

Also by Marty Appel

Pinstripe Pride: The Inside Story of the New York Yankees (for young readers)

Pinstripe Empire: The New York Yankees from Before the Babe to After the Boss

162-0: The Greatest Wins in Yankee History

Munson: The Life and Death of a Yankee Captain

Now Pitching for the Yankees

Slide, Kelly, Slide

When You're from Brooklyn, Everything Else Is Tokyo (with Larry King)

Great Moments in Baseball (with Tom Seaver)

Yogi Berra

Working the Plate (with Eric Gregg)

Joe DiMaggio

My Nine Innings (with Lee MacPhail)

Yesterday's Heroes

The First Book of Baseball

Tom Seaver's All-Time Baseball Greats (with Tom Seaver)

Batting Secrets of the Major Leaguers

Thurman Munson: An Autobiography (with Thurman Munson)

Baseball's Best: The Hall of Fame Gallery (with Burt Goldblatt)

CASEY STENGEL

BASEBALL'S GREATEST CHARACTER

Marty Appel

ANCHOR SPORTS
ANCHOR BOOKS
A Division of Penguin Random House LLC
New York

My brother, Norman Appel, a brilliant chemist, passed away during this project. I liked to tell people that I knew baseball trivia, and he knew everything else. In his honor, I dedicate this book to his three sons, my nephews, Scott, Andrew, and Brad.

FIRST ANCHOR SPORTS EDITION, MARCH 2018

Grateful acknowledgment is made to Robert Lipsyte for permission to reprint an excerpt from *SportWorld: An American Dreamland* (New York: Quadrangle, 1975); and *Sporting News* for permission to reprint excerpts from issues published on March 8, 1934; August 8, 1956; December 4, 1957; and October 1, 1958. All rights reserved.

The Library of Congress has cataloged the Doubleday edition as follows:
Names: Appel, Marty, author.
Title: Casey Stengel : the greatest character in baseball / Marty Appel.
Description: First edition. | New York : Doubleday, [2017]
Identifiers: LCCN 2016027618 (print) | LCCN 2016028538 (ebook)
Subjects: LCSH: Stengel, Casey. | Baseball managers—United States—Biography.
Classification: LCC GV865.S8 A66 2017 (print) | LCC GV865.S8 (ebook) |
DDC 796.357092 [B]—dc23
LC record available at https://lccn.loc.gov/2016027618

Anchor Books Trade Paperback ISBN: 978-1-101-91174-7
eBook ISBN: 978-0-385-54048-3

Author photograph by Ryan McMahon Photography
Book design by Michael Collica

www.anchorbooks.com

CONTENTS

viii Contents

CASEY STENGEL

INTRODUCTION

I F CASEY STENGEL HAD called it a career in 1948, after winning the Pacific Coast League championship with Oakland, he would have ridden off into the sunset with his beloved wife, Edna, proudly concluding a thirty-nine-year run in pro baseball.

And at fifty-seven (or fifty-eight) years old (his age was still in dispute at that time), he would have faded into that sunset and into baseball oblivion. At that point, despite the minor-league pennant, he was just a .284 career platoon outfielder who had played with five National League clubs over fourteen seasons, then served as a mediocre National League manager who was regularly in the second division. And let's face it, who remembers the managers of minor-league champions?

We fast-forward to 1965, when he retired, and he is a legend, bound for the Hall of Fame. And after he won ten pennants with the New York Yankees and then put the New York Mets on the map as their first manager, we see how patience, knowledge, and success can come together to rewrite the ledger.

Nobody ever did it quite like him. By the forceful combination of an unmatched baseball mind and an over-the-top personality, he ground it out for four decades before "suddenly" being recognized not only as a genius on the field, but as an American folk hero.

Casey Stengel had the genius to cultivate his friendships and associations, always looking out for "the next job" whenever he needed one. (And to get rich in the oil business while he was at it.) At last, his perseverance led him to the Yankees' managerial position, and five consecutive world championships. This feat is unmatched to this day. It may never be matched.

When the MLB Network's *Prime 9* named him "Baseball's Greatest

Character" in 2009, there were certainly a few generations of younger fans who were unfamiliar with him. But many more remembered him as a New York manager, and more yet—albeit in smaller numbers—still remembered his long and winding road to get there. Still, good for MLB Network, because the citation was spot-on. And it awoke a lot of younger fans who were interested in just what made this character such a character. He even out-Yogi'd his own protégé Yogi Berra to win top honors. (Yogi finished second).

My friend the late Robert Creamer wrote a landmark book about Casey more than three decades ago, and I was fortunate this time around to have an unpublished memoir by Edna available to me, as well as access to many digitized newspapers for online research that did not exist when Bob did his research. Newspapers in Casey's small minor-league towns were now available, offering newly discovered material. There was, in short, enough content to justify a new biography for this fascinating man.

I hope you enjoy the "splendid" life of Casey Stengel, to borrow one of his favorite words.

PART ONE

1

MAIL CALL

IT WAS TIME FOR the mail at the Stengel home.

Casey Stengel, now nearly eighty, loved this time of day. He would get up to three hundred letters every week, and since his home address—and phone number, of course—were listed in the phone book under "Stengel, Charles Casey," it was not hard to know where to send a fan letter: 1663 Grandview Avenue, in Glendale, California. He and his wife, Edna, had lived there since her father built the place forty-six years before, in 1924. People wanted his autograph, and he loved that they did.

Now, in 1970, in his retirement years, the home was a "splendid" place to be Casey Stengel. Old friends would visit, or new ones would just ring the bell, and he would regale them with stories, jumping with ease from Babe to Joe D to Yogi to Mickey to Marvelous Marv.

In his den, he would sit back in his ancient Yankee underwear (Edna was always on him to wear Mets underwear) and observe the world through six decades of baseball and worldly wisdom.

The home sat on a quiet two-lane street in a fashionable neighborhood, near the homes of the USC baseball coach Rod Dedeaux and Babe Herman, his fellow Brooklyn Dodger alum. Most people thought of Casey as either a Yankee or a Met, but of course he was a baseball lifer, who had played or managed almost everywhere and played with or against nearly everyone.

He batted against Grover Cleveland Alexander, chased fly balls hit by Babe Ruth, sent Ron Swoboda up to pinch hit, and moved Cleon Jones to left field. His career had spanned John McGraw and Tug McGraw.

Was there a ballpark he hadn't stood in? Never mind all those major-league and minor-league parks over more than half a century. For over fifty years, starting in 1910, the year of his first spring training, he had to check train schedules, road maps, and eventually flight schedules to get to his next training camp.

In 1910 and 1911, he traveled to Excelsior Springs, Missouri; then he went to Montgomery, Alabama (1912), Augusta, Georgia (1913–14), Daytona Beach, Florida (1915–16), Hot Springs, Arkansas (1917), Jacksonville, Florida (1918), Birmingham, Alabama (1920), Gainesville, Florida (1921), San Antonio, Texas (1922–23), Marlin, Texas (1923), St. Petersburg, Florida (1924–25), Jackson, Tennessee (1926–27), Biloxi, Mississippi (1928–29), Anniston, Alabama (1930), Miami, Florida (1931), Clearwater, Florida (1932), Miami (1933), Orlando, Florida (1934–35), Clearwater (1936), Bradenton, Florida (1938–40), San Antonio, Texas (1941), Sanford, Florida (1942), Wallingford, Connecticut (1943), Bartlesville, Oklahoma (1945), Boyes Hot Springs, California (1946–47), San Fernando, California, 1948), St. Petersburg (1949–50), Phoenix, Arizona (1951), and St. Petersburg (1952–60, 1962–65, and 1966–74 as a consultant).

And, of course, that excludes the road games and barnstorming games heading north that were part of spring training. One could learn a lot about people and a lot about America just by being Casey Stengel.

And his recall! Late in his life, some fan might come near the railing and say, "Casey! Casey! My dad sold you a pair of shoes in Biloxi in 1928!" Casey might rub his jaw and say, "I was almost out the door and he sold me a pair of socks, too. He was a good salesman!"

His home was not quite a mansion, nothing you would find in Bel Air, but it was grand in the upper-middle-class neighborhood in which it stood. Or "splendid," as he loved to say about almost anything that got his approval. Its forty-six hundred square feet (a bedroom and den were added in 1937 and 1956, respectively) sat on a lot that went back from the quiet street the length of a football field, with a swimming pool, a pool house, a tennis court, and an orchard. It was a two-story Spanish-architecture stucco dwelling, described in real-estate terms as "Spanish eclectic with a hipped roof." There were fourteen rooms, including five bedrooms, one living room with a barrel ceiling, two sitting rooms, maid's quarters, and five bathrooms, on one and a quarter acres.

"Eclectic." That was a good word for a Casey Stengel residence. Edna had styled a room or two into Japanese traditional after making tours of the Far East. It was an odd fit with the Spanish architecture, but it worked.

Casey sat at a big desk in his den, surrounded by trophies and souvenirs, including the school bell from Central High School in Kansas City. He had always been a walking advertisement for Kansas City—his nickname came from "K.C."

"To Charles (Casey-Dutch) Stengel, dentist, athlete, manager, raconteur," said the inscription on the bell. "For whom the bell tolled at Central High School, 1906–1910, from your many Kansas City friends."

There were autographed baseballs on shelves surrounding the room. Sometimes, if Edna was scolding him about something from another room, Casey might look up with those blue eyes and wink at his young assistant, Bobby Case. He'd whisper, "Whose name does she think is on the sweet spot of all these baseballs?"

But he'd say it for a laugh, because he loved Edna; theirs was one of the great love stories in baseball, a splendid marriage that lasted fifty-one years, till his death. They had no children, which meant she did a lot of traveling with him. She lived the life of a baseball wife.

On this day, Bobby Case had the day's mail and was "commencing" (another Casey word) to sort it out by priority. Business letters took precedence over fan letters, but eventually he would get to all of them. He would sign most anything, and if someone just asked for his autograph, he had paper disks with a photo of his wrinkled face topped by a Mets cap. He would sign "Let's Go Mets—Casey Stengel."

Bobby had been working as attendant in the visiting clubhouse for the Los Angeles Angels when they played at Chavez Ravine (which is what the Angels called Dodger Stadium). When the Angels prepared to move to Anaheim in 1966, Casey told him, "You don't want to commute to Anaheim. Come work for me."

He had been lucky enough to be nabbed to be Casey's "business manager," or assistant, which meant showing up each day to do whatever needed to be done. The mail was one of the few things that were part of a daily routine.

This particular day was early in 1970. Casey had been retired for five years from his last position, manager of the New York Mets. He would soon be off to St. Petersburg for another spring training, but these days he wasn't in uniform; he served as a vice president of the Mets, holding court, letting a new generation of sportswriters get to know him, and singing the praises of the "amazin' world champion Mets," who had stunned the nation with a miracle title in '69.

Bobby handed Casey one unopened letter. It bore a familiar logo and return address: New York Yankees, Yankee Stadium, Bronx, New York 10451.

Casey took a puff of his Kent cigarette and proceeded to slice open the envelope with a letter opener.

It was from Bob Fishel, the Yankees' public-relations director, one of the few team employees who went back to his days with the team.

Fishel was writing to invite Casey to Old-Timers' Day that summer at Yankee Stadium.

Just as he had every year.

Bob had added in his own handwriting at the bottom, "Really hope you and Edna can join us, Casey. The whole event would center on you, and we have plans to retire your uniform number as well."

Since that ugly day in October 1960 when Casey was told his "services were no longer desired," he had never returned to Yankee Stadium, save for an exhibition game while managing the Mets or as a fan at a World Series game. A decade in exile.

He was still bitter, despite the logo on his boxer shorts. Ten pennants in twelve years, then fired after losing a seven-game World Series? Because he had made the mistake of turning seventy?

The Yankees had just staged Mickey Mantle Day at the stadium in 1969, the year before. It was an enormous event, with over sixty thousand in attendance. Everyone of importance came back to honor Mantle and to see his number 7 formally retired. George Weiss, the general manager Mick hated, the man who had hired Casey and who was retired with Casey, came back. Mel Allen, the fired broadcaster who had given Mantle a bad medical reference, came back. Mick's minor-league managers, his scout, and illustrious teammates (except for Roger Maris) came back. Casey Stengel did not. He loved Mantle like a son, but he would not go back, not even for this.

But something told him that it was time for a return. Bobby Case was surprised—he had expected to hear another "no."

What was it? At seventy-nine, was his boss growing sentimental? Was it the appeal from Fishel, whom he liked? Was it the realization that the team's ownership had changed and prolonged anger was pointless? Was it that, with the Mets reigning as world champions, he was getting satisfaction out of seeing the Yankees down?

Edna had entered the room by now. Casey told her about the invitation, and about the note from Fishel saying his number would be retired.

"This is a big thing," he said to her. "Having your number retired, that doesn't happen every day. I'm thinking of going."

They always talked through big decisions. Edna remembered when Casey was managing Oakland in the Pacific Coast League in 1948 and the opportunity to manage the Yankees came up. They were so happy in Oakland. They needed a lot of discussion before finally saying yes—but maybe only for a year or two.

This wasn't going to be as important as that decision, but it did call for a conversation. And the answer was, again, yes.

The exile would end. A bad moment in Casey Stengel's history, and in Yankee history, would be set aside for a day.

2

KANSAS CITY

THE TERM "STENGELESE" FIRST appeared in print in the 1930s, but instead of describing his method of speech, it was a nickname for the players he was managing, as "Sudanese" would be used to describe the people of Sudan.

In 1940, *The New York Times* began to use it for his unique way of turning short answers into run-on sentences. Sometimes this was a tactic to bury what he really thought; at other times he might seem to be tangoing with the English language until he remembered what he wanted to say.

"They brought me up to the Brooklyn Dodgers, which at that time was in Brooklyn."

"Good pitching will always stop good hitting and vice versa."

"Sometimes I get a little hard-of-speaking."

"When you're losing, everyone commences to playing stupid."

He always had his own unique way of talking, but the term "Stengelese" wasn't really popularized until he went to the Yankees in 1949, and the New York sportswriters adopted it when quoting him at length or describing his speech patterns.

During spring training in 1940, while Casey was managing the Boston Braves (then called the Bees), the *Times*'s John Drebinger wrote:

> Life with the Giants these days seems to be pretty much up and down, and today it was down indeed as Professor Casey Stengel and his Bees polished off Colonel Bill Terry's vast army for the second time this Spring. The score was 4 to 3 and was achieved in typical Stengelese fashion.
>
> This consists of Professor Casey's engaging the enemy in some

of his most entertaining conversation while his helpers grab a few hits and run them out for all they are worth.

Because part of Casey's charm was surely in his colorful use of language, this seems like a good time to introduce it, as he described his childhood to a group of sportswriters in Kansas City in 1956:

> Lots of people think I was born in California because I live in Glendale and when they get you out there they forget where you come from and anything I read it states I was a Californian and when I am in Chicago I am taken for a fellow who was born in Illinois because no doubt I played there but it is never further than Davenport, Iowa, which is not too far off and which I also played in New York I never know where I was born to read it because they get all the stories there and I don't know if anybody is ever going to build me a monument, but I will bet they have some time to spend deciding where I was born because they put that on those things. What I know is a fact, that I was born right here in Kansas City but I ain't sure of the street but I think it was Agnes Avenue, because my father sold water from a truck and people said he was pretty smart to sell something that didn't cost anything but we had to move a lot of times to sell the water and we never had a cellar and we couldn't store the potatoes which they did when I was around here and that meant we had to do something with the potatoes and I guess I can tell you nobody was as smart with a potato as my brother Grant out there who was a much better ballplayer than I was and very smart.

We'd like to think that Casey (and his audience) took a breath here, but it's possible he continued right on, as though it was all one endless sentence.

> One day we were carrying around the potatoes in our pockets when we have to play a game and Grant is at second base when the pitcher tries to pick off a guy and he missed, but Grant just reaches in his pocket and throws it back to the pitcher and when the runner walks off the base Grant takes the ball out of his glove and tells the guy, "I have something to show you." I was never that smart but I remember we used to root for Central High and

we would beat Manuel High pretty good and then we would go
down and have a real fight, but I know I only won one thing at
Central High and that was a sweater with a letter on it and you
don't know how I loved that sweater because I was the seventh
man on the basketball team when they only needed five. I wore
that sweater you know how hot it is today and I wore that sweater,
a thick heavy sweater right through the summer so everybody
would see the letter from Central High.

As with all Stengelese, most of what Casey says here is essentially
true. But then comes the task of interpretation, and that indeed brings us
to Kansas City, Missouri, in the summer of 1890, when Charles Dillon
Stengel was born, the third and last child of Louis and Jennie Stengel.
Though various journals claimed he was born in 1889 or 1891, he settled
the matter in 1953 by admitting that the time had come to accept his
actual birth date as July 30, 1890. He had often said it was 1891—like
most players of his day, cheating a little off his age.

The idea, for him and many players, was that he might extend his
playing career if he was thought to be younger. But thanks to his early
wrinkles and a rather grizzly face, he was already being called "Ol' Casey
Stengel" by the early 1920s, an unfortunate development in a game that
always put a high price on youth.

The Stengels moved eight or nine times during Casey's childhood,
but Kansas City was always home until he got married—even when he
became a professional player. Before he married, at age thirty-four (I will
always use his real age when referring to events), he would spend off-
seasons living with his parents. And, yes, his nickname, "Casey," came
from the initials of his hometown, with a little bow to the popularity of
"Casey at the Bat." (When Casey was a member of the New York Giants
in the twenties, his manager, John McGraw, introduced him to DeWolf
Hopper, who had popularized the poem onstage). At home, he'd been
"Charlie," and at school "Dutch."

His birthplace was a modest-sized three-bedroom single-family home
at 1229 Agnes Avenue, which still stands, just off East Thirteenth Street
and just north of I-70, in the working-class Independence Plaza part of
town. The house was brand-new when the Stengels moved in. Charlie
would share a room with his brother, Grant, three years older; his sister,
Louise, four, could have a room of her own.

Even though their home was in the city, not a rural area, for a time they had a cow in the backyard; Charlie and Grant would peddle her milk around the neighborhood.

The family moved often, but eventually settled at 4149 Harrison Street, in the more fashionable South Hyde Park section. Here his parents continued to live long after Casey had achieved fame; Louise, who never married, would live there until her death. It was always "home."

It was a close family, and Casey often managed to work Grant into his stories, citing him as the better player of the two (and better cow-milker), whose potential baseball career was prevented by a horse-and-buggy accident that caused him to lose part of his foot. Grant married and had a stepdaughter, and eventually settled in Prairie Village, just outside Kansas City, to operate a taxi company and drive one himself. (Casey, early on, helped run the company as well.) He and Casey had a nice relationship, and Casey occasionally sent him money, but it was his big sister, Louise, whom he kept an especially close eye on, always calling to see if there was anything she needed, stopping in Kansas City to see her as his travels permitted.

Whenever Casey traveled by plane later in his life, he would buy an insurance policy and name Louise as beneficiary. Maybe this was payback of sorts: when they were kids and a touch of shyness overtook him, she used to introduce Charlie to girls he liked.

Charlie's most responsible behavior as a child was turning the pump of the organ at St. Mark's Episcopal Church—Episcopalianism being a religious compromise between Lutheranism and Catholicism in the Stengel home. He also entertained neighbors by having his dog Sport perform tricks.

In his early years, Charlie had curly golden hair, which his grandfather eventually had trimmed into a more boyish cut. The family story was that Louise raced to the barbershop to sweep up the lost curls and preserve them.

Charlie was a mischievous boy, playing Jesse James outlaw games with his friends, engaging in wrestling bouts, firing snowballs at men with pipes (seeking to dislodge the pipes), breaking the city's 9:00 p.m. curfew for kids, or swiping an ice cream freezer off the back of a parked truck while the driver was attending a party. He and Grant harbored a flock of pigeons, but also stole from a neighbor's collection to increase their own numbers. They sold watered-down milk from their cow. Inseparable and rambunctious, the brothers did manage to avoid any serious trouble as they traveled around on roller skates or a tandem bicycle.

Charlie nearly drowned when he was four. He fell off a small wagon Grant was pulling, landed in a deep hole filled with water, and had to be rescued. It was the first time he ever got his name in the newspaper. A second near-drowning came when he jumped into a swimming hole near a Milwaukee Railroad bridge outside of town and again had to be rescued.

There were only forty-three states in the Union when Charlie was born. It was before radio, before the automobile, before the Wright brothers' first flight, before there was an American League—even four and a half years before Babe Ruth was born.

In fact, it was because this was still the pre-automobile age that his father, Louis Stengel, found a profession.

Louis worked as an insurance agent with the Joseph Stiebel Company and eventually took full ownership of their road-sprinkling service. Leaving insurance behind, he would drive a horse-drawn water wagon around town, shooting water out of a tank with a foot pedal to keep the dust on the roads from invading people's homes, or the shops along Grand Avenue.

Not everyone signed up, so he had to take his foot off and on the pedal on each block and check off his customers' names. Of course, if one household was a "no," the dust in front of their home might blow onto the adjoining home of a customer.

That was considered tough luck, and led to disputes among neighbors.

It was also tough luck when rain or snow made Louis's water-sprinkling route unnecessary. But, as Casey pointed out, it was nice to have a business in which your goods cost essentially nothing. (This quip conveniently excluded the cost of feeding the horse.)

Still, "the city finally came in with modern apparatus and took over the job," wrote Casey in his autobiography, "and my father's business was what you'd call defunct."

Kansas City was the childhood home of some other notable achievers around this time, including Walt Disney (during his teen years, 1914–21), the future film siren Jean Harlow, and her companion of the 1930s, leading-man actor William Powell, who happened to go to Central High School with Charlie. He achieved fame in the *Thin Man* films in the thirties.

Although they were classmates, Powell and Stengel had little in common. In fact, other classmates would remember that when Powell acted in a Shakespearean drama on the Central High stage, Charlie and his friend Harold Lederman would sit in the front row and heckle him, teasing him about his "winter underwear" costume. But they did play varsity basketball together, and Charlie was surprised by Powell's tenacity.

Ivy Olson, a tough major-league infielder from 1911 to 1924, was five years older than Charlie, but they went to elementary school together, and were later teammates in Brooklyn.

The Hall of Fame outfielder Zack Wheat (along with his younger brother Mack, also a future major leaguer) moved to Kansas City when he was sixteen and Charlie was fourteen, and they became teammates in Brooklyn and lifelong friends.

CHARLIE'S ANCESTORS ON HIS father's side, the Schtengals, came from the Bavarian section of Germany, in the southeastern portion of the country. His mother's side was from Ireland. The pursuit of a better life sent both families sailing to America. The Stengels settled in Rock Island, Illinois. His mother Jennie's parents, descended from Dillons and Jordans, settled across the Mississippi River, eight miles from Rock Island, in Davenport, Iowa. That is where Louis and Jennie met and married.

Jennie Jordan, Casey's mom, was born in 1861, when Abraham Lincoln became president and the Civil War broke out.

His mother's uncle was John F. Dillon, counsel to the Union Pacific Railroad, a judge on the Iowa Supreme Court, and later a U.S. Circuit Court of Appeals judge, appointed by President Grant.[*]

The Dillon family is where Casey's middle name came from, and he was known to brag about his ancestry (on his mother's side) when people said that Edna came from a prosperous family. This could be a touchy subject for Casey.

Louis Stengel's father, Casey's grandfather, found his name changed from Karl Schtengal to Charles Stengel when he arrived in the United States. Louis was born in 1860 and was only four when his father died of tuberculosis. Louis's mother, the former Katherine Kniphals, remarried a gunsmith also named Charles—Charles Wolff.

---

[*] In 1868, Judge Dillon created the Dillon Rule, which is used to determine whether local governments may claim certain rights. There is a memorial statue to him in Davenport. Another relative, ornithologist-conservationist Sidney Dillon Ripley II, born in 1913, headed the Smithsonian Institution for twenty years and received the Presidential Medal of Freedom in 1985. His great-grandfather and Casey's great-grandfather were brothers, making Casey and Sidney distant cousins.

Louis and Jennie, both first-generation Americans, married in 1886 and settled in Kansas City, where Louis got his job with the insurance company. Charlie was probably named after both Charleses—his grandfather and his step-grandfather.

Kansas City was in a major growth spurt; its population almost doubled during Casey's childhood, from 133,000 in 1890 to 248,000 in 1910. The Atchison, Topeka and Santa Fe Railway helped make the city a bustling metropolis and home to the 1900 Democratic National Convention. The Parade Grounds and Exhibition Park were destinations for ball playing, but there were plenty of vacant lots in Northeast Kansas City, on whose rough terrain ball games were forever breaking out.

Charlie Stengel was hardly the Student of the Month at the Kansas City public schools; his two greatest takeaways were being forced to write right-handed, and his adventures with the McGuffey Readers.

At the turn of the century, left-handed students were indeed forced to write with their right hands, and for the rest of his life, largely thanks to his teacher, one Mrs. Kennedy, forcing lefties to write right-handed, Casey did everything left-handed except write. His handwritten letters, his autographs, his contracts were all done right-handed. He acknowledged the pain and annoyance of being forced to write right-handed, but claimed it made him a better player, because he was able to use both hands more effectively in catching baseballs.

Most American students of the time learned to read with the McGuffey Readers, and Casey latched on to "Ned," the male character from the third-grade edition. Throughout his decades of talking to the press, he would often compare a naïve comment or speaker to "Ned in the Third Reader." (Sometimes he would say "Fourth Reader," and indeed, Ned was there, too.)

His continuing use of turn-of-the-century expressions was one of the things that would endear him to generations of sportswriters, including those who had no idea who Ned was but were charmed by the references. With the turn of a phrase, he could sweep his audience back to the Teddy Roosevelt administration and prairie schools.

He went to the Woodland school and then to the Garfield school for elementary and middle school before moving up to Central High. "His friends sometimes called him Sails because of his big ears," recalled his sister, Louise.

"I guess we all had a grudge against the school," said his Central High classmate George Goldman many years later. "So we bought the school building some years ago, and we tore it down. And we sent Casey the bell, because we knew he had a special grudge."

They were the Eagles on sports fields, and it was there that Charlie Stengel made his mark. By now a broad-chested and muscular five foot eight, weighing 175 pounds, he played baseball, football, and basketball. Sports seemed to require nicknames, so Charlie became "Dutch," thanks to his German heritage.

Central High, at Eleventh and Locust (around where City Hall is today), opened in 1884. (It was razed and rebuilt in a different location in 1953, and today is called Central Academy of Excellence.) It called itself the largest high school in the West, which in itself would have made it hard to make a varsity starting team. "The West" has changed definition, of course, with the growth of California and the use of air travel, but even into the 1950s, it meant Missouri, and baseball teams making "Western trips" were referring to Chicago and St. Louis.

Dutch played only football in his junior year; at that point, one of the players was seriously injured, and the school suspended the sport. He had been a fullback and captain of the team.

"I played football before they had headgear," Casey later explained. "And that's how I lost my mind."

Dutch was a starting guard and occasional right forward on the basketball team; although not a high scorer, he was very athletic and a good defensive player. He claimed to be the "seventh man" on a seven-player roster, but newspaper box scores suggest he saw plenty of action. Basketball was played at a high level in Kansas City, and conference referees included Phog Allen, later the legendary basketball coach at Kansas University, and Ernie Quigley, later a National League umpire. Dutch played three years of varsity basketball, and in 1909 the Eagles won the city championship.

But baseball was his passion, from the days when he and his friends would copy batting stances and pitching poses they scrutinized on the colorful trading cards sold with cigarette packages. In 1906, he and his dad (and probably Grant) saw the future Hall of Famer Rube Marquard pitch in a minor-league game. Years later, Casey approached Rube, then a teammate in Brooklyn, and said, "When you were with Indianapolis, you came to Kansas City and my father took me to the ballpark to see you pitch."

Casey and his dad probably saw more than that one game at Association Park. The Kansas City Blues featured Smoky Joe Wood, just eighteen in 1908, as an up-and-coming pitcher, as well as another future Hall of Famer, Eagle Eye Jake Beckley, who was actually cross-eyed and lived in Kansas City. Beckley was a big name; he had just concluded a twenty-year major-league career with a .308 lifetime average and nearly three thousand hits. Casey probably had his tobacco card.

At Central, he was a left-handed-throwing second baseman and third baseman, and also an occasional pitcher. With his barrel chest and bow-legs, he had a body type like that of Honus Wagner, the greatest name in baseball at the time. Dutch was a grinder, a player who made the most of what he had. "He made himself a ballplayer," said Grant, many years later. "He never knew when he was whipped."

In addition to high school, Charlie played for several local amateur baseball teams. The first was for Harzfeld's, a department store, which had a team in the Merchants League. Dutch got $1.50 a game to pitch. Sieg Harzfeld was a business acquaintance of Louis Stengel's, and that probably led to the offer to pitch. Sieg liked to tell people in later years that he was Casey's first baseball employer.

Grant helped him get on the Armour Meat Packing team, then the Northeast Merchants, and then the Parisian Cloak Company team, who paid him three dollars a game. In 1908, he played for the Kansas City Bentons; a sketch of the eleven players appeared in the August 5, 1908, *Kansas City Star,* which called them "a strong amateur team."

He and his friends were starting to travel great distances in and out of state for games. Once, they made a train trip to Ogden, Utah, and Cheyenne, Wyoming. He was with the "Kansas City Red Sox" on those journeys, and what fun those kids had, hiding from the conductor to avoid paying their fares, and just generally enjoying life. A few of his Red Sox teammates also became professionals, including the pitcher Claude Hendrix, who would wind up pitching in Casey's major-league debut.

A classmate of Casey's, Ira Bidwell, organized the amateur games and made a strong impression on him. This got him thinking about the business side of the game. Bidwell died in an aviation accident over Oklahoma in 1919, but Casey never forgot him when his various jobs as manager included helping to promote the team. "He had a great knack about him," wrote Casey. "He was handsome; he had a good gab and a good line of talk. There's no doubt in my mind that Ira Bidwell would have gone on to own a big league ball club and been a tremendous man as far as sports were concerned."

In his senior year at Central, playing for the Missouri State Championship, Stengel pitched the full fifteen innings for a 7–6 Eagles victory over Joplin, a lofty achievement indeed. It turned out to be the last year for baseball at Central because of budget problems; Dutch Stengel left on a very high note, although two of his three sports were "defunct" by the time he left school.

And leave he did, despite being only a semester away from graduating. He had a chance to make real money playing baseball, and he felt he needed to take the offer at once.

His performance on the diamond and his high-profile victory in the state championship had brought him to the attention of the Blues, that high-minor-league team, just a step below the majors. And here was Dutch being offered a contract for $135 a month, contingent on his making the team.

"Money never seemed to mean anything to Casey," said Grant.

But $135 a month? This was real money. His father was earning about sixty dollars a month. Even though a high school diploma would be nice, this was too good to pass up.

Louis Stengel had to sign the contract—at nineteen, Charlie was still underage—and sign it he did.

"You never could change that boy's mind anyway," Louis later explained.

One neighbor of the Stengels (Casey said he lived "across the street") seemed to know a lot about baseball. He was another Charles—Charley Nichols. And it turned out he was worth listening to, because he was better known to baseball fans as "Kid" Nichols, a three-hundred-game winner in the National League (Boston, St. Louis, and Philadelphia) from 1890 to 1906, with a 361-208 record and seven thirty-win seasons. He lived in Kansas City from 1881 until his death in 1953. When Casey was a boy, only Cy Young and Pud Galvin had more career victories than Kid.

"Nichols always talked to me on his way to the park and I thought I was a big shot among the kids," said Casey, who would call him his boyhood idol.

Kid Nichols, realizing what a fine talent young Stengel was, took him aside one day to give him some timely advice. "I understand you get in a lot of trouble at school and in a lot of arguments. Now when you start out in baseball, the best thing you can do is listen to your manager. And once in a while you'll have an old player teach you. Always listen to the man. Never say, 'I won't do that.' Always listen to him. If you're not going to do it, don't tell him so. Let it go in one ear, then let it roll around there for a month, and if it isn't any good, let it go out the other ear. If it is any good after a month, memorize it and keep it. Now be sure you do that and you'll keep out of a lot of trouble."

By the time Casey became a manager, the name Kid Nichols might not have meant much to his young players. But there was a good chance that Casey himself remembered this advice and passed it on now and then to know-it-all prospects. The words of long-forgotten Kid Nichols may well have been spoken to young New York Mets prospects of the 1960s.

And so, in March 1910, while the rest of his class was in its final months before graduation, Dutch headed for Excelsior Springs, Missouri, twenty-eight miles from home, for his first training camp. He worked out with the Blues' player/manager, Danny Shay, an infielder who had been with the New York Giants as recently as 1907. He, too, lived in Kansas City, and he knew that Dutch wasn't going to be a left-handed infielder in the pros.

In an early exhibition game back in Kansas City, the Blues were to face Smoky Joe Wood and the Boston Red Sox—big leaguers. This was the same Smoky Joe that Dutch and his dad would have seen when he played for the Blues. Now Joe was a third-year major leaguer, not quite a star, but on his way to being one. Casey's family and friends came to watch, but Shay had Dutch simply carry the water bucket to the starters, and rub up the day's baseballs with mud. It was embarrassing, but Dutch was full of confidence and anxious for his opening. "There were a lot of them old fellers on the team I figured whose jobs I could take."

Back at Excelsior Springs, known for the power of its "healing water," Shay let Dutch pitch a couple of games, but he was not impressive. "I'm an outfielder, really," explained Stengel—even though his high-school career included very little outfielding. He didn't want to get cut on the basis of his pitching.

Shay gave him a chance in the outfield. He tried to explain the need to play the angles off the fences. "If you want somebody to play the angles, why don't you hire a pool player," Dutch allegedly said. Kid Nichols would have groaned. This could hardly have endeared him to Shay, either. Before the season could begin, Shay concluded that Dutch wasn't yet a Double-A player. (What we today call Triple-A.) "'You can't stay here, Dutch, you've got the biggest hitch of any man I ever saw.'"

He was sent to Kankakee, Illinois, in the Northern Association, though Kansas City still owned rights to him.

Kankakee wasn't Kansas City by any stretch, but the long professional baseball life of Charles Dillon Stengel was about to begin.

3

LUNATIC BEGINNING

SO CASEY STENGEL BEGAN his career as a Lunatic.

The Kankakee team officially called itself the "Kays," but newspapers in the league's cities took to calling them the "Lunatics." The ballpark was located across the street from the sprawling 119-acre Kankakee State Hospital, which until 1910 had been called the Illinois Eastern Hospital for the Insane.[*]

LUNATICS WIN FIRST, headlined the Decatur *Daily Review,* and the story read, "The Lunatics found them for nine safe hits in the sixth round, winning the game 7 to 6."

"There were a lot of things I couldn't do," Casey recalled of his days in Kankakee. "One of them was running bases. Instead of sliding into the bag, I'd come in standing up, and the manager showed me how to do it right and told me to practice every chance I got."

So, to the amusement of patients at the hospital who could see the field from their windows, Charlie (not yet "Casey"), would practice his sliding during batting practice, or while standing in the outfield between pitches.

"Stengel is one fellow who won't be here next year," said a teammate, Joe Gilligan. Asked if he was going to the major leagues, Gilligan reportedly responded, "No, he's going into that building over there," and pointed to the hospital.

"It's just a matter of time," said more than one teammate.

In the telling, Casey (and thus later biographers) would confuse

---

[*] It remains in use today as the Samuel H. Shapiro Developmental Center. The Negro League founder, Rube Foster, died there in 1930.

Kankakee with his next stop: Maysville, Kentucky, where there was no asylum near the ballpark.

CHARLIE STENGEL MADE HIS debut on May 10, batting cleanup and playing center field. He had a single and stole a base in a 3–2 loss to the Jacksonville Jacks. A teammate of note was Bobby Veach, who would go on to hit .310 over fourteen big-league seasons and share outfield duties in Detroit with Ty Cobb for most of those years.

Charlie's manager at Kankakee was Dan Collins, and the Jacksonville manager was Clarence "Pants" Rowland, who would later be a Chicago White Sox manager, an American League umpire, and president of the Pacific Coast League when Casey managed there. That three such prominent baseball figures as Veach, Stengel, and Rowland could one day wink at each other when one mentioned the Northern Association was no small coincidence.

"We did not draw and getting paid was quite an adventure," Casey later recalled.

"In those days a player in the minors had no protection against getting swindled, because there was no commissioner. You could write to the office of the chief of the minors, but that was a one-way thing."

The Class D Northern Association was brand-new to Organized Baseball in 1910. It consisted of eight teams and began play in May, but within a month, the Decatur team disbanded and the Joliet team moved to Sterling, Illinois. Clinton and Freeport dropped out soon after, and on July 7, a new schedule was cobbled together. Four days later, Elgin and Kankakee were done. "Owing to lack of attendance at week day games, the management of the Kankakee and Elgin teams called off games scheduled to take place here today and tomorrow," reported the Chicago *Daily Tribune* on July 15. "The members of the Kankakee team have received their releases and most of them have left to join different clubs with which they have signed."

The remaining four clubs went on for another week before the league formally disbanded.

When the club folded, Charlie was owed half of his monthly paycheck, fixed by the Kansas City contract at the salary of $135 a month. So he swiped his uniform—or several uniforms—to make up for the difference. And that wasn't all. The players were each given a meal ticket to eat at McBroom's in Kankakee, the best-known restaurant in town. Charlie still had $3.50 left on his ticket when the end came.

Stan McBroom himself showed up at the Yankees' spring training camp in 1959. Casey remembered him, and he remembered the $3.50. The restaurant was still in business—forty-nine years later—and Old Man McBroom offered him a free steak when Casey called him out on it.

In 1956, at his big birthday party in Kansas City, where they gave him the school bell, the Kankakee Federal Savings and Loan Association presented Casey with a check for $483.05—which was the $67.50—the missing half of his paycheck—plus forty-six years of interest. (He gave the money to the Kankakee Little League.)

For years, Casey's record at Kankakee was lost because of the dissolution of the league, and his stat line would show only "League disbanded in July." But Ray Nemec, one of the sixteen founders of the Society of American Baseball Research, was determined to piece together league records for the Northern Association, largely because Casey had this one line bare in his record. During the 1960s, after visiting newspaper archives in the league's cities, Nemec found the old accounts and box scores of those missing games. Casey played in fifty-nine games, batting .251 with one home run in 203 times at bat. A missing line on a baseball immortal had been filled in.

With the demise of Kankakee, Kansas City management assigned Charlie to another Class D team: Shelbyville, Kentucky, in the Blue Grass League. It was another struggling franchise in another struggling league, but he was glad to have a job to finish out his season. It would have been embarrassing to return home in midsummer.

The Shelbyville Millers were deep in last place, and just a month after Kankakee had slipped away, Charlie found himself surrounded by rumors that Shelbyville was also doomed. All of their home games were shifted to their opponents' ballparks. On August 26, *The Bourbon News* of nearby Paris, Kentucky, confirmed the sale of the team to new ownership, in Maysville, Kentucky, for six hundred dollars. That made two defunct franchises in three months for Stengel, just starting out. There were only a few weeks left of his first season in uniform—any uniform.

Charlie, perhaps because he was the youngest on the team, was chosen to return to Shelbyville, about 110 miles away, to collect the team's equipment. He filled a freight car with the bags and reported back to Maysville, with just a little railroad soot on the goods.

On August 26, Maysville hosted Paris at the East End Park. "The grounds have been hurriedly put in fair condition, bleacher seats have been erected, and 300 temporary and comfortable chairs will be placed as an extemporized grandstand until the real thing can be erected," reported the Maysville *Ledger*. "Preparations are already under way to have the Park fenced and other improvements added just as soon as work can be done. The general admission for both men and women will be 25 cents, children, 15 cents."

A few days after the opener, Maysville lost a home game 6–4 when "an automobile running across the field prevented [Warren] Fieber getting to a fly that would have perhaps saved the day for the home team."

Charlie's record—which sometimes shows only Maysville for 1910, not Shelbyville—says he played sixty-nine games and hit .223. A home run on September 4—the first in the new ballpark—earned him a five-dollar Duplex razor outfit and a five-pound box of candy as a prize. Another homer that week earned him a three-dollar hat.

The season ended September 22, with the team having finished deep in last place. Casey returned to Kansas City, where the Blues put him on the roster for the final week of their season. He got into four games and went 3-for-11. For his three teams in four cities, two of whom went broke, he played 132 games and batted .237—an inauspicious debut, but he did play that final week, at age twenty, at the highest level of minor-league baseball.

THE SEASON OVER, CHARLIE reunited with his Central High pals and caught up with their prospects and plans. A few were going to college; some were going to try business, or join their fathers in business. Charlie's contract with Kansas City was renewed for 1911.

An old teammate from his semipro days, Billy Brammage, decided to enroll in Western Dental College in Kansas City. Charlie thought about it, knew his father was all for developing a backup profession to baseball, and said, "I'll go with you."

"I have no objection to your playing baseball," Louis Stengel said to his son, "but some day you'll get married and have to support a family. You'll be in much better position to do that if you can sign D.D.S. after your name."

So Charlie enrolled in the dental college. He had enough high school credits to do so even without graduating, and enough money saved from baseball to pay for it. He supplemented his baseball money by driving a taxi, just like his brother.

Thirty-nine men and one woman were enrolled in the school, and though we don't know how many were left-handed, we know that Casey was, and he had trouble adjusting to the equipment. Today the equipment provides for greater maneuverability, and it's not so difficult to adjust it for righties and lefties. But in 1910, this was quite a barrier. Special left-handed dental equipment was available, but it would cost about $150.

The school president, a fellow named Workman, suggested that Charlie stick with baseball while going to school, so he could earn enough to open his own practice right away. He also suggested that Charlie look into orthodontic dentistry, which was just catching on.

Besides, as Casey noted, "in those days, you only got 50 cents a filling."

Casey liked to tell the story of the day a local bum came in to have a tooth pulled—bums got free dental care, and the students got to practice. Charlie didn't lower his chair enough, and by the time he had the tooth in clamps and ready to be yanked, his arm couldn't go any higher.

"The battle was on," he said. "And we hadn't settled on who was going to have that tooth—him or me! It took me an hour to wrestle him out of it."

It would be the only tooth he ever yanked.

4

AURORA, ILLINOIS

AURORA, ILLINOIS, ON THE banks of the Fox River, is still nick-named the "City of Lights." It was a big name for a relatively small town of thirty thousand, though it was growing, and could claim to be one of the first towns in America to be fully lit by electricity. As a railroad-manufacturing factory town in 1911, Aurora provided a tolerant home to a diverse population of laborers. Riverview Park was a great gathering spot for everyone.

Its proximity to Chicago—forty-one miles—would figure large in Charlie Stengel's advancement to the major leagues.

The Aurora Blues of the Wisconsin-Illinois League was in its second season of operation. Road games took them to Green Bay, Rockford, and Appleton. "We split the squad into parties which tried out all the res-taurants in town for rates and quality of food and then reported back and decided where is the best load of ptomaines at the cheapest prices," Charlie reported.

The players lived in rooming houses or modest hotels, and would take advantage of off-days to travel on the Aurora, Elgin & Chicago Railway (AE&C) to see the big-city delights of Chicago.

Kansas City had sold Charlie's contract to Class C Aurora in April, and this turned out to be a great stop for him. (The Kansas City owner, Patsy Tebeau, was the brother of the Aurora owner, Al Tebeau.) He turned twenty-one years old and led the league in hitting with a robust .352 average, forty-two points better than the runner-up. He also led in hits and stolen bases. Aurora finished seventh in the eight-team league, but Charlie experienced a full season and developed as an outfielder. The only games he missed all year came from a suspension: he had whacked the home-plate umpire in the rear with a baseball bat after a "disputed" third strike, maybe for the amusement of the fans as much as a display of his own temper on the field in the heat of a game.

The fans in Aurora loved the unpredictable Stengel, and the following year, 1912, when he was with Brooklyn and the Dodgers were playing in Chicago, Aurora fans went to West Side Grounds and presented him with a watch. "It had 23 jewels and it was one of those old-fashioned ones that you stuck in a vest pocket," he recalled some fifty years later.

Charlie was now making $175 a month; he had demanded a raise, threatening to stay in dental school if he didn't get it. He got his way and felt good about winning the dispute, but Al Tebeau noticed that Casey was not a very good card player and was regularly losing his money. "You'd better quit playing cards," he told him. "Because if you don't you'll be broke every payday." It was one of the best bits of advice Casey got as he set out on a life of baseball, baseball, and baseball, with virtually no other hobbies. Card playing was on a long list of things he didn't do.

One day, Larry Sutton, the chief scout for the Brooklyn Dodgers (they were more often called the Superbas then), found time on his hands while in Chicago and took the train to Aurora to see what he might spot. He always had an itch to go somewhere, to see a game, to see if there might be some lucky find there. One of the first full-time scouts in baseball, he was always on the hunt.

That day, down at the railroad station, I saw a sign that intrigued me: "Chicago and Aurora." On an impulse I grabbed one of those trains, intending to make a one-day visit to Aurora. I didn't come back for three days. I snared three players on that trip. You never heard of Somers or Madden, but the third was Casey Stengel. I paid $300 for Casey.

When I got to the ball park there I saw this kid Stengel and he had a good day. Better than that, he had blond hair and freckles, and a kid with that combination is always a fighter.

Amazingly, the circumstance of an easy train connection between Aurora and Chicago led Sutton to Stengel.

Later, Zack Wheat, who had already been signed by Sutton, claimed he tipped the scout off in advance of his trip to Aurora. "Our family and the Stengel family knew each other from Kansas City a long time," recalled Wheat, who was then in his third year with Brooklyn, though he had yet to blossom as a star. Zack and Casey would be friends for life. Give Wheat an assist on this one.

On September 1, the Dodgers purchased Casey's contract. Nevertheless, he finished the remaining days of the season at Aurora and returned to dental school.

Casey regaled his classmates at Western Dental with his baseball stories. In 1958, a fellow student who used to sit next to Stengel and was now a practicing dentist in Kansas City recalled in *The Kansas City Times,* "It was quite common for the students to gather around him as he brought them up to date on his extracurricular work on the baseball diamond."

Casey put in three off-seasons at Western Dental and as at high school, came within a few weeks of graduating. But by then, he seemed to be off on a major-league career, and he withdrew from school.

"My quitting with just a month to go was the greatest thing that ever happened to dentistry," he often said, with his famous wink.

Still, the question remains how he could spend three off-seasons in the program—and how the school could continue to advance him—if it was always apparent that because he was a left-hander dentistry wasn't for him. The high cost of specialized equipment should have dissuaded him—and the school—early on.

In the years to come, Edna was on him to resume school and graduate, especially every time he lost a minor-league managing job. But this was the end of the line for Charles Dillon Stengel, dental student.

THE SALE TO BROOKLYN made him prominent enough to be recruited by the barnstorming Nick Altrock All-Stars to play against the all-Negro Kansas City Royal Giants in an October exhibition at Kansas City's Shelley Park (a converted cemetery—don't ask). The veteran pitcher Altrock, now a Washington coach and famous "baseball clown," pitched, and Stengel led off and played center field. It must have felt very big-league to Charlie to be on the field behind Altrock in front of his friends and family.

Brooklyn changed Charlie's assignment from Toronto to Montgomery, Alabama, a team in the Class-A Southern League for 1912, and cut his salary from $175 to $150 a month. He wasn't happy about that development, but Sutton told him to take the deal: the total loss for the season—$125 over six months—would be made up when he got to the big leagues, and if he complained too much, it might slow his progress to that level. Sutton was being a good company man, as scouts always are; he was "looking after Stengel's interests" while saving the club money.

This journey to the Deep South would find Stengel playing teams in Atlanta, Birmingham, Chattanooga, Memphis, Mobile, Nashville, and New Orleans—exciting cities to visit for the first time. He would play games in brutally hot summer weather, but the crowds were decent and the competition was good. With an average of .290, Charlie led the Rebels in hitting. Montgomery, alas, finished sixth.

Charlie had an unorthodox batting style that seemed to work for him. He was unpredictable at the plate, which made him hard to pitch to. He would be all over the batter's box from one pitch to the next, sometimes deep in the box, sometimes crowding the plate. But it was working—he was making good contact, and hitting for a good average.

His baseball instincts still needed work, and he was lucky to find a Rebel teammate who took the time to work with him. Norm Elberfeld, "The Tabasco Kid," had spent thirteen seasons in the majors, scrapping and clawing his way to success. He was once the manager of the New York Highlanders (the Yankees' earlier nickname). He had played for Washington the year before and was a fan favorite, and a big name, on the Rebels. Elberfeld was only five foot seven and 158 pounds (Charlie was now listed at five foot eleven, 175), but the Kid taught him some fine points, such as not looking at the next base when he got on.

"That base isn't going anywhere," Elberfeld would say. "You're tipping off the defense that you're stealing. Pay attention to what the hitter is doing!"

Elberfeld—and his wife—were mentors to Stengel. When Charlie was summoned to Brooklyn in mid-September to make his major-league debut, the Elberfelds went to see him off and wish him well. And they told him to get rid of his cardboard suitcase and invest in a decent eighteen-dollar one.

"You won't come back," the Kid told him. "Never mind the money. And forget about dental school too."

Elberfeld's wisdom was heeded and appreciated. Two years later, he would come up one more time, joining Casey in Brooklyn. The two of them spent a lot of time together, the elder player taking the raw kid under his wing. The Kid had style, even if he had Tabasco sauce and chewing tobacco all over his clothes.

That was baseball continuity at its best: a Yankees manager from 1908 explaining things to the man who would go on to manage that same team from 1949 to 1960.

When the Southern Association season ended, Casey headed for Brooklyn and Major League Baseball. He stepped off the train and onto a platform at the sparkling new Pennsylvania Station on the morning of September 16, 1912, his first time in New York City, the city that would be home to his greatest fame as a player and as a manager.

He went directly to Washington Park in Brooklyn, where a day game was scheduled. He talked his way into the park and met the son of the owner, Charles Ebbets, who showed him around, no doubt telling him about the new park planned for next year. Stengel said he'd like to watch the game but not suit up until the next day, since he was weary from his long train trip.

After the game, he asked a cabdriver, not a teammate, where he might stay. The cabbie took him to the Longacre Hotel on West Forty-seventh Street. Times Square.

"It was dark and I was really alone," said Casey, although his uncle Charley Jordan, from Davenport, happened to be in town. "I was afraid to go out so I sat in the lobby. Eventually I walked to Forty-sixth Street, and then back to the lobby. I sat some more, then walked to Forty-fifth Street and back." Then he checked out Forty-fourth and Forty-third, and, at last, Forty-second Street, before he decided to turn in. He had ninety-five dollars in his pocket, and the team hadn't told him anything about what they covered and what expenses were his responsibility.

At eight the next morning, September 17, he headed back to Washington Park. The trip took him four hours: the elevated train down Broadway to Lower Manhattan, then a trolley over the Brooklyn Bridge, and another trolley toward Borough Park.

"I got to the office at Washington Park," said Casey, "and I commenced walking in. I was shocked. It was so run down I couldn't believe it. Wooden floor. They didn't expect me in the office, didn't believe I had really been told to report from Montgomery, and didn't know if they wanted me. I was afraid they'd send me home. Someone told me where the clubhouse was. I walked in, took a nail, and hung up my jacket."

His new teammates invited him to join them in playing dice on the floor.

"Superbas" was a strange nickname, the name of a vaudeville act that the former owner Ned Hanlon had had. But these Superbas were superb in name only, and by 1912 they were more frequently being called the Dodgers (because their fans were "trolley dodgers" on the streets of Brooklyn). The 1912 version of the team that Charlie joined was managed by a former Brooklyn shortstop, Bill Dahlen. When Dahlen spotted Charlie in the clubhouse, he quickly pulled him out of the dice game.

"What did you come up here to do?" he asked. "Shoot craps or play baseball?"

Add dice to the list of activities Charlie would not engage in.

Dahlen was a very hot-tempered fellow, hardly a role model for a young player entering the majors. He was thrown out of thirty games in his four years as manager, including one time for engaging in a fistfight with the umpire Cy Rigler.

The 1912 team lost ninety-five games and finished seventh, drawing attendance of fewer than thirty-five hundred a game. Zack Wheat was now their star, but the rest of the roster was loaded with no-names, save perhaps the first baseman Jake Daubert, the catcher Otto Miller, and the pitcher Nap Rucker. Casey would be penciled into center field that very day, in place of Hub Northen.

Foul-smelling Washington Park, in the Park Slope section of Brooklyn, was in its second incarnation, but was already run-down and something of an embarrassment for Major League Baseball. It was, in fact, running out of time: Charles Ebbets was overseeing construction of a new ballpark not far away, and had let go the upkeep on Washington Park. In fact, Ebbets Field was to have been ready for 1912—a few "last games" were planned in July and August—but the new place just wasn't ready. So they squeezed another full season out of Washington Park and made the best of it.

Washington Park—carved out between First and Third Streets, and between Third and Fourth Avenues—is today the site of a Con Edison parking-and-storage facility.* An outfield wall, once part of a 1914 renovation to accommodate the Federal League's Tip-Tops, is still standing. Though the area of the playing field is a vast concrete lot where trucks now park, it is possible to stand on it and imagine that, once upon a time, Casey Stengel played there.

In fact, a lot of great National League players stood there—including Honus Wagner, who would be on the opposing Pittsburgh Pirates the

---

* Con Edison is New York City's utility company.

very day Charlie Stengel made his major-league debut. Max Carey, another future Hall of Famer, was in the outfield for Pittsburgh.

In 1912, major-league teams still played in a lot of rickety old dead-ball-era wooden ballparks, and featured Ty Cobb, Christy Mathewson, Napoleon Lajoie, Shoeless Joe Jackson, Hal Chase, Walter Johnson, Grover Cleveland Alexander, and Tris Speaker. And now Stengel would join them all.

Zack Wheat had a special interest in Charlie and would remember his debut. "I was in left field and Stengel was in center," he later told the sportswriter Maury Allen. "He could run and played a shallow center field. Then Honus Wagner came up. He used to hit those sizzling line drives with spin. The ball would start low over the infield and rise. That was the dead ball, remember, and he would have hit many homers with the lively ball."

Wheat shouted to Stengel to play deeper. But Charlie ignored him, and even moved in a step or two.

"He didn't like to be told anything," recalled Wheat. "Sure enough, Wagner hits one of those sizzlers. Casey runs like hell, but it's way over his head, just like I figured. Casey finally gets the ball off the wall, Wagner has a double, and Casey looks over at me, grins, takes off his cap, and makes a deep bow. I had to laugh. We became good friends. Tell you the truth, there never was a day around Casey I didn't laugh."

Wagner surely made an impression, too. "Cobb was a greater ballplayer, I guess," reflected Casey in his old age. "Cobb's greatness, though, was on the offense. Defensively he was just an average outfielder with an average arm. It's an odd thing about greatness, however. Someone will say 'He was great but . . .' You see, there's always that 'but.' Yet Honus Wagner had no 'buts.' He could do everything."

His debut game was a day of stardom for Charles Dillon Stengel— one of the best in the history of baseball. He batted second and faced Claude Hendrix, who had been his teammate in semipro ball in Kansas City. His first time up in the big leagues, in the last of the first, Charlie singled to center. He told the first baseman, Dots Miller, "My name's Stengel, and I just came up."

In the second, he drove one past third for an RBI single. He singled to center his next time up to break up a tie game, which he followed with a stolen base, and then he singled to right and stole second again. Four straight singles.

His fifth time up, feeling a little full of himself, he turned around and batted right-handed against a lefty, Sherry Smith. Was this a clownish or defiant act in his first game? He would do such a thing in his first game?!

"Fred Clarke was managing the Pirates," he told *The New York Times* nearly forty years later. "And he's so shocked by my phenomenal batting that he yells over at me on my fifth trip to the plate, 'Why don't you bat right-handed, you fresh busher?' I guess I was a pretty fresh busher at that. I batted right-handed just to be obliging and walked for a perfect day."

The walk was followed by a steal. By the end of the afternoon, a 7–3 Brooklyn victory, Casey had gone 4-for-4. He had three stolen bases and two runs batted in, and had won over the small crowd, barely four thousand, with his hustle. The victory snapped a twelve-game winning streak for Pittsburgh. The only man who had ever bettered Stengel's debut was the man managing the Pirates that day, Clarke, who had gone 5-for-5 in his 1894 debut. (Through 2015, only twelve players have gone 4-for-4 in their debut since Casey did it, including Willie McCovey and Kirby Puckett.)

A few days later, Brooklyn played the Chicago Cubs—the Cubs of Joe Tinker, Johnny Evers, and Frank Chance. Casey would later recall:

Jimmy Archer was crouching behind the plate when I came to bat. "So you're Stengel," he said. "I hear you're pretty fast." I tossed out the old chest a foot or so and said, "You'll see when I get on base." I did get on base and I did go down, although I should have been fined for challenging an arm like Archer's. Johnny Evers had the ball ten feet ahead of me. There was only one chance so I slid into him hard. But he held the ball, although he was knocked to short left field. Until Evers got up and spoke to me I didn't have much of a vocabulary. He called me everything.

Stengel waited for Evers to finish screaming at him, and then said:

"That's the way I slid in the bushes and that's the way I'll slide up here. Take a good look at me because I'll be here a long time!"

That was in the fall, and I was proud the next time we saw the Cubs, Johnny came over and shook hands with me. I'd made him remember me.

Acceptance by his teammates was not so easy to come by. In the style of the day, veterans tended to shun rookies. He was shut out of batting practice. Finally, he printed up business cards that said "Hi. My name is Charles Dillon 'Dutch' Stengel and I would like to take batting practice." Daubert, the big first baseman, laughed and let him hit. Everyone else followed. And his new teammates showed him places to stay in Brooklyn, so he could avoid the four-hour commute from Times Square. He wound up living in the Park Slope section, in a furnished room near the ballpark, and had dinner each night at the Crown, where for thirty-five cents he could have soup, spaghetti, pot roast, pie à la mode, and coffee.

CHARLIE STENGEL WAS CATCHING on and fitting in. By the end of the week, *The Brooklyn Daily Eagle* was calling him the "New Superba Phenom." He soon got to bat against the Phillies' great Grover Cleveland Alexander, delivering a clean single. On a Sunday, playing an exhibition in Newark (Sunday ball was not permitted in New York), he won ten dollars for catching a greased pig in a pre-game contest.

Charlie played in seventeen games down the stretch and batted .316, which was tops on the team if you didn't count times at bat to qualify.

The final game in Washington Park was on October 5, 1912, with the Superbas losing to the World Series–bound New York Giants 1–0. Stengel played center field, batted third, and went 0-for-2 with a walk. Few of the ten thousand fans joined in the singing of "Auld Lang Syne," which was played by a live band—they had already done that the year before.

Three days later, he went to the Polo Grounds to see the first game of the 1912 World Series, the Giants playing the Red Sox. It was his first World Series game, and few men over time would attend more. Whether his team was in it or not, Casey could usually be found there. He loved being around the game and its people, and the perk of being able to attend for free was too great to ignore.

5

CASEY OF EBBETS FIELD

CHARLIE WENT HOME A hero, at least in his own mind. He was a major leaguer. He played in a few barnstorming exhibitions, including one in Coffeyville, Kansas, where Walter Johnson made him look so bad, he went back to the bench with only two strikes on him.

He hung out with friends at the YMCA and the local billiard room and waited for his 1913 Brooklyn contract. When it arrived, it was not for the salary increase Larry Sutton had told him to expect. Although he was a veteran of all of three weeks in the big leagues, he sent it back, unsigned, and would wind up being the last man on the roster to agree to terms, not signing until spring training was about to unfold in Augusta, Georgia. He would get about twenty-one hundred dollars for the year, and he had to fight Ebbets to get it. "The stars got $4,000," he would say. "And we all got $2.50 a day in meal money, which you tried to save. First class hotels do not like ball players in them days, so we'd sleep in second rate quarters and the ball club gives you $2.50 daily and says this is a lot of dough, don't spend it foolishly. You lived on meal money and did your best to save something for a rainy day. Of which we had many."

Dahlen didn't hand him the center-field job. He had to compete with another rookie, and he got banged up early and didn't do so well. But by the end of spring training, as the team began to barnstorm north, he found his batting stroke and won the job.

Ebbets Field was the tenth new ballpark to open in the last five years. This was an important time for major-league baseball; it was emerging from its infancy, exemplified by the more substantial architecture and building materials going into the parks.

The first test of Ebbets Field and its unique concrete outfield walls was an exhibition game against the Yankees, scheduled for Saturday, April 5. Stengel borrowed a bag of baseballs from the clubhouse man Dan Comerford and practiced fielding balls off the concrete.

He hit leadoff for the Superbas. More than twenty-five thousand turned out for the inaugural—a huge crowd for an exhibition game—and Charlie gave the fans their money's worth with an inside-the-park home run in the fifth; the Yankees' center fielder accidentally kicked it to the wall, enabling Stengel to scamper around the bases. Generous scoring called it a homer, and that was the first one hit in the new ballpark, albeit in an exhibition. It looked like the real deal in the box score.

The ballpark with its imposing round brick rotunda at Sullivan and Cedar welcoming arriving fans, this new sports temple in the Borough of Churches, was hailed as beautiful when it opened. Four decades later, it would be considered cramped and grimy. It was finally demolished in 1960, three years after the Dodgers' final home game before the team moved to Los Angeles. Though it came to be remembered as a wonderful temple of baseball, it was in fact always cramped and grimy. Still, for baseball fans in Brooklyn, it was home.

It was during these early days at Ebbets Field that Stengel seems to have acquired his nickname "Casey." One story was that a teammate in a poker game said, "About time you took a pot, Kansas City." Or maybe someone just said, "Where ya from, kid?" If he answered "K.C.," the nickname may have been born right then. The sportswriter Fred Lieb said he had "Charles Stengel—K.C." stenciled on his luggage, and that got picked up.

The hometown *Brooklyn Daily Eagle,* for whom Abe Yager was the beat writer (the first of many whom Casey would warmly embrace and call "my writers"—a term used both affectionately and politically to win them over), first used "Casey" Stengel in a photo caption on June 17, 1913. By season's end, the name was used more or less regularly.

On April 9, Casey played center field and led off in the first official game played at Ebbets. The pre-game celebrations were grand, although someone forgot to bring an American flag to the flagpole for the flag raising. (A batboy had to run and find one.) Every woman in attendance got a complimentary hand mirror.

Brooklyn lost to the Phillies 1–0, with Stengel going 0-for-4.

But Casey played well after that in April, enjoying a two-hit game against Christy Mathewson on the twenty-ninth. He got his average up as high as .352, and on April 26, he hit the "real" first home run in Ebbets

Field, this one clearing the wall onto Montgomery Street. In July, *Baseball Magazine*'s Bill Phelon wrote, "Few greater youngsters have been landed in recent years than Stengel, of the Brooklyn outfield."

By the season's end, Casey's play had faded, and he'd missed twenty-five games because of a shoulder injury. Another player, Bill Collins, came up from Newark to start against left-handers (Casey's first taste of being platooned). One afternoon, Louis Stengel went to Chicago to see his son play, and Casey was riding the bench in embarrassment. Nevertheless, he hit .272 with seven homers in his rookie season. But a sixth-place finish couldn't save Dahlen's job; they let him go in November.

Casey had grave concerns about his future when the shoulder injury ended his season. He didn't play until the off-season, in the annual "American Series," when he went to Cuba with a dozen Superbas to play fifteen games against teams from Havana and Almendares. Jake Daubert served as manager, and one can only imagine how the twelve Brooklyn boys bonded over the shared experience of being turned loose in Havana. Among the Havana players were Mike Gonzalez and Dolf Luque, of whom Casey would see more in the future. Brooklyn won ten of the fifteen games, and Casey played in all of them, batting .241. The shoulder was fine, and he had a great time.

He went home and brooded, anxious to see his next contract in the mail. His worries were short-lived. A new rival league—the baseball moguls quickly called it an "outlaw" league—was launched, the Federal League, which even had a franchise in Kansas City. Was Casey interested? Of course he was. He was seen making "mysterious trips" to St. Louis to meet with the Federal League founders.

HAVE BEEN MADE FLATTERING OFFERS BUT TO DATE CAN'T NAME CLUBS, he wired *The Brooklyn Daily Eagle* in response to their inquiry.

Ebbets was worried enough so he took trains around the country to sign up his players in person. Casey agreed to a one-year deal for four thousand dollars in early January, even though Ebbets wanted to lock him up for three. He was keeping his options open.

Also in January, Casey got an interesting invitation from his old Central High baseball coach, Bill Driver, who was now the athletic director and baseball coach at the University of Mississippi in Oxford: "Charlie, would you like to come down and help me coach our baseball team over the winter?"

It sounded immediately appealing, and so, at age twenty-three, he accepted his first coaching job. "Tell 'em I'm single yet," he told an interviewer for *The Daily Mississippian,* the college paper, thinking of the coeds on campus.

Since the position did not pay, he was also designated an assistant professor so he could draw some salary. This first coaching position would be long forgotten and seldom mentioned, but the nickname "The Ol' Perfessor" may have had its roots in his time at Ole Miss. When he returned to the Brooklyns, even some teammates, not surprisingly, called him "Professor."

His college team went 13-9 over six weeks, and his center fielder, Alexander Powe, later said that Casey was "a peach as a coach. Sometimes he would get me out in the field and knocked flies to me. He would get a kick out of pulling me in and then hitting one far behind me and shouting catch THAT ball. He was good with the pitchers too."

His players bought him a gold-handled cane at the end of the season, so he could strut around with it in the major leagues.

When he showed up for spring training after his Ole Miss season, he fell under the tutelage of the new Brooklyn manager, Wilbert "Uncle Robbie" Robinson. Kid Elberfeld came aboard as a coach, which went against Casey's observation that most coaches are "related to the manager's wife."

Uncle Robbie was already a baseball legend, although his reputation was largely as a sidekick to John McGraw. He had been the catcher for the legendary and innovative Baltimore Orioles, National League champions in 1894–96, the team of McGraw, Hughie Jennings, and Willie Keeler. Such terms as "butcher boy" (or "Baltimore chop"), used to describe chopping down on a pitch into a high bounce for a base hit, came from that club. These terms remained in Casey's vocabulary for the rest of his life.

THE ROTUND ROBINSON, AT the time coaching the Giants for McGraw (with whom he co-owned a business in Baltimore), questioned a decision by his boss after the last game of the 1913 World Series and found himself unemployed. They didn't speak for the next seventeen years. So, when Ebbets hired him to manage Brooklyn in 1914, a rivalry was lit.

Such a great Brooklyn character was Robinson that the team almost at once became the Brooklyn "Robins," and headline writers would call the team the "flock" for years to come—long after Robinson left and the team nickname reverted to "Dodgers."

Casey, needing to get his new manager's attention, made a fast impression in Augusta, hitting a much-talked-about home run over the spot where a center-field fence should have been (the wall had been knocked down by a storm). "The twenty-eight fans present gave a whoop of delight as they saw Boss Ebbets' dollar and a quarter piece of leather disappear into the beyond," reported the *Eagle*.

Facing a left-handed pitcher just starting his own career with the minor-league Baltimore Orioles, Casey hit two doubles against "Jack Dunn's babe"—a fellow named George Herman Ruth. (Dunn owned the Baltimore club.)

Robinson moved Casey from center to right, the position he would play most of the rest of his career.

Ebbets, meanwhile, wanted to tighten up discipline on the club, even though his new manager was anything but a disciplinarian. He identified "four rascals" as being most in need of "watching," including Stengel, and kept close watch on them. Fred Lieb, writing in his late-in-life memoir, *Baseball As I Have Known It,* said that Casey greatly resented this, and it became another irritant in his relationship with Ebbets.

Ebbets thought of Casey as the world's greatest ballplayer—"from the neck down." He had questions about his instincts on the field. He once fined him fifty dollars for sliding into second when the base was already occupied.

"The four rascals" according to Lieb, would take the trolley to nearby Coney Island after games, or on the Sunday off-days. Coney Island, with its honky-tonk atmosphere, its amusements, and its young visitors, was a natural destination for high-energy ballplayers.

"Every so often," wrote Lieb,

Ebbets would hold a Monday morning "court session" in his office. He usually started with Stengel. "You've been drinking and fighting again. We kept tab on you and you owned eight beers inside of an hour," he would bark. "No Mr. Ebbets," said Casey. "I had only four beers," said Casey holding up four fingers. "Who started the fights?" asked Ebbets.

"It was them other guys," explained Stengel. "Some of those toughs try to add to their reputation so they can say they licked a lot of Dodgers."

"Did they lick you?" asked the owner.

"No they didn't. We wouldn't have permitted that, for your

sake as well as ours. What would people say if a bunch of bums beat up some of your best players?"

"Well, you got a point there," said Ebbets. "Of course, you had to stand for the integrity of the club."

Case dismissed.

Lieb, who began covering New York baseball in 1909 and wrote his memoir sixty-eight years later, went on to discuss Stengel's drinking. "He wasn't a seasoned alcoholic. Every so often he would turn down his glass and say humbly, 'Doctor's orders.' He was a man with a very high capacity for holding alcohol. He didn't get stupid or slovenly in his speech when he drank. His mind seemed as keen after eight drinks as after one, and his memory remained keen after a night of drinking. In that respect, he was a man in a million, or maybe a hundred million."

Indeed, Casey's capacity to drink a lot without showing any more effect than prolonged talking was legendary in baseball circles. Most people simply marveled at his capacity for drink and his ability to go on till the early morning, continuing to hold his own while closing up bars around the country.

Uncle Robbie, who had owned a billiard parlor/saloon with McGraw, could tell the good drunks from the bad. It was pretty certain that he had no problem with Casey. Ebbets was the thorn in Casey's side on this issue.

"Wilbert Robinson was a lot of fun to work for," said Casey.

In July, during an exhibition in Bellaire, Ohio, Casey took a perch in the infield before the start of an inning and initiated a phantom infield drill, throwing and catching in rapid order with his teammates, none of whom actually produced a baseball. The fans loved it, and it went on for nearly ten minutes. Casey was settling into his role as a very entertaining ballplayer.

By the end of Robinson's first season, the team had moved up a notch, to fifth, but still played under .500. Casey, though, was a revelation. His .316 average was fifth in the National League, and his on-base percentage (which no one gave a thought to in 1914) was a league-best .404.

Robbie showed some previously untapped skills as a communicator and a manager. If he benched a player and the substitute didn't deliver, he might tell the benched player (sometimes Casey), "I couldn't sleep all night. I messed up. I should have played you." This kept morale high. (Casey, as a manager, would never do anything like it. He was from the McGraw school of "no excuses.")

Casey earned raves for his outfielding, and at twenty-three he was one of the league's shining faces. He could certainly feel secure in his standing. Sure enough, with the threat of Casey's jumping to the Federal League still out there, Ebbets signed Casey to a two-year deal at six thousand dollars a year right after the 1914 season ended. For Casey, it was big-time money.

For Ebbets, always just a step ahead of creditors, it was a bold move.

6

THE GRAPEFRUIT
FROM THE SKY

WHEN CASEY REPORTED TO the Dodgers' new spring training site in Daytona Beach, Florida, in March 1915, he looked
awful. He had lost a lot of weight, and was no longer a
barrel-chested figure of powerful manhood.

"He has lost fifteen pounds through sickness, but is rapidly recovering," reported *The New York Times.*

The *Eagle* put it in worse terms when he reported to camp. He was "a
mere shadow of himself," they reported. "From a husky athlete weighing in in the neighborhood of 185 pounds, Stengel now tips the scales at
about 157, which is no heft for an able-bodied big leaguer. . . . It will be
a long time before the loyal youth from Kansas City will be able to slam
out his customary hits." On April 4, he was still reported to be "in bad
health and there is no telling how good he will be through a string of 154
games."

He was recovering from typhoid fever, which might have explained
it all, but he was also depressed. This was not the outgoing, fun-loving
figure his teammates had come to know.

George Underwood, a former Olympic gold medalist (1904 games,
track), was covering baseball at the time for a New York daily. In a
remarkable (but uncorroborated) story, which did not come to light
until years later, Underwood claimed to have encountered Casey around
midnight one night, leaning over the edge of the wooden-plank low-rise
South Bridge, which spanned the Halifax River, connecting Daytona to
Daytona Beach.

According to the story, which was later repeated in Fred Lieb's
respected 1977 memoir, Underwood spotted Casey and said, "What the

hell are you doing? You're supposed to be in bed! Uncle Robbie will slap a big fine on you if he ever hears of this, but it won't be from me!"

To which Casey apparently said, "George, I was trying to get up the guts to jump into the deep water."

"What gives you such a crazy idea?" asked Underwood.

"Oh, I'm not hitting. Besides, Uncle Robbie doesn't like me. Besides, I've got the clap."

"You better jump in my car and I'll drop you off where you live," Underwood responded. And Casey went with him. There would be no suicide that night.

Psychiatrists today might tell you that it is hard to find a better-adjusted, more self-confident guy than Casey Stengel. He was quite comfortable being Casey Stengel, and seemed not to suffer much self-doubt—or even self-reflection. But a suicide attempt off a bridge? If the story was true, what a surprise this would be to people who knew him. It seemed wholly against type.

As for Casey's having the clap, there are no known medical records to support this, but gonorrhea was especially terrible to get in the days before penicillin. (How is Alexander Fleming, the inventor of penicillin, not in the Baseball Hall of Fame?) The disease was not uncommon among players, given the rather reckless way they tended to live their lives, and the "fast" women they encountered. But there was shame and humiliation associated with it, along with great discomfort and painful treatments. It could well have humbled Casey. Some have suggested that he may still have been confused as an aftereffect of typhoid, but the pain in urination from gonorrhea is pretty much unrivaled. If true, this could have been unsettling enough to send him onto South Bridge's wooden trestle that night.

Not surprisingly, Casey makes no mention of this in his autobiography, nor was it ever a story he told "his writers." It was Underwood telling Lieb, and Lieb writing it so many decades later, that make it part of the tale, true or not.

Fortunately, the first great Casey Stengel legend—one that could be told—occurred that same month.

The story has its origins in 1908, when the Washington Senators' catcher Gabby Street caught a baseball—on his thirteenth try—that was dropped from the window at the top of the Washington Monument, some 555 feet high. This became part of the game's lore.

Legend had it that Casey participated in "beating" that record by dropping a baseball from an airplane to Uncle Robbie. And they used a grapefruit, not a baseball. Robbie, a catcher before he managed the Dodgers, was then over fifty, and very overweight. (Casey said he wore a "stomach band.")

Ebbets wanted to drop a real baseball, but the team's trainer, Frank Kelly, talked him out of it. The story grew until Casey was not only aboard, but actually sitting in a chair strapped to one of the wings!

Ruth Law, who was famous simply for being a woman pilot, had been hired by the Daytona Chamber of Commerce to fly over the beach in a Wright Brothers Model B airplane. "The idea was that my exhibition flights and passenger-carrying would attract people to the Nautilus Casino at the end of the trolley line," she said. A number of players had flown with her that spring. In this small town, she came to know the guys on the team. Casey even danced with her at the Nautilus the night before the stunt.

So Casey, presumably sitting on the wing of an airplane, dropped the grapefruit, and it exploded onto Robbie's expansive chest. Robbie yelled, "Jesus, I'm killed, I'm killed!"—which is not something you hear every day.

Some forty years later, the sportswriter Harold Rosenthal located Ruth Law and interviewed her about the event. She was then Ruth Law Oliver, and this was a journalistic coup in that he ignored the adage "Don't let the facts get in the way of a good story." Said Ruth:

A messenger was sent to me with a request that I drop a baseball from my airplane, at a little over 500 feet altitude, and one of the Dodgers would attempt to catch it with the hope of establishing a new record. . . . Time arrived for the demonstration, my plane was rolled out on the beach, and I was ready to fly. But alas, I had forgotten to bring along the ball. . . . What to do? Time was running out; no time to send anyone for the ball.

While I was considering the dilemma, a young man working in my outfit brought me a small grapefruit that he had intended to have with his lunch and suggested that I drop that. It looked about the size of a baseball and I thought what difference would it make if I dropped the pretty yellow fruit? Dummy that I was, I hadn't thought of the difference in weight of its juicy interior.

I took off, flying to about 525 feet altitude over the park, and zip went the fruit to the fellow who was standing in the middle of the field waiting to make the catch. I didn't stay to see what the result of my first and only pitch of a "baseball" would be. I was busy with my flying activities the remainder of the afternoon and gave no further thought to the stunt, which hadn't seemed important, anyway.

The next day the storm broke. Word got around that I had played a practical joke on the Dodgers, their manager had nearly been killed by a lethal weapon dropped from an airplane with malicious intent, etc. I was warned by a friend that if a Dodger ever caught me off my home base I would be shot on sight. The rest of that winter season I was careful not to fly over or near the Daytona ball park.

Many years later, Casey offered this addendum:

I want to make a correction in baseball history. I have read time and again that I went up in a plane at Daytona to throw a ball down to Wilbert Robinson, who wished to duplicate Gabby Street's stunt of catching a ball dropped from the top of the Washington Monument. The story is that I dropped a grapefruit and that it splashed all over Robbie and got me in a jam. Well I was up in the plane. But I did not drop the grapefruit. The man who did it was the club trainer, a guy named Kelly, which he always wore a diamond horseshoe stick pin, and getting your arm worked on by a trainer wearing a diamond stick pin was quite an experience which nobody nowadays possibly can undergo. Robbie found out it was this Kelly and Kelly did not get signed the following season. So there is a funny story, a trainer fired by a grapefruit.

Was Casey even on the flight? It seems unlikely.

Eventually, in his autobiography, Casey tried to set the record straight. The "drop" would be over the ballpark during practice. Robbie was not the intended catcher; it could have been anyone. But he waved everybody off and said, "Look out! I got it!"

By then, he had stopped suggesting that he might have been on the plane. Kelly was the fruit dropper and Casey seemed like an organizer. With the noise of the plane, Ruth Law probably didn't even hear that Kelly was a last-minute substitute.

Casey loved to tell this story over the years, and whether or not he was on the flight became extraneous information.

Casey was the guardian of the tale.

And that was good enough.

"When you are younger you get blamed for crimes you never committed," Casey observed in his older age. "And when you're older you begin to get credit for virtues you never possessed. It evens itself out."

7

GOOD PLAYER? BAD PLAYER?

ASEY LOOKED MUCH RECOVERED by July, when he made a remarkable catch at Ebbets Field that called for an extra measure of superlatives in the *Eagle*. "It seemed as if nothing but a ten-foot giant with a forty-foot net could reach that ball, but Casey Stengel breezed out of nowhere in particular, and, in a mighty lunge, captured the flying missile."

But even though there were moments at bat and in the field that reminded people of his many talents, the 1915 season was a struggle. On August 25, he got into a fight with a teammate, Ed "Whitey" Appleton, after a party at Coney Island. Casey's recollection of it:

> He gets into the punch [bowl] and starts sayin' a few things and he ain't actin' right. So I get him out of there and tell him we're going home. We're on the trolley and he looks all right except he doesn't say much.
>
> Him and I roomed together and by the time we got to where we lived [the Fulton Arms on Washington Street] arounds Borough Hall he probably figured I was his worst enemy in the world. He don't say nothin' until we climb the five flights of stairs to where we live and then he starts in.
>
> I give it back to him and we started to fight our way down the stairs. By the time we got to the bottom both of us have bumps all over our heads and I got this lip.
>
> The next day our heads were so swelled up we could hardly put our straw hats on. We made up some kind of a story about getting into a fight with some third guy in a restaurant for Robbie's ben-

efit and he says, "How come every time I see you guys with black eyes there was always a third guy somewhere?"

When Casey told this story to Harold Rosenthal forty-three years later, he was still able to display a deep furrow running at an angle from the side of his mouth.

"He ripped me," explained Casey. Got his hand right into my mouth and pulled. Forgot how many stitches they had to put into it."

Rosenthal checked out the story with Zack Wheat, who said they actually lived on the second floor, not the fifth. Otherwise, it checked out.

WHETHER IT WAS THE lingering effects of typhoid, other injuries or ill-nesses, depression, his feeling ill-at-ease with his manager (who actually liked him a lot), or just an unexplained off-year, Casey's 1915 average fell from .316 to .237. The Robins finished third, and finished over .500 for the first time in twelve years, but it was despite Casey, not thanks to Casey. In fact, his .237 ranked forty-second in the league among the forty-five players who had enough at-bats to qualify for the batting title.

Suddenly he was one of the worst players in the league.

Feeling down and uncertain of his future, he took the train home, disembarking at Kansas City's recently opened Union Station.*

So who was Casey Stengel, after one fine year and one bad one? Were there long careers ahead for players who clowned around, fought with teammates, and hit .237? He was lucky to have signed a two-year con-tract after 1914, but he was going to have to come back big in 1916 to prove he was worth keeping. There was no longer a Federal League offer-ing players big bucks to jump.

---

* Exactly one hundred years later, the station served as the backdrop to the Kansas City Royals' World Series celebration before an estimated eight hundred thousand fans.

8

A PENNANT FOR
UNCLE ROBBIE

THE BROOKLYN DODGERS, (or Robins or Superbas), meanwhile, had not finished first since 1900, and had never been to a modern World Series. (The modern World Series as we know it began in 1903.) Their improvement in 1915 stirred some optimism in Brooklyn.

For Wilbert Robinson, of course, it was also personal. John McGraw's Giants finished last in 1915; that had to give Robbie pleasure.

Stengel, at twenty-five, was a veteran in 1916, but still the youngest man in the regular lineup on this pennant-contending team, which included an infield of Daubert (first base), George Cutshaw (second base), Casey's old schoolmate Ivy Olson (shortstop), and Mike Mowrey (third base); Stengel, Jimmy Johnston, and Wheat in the outfield; and thirty-five-year-old Chief Meyers catching. Jeff Pfeffer (19-14 in 1915) was the ace of the pitching staff, backed by Larry Cheney, Sherry Smith, Rube Marquard, and Jack Coombs.

Meyers was one of the storytellers in Lawrence Ritter's 1966 classic book about the early years of baseball, *The Glory of Their Times,* and he had high praise for Casey as a team leader. "Robbie was just a good old soul and everything," said Meyers. "[But] it was Casey who kept us on our toes. He was the life of the party and kept us old-timers pepped up all season."

Casey had a fine spring training. At full playing weight, with his health restored and his batting eye working again, he was returning to star form. He looked robust in the team's new checkered uniforms, and he experimented by wearing sunglasses in the outfield, a practice seldom observed at the time. He appeared on two advertising posters for tobacco brands—Piedmont and Fatima—a testament to his renewed marketability in the game.

Right from the start, the Robins took off. They moved into first place on May 1, and stayed there (save for a day or two) the whole season, winning ninety-four games.

"We knew so much baseball that we just outsmarted the rest of the league and walked off—or you might say limped off—with the pennant," said Meyers. "I always maintain that Stengel won one more pennant [as a manager] than the record books show—that was in 1916 with Brooklyn."

In July, sportswriter W. R. Hoefer contributed a fan's-eye view of Casey's return to form in the *Eagle,* and with it the feeling of being in the stands at Ebbets Field at this time in history:

> The grand stand and bleachers were booming with shrieks of mad, pop-eyed creatures and wild, yowling geeks. Professors and brokers exhaled their mad cries with butchers and stokers and bakers of pies. The yells the mob uttered reached Medicine Hat, for the bases were cluttered, with "Casey" at bat. Aye! There at the platter stood "Casey the Great." Famed "Casey," the batter! He crowded the plate; but unlike the famous great Casey of verse, Charles D. didn't shame us or cause us to curse. Instead, he adjusted his batting lamps right, took two and then busted the ball outa sight. I turned to a grocer, who sat on my hat, and said to him, "Oh! Sir, when Stengel's at bat, does Charles always pickle the pill out the park, or did he just tickle that one for a lark?" But the rude grocer fellow, who ruined my lid, just roared, with a bellow, "WOW, STENGEL, OLD KID." And a shy girl who wriggled around in her joy, in ecstasy giggled and cried, "ATTA BOY." And then a most charming old lady arose, with gestures alarming that fractured my nose, as a grandfather clamored, with swings of his cane that joyously hammered my back, and my brain. Oh! Well may the happy fans warble his praise and cheer Stengel's scrappy and fence-breaking ways; for Charlie's great fielding and walloping skill have kept the Superbas up near Pennantville.

The pennant was even more laudable because this was the season when the Giants won a record twenty-six straight games. Indeed, that winning streak (there was a tie in there as well) began with a win over Brooklyn, but failed to move the Giants up in the standings at all. They started the streak in fourth place and ended it in fourth place, which is where they finished five days later.

McGraw wound up calling his own team quitters. Uncle Robbie, enjoying all this a great deal, said, "That's a lot of shit. The fact is, we're a better club and McGraw knows it. Tell him to stop pissing on my pennant."

Casey was the hero of the game that was thought to decide the season: the second game of the doubleheader on Saturday, September 30, against the defending champion Phillies and their great hurler, Grover Cleveland Alexander. After losing the opener 7–2, Brooklyn was briefly out of first, behind the Phillies. Only five games were left in the season.

Stengel led off the fifth inning against Alexander (who won thirty-three that year, with sixteen shutouts), and he unloaded on a 1-0 pitch. Wrote the *Eagle:* "The second pitch fell upon the pavement outside the right field wall. It was a home run!"

Enjoying the moment, which he would call one of his greatest baseball memories, Casey stopped at both second and third bases to remove his cap and dust off the bags before moving on.

The victory put the Robins a half-game ahead of the Phillies, and they held on, clinching the flag on Tuesday against the Giants and winning by two and a half games in the end.

They were going to their first ever World Series.

Although Casey's heroics seemed to indicate he had a year of big power, this was still the dead-ball era, and he hit only eight home runs. He had fifty-three RBIs, and hit .279, a forty-two-point improvement over the year before. The Spalding Baseball Guide called him the best player on the team.

"Pitchers had all the advantages back then," he later ruminated. "They used about four balls every game. When I broke into the business, the pitcher would throw the ball to the third baseman who would blacken it with tobacco juice, toss it to the second baseman who would blacken it further with more tobacco juice, pass it to the shortstop who would rub it in the dirt and then throw it back to the pitcher."

The players were heroes, and on the day they left for Boston, to face the Red Sox, October 5, thousands of people gathered along the streets for a grand send-off, from Ebbets Field at 11:00 a.m. to Grand Central Terminal in Manhattan two hours later.

The procession included eighteen open "touring cars" carrying team management, with Robinson and his twenty-three players all waving hats to the multitudes. The line of vehicles headed from Ebbets Field for Borough Hall in downtown Brooklyn, where thousands more awaited them. They moved on to the front of the *Brooklyn Daily Eagle* building, where a band played "Hail to the Chief." Outside the *Eagle* building, a large scoreboard would be displaying the batter-by-batter results as they arrived by telegraph.[*]

Then it was on to the Bedford Avenue branch of the YMCA, where the St. John's Orphan Asylum band played, and public officials spoke. Uncle Robbie said, "Mr. Ebbets makes the speeches for his club and I don't. However," reported the *Eagle,* "I am sure we will prove to the fans that the team can be tried and not found wanting."

Ebbets spoke little on this trip; he was dealing with loud public criticism over his pricing of World Series tickets at five dollars per box seat.

At Grand Central, the players "had to fight to get to their cars, so great was the crush of fans to see them. All of the men were in the best of spirits and quietly echoing the confidence of Robbie, who said, 'We are sure that we will make a better showing in this series than the croakers would give us credit for.'"

Unfortunately, the croakers knew what they were croaking about.

Robinson chose Marquard to start the first game at Braves Field (used because it held more people than Fenway Park), on Saturday, October 7, but the Red Sox won it 6–5 despite a four-run rally by Brooklyn in the ninth. Casey played right and batted third. It would be the first time that he ever lined up with his teammates for the first game of a World Series. He would do it fifteen times in all as a player and a manager, but there would only be one "first."

Sunday, the off day, found the players hanging around the Brunswick Hotel, eating and smoking. Casey was spotted reading *The Brooklyn Daily Eagle* over two stacks of wheat cakes, half a dozen rolls, bacon and eggs, and coffee. The players were happy to have the diversion of an automobile trip to Concord to see the Minuteman Monument.

Casey didn't play the second game, on Monday, against the lefty for Boston, Babe Ruth, who had gone 23-12 with nine shutouts during the season. And all the Babe did was pitch a 2–1 win in fourteen innings, a heartbreaking loss for the Robins, whose Sherry Smith matched Ruth inning for inning. But Ruth gave up only six hits, and no runs after the first inning. It was a masterful pitching performance on both sides.

---

[*] The World Series scoreboard display outside newspaper offices was an American tradition before mass media took hold. One might call these displays the first "sports bars" in the country.

Casey knew all about Babe. Everyone did—his reputation was growing by the day.

"It was during the following spring that I first suspected Ruth could hit. We played the Sox an exhibition game down South and in center field I played the Babe about as I'd play any husky pitcher. He socked one over my head. Back on the bench, grand old Uncle Wilbert Robinson gave me the very devil. I was sore at Robbie and to show him up I dropped back least 50 feet the next time Ruth came up. I only succeeded in showing myself up. He blasted another one over my bean."

Asked about the rather heavy bat Ruth employed, Casey said, "He could have used his sleeve or a rolled up copy of the Police Gazette. Wouldn't have made a bit of difference."

Tuesday, October 10, would prove to be the Robins' high point in the series. Back home at Ebbets Field, before 21,087 fans (seating capacity was about thirty thousand—take that for your high ticket prices, Mr. Ebbets!), Jack Coombs beat the Sox 4–3.

Casey ("That box of pep who plays right field," wrote the *Eagle*) was a hero for a dazzling throw to third base. He could be heard loudly cheering in the dugout, "We got Boston on the run!"

"The boys feel much encouraged now," Casey told the sportswriters after the game. "I hope we can all get together now and play winning ball for the rest of the series!"

But it was not to be. The Red Sox won game four at Ebbets Field 6–2, as Casey sat again against a lefty, Dutch Leonard. The next day, at Braves Field, Brooklyn lost 4–1, which would be the same as the games-won margin for the series. It was over, an easy championship for the Sox. The largest crowd in baseball history up to that point, 42,620, witnessed the action—the largest until Yankee Stadium opened in 1923 to break that record.

Casey led all hitters, with a .364 average, and got a losing player's share of $2,835—nearly half of his season's salary.

He gave the money to his dad—investing, as it were, in the Improved Street Sprinkling Company, which was experiencing rough times as more and more roadways were being paved in Kansas City.

Casey's parents couldn't be more proud. His father told friends that his son was the best outfielder in baseball since Wee Willie Keeler.

9

THE PIRATES AND
THE PHILLIES

NOTHER WINTER, AND ANOTHER holdout for Casey, as Ebbets cut almost everyone's salary following the demise of the Federal League. Casey expected a raise after a pennant-winning season; instead, he got a two-thousand-dollar cut. "If [Ebbets] lost money last year, or even had a poor year financially, I would think he was doing this to cover up the deficit," Casey told the *Eagle*. "But I can't see any reason in the world why he wants to cut the boys who made it possible for him to collect a goodly sum of money last season as his spoils of the World Series. And besides, he charged more for admission . . . than any other owner in the National League. It seems reasonable that if he charges such prices to see his players perform, he should meet the fans halfway by giving them the opportunity to watch high-priced players."

Casey was a supporter of the rather powerless Baseball Players' Fraternity, which in January threatened to strike spring-training camps. This union was headed by the lawyer and former player Dave Fultz, whose demands did not extend to ending the reserve clause, that item in the player contracts that bound them to their team for life, or at least until they were released or traded. In fact, the only one of the four demands it made that directly affected major-league players was the elimination of a rule allowing clubs to suspend players without pay after certain periods of disability. Casey would not publicly state whether he supported a strike, but his feelings were growing hostile over the big pay cut he was to receive.

Not surprisingly, Ebbets opposed the Players' Fraternity and stood fast in opposition to strike threats. There was no strike, and, not much later, the Fraternity died.

Ebbets now sent Casey a contract calling for an additional cut of

thirteen hundred dollars. Casey wrote back that by some mistake he
had received the clubhouse attendant's contract. Ebbets then offered a
seventeen-hundred-dollar cut. Casey considered his options and wrote
back to say he'd take the one calling for the thirteen-hundred-dollar cut.

Stengel and Wheat (another holdout) stayed home and didn't sign
until two weeks before the season. The signings took place when the
Robins and Red Sox met in Kansas City (where both players were holed
up) for a pair of exhibitions, a match of the World Series opponents.
(This was the series in which Ruth socked two over Casey's bean.)

The 1917 holdout was just the start of a year of skirmishes and mis-
steps for Casey that doubtless set him back with Ebbets and Robinson.
Later, looking back, he said:

> When we came to Ebbets Field to start the season, I took one
> of the contracts they'd sent me, and took a pair of scissors and
> started down to right field during practice. People would yell to
> me, "Did you get your money back, Casey? What kind of contract
> did you get?"
>
> And I'd hold up the contract and cut a piece off it with the scis-
> sors to make it shorter. "I didn't get such a big one," I'd say.
>
> Well, in the Brooklyn office they didn't think that was so smart.
> They said, "He's getting too fresh, and he don't use enough tact."

Casey was considered part of the unit of players known as the "grum-
blers." This was a newspaper term, and perhaps a successor group to the
"four rascals" of earlier days. Casey managed to be part of both groups.

In August, feeling the Giants' Jeff Tesreau had intentionally thrown
at his head, Casey threatened to "get somebody myself." That turned out
to be Art Fletcher, who was the victim of Casey's nasty slide into second,
leading to a fight. Though newspapers speculated over suspensions, the
league president, John K. Tener, decided not to suspend anyone: "The
two players simply lost their tempers in the stress of a keen battle. They
were surely doing their very best for their clubs and scrapping for every
inch in the game."

BY THE END OF the 1917 season, the Robins had fallen to seventh place,
a terrible tumble for the defending league champions. Casey hit an undis-
tinguished .257 but led the team with seventy-three RBIs, sixty-nine

runs, six home runs (tied), twenty-three doubles, and twelve triples. He also started eight double plays from right field, which tied a major-league record, and led the National League with thirty outfield assists, a total that has been bettered only three times since then. Not even Roberto Clemente, whose peak was twenty-six, bettered it.

Why the high assist total? It was largely because Casey had mastered the concrete wall in right field.

As the *Pittsburgh Post-Gazette* wrote:

> Stengel plays the concrete barrier almost as well as a good billiard player behaves while manipulating the smooth ivories. The clever Dodger is such a fine judge of distance that he can tell in a flash whether it will be possible for him to capture a low-flying sizzler or be forced to take it off the fence.
>
> It is a rare pleasure to watch Casey turn deftly with his back to the diamond, gather in the ball as it rebounds off the hard concrete and stop a surprised runner who thinks he has an easy two-base hit. Of course the seasoned player soon gets on to Casey's little trick, but he does it so cleverly that even a veteran is likely to be nipped any time.

But his time in Brooklyn was over.

Ebbets thought Casey was disrespectful and rude, and resented his running his mouth off to the newspapers. Ebbets was pretty much done with him.

In December, choosing to be an eyewitness to what he presumed to be his own trade, he went to the winter meetings in New York, campaigning a bit to determine his fate. "I'd like to wind up in the 'Big Town,'" as he called New York. "They can send me to Pittsburgh or Chicago or any old place, but give me the Big Town. That's where we all want to land."

It didn't happen at the winter meetings. But on January 9, he and George Cutshaw were traded to the Pittsburgh Pirates for Burleigh Grimes, Al Mamaux, and Chuck Ward.

"I know'd I shouldn't of been such a smart aleck," said Casey, now a member of the only team to finish behind Brooklyn in 1917.

> I'm glad and I'm sorry that the deal has been consummated. It affords me much joy to know that I won't have to play for Ebbets next season, that is, if my services are not wanted by Uncle Sam

[the United States had declared war on Germany in April 1917], but it causes me much regret to realize that I have to leave a city of fans that have treated me most royally even when I chanced to fall into a slump.

Since my debut in Flatbush in the fall of 1912, I can say with much sincerity that Ty Cobb in Detroit or George Sisler in St. Louis never enjoyed any better treatment than was accorded me in the Dodger village. It causes me an exuberance of sorrow to even think that I have to leave such a square, sportsmanlike, considerate body of baseball followers as those that inhabit the ball emporium of Ebbets . . . but the best of friends must part and I guess fate decided that I was a popular idol long enough.

Certainly, up until the time that the "Boys of Summer" came along in the late '40s, any discussion of memorable Dodger players would have included the colorful Casey. He gave them five full seasons plus a month in 1912, helped to open Ebbets Field in grand style, helped them to their first World Series, was a "popular idol" and a genuine gate attraction. Had there been All-Star teams then, he likely would have made at least one. He hit a respectable .272 for them, and would one day leverage his popularity to come back and manage them. But for now, it was time to move on.

Casey wasted no time before sitting down with the owner, Barney Dreyfuss, in Pittsburgh. "I'm playing for the same money I got in my third year," Casey said. "For heaven's sake, I want more money. That was my problem in Brooklyn."

"More money? How do I know you're that good?"

"I must have been or you wouldn't have traded for me," Casey responded.

"You didn't do it for me," Dreyfuss said, according to Casey. "Show me you're that good this year."

Casey sighed; he would remember Dreyfuss as always having an answer for everything.

The trade was very popular in the Pittsburgh newspapers and among fans. "Casey probably has more friends in the bleacher populations of the National League cities than any other player in the circuit," wrote the *Post-Gazette.*

And Casey was feeling good about showing up the Robins for their bad deal. "I'm not bragging about the size of my income tax or anything like that," he said, "but I think I can afford to lose $500 if anybody sees fit to back the Dodgers over the Pirates. I have $500 right now that says we will be ahead of Brooklyn in October and the bet is open to anybody."

Brooklyn finished fifth, Pittsburgh fourth. (Honus Wagner had retired the year before.) He would have won that bet.

On opening day, Casey's double off Pete Schneider of Cincinnati was the Pirates' only hit in a 2–0 loss. This would have otherwise been the first opening-day no-hitter in history. (There has only been one since—by Bob Feller in 1940.)

He would, however, play in only thirty-nine games for the Pirates in 1918. On June 3, at the Polo Grounds in New York, he was ejected for arguing, and while taking that long walk to the clubhouse in deep center field, he took off his uniform jersey and flung it over his shoulder, leaving him in his flannel baseball undershirt. The next day, a telegram arrived informing him that he was being fined by the league office for his "shocking conduct in disrobing on the ball field."

The Pirates next went to Ebbets Field—his first time back—and Casey pinned his telegram from the league to his jersey. He figured he would be in for more trouble, and that night talked himself into enlisting in the war effort.

"My brother and everybody said later that showed how smart I was, because to keep from paying a $200 fine, I gave up a salary of about $4,000 a year for Navy pay of $15 a month." He left the team on June 10.

"The doc took one look at me and pronounced me perfect," said Casey. He passed his physical and enlisted in the navy without even informing his Pittsburgh manager. In all, 103 players left their major-league teams, including fourteen Pirates.

Casey did not go overseas. He was stationed at the Brooklyn Navy Yard, and his war duty consisted of being a player/manager for the Navy Yard's baseball team. Sometimes he helped to paint ships.

"I managed a ball club of gobs [sailors] and this gave me an opportunity to institute a training table at which we ate like admirals. My faith in human nature was somewhat upset in the course of one of those battleship games. At the Prospect Park Parade Grounds, I asked a youngster to look on, to hold my wallet. As I slid into second base in the first inning, I caught sight of the kid about a quarter of a mile away, on a bicycle and pedaling like blazes. That taught me a rule I have followed ever since. I never again will trust my roll to anybody who owns a bicycle."

Casey was not just a manager, he was the one who organized the games. "I made it my business to board every ship as it came in, and I scheduled a game with their team for the next day. That way we got them before they could get rid of their sea legs."

His highlight moment playing service ball came when he led Navy to a 1–0 victory over Army before five thousand fans at the Polo Grounds, with Casey driving in the only run of the game.

Casey never saw action (although he would tell people that he guarded Brooklyn's Gowanus Canal and not a single submarine got into it), and his service was complete when the war ended in November, five months after his enlistment. "I never ate better in my life than at the training table of my sailor ball team," he would say.

THE 1919 PIRATES TRAINED in Birmingham, Alabama, but they trained without Casey, who held out the entire spring, not joining the team until they got to Louisville on their way north to open the season. Dreyfuss counted on the fact that players, with no leverage, always come around. He tried to trade Casey, without success. As with Ebbets, there was no love lost between Stengel and Dreyfuss. Casey wanted out.

One day in Pittsburgh's Forbes Field he made a bad play, and the bleacher fans were all over him. Casey turned to them and said, "Please don't yell at me that loud. I am not strong any more. I don't get much money and I don't get enough to eat."

Another time, fans and writers noticed that he wasn't sliding when he should. "With the salary I got here, I'm so hollow and starving that I'm liable to explode like a light-bulb if I hit the ground too hard."

The season highlight for Casey came at Ebbets Field on Sunday, May 25. This was the first year in which Sunday baseball was allowed in New York, and a big crowd was on hand. What happened that day would be remembered as Casey's zaniest moment as a player.

Casey's heart had never left Ebbets Field, and he was in a good mood that day. He was hitting over .300 and life was good. He had struck out twice and had semi-jogged after a long fly ball that let three runs score. The fans were playfully picking on him, although happy that their Robins were the beneficiaries.

After the Robins batted in the sixth, Casey went to their bullpen in right field, instead of to the Pirates' dugout. He had old friends there, including the pitcher Leon Cadore.

Cadore had just picked up a small sparrow, which had flown into the wall behind the bullpen and knocked itself senseless. "The bird was stunned," said Casey. "He commenced shaking himself a little to see if his head was still on."

"Lemme have it," said Casey to Cadore, and he proceeded to run in from the bullpen with the bird under his cap. When he came to bat, the Brooklyn faithful greeted him with some good-humored boos mixed in. He was, after all, an opposing player.

Casey proceeded to face the fans and, in one motion, took a deep bow and removed his cap, permitting the now recovered sparrow to fly off triumphantly. "The bird commenced wiggling and I had to get rid of it," said Casey. The home plate umpire laughed. Even the staid *New York Times* loved it. "Stengel . . . turned magician in the seventh inning. He doffed his cap and from out of the darkness of the headpiece there flew an irate but much relieved sparrow."

Caps were much flatter then than they are now; how he kept the bird in place without letting it flutter its way out might make one skeptical, but there were enough eyewitnesses on hand that day to assure that this was a wholly true story, not a fable. His signature moment had been achieved. With good humor, he had given the ol' Brooklyn fans "the bird" in response to their taunting. And they loved it.

(He did it again in Philadelphia a year later, releasing a bird after catching a fly ball, but the crowd was only about five hundred, and this moment was pretty much lost to history.)

"I was fairly good at times," he reflected, "but a lot of people seem to remember the stunts I pulled better than they do the ball games I helped win." More than fifty years later, a children's book called *Baseball's Zaniest Stars* featured an illustration of the bird-in-cap moment on the cover.

Casey hit .293, which would have led the team had he had enough plate appearances, but on August 9, Dreyfuss finally managed to trade him to the Philadelphia Phillies for outfielder Possum Whitted.

"We showed Stengel every consideration and tried to trade him to an Eastern club," said Dreyfuss, who had verbally promised Casey a thousand-dollar bonus if he reached certain statistical plateaus at bat.

Said the *Post-Gazette*:

Casey had it in him to be a star of the first order here. But he was not satisfied with his surroundings and wouldn't play his best. Repeatedly he "loafed" on balls hit in his direction and in other ways demonstrated that his efforts were of only an indifferent brand. He simply did not want to play for the Pirates and it did not take long for his admirers to turn against him. Even the right field bleacherites, who once fairly worshipped him, resented his actions and turned upon him. He outlived his wonderful popularity and usefulness and virtually made a trade imperative.

Casey has a wonderful personality, but even that wasn't enough to cause the fans to overlook shortcomings for which there was no excuse. The fans expect the players to do their best at all times; that is what they pay for and what the players are paid for. They will not tolerate willful shirking on the ball field.

Although it was midseason, Casey wired the Phillies' owner, William Baker, and asked that he honor that thousand-dollar bonus. Casey was well below his six-thousand-dollar peak from 1915–16, and still agitated about it. Baker wouldn't honor the bonus (not unusual behavior by an owner in those days), so Casey quit. Quit! He went home to Kansas City and sat out the rest of the season. This was an unthinkable gesture for a major-league player.

He didn't sit home for long, however. He put together a barnstorming team made up of former minor leaguers and even old Central High teammates and proceeded to set up a schedule of games with a local promoter named Logan Galbreath. They played twice a week, and the manager was Roy Sanders, a Pirates holdout. He was lucky that major-league baseball didn't suspend him for this action, but there was no commissioner yet, and he seemed free to do as he chose. One of his games was against a "colored" team on which Bullet Joe Rogan was a dazzling pitcher. Casey later noted, "They were as good as any major-leaguers, but colored players couldn't be in the big leagues then."

When Rube Foster founded the Negro National League in 1920 and a team was placed in Kansas City under the ownership of J. L. Wilkinson, Casey suggested he sign Rogan for the club. Wilkinson and Rogan are both in the Hall of Fame today, and the Negro Leagues Baseball Museum is in Kansas City.

Casey looked back at the evolution of the game in his 1961 memoir.

When I broke into baseball, we used to have Irish and German and Polish players. And then the greatest players came from the South. Then they came from Texas and then they came from Chicago.

Today it's the colored player. He's a good runner, and he's very quick with his wrists. He's the best hitter. The Italians are the second best hitters. The Polish player is sometimes slow and sluggish swinging the bat. The Germans are passing out, the race has gotten mixed up so much, and it's the same with the Irish. They don't talk and act like the ones that had just come from Ireland.

Casey was, of course, German-Irish.

AND THEN HE WAS a Phillie.

Casey wanted to be "back east," but he was savvy enough to know that this was a sad entry in major-league baseball.

"Some teams," he later reflected, "like the Phillies when I was there, don't aim for the pennant, they was glad to aim for fourth place."

His observation, though he couldn't know it, would cover the time from their 1915 pennant until their 1950 pennant; this was only 1920.

They played in Baker Bowl, a bandbox of a ballpark that was only 280 feet to the right-field foul pole, with a shabby clubhouse in center field. A sixty-foot fence was added to a low right-field wall the year Casey arrived. He would have to learn to play that wall much as Red Sox left fielders learned to play the high wall in Fenway Park—except that the Fenway wall was just thirty-seven feet high. Baker Bowl's wall was tougher to play than Fenway's, because it was made of different construction materials and the ball would rebound differently depending on where it hit. This was a challenge for anyone who played there.

Living in Philadelphia and playing in Baker Bowl was the kind of experience that could drive a ballplayer to drink. Except this was 1920, and the Volstead Act—aka Prohibition—made such a pastime illegal. Ballplayers, just like everyone else, had to break the law to purchase a distilled beverage.

The Phillies were not without some notables in 1920, despite their last-place finish for the year. Casey's pal Irish Meusel was on the club; he had played for Casey over the winter on his touring team, and would be a lifelong friend.

Now thirty years old, Casey had a good season, hitting .292 with nine home runs (a career high, thanks to Baker Bowl). Still feisty and competitive, he was fined twenty-five dollars in May for arguing too vehemently.

Casey, of course, also continued to be a bench jockey and a provocateur in on-field scrapes. One day, Dolf Luque, the pitcher against whom Casey had played in that 1913 Cuban-American series, and who was now playing for Cincinnati, walked over to the Phillies' bench and flat-out punched Casey in the mouth for his persistent heckling. Except he got the wrong guy. Told it wasn't Casey, Luque said, "Stengel pop off too much anyway."

The two would battle another day.

When Brooklyn won the 1920 pennant, it could not have made Casey feel any happier about his situation in Philly.

Gavvy Cravath was fired as manager after 1920 and replaced by a former Yankees manager from 1915 to 1917, Wild Bill Donovan.

Casey found himself riding the bench a lot in 1921. He let everyone in Brooklyn know how much he missed those days with the Dodgers, and how he would rather be "back home at Ebbets Field than anywhere else in the universe." This was going to be another last-place season for Philly, one in which they would draw fewer than four thousand people a game. It was not a happy environment.

Both Casey's legs and his back were acting up—traces of pain he first experienced the year before—and he had gotten into only twenty-four games by the end of June. When he did play, he sometimes got silly. The Philadelphia sportswriter Stan Baumgartner remembered him catching fly balls behind his back to amuse the fans.

Additionally, the Phillies pitcher Jimmy Ring said he saw Casey make "the finest catch that it has been my fortune to witness." He was running down a fierce drive by Rogers Hornsby when "his shoulder hit the wall at the same time [as the ball] and he went over on his face, but hung on to the pill. It was a wonderful effort and saved the game when it appeared hopelessly lost."

CASEY'S TURN TO LEAVE came on July 1, when he and the infielder Johnny Rawlings were traded to the New York Giants for three fairly nondescript players—Lee King, Goldie Rapp, and Lance Richbourg. The value of the players, plus cash, was said to be seventy-five thousand dollars.

The Phils were in last place, twenty-five games out of first on the day of the trade. The Giants were in first.

What a great day that was for Stengel. His "exile" to Pennsylvania was over. He had grown "baseball old" in those towns, watching losses pile up. Donovan was forever shouting at his players' ineptness, so much so that Casey had moved his locker as far away from the manager as he could. When the club's road secretary found him to inform him of the trade, Casey let out a wild cheer and leaped from the trainer's table.

"I thought your leg hurt," said the road secretary.

"Not anymore," said Casey. "I've been traded to the Giants!"

Dressed only in his shorts, he ran onto the field and circled the bases, sliding into each base as he went. He caught the 6:41 from 30th Street Station in Philadelphia to New York, and then a midnight train to Boston to meet the Giants. He wanted to report right away; he didn't want anything to go wrong with the deal, even though the Giants' next game was in New York.

The Giants were hosting the Braves on a July 3 Sunday doubleheader. He was immediately put into the lineup—batting sixth, in center field—in both games. There were twenty-eight thousand people in attendance. This was big-time baseball, back in the big town! This was more like it!

10

MCGRAW AND
THE GIANTS

NEW YORK WAS THE nation's most exciting city, the Polo Grounds was the most majestic ballpark in the land, the Giants were baseball's glamour team, and John McGraw, at forty-eight, the most celebrated manager in the game. He had already won six pennants and finished second seven times. The Giants were the toast of the Broadway crowd, and now the colorful Casey would be joining a star-studded roster that included Frankie Frisch, George Kelly, Dave Bancroft, Irish Meusel, and Ross Youngs. Casey and Irish would be roommates.

McGraw was still a scrapper, the kind of guy Casey admired. He was a member of New York's prestigious Lambs Club—and missed a chunk of the 1920 season "through injuries sustained in a brawl" at the club, according to *Reach's Base Ball Guide*.

On August 24, Casey was on the bench for a game against his old Pirates. It was a "learning moment" for him.

The Pirates were up 2–0 in the seventh, with Babe Adams on the mound for the Bucs. The Giants loaded the bases, and George "High Pockets" Kelly was up. The count went to 3-0.

"Look at those clowns," muttered McGraw so his players could hear him. Casey later said:

> I almost didn't bother to look, because I know McGraw will flash the sign to take the next pitch. But I nearly fell off the bench. McGraw is giving him the sign to hit, and Kelly hits a grand-slam home run.
>
> It bugs me, though. I can't figure it out. It worked, but why should Mac go against the percentages? So after the game, I ask him.
>
> "I'll tell you why," shouts McGraw. "Kelly couldn't hit Adams'

curveball if he stood at the plate all day. But on this one pitch Adams has to come in with his fastball. And since it would be the only fastball Kelly would get all day, I let him hit it."

McGraw and Stengel. Teacher and student. Casey was about to learn a lot about managing. It was the start of a beautiful era in his life. Casey recalled:

Some men didn't play good for McGraw—at least they said they didn't. They'd say, "Why this man's never satisfied with me." I thought that McGraw did great with me because I had to run out every ball; I had to play good. And if I didn't play good, he thought that there was something wrong with me or that I wasn't putting out enough. I thought I was hustling all the time, but he'd see where I could have put out a little extra.

One day we are playing the Cardinals and we have them 4 to 1 and sailing along easy, when things begin to pop. In the eighth, the Redbirds score five and beat us. In that eighth, a hard grounder is hit to Frankie Frisch's left. He dives for it. He throws the man out. But what we needed was a double play.

When we return to the bench, I say, "Frankie, you made a wonderful play. It's a long time since I saw one as good."

McGraw is sitting next to me and he grunts. I know that he doesn't agree. I know that grunt.

McGraw looks at me and says, "Stengel, no wonder you are traded off one club after another. You don't know a damn thing about baseball."

This is a big shock on account of I figure I know plenty about the national pastime.

"A player with the best legs in the National League, like Frisch, doesn't have to dive. All he has to do is get the jump on the ball and dash into the play.

"If he handles the ball right, he gets a double play and the Cardinals get no five runs. Since he dived, we may lose this one."

I sat back and studied his remarks and said to myself, "Hey, the old guy is right."

As Casey turned thirty (really thirty-one), and as he kept seeing himself called "Ol Case" in the paper, he knew that his peak playing days might be winding down. He was going to get a heavy dose of platoon baseball, as Meusel, Youngs, and George Burns did most of the outfield time. But he was going to school on this, observing McGraw's tactics, learning about moving players in and out of the lineup. What he learned would one day come to define his own managing style.

Over the final three months of the pennant-winnning season, Casey played in only eight games in the outfield, and had five hits. He still had problems with his back. And even though he was among the twenty-five eligible players for the World Series, he did not get into any games. He did, all the same, manage to get thrown out of one of them for excessive arguing from the dugout of umpire George Moriarty's call at first base. The Giants won the world championship, beating the Yankees. In fact, if there was an example of *no* platooning, this was it. McGraw used only thirteen players in the eight games, including the exact same starting lineup in each game (except for alternating catchers) and four pitchers. Still, each winning player on the Giants received a record $5,265; Casey got a half-share, commensurate with his time on the team.

He was happy to be a Giant, but probably had some concern about his status for 1922, after barely making eye contact with McGraw during the series.

He was still young at heart, a bachelor enjoying the big city, but lines were appearing in his face that made him look older than he was. The press enjoyed picking on his age. Will Wedge of the New York *Globe and Commercial Advertiser* wrote a poem in *The Sporting News* called "Lines to Casey Stengel":

> You wouldn't let 'em count you out;
> You wouldn't warm the bench:
> Thought thirty years or thereabout
> Your spirit would not quench
> And thirty's old in baseball land—
> And you admit to more—
> Yet bounce with pepper of the brand
> Of birds of twenty-four
> It seems they cannot tie the can
> To guys from Kankakee
> You played there, yes, you did, old man,
> When was it, 1903?
> You came from Kansas, wasn't it?

From Kansas City, Mo.
"K.C." they called you, and it fit;
Eh, Casey, long ago?
Since then you played in Brooklyn town,
In Pittsburgh and in "Phil";
Now in New York you earn renown
Ey keeping at it still
Your limbs may feel the stiffening
Of age that mounteth slow;
You keep it, though, a secret thing
And never let it show
How do you do it, Casey, how
Still swing so mean a mace?
So old! (or young?) Well, we will vow
That Casey, you're a case!

The Giants trained in San Antonio in the spring of 1922. On the way north, to play a game in Wichita Falls, Casey had some fun. He pulled a pair of dirty blue overalls over his uniform, donned a straw hat and an old coat, and heckled the players from the stands. "Tramps! Bums! Rotten players!" he shouted. "Go get a real job!"

His teammates were in on the joke and played along. One shouted back: "If you can do better, you fresh appleknocker, why don't you come down and do it!"

"Well, give me a suit and I will show yer," said Casey. And with that, he threw off his costume and raced to the field in his Giants uniform to play the rest of the game, to the delight of the fans.

Casey was thought of as a fourth outfielder, and some thought his place on the team might be tenuous. But the Giants had paid seventy-five thousand dollars in cash and players for him (and Johnny Rawlings), and that at least seemed to secure his spot on the roster for '22. Youngs and Meusel both hit .331 and were secure in the outfield. Bill Cunningham (.328) was now the third man. Casey appeared in only four games in all of April and May. But at one point both Cunningham and Youngs were injured, and Casey got more playing time. And, oh, did the hits start to fall.

As late as July 29, Casey was hitting .402. And this came after a pitch from the Cubs' Virgil Cheeves on July 11 that hit him in the face. They feared that his cheekbone was fractured, but the X-rays were negative. He spent a few days in the hospital and was back in the lineup ten days after being hit—playing with a swollen face, but with his usual gusto. His average continued to rise after he returned. He led the league in hit-by-pitch that season, with nine, in just eighty-four games.

He batted a robust .368 for the season, the highest mark of his career, and the highest mark on the Giants that season. In the National League, it was topped only by Rogers Hornsby of the Cardinals, who hit .401 (although Casey did not have enough plate appearances to qualify among league leaders). His average at home was .397, and he struck out only seventeen times all season. Long a right fielder, he adjusted to center and earned McGraw's admiration by playing the sun so well—tilting his cap just so to shield his eyes from the rays, frequently using sunglasses. His popularity soared, and he was the toast of another pennant-winning Giants team.

Adding to his joy in the big season was the summer-long presence of his mother and sister at the Polo Grounds. He set them up in a rental apartment on Riverside Drive in Manhattan, overlooking the Hudson River. "Charlie is a home boy," said his mother. "And I guess he likes to have us around."

Unfortunately, nine days before the World Series began, he pulled a muscle in his leg and, just like that, he was an old man again. The fountain of youth he had discovered in June was gone.

In the World Series, he only started the first two games, and McGraw sent Cunningham in to run for him in the second inning of Game Two, after seeing Casey limp to second on a ground ball. McGraw was angry that Casey had faked being fine, instead of letting a pinch runner go in when he was at first base. "His run could have scored," groused McGraw. "It cost us a win."

Whether or not McGraw's analysis was completely on the mark, the Giants didn't get the win. The game was called for darkness—despite bright sunlight—a very controversial tie in which Commissioner Kenesaw Mountain Landis awarded the gate receipts to charity. McGraw's feelings on the matter were pretty clear; this was the only mention he made of Stengel in his memoir *My Thirty Years in Baseball*.

The Giants won the series in five games, and Casey whooped it up in the clubhouse like the kids on the team. He chased after a teammate who had swiped his detachable shirt collar and, curiously, recited lines of classical literature as he paused in pursuit. He had just won another world championship, and a World Series share of $4,546.

11

WORLD SERIES HEROICS

ELEVEN DAYS AFTER the World Series ended, fourteen players (and six wives) gathered in Vancouver, British Columbia, to embark on a journey to the Far East for a series of exhibition games. It would be the first visit to Japan by an American team. This trip, which was endorsed by President Warren Harding, was to include players selected not only for their playing skill, but for good deportment.

Commissioner Landis was vocal on this point, knowing as he did that turning these players loose in a foreign land could be risky. And this was even before Casey was added to the roster. "The players appreciate the necessity and importance of maintaining the high standards of play and sportsmanship and of personal conduct on and off the field which they observe during the regular championship season," Landis stated.

Landis sent umpire George Moriarty to be "house mother" and supervise behavior. A few sportswriters also went, including Fred Lieb and Frank O'Neill.

Casey replaced Joe Sewell of Cleveland on the roster at the last minute. The team also included Fred Hofmann, Joe Bush, and Waite Hoyt from the Yankees; Luke Sewell and Riggs Stephenson of the Indians; Herb Pennock of the Red Sox (who was traded to the Yankees during the trip); Kelly and Meusel of the Giants (after overcoming objections from McGraw); Bert Griffith of the Robins; John Lavan of the Cardinals; Bibb Falk and Amos Strunk of the White Sox; and ex-player Herb Hunter as the organizer and substitute if needed.

One newspaperman—Jack Keene of the *Times Herald* of Olean, New York—wrote, "There are precious few like Stengel. . . . He is one of baseball's real clowns on and off the field. The fact that he is to appear before people whose language he does not understand will not bother him in the slightest for he is quite as funny in pantomime as he is with the spoken line. . . . Turn him loose in a field with nothing on his mind but his hat, and there will be many a laugh in store for the spectators." The headline said STENGEL IS JOY BOY OF TEAM TO TOUR ORIENT.

The players went for the adventure, not for any guaranteed payment. They got first-class treatment at every stop and stayed in fine hotels, but each player had to post a thousand dollars into an escrow account to make sure they completed the trip. They likely received a portion of the gate receipts, but were not otherwise compensated—which may explain why Babe Ruth didn't go along. The team wore uniforms with a "U.S." patch on the jersey, and each player also got a "U.S." pullover sweater. The caps bore no logo.

There was risk to this, and no insurance policies were written. The players agreed not to sign 1923 contracts until they returned home and showed that they had not suffered any serious injuries. Still, those who took the risk thought it was worth it.

The "All-American Team" sailed on the *Empress of Canada* and reached Yokohama, Japan, on October 30, after an eleven-day voyage. The team scheduled thirteen games in Japan, some played in the snow, plus some hastily scheduled ones (overall record: 15-1), covering a number of Japanese college teams. There was plenty of time for sightseeing, including a two-week stay in Tokyo.

The only blemish was a 9–3 loss to Keio University alumni who came from Mita, a district in Tokyo, on November 23. Judge Landis took it as a sign that the team was not taking the game, or their role as ambassadors of baseball, very seriously. The Japanese press reported that the Americans in essence threw the game, making four errors. And that certainly could have been. The implication in the local press was that this was an unsportsmanlike ploy designed to drive up fan interest—and gate receipts.

They toured Osaka and Nagasaki, then went to Seoul, Korea, and played in Manchuria, North China, Peking, Shanghai, Canton, and Hong Kong, and sailed to the Philippines (a U.S. territory) for two games against Filipino Railway and Manila Americans (largely American military and civilians) at the Manila Carnival Grounds. At a banquet after one game, Casey stood up and pretended to give a speech, a delightful bit of pantomime that made him the hit of the evening.

"He started by smacking his right fist in his left palm," wrote Boston's Hy Hurwitz, re-creating the scene years later. "He raised his arms skyward. He placed his right hand on his heart. He took a swing at an imaginary baseball. He went through the motions of sliding. He kept up his gestures for 20 minutes but didn't say a word. People down front realized the gag, and those in the rear also caught on. When [he] was finished he was wildly applauded."

When they stopped in Hong Kong before sailing for Hawaii, most of the players purchased Chow dogs. Unfortunately, most of the dogs died in an improvised kennel belowdecks on the trip home, but Casey's lived. Ah Ming lived in Kansas City with the Stengel family on Harrison Street for about eight years. Louis Stengel used to tell people it was a baby lion.

In Hawaii, on the return trip, they played one game (in which Casey homered) and visited the tomb of Alexander Cartwright, a founder of the pioneering 1845 Knickerbocker nine, those amateur players who laid out their diamond at Elysian Fields in Hoboken, New Jersey. They landed in San Francisco on February 2, 1923, after nearly fourteen weeks on the road.

The tour was a success by all accounts, and not one "untoward incident in playing or conduct" marred the trip. Plans for another trip in 1923 failed to materialize when Japan was hit by a big earthquake in September.

WHEN CASEY REPORTED TO spring training in San Antonio in 1923, McGraw assigned him to manage the "B" team on split-squad days; with these added responsibilities came the implication that Casey might one day coach under McGraw. He often coached first base on days when he wasn't playing.

There was a problem, however. Managing the "B" team was an everyday task that sent Casey to a camp in Marlin, Texas, a hundred and sixty-one miles north of San Antonio. In short, Casey was out of McGraw's sight, just as newly acquired Jimmy O'Connell took over center field in the "A" games.

Also, many of his "B" squad players were fat and out of shape from the long off-season.

"Players back then," he later explained, "had no skills off the field. So they became bartenders, and from tending bar to sampling the wet goods wasn't much of a jump. So when you gathered the players for spring training, you saw pot bellies, rum blossom noses and other evidences of the free and easy life.

"In them days, the training season was supposed to be mainly for melting the lard off the fatties and getting the boozers ready to run 90 feet without being winded."

Casey sent a letter to his boss. "Dear Mr. McGraw," he wrote. "It's very nice and wonderful of you to want to make me a coach later on in life, but I think it's time I came back and got in good shape so I can be ready to play for you—or ready to play for some other ball club if I am traded. So I think someone else can run this team better and I would say Cozy Dolan. So I'm going to have Mr. Dolan run the team the rest of the way."

The two didn't meet up until they arrived together at West Point for a final pre-season exhibition. McGraw was grumpy.

"How in the world could you fire yourself?" he asked. "That's another smart-aleck thing you did. Now I'll tell you what you'll do tonight. You'll stay out here at West Point after the game and tell those officers stories about the Giants."

Only Casey stayed behind as the team headed to New York. After his big season in 1922, his position was suddenly precarious.

Another setback came on May 7, when the Phillies pitcher Phil "Lefty" Weinert, an old teammate, hit Casey hard in the back with a pitch at the Polo Grounds.

Casey threw his bat at Weinert. Benches emptied.

"Someone got hold of my Adam's apple and squeezed it, and to this day," he said in 1961, "I have about the largest Adam's apple you ever saw."

Casey was thrown out of the game, and four New York City policemen appeared, to quell the fracas and escort him off the field. The photo of him being led off by a police squad made its way into the nation's daily newspapers.

McGraw was furious. This was only the ninth game all season when he had started Stengel—he wanted to give Meusel the day off—and now this. "That's the most asinine stunt I ever saw in my life," said McGraw. "If you're not suspended by the president of this league, I'm going to suspend you myself."

And they both issued a suspension. He didn't play another game until June 2.

Adding insult to injury, that very morning in his hotel he had gotten "the works" at the barber—two dollars' worth. After the fight, the "aroma of the hair tonic stayed with me," he said. McGraw smelled it, thought it was cheap gin, and fined Casey a whopping two hundred dollars.

He batted only nineteen times in April and twenty-eight times in May; in June, he had nine pinch-hitting appearances without ever taking the field. But he made the most of the limited playing time and took a .327 average into July 4.

Then, on August 7, the Cincinnati pitcher Dolf Luque approached the Giants' dugout after getting heckled all afternoon, and decided that Stengel would be on the receiving end of another punch in the nose. (He had first gone after him in 1920.) The sucker punch actually hit the stunned Casey in the shoulder (he never rose from his seat), and Ross Youngs wrestled Luque away. Both Luque and Stengel were ejected; Luque was suspended. McGraw came to Stengel's defense, claiming it had been another outfielder on the team who was yelling at Luque.

Players sometimes spoke of who the best-hitting pitchers in the game were. Casey had a fast answer to that one. "Weinert and Luque," he'd say, and everyone knew what he meant.

Casey wasn't yelling that day, but one thing McGraw did like about him was his ability to "give it back." Casey remembered:

> There used to be a middle-aged woman who attended all the Giant-Brooklyn games at Ebbets Field.
>
> One day I'm sitting on the bench when she's unloading on McGraw and he's burning up. So the happy thought strikes me to just come out of the dugout where she can see me and start moving my mouth, but not making a sound and gesticulating with my fingers for a change of pace.
>
> That does it. She nearly falls out of the box in her rage. Ol' John J. thinks that is great. For the first time since I joined the team, he actually grins. Whenever she started her tirade, he'd say, "Casey give that old buzzard the works." Then he'd relax as though watching a musical comedy, while I went into my act.

There were things about Casey that McGraw liked, and there were periods of friendship between them, especially after Casey got married. But as a player under McGraw, Casey just seemed to annoy him a lot. Casey had yet another act that did not sit well with McGraw.

Players were supposed to acknowledge that they were in their rooms when the trainer did a room check and knocked on their doors. One night in early June, at the Auditorium Hotel in Chicago, Casey used a second voice to cover for his absent roommate, Hugh McQuillan. It was not an uncommon trick, to be sure.

The next morning, the room was a wreck; McQuillan had returned at last, but badly trashed it. Casey got blamed. On June 7, waiting at Union Station in Chicago after a game against the Cubs, Casey was told that he, Jesse Barnes, and Earl Smith were being traded to the Boston Braves. In fact, Judge Emil Fuchs, the Braves owner, was at the station with his coach Dick Rudolph, and told all three he was giving them a raise. (The Braves were arriving to play Chicago as the Giants were leaving.) Barnes and Smith happily took the raise and joined Boston. Casey did not. "I'm not going to join you," he told Rudolph.

Instead, Casey went to McGraw and, remarkably, talked him out of including him in the trade. He would remain a Giant and forgo the raise. The trade would be Barnes and Smith for Hank Gowdy and Mule Watson, and there was no Stengel in the deal.

Something else was happening to Casey Stengel that summer. He was falling in love.

Edna May Lawson Stengel tells the story in her unpublished memoir, written in 1958, with her friend Jeane Hoffman, warmly capturing her three decades plus as the wife of Casey Stengel:

> I was a tall, lanky California girl, aged 26 . . . and I didn't know a thing about the national pastime. I'd never seen a game.
>
> But I can't say, in all honesty that I didn't know anything about this Casey Stengel, the Giants' star outfielder, because I'd spent the previous week-end in Atlantic City with Van [and Edith Meusel, wives of brothers Irish and Bob Meusel] hearing about him.
>
> All the baseball I knew I'd learned from Van and Irish, who made their home in Los Angeles. The Meusels were old friends, in fact, their parents and my parents had been neighbors back in Menominee, Wisconsin before they both moved west.
>
> "You simply must meet Casey Stengel, Edna," Van kept telling me. "He's a lot of fun, a good spender, and the life of the party. You two will get along great!"

But Edna had come east and was to meet up with a Brooklyn doctor for a date. His name was Robert Darrell. He'd been stationed in Arcadia,

California, with Edna's brother Larry. She was to meet Dr. Darrell that night.

"Edna had this handsome Jewish doctor from Brooklyn," Casey said, "and I swept her off her feet so the doctor never married anybody and went on to do some splendid operations while he was waiting for me and Edna to split up, but he's still waiting and I don't know how good his operations are anymore and why would you go to him if he couldn't concentrate on his work."

Edna's version: "The Jewish doctor was just a date, nothing serious. Casey always made it out to be more than it was because he wanted people to think he swept me off my feet and stole me away from somebody else. You know Casey, it has to be a good story or it wasn't worth telling.

"Once I met Casey, I never really saw anybody else. He saw to that."

We know that Casey's sister used to introduce him to girls he liked, because he was shy. But the Stengel charm could be overwhelming, and it appears he gave it his all when he met Edna Lawson.

"I think now that Irish," Edna continued, "must have given Casey the same sort of pep talk that Van had given me. Casey apparently spotted me from the outfield, sitting back of first base with the girls, because it seemed that the instant the game was over he was standing beside us, waiting for an introduction.

"I will never forget my first sight of Casey, running down the ramp to our box seat. My first impression was that he was one of the best-dressed men I'd ever seen. His blonde hair was slicked down, and he wore a straw hat, slightly tilted. Nobody could ever wear hats like Casey. He had on an expensive brown suit and an expansive grin."

This was a wonderful portrait of Casey as a fashion plate, ready for perhaps the most important introduction of his life. Edna's narrative continued:

"My," gasped Van, "it certainly didn't take you long to get here, Casey!"

"I saw enough from the outfield," he grinned, looking right at me.

Van introduced us, and we smiled at each other. Something seemed to click. I don't know what it was about him. At 32, Casey wasn't handsome, [but] he had a quick grin, laughing eyes and rather sharp features. But he was definitely different from all the other players, although I'm not sure how I arrived at that conclusion because I never got to meet any of the others. I guess what intrigued me was Casey's personality. (It certainly wasn't his money—he didn't have any!)

How could I know that this personable, rather cocky young man would change my whole life and lead me through [thirty-three] exciting years in baseball, because certainly, any trail Casey blazed would have to be exciting. I couldn't foresee that this casual meeting would take me to dozens of strange cities, to Europe, the Orient, to the top of the baseball world—the Yankees—and to everything from hostessing the Duke and Duchess of Windsor to milking a cow in Milwaukee.

They would have fifty-one years together in all, a remarkable run, considering how old they were when they married. When Edna wrote this memoir, they still had eighteen years to go.

Casey walked with the Meusels and me to their Edgecombe Avenue apartment, where I was staying, and rather shyly asked me for a date the next evening. He made an evening of it. He came over, dressed to the teeth, and took the Meusel couples (Bob played for the Yanks), the Herb Pennocks, the Jimmy O'Connors and me out for an evening of dining and dancing. He was a lavish spender, jolly host, and a marvelous dancer. I was impressed.

I thought he was very good company, and my, how he could talk! During my stay in New York, I had but two dates with him—and those with the Meusels. Although Casey talked a lot, it was always about baseball, and he was astounded to find out how little I knew about the game. When the Giants journeyed to Philadelphia, I made the trip with Casey and the team, and promised to meet him in Chicago later on my way home to California.

Casey said it was important that he see me because he wanted to improve my knowledge of baseball.

Dr. Darrell, whom I'd come east to see—and saw very little of—put me on the train for Chicago. "Edna," he warned me, "you'd better forget about this ball player. He's not good enough for you."

But I'm afraid it was the doctor I forgot about.

The Ol' Perfessor won out over the good doctor.

When the Giants arrived in Chicago to play the Cubs, Casey and I had our first date alone. We both loved to dance, so Casey took me to an expensive night spot for dinner and dancing, and now that I look back on it, I think he was trying to propose.

But he kept double-talking me, and I was doubly hard to convince. Casey, such a glib orator on baseball, was tongue-tied when it came to tying romantic sentences together. I think he was giving me "early Stengelese", although of course I didn't recognize it as such, because I never heard Casey talk "Stengelese" until he came to the Yankees.

Anyway, I'm afraid I didn't encourage him much. I still had the romantic idea of marrying some tall, distinguished-looking man. Casey wasn't tall, and in his 13 years in the majors, he'd earned a reputation as something other than distinguished. The bird-in-cap stunt in Brooklyn, cutting up the blank checks in Pittsburgh, jumping in an outfield hole at Ebbets Field, were feats already behind him when I met Casey.

Besides, I was anxious to get home. I was a working girl, and I wanted to return to my job and family. It wasn't that I wasn't intrigued with Casey, and this new world of baseball, but because my interest lay elsewhere. I loved the business world, as well as my family.

THE GIANTS WERE HAVING another big season in 1923, en route to a third straight pennant. With the Yankees departure for the Bronx, they had the Polo Grounds to themselves now. They expanded it to fifty-five thousand seats, and added new clubhouses in deep center field. This was Yankee Stadium's first year. McGraw hated everything about the Yankees, and now that his team didn't have to share the Polo Grounds, he wanted the quality of the ballpark to be competitive, too.

The Giants won ninety-five games without any top-tier pitchers. But with Kelly, Frisch, Bancroft, Youngs, and, yes, Casey in the lineup, they were formidable. (Bill Terry, then a rookie and a future Hall of Famer, joined the team on September 24, time enough to say that he and Casey were briefly teammates.)

Casey and McGraw were getting along much better. He was one of the few who called him "Mac" instead of Mr. McGraw, and was a frequent house guest in John and Blanche's Pelham, New York, home, whipping up his fried-eggs specialty in the kitchen. Casey could always turn on the charm, and it made him a favorite of Blanche McGraw.

On September 16, with Casey batting .338 and reclaiming his center-field job, he landed hard against a concrete portion of the Wrigley Field wall, sending a rivet that held a spike on his shoe into his heel. Because of this "stone bruise," he had to tape a soft rubber pad inside his shoe for protection.

He missed seven days, and then played the final two games of the season in center, finishing at a robust .339.

The Yankees won their pennant again, so there would be another New York–New York World Series. (Just before it began, the Giants played a benefit game at the Polo Grounds, and Babe Ruth, always game for anything, joined the Giants for the day. Thus, for that one day, he appeared in the same box score as Casey.)

The 1923 World Series opened on October 10 in Yankee Stadium— the first World Series game to be played in the sparkling new ballpark. The attendance was 55,307, the biggest crowd Casey had ever played in front of.

McGraw still hated everything about this World Series, and he had his players dress at the Polo Grounds and take cabs to and from Yankee Stadium, across the Harlem River, over the Macombs Dam Bridge. He was cranky about all the attention Babe Ruth was getting, but felt deservedly proud of being a two-time defending champion.

He even suspected that the Yankees might plant a recording device—a Dictograph—in the Giants' clubhouse. He also suspected that the Yankees would use binoculars to peer into his dugout and read lips. And so he cooked up a scheme—the reserve infielder Freddie Maguire would flash the signs, not McGraw, and Casey would room with Maguire and make sure he was alert at all times.

Casey played center field that afternoon and batted fifth. The score was 4–4 in the top of the ninth, with Joe Bush, who had been on the Asian trip with Casey the winter before, on the mound for the Yankees.

Bush retired Youngs and Irish Meusel. Casey was up.

Now Casey stood in—Casey at the bat—and swung at a changeup, driving it to the farthest reaches of the stadium, left center field.

There was joy in Mudville on this one, at least among Giants fans.

It was chased down by Bob Meusel (Irish's brother) and Whitey Witt, the center fielder. Casey pushed himself hard, and as he rounded second, he thought he felt his shoe come off. He began hobbling as much as running, continuing the mighty effort, huffing and puffing his way along.

Witt was first to the ball, but he was so deep he had first to relay it to Meusel, who then threw to the shortstop, Ernie Johnson. Johnson threw to the catcher, Wally Schang.

When Casey at last slid home ahead of the throw, he had the first World Series home run ever hit in Yankee Stadium, an inside-the-parker. And he shouted to the waiting George Kelly and Hank Gowdy, the next hitters, "I lost my shoe!"

Gowdy said, "How many were you wearing, Casey? You have two on!"

It turned out that the rubber pad had come loose and slipped out. He didn't really lose a shoe, but that became part of the lore.

In the New York *Sun,* Damon Runyon wrote an inspired piece of journalism, which has been reprinted many times over the years, in Runyon and baseball anthologies.

This is the way old Casey Stengel ran yesterday afternoon running his home run home.

This is the way old Casey Stengel ran running his home run home to a Giant victory by a score of 5 to 4 in the first game of the World Series in 1923.

This is the way old Casey Stengel ran running his home run home when two were out in the ninth inning and the score was tied, and the ball still bounding inside the Yankee yard.

This is the way—

His mouth wide open.

His warped old legs bending beneath him at every stride.

His arms flying back and forth like those of a man swimming with a crawl stroke.

His flanks heaving, his breath whistling, his head far back. Yankee infielders, passed by Old Casey Stengel as he was running his home run home, say Casey was muttering to himself, adjuring himself to greater speed as a jockey mutters to his horse in a race, saying, "Go on, Casey, go on."

. . . The warped old legs, twisted and bent by many a year of baseball campaigning, just barely held out under Casey as he reached the plate, running his home run home.

Then they collapsed.

They gave out just as old "Casey" Stengel slid over the plate in his awkward fashion with Wally Schang futilely [*sic*] reaching for him with the ball. "Billy" Evans, the American League umpire, poised over him in a set pose, arms spread wide to indicate that old "Casey" was safe.

Half a dozen Giants rushed forward to help "Casey" to his feet, to hammer him on the back, to bawl congratulations in his ears as he limped unsteadily, still panting furiously, to the bench where John J. McGraw, the chief of the Giants, relaxed his stern features to smile for the man who had won the game.

Casey was too winded to play center field in the last of the ninth, but the Giants held on and won the opener 5–4 on Stengel's mighty blast. The World Series, broadcast on radio and headlined in every newspaper in the land, was by now the biggest sports event in America save perhaps for the Rose Bowl or a heavyweight fight. In uniform, the Giants took taxis back to the Polo Grounds, no one feeling better about this victory than Stengel.

When the Giants got back to their clubhouse in the Polo Grounds, McGraw couldn't find Maguire. That set him off into berating Stengel for losing Maguire. And that's how the glorious day ended for Casey.

CASEY WAS ONLY A defensive replacement in Game Two at the Polo Grounds when the Yankees evened the series. He was back in center for Game Three, which saw Artie Nehf in a taut pitching duel against the Yankee ace Sam Jones. This time, the attendance was reported at 62,430.

The game was scoreless in the seventh inning when Casey faced Jones with one out. He chose another changeup and hit a shot into the right-field bleachers. (When Yankee Stadium opened, the bleachers extended from foul pole to foul pole; there was no triple deck for fair balls.) As he circled the bases, he gave Jones a five-fingered salute with his thumb on his nose, a gesture thought to be fairly risqué for the better-mannered in the stands. Jacob Ruppert, owner of the Yankees, wanted a reprimand from Commissioner Landis.

"No, I don't think I will," Landis responded. "A fellow who wins two games with home runs has a right to feel a little playful, especially if he's a Stengel."

The shot gave the Giants a 1–0 win and a 2–1 series lead. Casey had won both of their victories with home runs.

How many baseball players have ever had a week quite like this one!?

Back in Kansas City, reporters sought out Casey's mother, who was following the series on the radio.

"I am mighty grateful to McGraw for giving Charlie a new chance. I guess for a while Mr. McGraw and I were the only ones who thought the boy could play baseball. Our confidence in his ability has now proven warranted."

His dad watched on a big scoreboard in front of *The Kansas City Star,* as proud as could be.

The Yankees went on to win the next three games and earn their first world championship, so Casey's star turns proved to be their only victories. He hit .417 in the series, for a lifetime World Series average of .393 in twelve games. His losing share was $4,363, the most ever for a losing team up to that point, thanks to the two spacious ballparks. His full season salary had been sixty-five hundred dollars.

His lifetime regular season batting average for the Giants: .349.

THE SERIES ENDED ON October 15. On November 13, Casey was (again) traded to the Boston Braves, with Dave Bancroft (who had missed a chunk of the regular season with pneumonia) and Bill Cunningham, for Billy Southworth and Joe Oeschger.[*] Bancroft would become player-manager in Boston.

What happened? Why was Casey traded?

Some thought McGraw was trying to help out his old ace, Christy Mathewson, who had been named president of the hapless Braves. Some thought he was trying to get rid of his troublemakers; he had taken the World Series loss hard.

Casey, back in Kansas City, was understandably distraught. His time as a Giant was over. "Good thing I didn't win any more ball games for him. If I had he'd probably had me sent to jail," he said. "It's lucky I didn't hit three home runs in three games, or McGraw would have traded me to the Three-I League."

But, on reflection, recognizing that sentiment played no role with

---

[*] A coincidence: of nearly nineteen thousand major-league players, Baseball-Reference .com computes that Southworth's record was the most statistically similar to Stengel's.

McGraw, Casey could speak of him only with praise: "Uncle Robbie was very jolly and wonderful to work for. He would make you think he thought you were better than you were. But McGraw was the greatest manager I played for."

Meanwhile, Judge Fuchs told his Boston fans, "With the added strength just announced, the Braves of 1924 will be fighting it out with the best of them for the highest honors of the game."

12

EDNA LAWSON

CASEY WAS SMITTEN BY Edna and already thinking about proposing, despite their very limited time together. He may have thought his charm and style were all he needed. But now he was a national hero, all over the newspapers, because of his World Series triumphs. The problem was, everyone wrote about "Ol' Case" and "Methuselah," and Casey didn't like it. He was afraid his prospective in-laws would wonder what the hell Edna might be marrying, and whether he'd live to see a wedding day.

There was no cause for concern, however. Out in Glendale, California, Edna's father, John Lawson, saw Casey's bow legs in a newspaper photo and thought he reminded him of his favorite player, Honus Wagner.

John Lawson was a contractor and developer from Menomonie, Wisconsin; he built its City Hall, where he then married Margaret Forvilly. In 1906, they moved to Glendale, where he helped lay out the city and built some 250 homes and offices—a good part of the city's main artery, North Brand Boulevard. His contracting work brought him into movie-lot construction; on occasion, Edna was an extra in films.

It may sound as if Lawson was a rich man, but he lost most of his money around this time to some bad investments. Edna was by now working at the Hall of Records in Los Angeles, and she turned over her savings—$250—to her father so he could start over. He began to buy up decaying homes, repair them, and flip them for a profit. He continued this practice, buying more substantial properties, until his wealth—and position in society—returned.

—

OVER THE WINTER, CASEY wrote often to Edna in Glendale, but "no sentence was ever finished that would make me think it was a love letter," she said.

He would call, but if she thought it was going to be a romantic call, she was wrong. "How's the weather there?" he'd ask her.

He reported to spring training in St. Petersburg in March to play for his former teammate, Dave Bancroft, who was younger than he was. His head may have been filled with thoughts of an upcoming managing or coaching career, based on his experience with McGraw, but on the Boston team he was just another outfielder on a bad roster.[*]

On April 16, he hit a tenth-inning home run in Philadelphia to beat the Phillies 4–3. On April 19, their first return to the Polo Grounds, Bancroft got a "loud and vociferous cheer when he stepped to the plate," as reported in *The New York Times*, "but no louder than that accorded to old Casey Stengel, who had to lift his cap a number of times. Baseball memories are short, but not so brief that the fans can't still remember as far back as last October." For a while, the Braves stayed out of the cellar, but a ten-game losing streak in July doomed them, and they never got out of last place after that. The team hit only twenty-five home runs the entire season. So much for Judge Fuchs's prediction.

Bancroft developed appendicitis on July 1 after being hit in the stomach by a batted ball, which meant that the Braves were out their manager and shortstop until mid-September. If Casey thought he might be named "acting manager" while Bancroft was hospitalized, he was wrong. The coach Dick Rudolph, who had been a pitcher on the "Miracle" 1914 Braves for their amazing run from last to first after July 4, ran the team.

The fans, what few there were, seemed not to care. The Braves drew 177,478 at Braves Field that season, about twenty-five hundred a game. It was tough for Casey to offer peak performance with so many empty seats, after those glamour years at the Polo Grounds.

CASEY MAY HAVE BEEN a little tongue-tied in the romance department when he first met Edna, but he was on top of his game in plotting his next move. Learning that Edna's brother Larry was stationed with the U.S.

---

[*] The Yankees moved their spring training site to St. Pete in 1925, sharing facilities with the Braves, which meant that the Murderers' Row Yankees of Babe Ruth would also share the area's nightlife with Casey and the Braves.

Army Air Service in Belleville, Illinois (he was later promoted to general), Casey reached out to Larry to suggest inviting Edna the next time the Braves were in St. Louis, seventeen miles north.

Larry was good with this, writing to his father, John Lawson, "Casey Stengel seems real interested in Edna. He's a very personable, presentable fellow, well dressed and mannered, and I like him." Edna wrote:

> Casey never really proposed to me. I had to assume he proposed, because he never said, "Edna I love you, will you marry me?"
>
> What happened was that he worked through a "middleman"— my brother Larry. The two of them connived for me to come east and visit Belleville the following summer, 1924, on the grounds that I needed a "change."
>
> Wrote Larry to my father, "Casey and I have arranged things, and it's up to you to see that Edna makes the Braves next road trip to St. Louis."
>
> I came east a week before Casey was scheduled to arrive and went to a few parties. Casey let it be known he might drop around—to see my brother.
>
> The Braves arrived in St. Louis on a Monday morning, and Casey took a taxi directly from the depot out to my brother's house. Did he know his way around? Well, he had the master's touch, even then. By this time he had already been a house guest of Larry and his wife, Nancy, and won them completely over with his charm, and he had everything "arranged." There was no doubt which side my brother and sister-in-law were on. When Casey arrived at noon, I discovered that Nancy was out shopping, Larry was at the air base, and Casey and I were completely alone in the house!
>
> The exact details are a little vague to me, but I do remember that the morning was yellow-bright, the house was deathly-still, and that Casey, as immaculately dressed as ever, was slightly nervous as the two of us sat down for coffee in the dining room.
>
> For a few moments, there was only the sound of our teaspoons stirring coffee, then, abruptly, Casey started in out of nowhere with "Well, do you want to be married in a church, or where? Should I become a Catholic, or what?"
>
> That was my proposal.
>
> I didn't say "yes" the first day, not that I intended to say no,

but he kept talking—throwing in a baseball honeymoon trip to Europe—my relatives kept disappearing, and by the third day we were officially engaged. Casey had to talk fast because the Braves were scheduled to pull out of St. Louis and he was supposed to go with them.

That night, we had dinner in St. Louis to celebrate, then called on Dave Bancroft, the Braves manager, in his hotel room.

"Dave," began Casey, excitedly, "could I stay over an extra day so that Edna and I can get married?"

"Married?" Dave jumped to his feet. ". . . why wait a couple of days? Get married tomorrow!"

The Stengels wanted a quiet wedding, with no publicity. On August 15, Larry accompanied them to the Belleville City Hall to get a license. They went to a local jeweler for a wedding band—the engagement ring, a huge three-carat diamond, would follow weeks later. Casey, so recently a World Series hero, was recognized. He wound up telling the press, "This was the best catch I ever made."

They were married in a Catholic ceremony on Saturday, August 16, at the home of the local bishop, with only Larry and Nancy present. (Casey remained an Episcopalian.) They had dinner at the Chase Hotel in St. Louis and took a midnight train to Chicago. In his first day back with the team, he went 4-for-7, with two doubles, a home run, and four RBIs, in a doubleheader sweep (both shutouts) of the Cubs at Wrigley Field.

On September 10, the Braves went to New York for a doubleheader, and his friends on the Giants gave him and Edna the wedding party they hadn't yet had. They danced the night away.

"If Casey's dancing helped win Edna's heart," said Ann Mulvey Branca (whose husband, Ralph, later played for the Dodgers and briefly for Casey with the Yankees), "then my mother, Dearie Mulvey, was the one who taught him. Dearie was the daughter of Steve McKeever, a Dodgers owner. And for the rest of her life, every time Casey saw me, he said, 'Your mother taught me how to dance!'"

Since the Yankees were also at home, the party, at Hunter's Island Inn in New Rochelle, was attended by about a dozen players, including Babe Ruth, although Ruth, being Ruth, had come there for another party and was a drop-in at the Stengels'.

Casey and Edna stayed at the St. George Hotel in Brooklyn. They would live in hotels for a good chunk of the next forty years. Having no children to keep her home, Edna was generally by Casey's side throughout his baseball career, spring training and all.

In researching his book on Casey, Maury Allen asked Edna's brother about their being childless.

"I think they simply never wanted any," he told Allen. "Casey was a little old when they got married and in those days it was considered dangerous to have children after thirty. Edna was also getting up there in age when they married and I think they felt they didn't need children. Maybe Casey was too great a man, too busy with other things. They did so much, traveled so much, met so many people, they probably figured children would change all that and they didn't want to get involved with them. Casey traveled all summer with the team and was away a good deal in the winter with banquets and dinners and such, and children had no place. I never heard them discuss it and as far as I know, they never seemed to miss having children."

Casey was always courteous and polite with Edna, but he was far from a romantic. She wrote:

[He] turned his first pay check over to me, and he made a sort of speech. He said, "Edna, I understand that the average ball player brings gifts to his wife —you know, stockings, lingerie, and that sort of thing. I don't know how to pick out that stuff, so you take the money and buy yourself anything you want."

When I thought it over, I just couldn't see Casey browsing in a department store, fingering lingerie or perfume either, so I accepted the understanding. From that day to this [1958], he has only bought me two gifts: a gold fountain pen the Christmas before we were married, and he came home carrying an orchid 15 years later, for some unknown reason. Oh yes, once he sent me a wire at Easter. But there has never been any other gift. No birthday, anniversary, or Christmas presents.

What does he give me? His love and affection. He is the most generous man in the world. He has always turned over his pay check to me to bank, and I know the money is mine for anything I want, without questions. I guess I've gotten out of the habit of giving Casey presents too. This last Christmas I gave him a $3.50 ashtray. But there's nothing I can't have if I want it.

—

CASEY HIT A RESPECTABLE .280 in 131 games in 1924, led the club with thirteen stolen bases, and tied for the club lead in runs scored, aging legs and all.

It couldn't have been easy for Casey to see the Giants win their fourth straight pennant in 1924. When the World Series ended, McGraw's Giants and Charles Comiskey's White Sox were to leave on a tour of Europe; the two teams had taken a world tour together in 1913–14. But McGraw invited the Stengels to rejoin the Giants for the trip! It would be their honeymoon. Thirteen Giants and fifteen White Sox players went, with two umpires, two sportswriters, and McGraw as manager.

Not only were any lingering bad feelings between McGraw and Stengel gone, but the four of them—John and Blanche, Casey and Edna— grew in their friendship. The two wives stayed friends for the rest of Blanche's life. (She died in 1962, after the Mets' first season. Her husband died in 1934.)

"I never saw a happier pair," said Blanche of Casey and Edna.

Among the players who went along were Ross Youngs, Frankie Frisch, the retired Johnny Evers, Red Faber, Sam Rice, and Bancroft, the latter two loaned to Chicago for the tour. The Stengels spent much of the time with Irish and Van Meusel. Casey wore a Giants uniform again.

The tour began with four games in Canada, and then a voyage to Liverpool on the *Mont Royal;* after that, it was on to London by way of Dublin. Crowds were small, including a reported "crowd" of twenty for the Dublin game.

On November 6, during a well-attended game at the home of the Chelsea football club, Stamford Bridge Grounds in London, a royal emissary came down to the field-level seats to find Edna. "Queen Mary would very much like for you to join her for tea." (This was Queen Elizabeth II's grandmother.) At tea were also no less than King George V, his son the Prince of Wales (who would abdicate the throne in 1936), and Prince Henry (the future governor-general of Australia). After the game, all the players lined up and were introduced, and Casey was believed to have said, "Nice to meet ya, King." This sounds more like something Babe Ruth might have said; the tale is another one that is best left uncontested.

They proceeded to Paris for a final game on November 13—games scheduled for Brussels, Nice, Rome, and Berlin were canceled because the European crowds were unenthusiastic. This meant the Stengels' honeymoon was also "abridged," but they had time to visit Rome before returning to Paris to embark on the trip home—a seven-day voyage with first-class accommodations on the *Leviathan*. They stayed with the McGraws in Pelham for a week, then visited Casey's family in Kansas City (where the family met Edna), and then went to Glendale (where Edna's family met Casey). Edna's father had built a nine-room home for them there, on Grandview Avenue, near the foot of the Verdugo Hills, for twenty-five thousand dollars. It was the house Casey and Edna would live in for the next fifty-one years.[*]

---

[*] Casey and Edna did not own the house, or live there alone, until John Lawson died in 1947. John and his wife, Margaret, who predeceased him by four years, lived there, too. Casey and Edna occupied their own bedroom and enjoyed the benefits of the home until they took full ownership. Most Stengel biographies suggest the home was a wedding gift and the Stengels owned it from the start. That was not correct, although the Stengels could frame the answer to make it appear it was always theirs. "It was meant for us alone . . . and we asked them to move in with us," wrote Edna. With all of Casey's travels, owning a permanent residence seemed unnecessary.

13

MANAGING IN
THE MINORS

O L' CASEY'S" PLAYING DAYS were coming to a close. He was entering his fourteenth season, and he would turn thirty-five in July. His body looked and played old. He had been with five of the eight National League teams.

He went through the paces in spring training.

When the Braves' opening-day lineup included an outfield of such unknowns as Bernie Neis, Dave Harris, and Jimmy Welsh, Casey could see the writing on the wall. If he wasn't better than one of them . . .

He was strictly a pinch hitter (he went 0-for-9) and had one start in right field, a May 14 game in Boston against Pittsburgh. In that game he had a base hit, his last. Three more futile pinch-hit appearances followed; his last was on May 19, when he was retired by none other than the Reds' Dolf Luque in a 7–3 Boston loss.

It was his 1,277th game over fourteen seasons, and his lifetime average was a respectable .284, with sixty home runs and 535 RBIs. He earned four World Series "rings" (they didn't actually present rings when he played, except for 1922).

In May, Judge Fuchs entered into discussion with the owners of the Eastern League's Worcester, Massachusetts, franchise, with an eye toward buying the team, fifty miles west of Boston.

Even though the decision to transfer ownership to Fuchs was not approved until June 8, Casey had been released by the Braves by May 22 and made player-manager and president of the Worcester Panthers. (Because of the delay in Fuchs's ownership, there were rumors that Casey himself had purchased the team.) A number of Casey's Braves teammates went with him to Worcester, relieving the parent team of some dead wood. Casey received a reported seven thousand dollars for his three roles, although the presidency may have been in lieu of a cash bonus, which was then customary when a ten-year veteran was sent to the minors.

He would be replacing Eddie Eayrs, starting out on a managing career that would eventually take him to Cooperstown.

Worcester was in seventh place when he arrived, and he guided them to third, going 70-55 in the process. He also played every day—batting .302 with ten home runs. He was the leading gate attraction in the league—just nineteen months removed from his World Series heroics, and still feisty and scrappy with umpires, which the fans loved.

One of the "touches" brought to the Panthers ball club was a team bus, purchased by Fuchs. Casey loved it and believed it to be one of the first team-owned buses in the minors. He and Edna would sit up front and enjoy the scenery, as the relatively short trips took them to Albany, Bridgeport, Pittsfield, Springfield, Waterbury, Hartford, and New Haven. The New Haven owner was George Weiss, who was as introverted as Casey was extroverted. But they liked each other, and would spend time together when they visited each other's ballparks. Casey, the man of a thousand baseball friendships, added another important one on this stop.

As for the bus, Casey also drew a lesson from the experience—"Never let a losing pitcher drive the bus—especially a left-hander. A guy who has just blown a tough one shouldn't be allowed behind the wheel. He just has no regard for the life and limb of others." This wasn't the first time Casey spoke out about his fellow left-handers. He had written a playful guest essay in *Baseball Magazine* in 1918 discussing why left-handers are "nuts," although it really drew no conclusion.

He would sit in the front of the bus with Edna and lecture the players on the finer points of baseball. Edna wrote that, by not turning around, he remained unaware that most of the players were fast asleep.

WORCESTER WAS NOT A success at the gate—the nearby College of the Holy Cross's baseball team drew more fans—and Fuchs decided to move the team to Providence, Rhode Island, in 1926. The assumption was that Casey would still be the manager, but before the year was over, he had received an offer to manage the Toledo Mud Hens of the American Association—for more money. (McGraw was the catalyst; he had an ownership stake in the team and recommended Casey.) In fact, Toledo would pay him ten thousand dollars a year, which was similar to a major-league manager's salary.

He asked Fuchs to release him, but was turned down. Fuchs wanted him in Providence.

So, pure Casey, he wrote himself a letter as manager to the club president (himself), resigning as manager, and received a quick letter back from himself accepting the resignation.

> Dear Mr. Stengel:
>
> Having an opportunity [to] improve my position by going to a higher classification as manager, I hereby tender my resignation as manager of the Worcester club. I cannot leave without thanking you for your courtesy, consideration and advice, which was of great help in running the club.
> Very truly yours,
> Casey Stengel

> Dear Casey:
>
> Your letter came as a surprise but we realize that ability should be rewarded. Therefore, I join the fans of Worcester in expressing our appreciation for your outstanding services rendered and wish you luck in your new position. We congratulate Toledo on getting your valuable services.
> Very truly yours,
> Charles D. Stengel

Then came a wire to Fuchs:

> MANAGER CHARLES DILLON STENGEL IS
> HEREBY AND AS OF THIS DATE DISMISSED AS MANAGER
> OF THE WORCESTER, EASTERN LEAGUE CLUB.
> CHARLES DILLON STENGEL, PRESIDENT,
> WORCESTER BASEBALL CLUB

Fuchs really liked Casey and regularly played cards with Edna (since Casey wasn't a card player), but now he was furious, and informed Judge Landis of Stengel's impetuous move. Landis again exonerated Casey: "Let him go. . . . Better off without him."

—

THE DEPARTURE FROM WORCESTER was a relief to Edna. She was used to mansions and big houses; here they had lived without plumbing in a rented home before moving into a small hotel. There were no convenient cleaning facilities; Casey had to hang his sweaty uniform out the window to air out after games. And the ballpark was in a bad section, so that Edna got pelted with stones by some neighborhood boys on her way to a game. However, she maintained her dignified, ladylike presence at all games, dressing fashionably in hats and cocktail dresses, even though the ballpark attire around her bordered on slovenly.

Meanwhile, the winter of 1925–26 was the Stengels' first prolonged stay in their new Glendale home. Edna, in charge of the couple's finances, decided to invest their savings—about thirty-five hundred dollars—in what seemed like a safe bet: a cemetery, her father's idea. But it went bankrupt. They lost their nest egg, modest though it might have seemed.

Here is where Edna the businesswoman first impressed her husband.

"In desperation, I sought out the owner [of the cemetery] and begged, pleaded and wheeled [sic] every cent of our $3,500 out of him," she wrote. "When he heard I had the money back, Casey looked at me admiringly. I think I went up several notches in his esteem."

CASEY SPENT SIX YEARS in Toledo, winning his first championship as a manager and the team's first pennant. In doing so, he learned to platoon as McGraw had taught him, and to handle players both on the way up, and on the way down.

Unfortunately, he had more heading down, and did not develop many future big leaguers. A lot of openings for managing jobs on the big-league level came and went. He got no calls.

Among the better known "on the way down" players who wore Mud Hens uniforms were Carl Mays (the former Yankee, whose pitch at Ray Chapman's head in 1920 had resulted in the only on-field fatality in Major League history), Rosy Ryan, Bevo LeBourveau, Jocko Conlan (later a Hall of Fame umpire), Johnny Neun, Bobby Veach (Casey's old Kankakee teammate), Johnny Cooney (of whom we will hear more), Casey's pal Irish Meusel, and Wilbur Cooper. The few prospects on their way up included Dixie Walker and Bill Werber.

The Meusel signing should have been a happy one, given Casey and

Edna's friendship with Irish and Van. But even though he hit .354 in forty-seven games, the fans saw a lackadaisical, out-of-shape Meusel, and he was immediately unpopular. His release could not have been easy for Casey, but their friendship survived.

And there was Casey himself. He stayed active, played the outfield, and pinch-hit from 1926 to 1929, and came back for eight at-bats over two games in 1931 at the age of forty-one, to complete his professional career. He was still productive in his first year, batting .328 in 88 games, and he hit .438 in 26 games in 1928. The fans loved his appearances—they would cheer wildly when he went into a game.

"[Casey's] transition from player to manager had altered his personality not a whit," wrote Edna. "In fact he was a long time making the transition, because he still played spasmodically. He ate with the players, joked, laughed and worried with them—everything but play cards with them.

"[Toledo] began the six happiest years of our lives."

Casey also got a liberal expense account to entertain scouts, since selling players to major-league teams was among his chief responsibilities. To stay solvent, the team had to sell four or five players a year to major-league clubs. Scouts were regularly in attendance—even Larry Sutton, the man who had signed Casey, was still on the job.

The best news about joining the American Association was that Kansas City was in the league, and Casey could go home and visit with his family and friends three times a season. Casey's pal Dutch Zwilling was the manager of the Kansas City Blues from 1927 to 1932, and Casey might have envied him for getting that position in their hometown, but Toledo was absolutely a great stop for Casey. He was treated well, he liked the city, he experienced success, and he had a good time.

Success came in his second season, as the '27 Mud Hens went 101-67 to win their first American Association pennant, beating Milwaukee on the final day of the season to take the honors. The team drew 324,000—more than the population of the entire city—in a ballpark, Swayne Field (now a shopping center), that had a capacity of only forty-five hundred. (Ten thousand seats were added after this season.)

ONE STAR OF THE 1927 championship team was the outfielder Bevo LeBourveau, Edna's favorite player. He had a great name, and enough showmanship and ability to be one of Casey's favorites, too. The fans took to him. A teammate of Casey's with the Phillies in 1920–21, he joined the Mud Hens in 1926 and 1927, returning in 1930–31. A lifetime minor-league hitter of nearly .340 over fourteen seasons, he was what some came to call a "Four-A player"—too good for Triple-A, and not quite good enough for the majors.

"I sold Bevo three times," recalled Casey. "Once to McGraw, once to Connie Mack, and once to Branch Rickey. Each time I got him back."

One high spot of the 1927 season came on June 22, when Casey, pinch-hitting, hit an eleventh-inning grand slam on a 3-2 count for a 10–9 Hens victory—his last professional homer.

Five days later, he was indefinitely suspended for umpire abuse. On Labor Day, while losing a game to Columbus, he got into such an argument that hundreds of fans came out of the stands, forcing the umpire to flee for the dugout, where he received police protection. Casey was again suspended; after this one was lifted, the Mud Hens rallied for ten straight wins, and went on to win the pennant.

That put the team in the post-season, the Little World Series, which pitted the American Association champ against the International League champ.[*]

The Mud Hens defeated the Buffalo Bisons five games to one, the clinching victory coming at home on October 6 on a 4–0 shutout by Emilio Palmero, a thirty-two-year-old Cuban southpaw. *Reach's Base Ball Guide* described the Toledo fans as having enthusiasm that was "abundant and sincere."

The winning share was a thousand dollars per player, and manager.

OPERATING WITH ONE-YEAR CONTRACTS, and now under local ownership without McGraw's involvement (although John's brother Jim was the club's business manager), Casey put eight thousand dollars of his own money into the team to help keep it afloat once local interests took control.

It is hard to repeat a minor-league title because the rosters change so dramatically every year, as they did for Toledo in 1928. The team looked more and more like a McGraw team, with fifteen ex-Giants, including Casey, who signed another one-year contract.

---

[*] The Little World Series dated back to 1904 (although it skipped some years), and after changing its name to Junior World Series in 1932, continued until 1975.

The players came and went, and Casey, alluding to the then bullish stock market, walked into the Toledo clubhouse and said to his assembled players, "Buy Pennsylvania Railroad! I'm going to ship so many of you birds on the Penny tonight the railroad will be able declare an extra dividend!"

The Hens finished sixth, falling under .500, but attendance was up in the expanded ballpark, and fan enthusiasm remained high. Casey signed his fourth one-year contract in December.

In 1929, the last year of economic "normalcy" in the country, Toledo plunged to last place, losing one hundred games. Casey was involved in three fights and two suspensions during the year, and as he approached forty, this was thought to be unbecoming. In May, a fan in Toledo named Samuel J. Howe charged Casey with assault after Stengel went after him to return a batting-practice foul ball. In July, he was suspended for punching infielder Lute Boone of Columbus.

When he wasn't under suspension, he was in full entertainment mode, mimicking the opposing pitcher's delivery from his perch at the third-base coach's box, reveling in those that were especially slow, blending in yawns and stretches with each phantom pitch.

DURING THE SUMMER, HE wrote to his mother:

> My club is drawing terrible and playing worse. . . . E.L.O. is a
> good stock and making money. Regarding money arrangements
> tell L.S. [his father] if you or Aunt Lille needs any money to use
> that mortgage on Belleview if you have to. Oscar & John need
> money—so why ask them for our loan but this fall expect to get
> paid up. Love & good wishes to all so don't worry. C.D.S.

ON OCTOBER 29, THE stock market crashed.

"Our stocks went crashing, the merry-go-round came to a halt and the Stengels were broke," wrote Edna. "That winter of 1930 we were down to $34.16 in our savings. At this period we had as much life between us as a pair of battered book-ends. I, especially, was gloomy. I'd invested in stocks along with Casey, and I was inconsolable at the prospect of being wiped out."

"I'll tell you what you need. A party," she told Casey. "And we withdrew the entire $34.16 and invited 20 friends, and served cold cuts."

They were down to zero, except for the salary Casey would draw for 1930. He was happy to sign another one-year deal.

IN 1930, CASEY TURNED forty (although everyone thought he was thirty-nine), and he was just as scrappy as ever. He was even called before Judge Landis in Chicago to review his latest suspension for inciting a near-riot during a game with the Milwaukee Brewers.

He may have been preoccupied. Back home, his brother, Grant, had been abducted, bound and gagged, and placed in an abandoned barn by two men, one of whom went on to shoot the sheriff in St. Joseph, Missouri—Wild West stuff. Grant was rescued, unharmed.

Toledo finished third in 1930 with an 88-66 record, but then plummeted to last in 1931, losing a hundred again. Money was tight all around, and Casey found no buyers for his better players. The team's finances were tottering.

On October 5, he wrote his mother:

Dear Mother:
. . . spent Saturday with Robby [Wilbert Robinson] . . . They
also introduced me to Mr. McKeever [the Dodgers owner] & he
gave me a good welcome but did not ask me to manage their
club. . . . Spent Sunday at Polo Grounds saw Meusel & boys &
took dinner at McGraw's. . . . Don't worry about stocks etc.,
they will come back as the country comes out of this spell. . . .
Charles D. Stengel.

JOHNNY COONEY, WHO WOULD prove to be a longtime Casey confidant, joined the team in 1931, at the age of thirty. He had been an outfielder and pitcher with the Braves from 1921 to 1930 (and Casey's teammate in 1924–25), and was transitioning to his "next life" after being a major leaguer. Though Casey was about a decade older, they formed a strong friendship, and their lives would intersect at more places than Toledo.

At Toledo, Casey made Cooney into an everyday outfielder, and a good one. Casey was able to sell him to the Giants. He would later play for Casey at Brooklyn in 1935–37, and the Kansas City Blues in 1945.

Casey would later say that the money he himself had put into the franchise to keep it afloat was all worth it for the fun and the friendships he had there. He ultimately settled his investment for a used car and a small chunk of cash. But at this point, in 1931, the team was bankrupt. Edna wisely withdrew five thousand dollars of Casey's salary from a Toledo bank, just as it was about to close down. She put it into government bonds and stabilized the family savings.

"We were so hard up we stayed in Toledo instead of going to Glendale," wrote Edna. "We went to New York to seek work; and we moved into the smallest and cheapest hotel room we could find. [Not even a private bathroom.] Often, we went to Pelham for home cooked meals with the McGraws."

The Mud Hens were put into a receivership (the bank taking ownership), and just before Christmas, a judge signed an order granting the bank permission to release Stengel. On the last day of the year, it was inaccurately reported that McGraw had hired Stengel as a coach for the Giants. The two had apparently discussed it at baseball's annual Winter Meetings—the industry convention, which Casey seldom missed, and where jobs were often filled.

"We left the small hotel and moved in with the Rosy Ryans."[*]

The report of the Giants job proved to be premature, or false; it was the Dodgers who eventually threw him a lifeline. The Stengels were having Christmas dinner with the Ryans when the call came—long-distance, from Brooklyn.

"For a moment, Casey just looked at us," wrote Edna. "Then a big grin spread over his face.

"'The job's mine,' he announced."

Casey had approached the new Dodgers manager, Max Carey, at the Winter Meetings and asked if he needed a coach. Coaches in those days would hit fungos, throw batting practice, and go out for dinner with the manager. Teaching skills were considered a small requirement.

"We were so delirious with excitement," Edna continued, "that we nearly threw the food into the air. . . . We hurried through dessert, then

---

[*] The Ryans' son, Bob, who slept on the couch, became a popular newscaster in Minneapolis, and Rosy, Casey's teammate with the Giants, landlord in Worcester, and pitcher in Toledo, became a longtime manager and general manager in the minors.

we all went to midnight mass to celebrate—even Casey, and he's not a Catholic."

Max Carey had become manager of Brooklyn, replacing Uncle Robbie, after the 1931 season. Robbie's two-year contract expired after that season, the team had not improved in recent years, and the owner agreed it was time for a change. Robinson resigned, after eighteen years. Carey, a Robins coach in 1930 who sat out '31, would now return at the helm. He would be the anti-Robinson—a disciplinarian, not much of a drinker, proud of being fit and in good shape.

Casey would make seven thousand dollars a year, his smallest salary in many years. And he would be happy to get it.

Casey would coach first base, his pal Otto Miller would be the pitching coach, and, as was customary (except for Uncle Robbie and a few others), the manager, Carey, would coach at third.

Casey was back in the big leagues, after seven years at Worcester and Toledo.

Thirty-four managers had been hired for major-league teams during Casey's seven years "away." Everyone knew him to be a very smart baseball man, and great with the press. Alas, being known as a "clown" must certainly have helped keep him down in the minors.

The sportswriter Dan Daniel couldn't have been happier about the team's new "Assistant Manager," as he described it for his readers in *The Sporting News*. "Brooklyn fans will hail the coming of Casey both as a sentimental gesture and a utilitarian move. The Old Guard, a trifle shocked by the passing of Uncle Robbie, no doubt will be somewhat appeased and will regard the signing of Stengel as the return of an ancient Flatbush landmark. . . . And now, Rip Van Stengel is back with the Dodgers—back in a setting that is old and familiar, and yet looks as different as the picture which confronted Rip when he came down from the mountain. He is a clown, one of the funniest men connected with the game and yet he is a wise, crafty leader, sound strategically, and keen in the development of young players. Those qualities stood out in his regime at Toledo, which crashed last season with the financial collapse of the club."

Another sportswriter, Tommy Holmes, wrote, "The greatest quality that Casey brought into the major leagues was his fighting spirit and his hard-shelled ability to play winning baseball of a high order in the pinches. He always was a 'hell-for-leather' chap who never spared the whip, least of all on himself. Now, at 40, Stengel shows some effects of his rough-riding career. He looks prematurely old with his graying hair, his weather beaten countenance, his double chinned face."

William Baucher, a sports columnist in Kansas, wrote, "Casey is one of the hard guys of the old school. Umpires dread the sound of his name. Opposing pitchers tremble when Casey starts his 'Quack, quack' or maybe 'baa, baa' or maybe again 'Cuckoo, cuckoo' from the bench."

Brooklyn was delighted to welcome home the man who had patrolled right field so well in his day. He was already a fount of baseball history. He could regale writers and players with his tales. Like this one:

> I am at a circus in Kansas City, see. And the announcer brings out a freak, which he says is a man who GROWS before your eyes.
>
> He is a pretty average-size fellow but he begins to swell until he is over six feet and very broad. I am amazed. I look close and I recognize the fellow, and who do you think it was?
>
> Why, he was the announcer at Ebbets Field many years before— in 1912 and '13 when I was there. Irving O'Hea. We meet after the circus and have a long chat.

14

BACK TO BROOKLYN

WHEN THE STENGELS ARRIVED for spring training at Clearwater, Florida, in 1932, they learned that Max Carey was introducing calisthenics into the daily regimen. Edna wrote:

I believe it was the first time that calisthenics were ever used in baseball. Certainly they were unknown to my startled spouse.

He stared in disbelief as the pudgy Max flopped down on the floor, kicked his legs in the air, and rolled his body from side to side.

"Like this, see?" grunted Max, between breaths.

"You want me to do that stuff?" [said] Casey, who privately must have thought his old teammate had gone crazy.

"Yup," continued Max, "You gotta teach those kids!"

Casey was appointed to lead the team in calisthenics each day.

The Stengels found a twenty-five-dollar-a-week apartment, rented a car, and toughed it out until opening day—there was no pay during spring training.

Once the season began, Casey and Edna found a hotel room in Brooklyn. But in July, Edna's mother was seriously injured in an auto accident in Reno. Edna rushed to her side; she not only cared for her crippled parent, but also assumed more responsibility in the Lawson family business of property holdings. This was the start of an eleven-year period during which Edna carried a dual burden. Until her mother's death in 1943, Edna could only make two trips east a year to be with Casey; they were apart for very long stretches.

—

CASEY COACHED FIRST BASE in 1932–33, as the Dodgers (no longer the Robins) finished third and sixth. The team was not quite the "Daffiness Boys" of Uncle Robbie anymore, especially after trading colorful Babe Herman during spring training of 1932 following a prolonged holdout.

The owner, Steve McKeever, brought in Bob Quinn to run the team, but the front office was still at odds with itself, perhaps the residue of infighting over whether to retain Robbie in his final seasons.

The '32 Dodgers were not without their colorful characters, including Hack Wilson, who had belted fifty-six homers just two years earlier; Van Lingle Mungo; Dazzy Vance, now forty-one but with three more years remaining in his career; Lefty O'Doul, who batted .368, to lead the National League, and future managers and club executives Paul Richards, Clyde Sukeforth and Fresco Thompson. One outfielder, Maxie Rosenfeld, hit .359 in thirty-four games; he had been one of Casey's players at Toledo.

Waite Hoyt, a star on the Yankees in the Murderers' Row years, was on the pitching staff (he was the opening-day starter), but when they wanted to release him, on June 7, Max Carey asked Stengel to do it. This did not please the Brooklyn-born Hoyt, who complained bitterly that the manager hadn't handled it "like a man" and had dispatched a "clubhouse boy" to do it (thus insulting Casey).

Al Lopez, age twenty-three, was the Dodgers' catcher. Although they were seventeen years apart in age, Casey and Al hit it off. This was Lopez's third full season with the team, and Casey was impressed by his baseball wisdom. They would not only share a long friendship, but would become rival managers in the American League in the 1950s.

Ring Lardner, who blended baseball fact and fiction so well in his popular "Alibi Ike" and *You Know Me Al,* wrote about the '32 Dodgers and used Casey—not Max Carey—as the real-life figure he blended into the story. This allowed him to tap into colorful Casey stories and enhance the personality of the man even more.

At season's end, the Dodgers gave Carey a two-year contract for 1933–34, and Casey's was extended as a coach for 1933, at six thousand dollars.

In '33, the Dodgers added Casey's pal Rosy Ryan to the pitching staff, but the year did not go well. By August, they had settled into seventh place, some twenty games out of first, and newspapers were already speculating that Carey might be dropped—despite having a contract for 1934—if things didn't turn around quickly.

Firing Carey, which would essentially mean paying two managers in 1934, was not a prescription for financial success. But the papers were throwing out names for Carey's successor—including Casey, Burleigh Grimes, and Gabby Street—and Carey was feeling the pressure. The Dodgers finished sixth, twenty-six and a half games out of first. With the Great Depression showing no signs of recovery, and the team mediocre at best, attendance was down about 20 percent, to 527,000.

Casey and Edna were home in Glendale, waiting for a call or a letter from the Dodgers regarding his status for 1934.

Nothing arrived. Christmas season was one of mixed feelings—would he be unemployed? Do they write you to tell you that you won't be on the coaching staff?

And they waited. Carey was still the manager.

In January 1934, during an interview with Roscoe McGowen of the *Times,* the Giants' manager, Bill Terry, was asked about his seven opponents for the upcoming season. He gave McGowen a joke line: "Brooklyn? Gee, I haven't heard a peep out there. Is Brooklyn still in the league?"

At the Dodgers' offices at 215 Montague Street in Brooklyn, the club officials seethed. No public response from Carey? This insult by Terry could really kill any enthusiasm Brooklyn fans had for their team. C'mon, Max, fight back! This is Brooklyn! Our fans don't sit back.

There was no response from Carey.

On February 21, 1934, just before spring training, Carey was fired. This was very late to take such an action. It meant Carey had represented the team at the Winter Meetings and had helped them shape their spring roster. Now he was done, and it was too late for him to find another job for 1934. Baseball usually didn't work quite this way.

The general manager, Bob Quinn, summoned Stengel east from Glendale to his New York apartment. He offered him the job just hours after Carey had been fired. Spring training was weeks away.

"Is Max going to be paid the last year of his contract?" Casey asked. Told he would be, Casey asked to speak to him on the phone in Florida.

"Take the job," said Max. "If you don't take it someone else will."

He got a two-year contract, for ten thousand dollars a year—the same money he had made in Toledo. But this was the Depression. Having any salary was considered good fortune.

This was an enormous moment in Stengel's career—his first major-league managing job.

On February 24, the press was summoned to the Hotel New Yorker, on Eighth Avenue in Manhattan, to meet the new Brooklyn manager, someone well known to them all. Training camp would open March 5 in Orlando.

"The first thing I want to say is, the Dodgers are still in the league," he told them. Team officials smiled.

At forty-four, he was about to begin his major-league managing career.

15

DEATH OF KOENECKE

ONE OF THE FIRST wires of congratulations Casey received came from Wilbert Robinson, who was now president of the Southern Association's Atlanta Crackers. "I am sure pleased you have the position as manager of the Brooklyn Club," he wrote. "I know you will do well, in fact better than anyone I know of, with the material you have."

Casey's other mentor, John McGraw, was too ill to issue a comment. He died the day after the announcement.

On February 27, Casey was among those named as honorary pallbearers for McGraw's funeral at St. Patrick's Cathedral, a list that also included George M. Cohan, DeWolf Hopper (of "Casey at the Bat" recital fame), Jacob Ruppert, Wilbert Robinson (who would himself die five months later), Will Rogers, Tim Mara (owner of the football Giants), Bill Terry, and many more. Elite company.

The next day, Casey arrived in Orlando, five days before camp was to open. In fact, he opened it a day early; enough players were present to run a light workout. "The camera boys are eager to get some pictures," he said. He knew the newspapermen's need.

He adopted a pet snake, who roamed the Orlando outfield and seemed to settle in for the whole spring; one of his players clobbered it with a bat, and that was the end of Casey's mascot.

The team went north with "interesting players" and not much pitching. It was clear that the club's directors were not going to spend the money for better talent.

The Dodgers went to Ebbets Field in anticipation of their April 17 home opener against the Braves. When he entered the clubhouse, Casey made a right turn, to head for the corner office. In the minors, few clubhouses had "offices"; the manager had an end locker. Now Casey settled behind his desk and chatted with his clubhouse manager, the rotund, cigar-smoking "senator" John Griffin. The "senator," who had broken in as a batboy when Casey played for the Robins in 1916, made sure there were blank lineup cards in the desk. Casey pulled one out and began to tinker with his first big-league lineup.

He penciled in Danny Taylor, cf. Jimmy Jordan, ss. Joe Stripp, 3b. Johnny Frederick, rf. Hack Wilson, lf. Sam Leslie, 1b. Tony Cuccinello, 2b. Al Lopez, c. Van Lingle Mungo, p. The task was done. It would be his first of more than 3,600 major-league lineup cards.

Twenty-eight thousand turned out for opening day, to see the Dodgers wearing new uniforms with BROOKLYN in block letters. And they won, 8–7, with Wilson and Taylor homering; Casey stuck with Mungo in the ninth even though he yielded three runs, putting a scare into things. This was indicative of his lack of confidence in his other pitchers.

The first time the Dodgers played the Giants, April 30, photographers wanted Casey to pose with Terry, whose "still in the league" remark was already part of baseball lore. They posed. And the Giants won three straight.

In May, when the team had lost thirteen of their first twenty-one, *The Sporting News* wrote, "The situation is so desperate that manager Casey Stengel is willing to trade anybody on his ball club, value for value if he can get pitching in return."

That month, the team settled into sixth place—where they would finish. Casey platooned his players as best he could, but the Depression had led to teams' having only twenty-three-man rosters, which limited maneuverability. He had only eight pitchers on the roster.

The game Casey always loved to talk about came in Baker Bowl in Philadelphia.* Hack Wilson was in right field. Walter "Boom Boom" Beck was getting pounded, letting the Dodgers give back an early lead, and Casey went out to the mound. "Now listen," said Beck (according to Casey), "don't go thinking of taking me out. I just commenced feeling good on those last hitters." ("Commenced" would have been a Casey word, probably added in the storytelling.)

So Casey let him pitch, but he kept getting into more trouble.

---

* This is another story in which the the facts as he remembered them don't all match, but the story has taken on a life of its own over time.

In the fifth, I had enough and said, "Walter give me the ball." He said, "no sir you let me pitch to this next hitter." I said "Walter let me have that ball." And he turned and threw the ball out to right field, where [Hack] Wilson was playing. The ball hit that tin fence and bing, it dropped off the ground.

Hack evidently had been standing out there thinking about what he was going to do that night or something, because he heard the ball hit the fence and he turned around and chased it and fired it into second base. And he was good and mad when everybody started to laugh and ridicule him.

Meanwhile Beck came in to the bench and I said, "Well, Walter, you were right about one thing. There's nothing wrong with your arm or you wouldn't have been able to throw all the way out to that fence." He didn't say anything; he just went over and kicked the pail of water. I said "Walter don't you dare kick that bucket again. He said why wouldn't I kick it? I said because you might break your leg and then I won't be able to sell or trade you."

TERRY NAMED STENGEL AS a coach for the 1934 All-Star Game at the Polo Grounds, giving Casey a good seat for that historic afternoon when Carl Hubbell struck out Babe Ruth, Lou Gehrig, Jimmie Foxx, Al Simmons, and Joe Cronin in order.

If there was such a thing as a season highlight coming long after the team had been eliminated, it came in the final two games of the season, September 29 and 30, when the Dodgers went to the Polo Grounds; thousands of their fans followed them into Manhattan, holding signs: "Still in the league!"

The Giants needed to win those games to defend their pennant. They were deadlocked with the Cardinals, both teams 93-58. But on Saturday, the twenty-ninth, Mungo stopped the Giants for his eighteenth win, a 5–1 triumph, and on Sunday, the last day of the season, the Dodgers scored three in the tenth to beat New York 8–5 and eliminate the Giants from the pennant. What sweet victories those were for the boys from Flatbush.

Casey and Terry had an off-again, on-again friendship, generally off. But Casey remembered one day when they were both with Walter Johnson, and both wanted to be photographed with him for the press photographers.

"We have the darndest time," said Casey, "as Terry wants to stand in the middle and I also want to stand in the middle because you know when those pictures is printed in the newspapers sometimes they chop off the guy at one end. Which is what happens—Walter Johnson finally stands at one end and when the picture is printed in the paper he is the one chopped off and the picture is just of me and Terry which we didn't want took together except with Walter Johnson."

IT HAD BEEN A tough first season for Casey, producing only seventy-one wins.

Despite the sixth-place finish, Casey got a two-year extension to his contract. The fans liked him, the writers loved him, and since the Dodgers were in no position to surround him with good players, they felt they had a good thing going.

The talk of spring training in 1935, apart from the return of the forty-four-year-old Dodger legend Dazzy Vance (who would be a seldom used reliever in his final season), was the arrival of Stan "Frenchy" Bordagaray. He had come over from Sacramento in December, and arrived in camp with an astonishing mustache and beard. The beard disappeared soon, but the mustache was so out of place for the time that newspapers all around the country couldn't help running photos of him. Casey was okay with it, but warned him that if he didn't produce, it would really be an object of derision.

Bordagaray was a great Casey character. Once, he was tagged out while standing on a base. Casey said, "How could you be out!?" And Frenchy told him, "I was tapping my foot and he tagged me between taps."

A twenty-one-year-old shortstop named Rod Dedeaux, who would become one of the nation's leading college baseball coaches, and a great friend of Casey's, got into two games in late September.

And then there was outfielder Len Koenecke.

Koenecke, had given Casey a .320 season in 1934, but in '35 that average was down thirty-five points. He didn't run well, his home runs were down from fourteen to four, and Casey decided to release him while the team was in Chicago.

There were only seventeen games left in the season. He had hit .294 over his last eleven games. He didn't see this coming. Maybe after the season, but with two weeks left as the team played down the schedule?

Koenecke did what many players of that era did: he got drunk. He got himself to Detroit on his own, and then chartered a small plane to fly him to Buffalo. It was late at night.

On the plane, he got into an altercation with the pilot and copilot. Some accounts suggested he might have attempted a sexual attack. In any case, to save the plane from crashing and to restrain Koenecke, the pilot, William Mulqueeney, grabbed a small fire extinguisher and hit the ballplayer over the head with it.

"He seemed to be under great stress when we began the flight," the crew reported, "and he was quiet at first. But about 15 minutes in, he moved into the cockpit and began poking the pilot in the shoulder. He then bit the co-pilot [Irwin Davis], and a struggle went on for 10 to 15 minutes before they had to use the fire extinguisher."

Koenecke was knocked dead, at thirty-one.

Inside his clothing was a check from the Dodgers for $680, which was how identification was quickly made. The death was listed as having happened over Toronto. The pilots landed on a racetrack, and were charged with manslaughter and imprisoned, but the charges were dropped after a review of the facts.

Casey, in St. Louis with the team, got the news by telephone and was understandably shaken—and feeling guilty.

Tommy Holmes wrote in the *Eagle:*

Saner minds on the ball club swiftly corrected an impulsive and hysterical feeling that his death was the fault of Manager Casey Stengel because Stengel shipped him East. . . . No one feels worse about Koenecke's fatal frenzy than Stengel. While he cannot bring himself to admit that he was wrong in sending the moody player East, he'd probably give anything to recall the move that ended so tragically for the sensitive, temperamental yet thoroughly likeable athlete.

"I can't believe it," Casey said. "I won't believe it! How could he have been on a plane at Toronto when he left on one that doesn't go near there?"

In author Robert Creamer's account of the night, when newspapers wanted a statement from him, he was unable to deliver one. It was not often that he was speechless.

He went to Sportsman Park early in the morning and spoke to the players without any newspapermen present. Each Dodger wore a black band on his left sleeve for the remainder of the season.

According to Creamer, the general manager, Bob Quinn, persuaded the *Times*'s Roscoe McGowen to pretend to be Casey (they had similar deep, gravelly voices) and read a statement to the Associated Press.

"I am sorry about this," said McGowen-as-Casey. "I was upset when I first heard the report and I couldn't believe it. I can hardly believe it now. Koenecke was a good player last year. He was not quite so good this year and was one of the players sent home so we could try some of our new players. I deeply regret his death and can't explain his actions, for when he left yesterday he seemed all right and in good spirits."

McGowen pulled it off.

A lawyer for the pilots insisted that Casey be subpoenaed to testify at the coroner's inquest as to Koenecke's mental condition, but he was never called to testify.

The Koenecke story would fade away, and it's barely known today, but Casey thought of it often in his later years, still with deep personal regrets.

THE DODGERS WON ONE less game in 1935 than the year before, but moved up a notch in the standings to fifth. The owners then allowed Bob Quinn to leave and join the Boston Braves as team president. Casey got a raise to $12,500 for 1936.

Spring training of 1936 was its usual challenge for Casey, as he tried to cobble together a roster when he had little to work with. Buddy Hassett, a rookie first baseman, played 156 games that season (there were two ties) and batted .310. And he was also quite a baritone singer. One day, when the Dodgers were traveling by train, he sang a lullaby to a crying baby on the train and put the baby to sleep. Noted Casey, "I know how to get the most out of my players."

This team would not be known for its power. They hit only thirty-three home runs all season, the fewest in the majors, with catcher Babe Phelps leading the club with just five.

Phelps replaced Al Lopez behind the plate. Casey hated to make this trade; he really valued Lopez, who had been an All-Star in '34 and was a friend as well. But in December 1935, he went to the Braves in a trade that brought the outfielder Randy Moore to the Dodgers. Moore would be an important addition for Casey—for reasons to emerge later on.

When spring training ended, fourteen players went to Casey to ask permission to drive north. He refused: he wanted the team to travel together. So a few of the fourteen went to a front-office official, possibly the new business manager, John Gorman, and got permission. That was a bad start to the season—undermining Casey by going behind his back on such a thing.

In May, the Cardinals' Leo Durocher and Casey got into a brawl under the stands after a game, leaving Casey with a cut lip. The police had to break it up.

On June 9, Mungo left the team, after an ineffective start in which the Dodgers had lost their sixth game in a row.

Casey and Mungo had their issues. Once, after refusing Casey's order of an intentional walk to Dick Bartell of the Giants, Mungo jumped the team and was fined six hundred dollars. He returned to pitch well, but the episode turned the Dodger fans against Mungo, who had been one of the few popular players on the club.

One day, the Dodgers were playing the talent-laden Cardinals, and Dizzy Dean stuck his head into the Dodgers clubhouse while Casey was going over their hitters. "C'mon in," invited Casey, and he let Diz listen in. In return, Diz told the Dodgers how he would be pitching to each of them that afternoon.

He shut them out.

DURING THE SUMMER, THE Dodgers held an open tryout at Ebbets Field for amateur players. Maybe they would get lucky; maybe some local discovery would emerge.

One of the players was a little eighteen-year-old infielder named Phil Rizzuto. As the story came to be told, Casey took a look at him and said, "Go get a shoeshine box, kid." It would seem that Casey had made a grievous scouting error, for Rizzuto eventually made the Hall of Fame. And, truth be told, Phil told the story himself, just that way, over his lifetime. But occasionally he'd tell what really happened: "I was one of about 150 kids invited to try out at Ebbets field," he said. "We began with a running drill, running from left field to right field. The first 50 to finish were told to stay, and I was one of them. But Casey never saw me. One of the Brooklyn coaches eventually told me I was too small. He told me to try something else, and forget baseball."

—

THE SEASON ENDED WITH a seventh-place finish. The Dodgers drew just under five hundred thousand fans, which was third best in the league.

Casey stayed in town for the World Series, between the Yankees and the Giants, taking advantage of an opportunity to offer his insights for a New York newspaper. He sat in the press box with his newspaper pals, watching the two New York rivals battle it out.

On Monday, October 5, after the Giants won a 5–4 game in ten innings to extend the World Series to a sixth game, Casey was leaving through the Yankee Stadium press gate when he was told the Dodgers management wanted to see him downtown at the Commodore Hotel.

James Mulvey, the team's vice president and secretary, and Joseph Gilleaudeau, the treasurer (and son-in-law of Charles Ebbets), broke the news. He was being fired.

John Gorman put out a statement at the World Series press headquarters: "The Brooklyn Baseball Club announces that Casey Stengel will not return to Brooklyn as manager next year."

A writer shouted, "Will Casey be paid for 1937?"

"Of course he will," said Gorman.

For a team that struggled to make a buck, this was a very strange business decision—like paying Max Carey not to manage in 1934. Once again, they would be paying two managers, one to manage and one not to manage.

They tried to get him to take a lump sum payment—at a reduced price—but Casey insisted on his full fifteen thousand dollars, payments to be made on the first and fifteenth of each month.

Phil Dooley of *The Philadelphia Inquirer* had good sources in the New York banking community. "The board decided Stengel hadn't done a good job with the Dodgers. I take it that the decision was based on what the Dodgers drew at the gate, which wasn't enough to pay off any of the principal on the mortgage. The Dodgers were in hock for the tune of $380,000. Instead of placing the onus where it belonged, on the ham talent Stengel had to work with, they decided the trouble was all with the manager, and presumably with a shout of ipso facto, non compos mentis, demanded his head. The officials of the Brooklyn Dodgers aren't responsible to the rude hustling out of the picture of Casey Stengel, but the credit of cooking it up goes to a group of bank directors."

Casey went back to the World Series the next day, sat in the press box, and received congratulations and condolences all around. He was being paid to offer his expertise, and he was going to meet his obligations.

The firing caused a storm. Tommy Holmes wrote, "The National League must be stunned by the good will the club has lost by firing an intensely popular figure."

On October 8, a testimonial dinner was held in Casey's honor at the Hotel New Yorker, thrown together by the New York press. Among those present were George Weiss, farm director for the Yankees, generating some guesses that Casey might be asked to manage the Yankees' Newark farm team. Meanwhile, Casey said to the gathering about his being fired, "Such things happen in baseball, but I've been down and have come up again. I'm down now, and I'll be up again if I want to."

Speculation on Stengel's successor in Brooklyn immediately included Burleigh Grimes, the old spitball pitcher, and Babe Ruth, who had retired in 1935 and made no secret of wanting to manage. Grimes got the job; Ruth was hired as a coach in 1938.

In December, when he was back in town for the Winter Meetings (even without an employer to pay his expenses), fans in Brooklyn booked the twenty-five-hundred-seat ballroom at the St. George Hotel in Brooklyn Heights and threw him another testimonial.

A letter to his mother in a Dodgers envelope from around this time survives:

Dear Mother:
. . . The father [Edna's father] got a load on today & they have him down town trying to sober him up. Guess he will be o.k. for Thanksgiving. . . . I have not signed with anyone; have not heard about my contract but will lay idle if I have to pay back all my salary from another job. I intend to take care of that business but I know best for a number of jobs will come up later during the season if I don't get what I want. Well love & good health to all and stop worrying about my job. Your loving son, C.D.S.

Thus ended Casey's association with the Dodgers as player, coach, and manager. He always loved the borough, the neighborhood, walking to work, the fans, the atmosphere, and the writers. But for the rest of his career, they would be "the opponent," and younger fans would forget how tied he had once been to this team, his first major-league club.

16

OIL!

PERSONALLY, CASEY WASN'T QUITE down. Coinciding with this professional setback, some wonderful news emerged for Casey and Edna, almost immediately after the firing.

As Casey remembered it, he was at a dinner at Joe's Restaurant, under the Brooklyn Bridge, when his former player Randy Moore told him, "My father-in-law has some oil wells back home in Naples, Texas. I might get involved with that."

Casey said: "I might be interested in investing in that if you have room." Moore agreed to speak to his father-in-law and Casey added, "Let's put the Mexican in it too," meaning Al Lopez.*

Edna tells the story in her memoir:

One day, during pre-game practice, Moore mentioned to Casey that his father-in-law, a banker in a small Texas town, had discovered oil on a peach grove. He was going to run a wildcat well, and was Casey interested in going into the venture with him?

Casey sure was, but it took more spare dough than he had at the time. He wrote me saying he wanted to go in on the deal. My family, who knew Casey was a good bet and shrewd as they came, backed him.

"How much does he need?" was all my father asked.

Father entered whole-heartedly into the gamble. So did a few of the more venturesome players—Johnny Cooney, who was with Casey much of his baseball life, Al Lopez, later Cleveland man-

---

* Lopez's parents were from Spain; they emigrated to Cuba, then the United States. Al was born in Tampa.

ager, Watty Clark, a pitcher, Freddie Frankhouse, Bill McKechnie, the Braves manager, and John [Bob] Quinn.

The well was located on a farm near Mt. Pleasant, Texas and was called the "All-Star." It was a lucky star for us, and the turning point in Casey's life.

When the season ended—and it really ended for Casey, because he had been fired—we started a leisurely drive back across the country with my niece, Margaret Hunter. We were there on a Sunday in October 1936 [just days after his firing], when that first well came in. We stood so close that the beautiful, black blood splattered all over my white blouse and Casey's clean shirt, and we didn't even notice. We couldn't take our eyes off that oil well.

It was a strange sensation to stand there, with your feet firmly planted on solid earth, and realize that one minute you were poor the next instant, you are rich. Or at least, Casey and the boys were. This was one venture in which I had no part.

The oil strike made history; it was the first group of ball players who ever cashed in on a big strike, and it set most of them up for life. They were touched with luck: there wasn't a dry well in the entire Talco Oil Field! This, combined with his shrewd manipulations in stocks, started Casey on his way to being a wealthy man.

Attention had been drawn to East Texas since the discovery of oil in the East Texas Field in 1930, the biggest oil discovery in the world up to that point. And even though the "Casey find" wasn't part of that, it was a sensation unto itself. The oil field, crescent-shaped and covering about thirty-five miles along U.S. Highway 271 in Northeast Texas, eventually had over seven hundred drilling operations going. Talco became an oil boomtown. The grade of oil was not suitable for petroleum production, it was perfect for asphalt, and Talco came to be called the "Asphalt Capital of the World."

There was a certain irony in this. Casey's father's street-watering truck had gone out of business when the streets of Kansas City began to be paved. Now Casey was becoming a rich man on the material used for just such paving.

Al Lopez went in for about one-tenth of what Casey did (though he added more later), and said that even twenty years later it was producing seven hundred dollars a month. The investment did not make Casey a millionaire, but it gave him financial credibility with Edna's family, and provided a fine income for the Stengels for the rest of their lives. His 1938 tax return showed he had received $16,740 from the wells that year (about $285,000 in today's money), and that might have been the peak. He was not making "millions," as baseball people whispered, but he was making more from the wells than he was from baseball.

Casey told it this way in his autobiography: "I took the $15,000 the club had to pay me for not managing in 1937 and used it to go in the oil business in Texas with Randy Moore, who had played ball for me in Brooklyn. I'd go into separate wells and take a small fraction of them. It turned out to be a profitable business for twenty years or more, in fact, some of the wells are still going. Randy Moore has been very successful down there and he's been a wonderful friend to me and some of his other baseball pals he brought into the oil business. . . ."

On December 2, 1936, the Associated Press reported, "Casey Stengel is doing all right in Texas Oil." That would be putting it mildly. Word was out.

For the rest of his life, Casey accumulated wealth off that investment. Most people who knew him—sportswriters, players, club officials— knew that he was well off, but tended to attribute it to Lawson family money, particularly the banking business in Glendale. Not true.

AND SO CASEY AND Edna were out of baseball in 1937. This would be the only summer of Casey's adult life between 1910 and 1960 when he would have such "idle" time. Though he got some managing and coaching inquiries, he was content to learn the oil business and otherwise stay home.

To be sure, Casey absolutely missed the game. He had no other hobbies: not golf, not card playing, not reading, not swimming, not tennis. But he couldn't be certain of a return to baseball; it might actually be over. So he made numerous trips to the oil fields in Texas and Oklahoma that he had invested in, while Edna sharpened her skills as a businesswoman.

THE GENERAL MANAGER BOB Quinn, who had gone from Brooklyn to Boston, needed a manager for 1938. Bill McKechnie, one of Casey's oil partners, had been named Manager of the Year by *The Sporting News* in 1937 for merely bringing the Braves in fifth. He took his award and accepted an offer to manage Cincinnati.

Quinn called Casey in Omaha, Texas, and offered him the Boston job on October 25, 1937.

Casey had been in touch with George Weiss about possibly taking a job at the Yankee farm clubs of Kansas City or Newark. He had also spoken to Bill Terry about a job in the Giants organization. But he leaped at Quinn's offer. They didn't even discuss salary.

CASEY WASN'T QUINN'S FIRST choice. That was Donie Bush, who was happy in Minneapolis and turned him down. (Bush had won the 1927 pennant with Pittsburgh.) Other names considered were Rabbit Maranville, Roger Peckinpaugh, and yes, Babe Ruth. But Casey had a reputation for attracting fans, and the Bees (they had dropped "Braves" after 1935), were the second team in town, after the Red Sox. It had been twenty-three years since they had won a pennant. The Bees in fact had drawn only 385,339 in 1937, a little over five thousand a game.

On November 22, at the Copley Plaza Hotel, Casey was introduced to the Boston baseball writers at a luncheon. Seventy-five journalists turned out—it seemed like most of New England. The reaction was, well, mixed. "Called a 'crackpot' and a 'screwball' by thousands of fans, Charles Dillon 'Casey' Stengel, the newly-appointed manager of the Boston Bees, has earned the respect of those who make baseball their livelihood because of his shrewdness," wrote Hy Hurwitz in the *Globe*.

Casey went to the Baseball Writers' Dinner in Boston in January 1938 and was, predictably, a hit, with his stories, pantomime, and predictions. The writers were happy to have him: good copy was sure to follow.

The team's second-class citizenship would be evident in the difference between Braves Field and Fenway Park, but it was also immediately apparent to Casey in spring training. Quinn himself called the clubhouse at Waterfront Park in Bradenton, Florida, a "kennel." Both the stands and the field were run-down. The hotel was a loser.

Stengel brought in two unrelated coaches named Kelly: George ("High Pockets") Kelly, who had been Casey's teammate with the Giants, and the less famous Mike Kelly. He had two pitchers who would stand out: Jim Turner and Lou Fette. Turner had won twenty games as a thirty-three-year-old rookie the year before. Not only would Casey quickly see

Turner's wisdom as a pitcher; he would make Turner his pitching coach when he later went to the Yankees.

There were some familiar faces on the club, to be sure. Al Lopez, Joe Stripp, Bobby Reis, Tony Cuccinello, and Johnny Cooney were all players he had managed in Brooklyn. A sophomore in the outfield was Vince DiMaggio, older brother of Joe, who had led the league in strikeouts in '37 with 111 and would do it again in '38 with 134—extraordinary numbers for the times.

Vince would be sent down to Kansas City in February 1939, as Casey admitted his own failure to curb the strikeouts and suggested someone else might do better. (The someone else turned out to be Casey when he had Vince again, with the minor-league Oakland Oaks in 1947.)

Lopez, catching, took a foul ball off his thumb one day; he knew it was bad, but decided to soldier on. Lopez described what happened next:

> Casey rushed out to look at it, but I said, "No, it'll be all right." He demanded to see it.
> "You really want to see it, Casey?" I asked.
> He said, "Certainly."
> I stuck the thumb right in front of his face. He took one look, turned green and then passed out.

Lopez was out from May 24 to July 26. Injuries took a huge toll on the team. There were days when Casey had as few as sixteen able-bodied men to work with.

ONE OF CASEY'S FEW players who could rightly be called a star was the outfielder Max West, who broke in in 1938, and started the 1940 All-Star Game, hitting a three-run home run off Red Ruffing in the contest, which the National League won 4–0. (McKechnie, the National League manager, named Casey as one of his coaches.)

Casey also had a left-handed hitter named Debs Garms, who had batted .259 in 1937. Garms would remember:

> The following spring, Stengel came to the club. I remember we were training at Bradenton, Florida, and Casey said to me: "They tell me there's a man on that infield you like pretty well." I knew

he meant the second baseman. I must have hit 150 or 200 balls down that way the previous year.

Then Case said, "Young man, if you're ever going to make a living up here in the big leagues, you've got to learn to bunt and hit the ball by the third baseman."

By the time Casey had started working on me, I realized that it was up to me to do something or lose my job. A .259 average wasn't good enough. He told me to make the third baseman my target, and hope that I missed him. If I aimed at him, enough balls would go to either side and be safe. I owe Casey a great deal for the way he likes to sit around and talk baseball.

In 1940, Garms led the National League with a .355 average. Unfortunately, by then he was playing for Pittsburgh.

On June 11 in Cincinnati, the Bees were no-hit by Johnny Vander Meer, which might not have been as historic had he not no-hit Brooklyn his next time out (in the first night game at Ebbets Field), the only pitcher in history to throw consecutive no-hitters.

Casey was far more accustomed to losing than to winning by now, and his six years in Boston would not change that pattern. His fifth place finish in 1938 was his high-water mark with the team. Alas, attendance fell to 341,149 in 1938, even though the Bees finished only twelve games out of first. After that, he was seventh four years in a row, and then sixth. He never tasted the first division.

"People often ask me if this affected his personality—did he snap at the dog, glower at the toaster, snarl at his wife?" wrote Edna. "No, never. Casey would start talking baseball the minute we left Braves Field, and he'd gab, non-stop, until we reached our hotel. He might be temporarily upset about losing a tough one, but his tremendous love of baseball and people always brought him back to even keel. He thinks always of tomorrow's chance, not yesterday's loss."

CASEY'S MOTHER, JENNIE STENGEL, suffered a heart attack and died at seventy-nine years of age in Kansas City on December 5, 1938. Casey barely missed a flight from Dallas (the Winter Meetings) that would have gotten him home in time to say goodbye.

Louis Stengel died sixteen months later, on April 7, 1940, also at seventy-nine. After Casey got the phone call from his brother, Grant, the Bees' traveling secretary, Duffy Lewis, arranged for Casey to get from spring training in Augusta, Georgia, to Atlanta, from which he could travel by train for the funeral. The report was that Louis had suffered "a shock," which probably meant a heart attack, or perhaps a stroke.

Although his parents would have been proud and happy to see Casey become a dentist, they had rejoiced in his celebrity in baseball, and often went to Chicago, or even to New York, Philadelphia, Pittsburgh, or Brooklyn, to see him play. They were baseball fans, and though they didn't get to see Casey's finest hours as a manager, they did get to delight in his major-league status and celebrity.

"BUCKETFOOT" AL SIMMONS, WHO had had a great career in the American League, joined "the Swarm" (the newspapers' sometime name for the Bees) in 1939. And then there was Paul "Big Poison" Waner, who was on the Bees in 1941 and 1942, collecting 168 hits in those two years, including the one that made him the seventh member of the 3,000-Hit Club.

His three thousandth hit came on June 19, 1942, in Braves Field, off Rip Sewell of Pittsburgh (Waner's longtime team), and would probably have been viewed as a bigger moment if anyone had realized that he would be the only player in thirty-three years—between Eddie Collins in 1925 and Stan Musial in 1958—to accomplish the feat.

The game was halted so that Waner could retrieve the milestone baseball, and the Pirates came on the field to join the Bees and congratulate him. Casey, coaching third, was among the first in a Boston uniform to get to him and slap him on the back.

It was fairly well celebrated by 1942 standards, even before fans and writers really bore down on baseball statistics.

BECAUSE CASEY'S BOSTON SEASONS produced few positive highlights, some games remained etched in fans' minds. The Bees, for instance, played a twenty-three-inning game on June 28, 1939, the third longest in history to that point, which ended in a 2–2 tie five hours after it began. It needn't have gone that far, but a Bees pinch runner named Otto Huber fell down trying to score the winning run in the thirteenth. To Casey's total dismay, it turned out that Huber lost his footing because his spikes were worn down to nubs. There was no record of how many of the 2,457 fans in attendance that day stayed to the finish.

"Otto got us into the Little Red Book of Baseball," said Casey, referring to the game's record book.

A year later, the Bees lost to the Dodgers a twenty-inning game that lasted five hours and nineteen minutes; Brooklyn ended it by scoring four in the twentieth inning.

In September 1939, Casey was in Chicago to play the Cubs when he agreed to manage the Bees again in 1940. He wired Bob Quinn: "Am more than pleased to accept the management again and want you to know that I never have entered into a conversation or looked elsewhere for a position because the treatment and cooperation I have received from you has been more than any place I ever held a position and only hope my plans for a young ball club for the Boston public will be realized in 1940."

At the end of the season, Mike Kelly went to coach Pittsburgh, and the ever-present Cooney replaced him as a player-coach. (A fictional "Cooney," it might be noted, "died at first" in line three of "Casey at the Bat," which people still associated with Stengel.)

Casey tried something different in February 1940, when he opened an early-spring training camp in Bradenton. It was an experiment he would come to repeat during his glory years with the Yankees. He would instruct and observe the youngest of the organization's prospects, which at that time included twenty-three "Baby Bees," including Sibby Sisti and Phil Masi, who had just come up the previous summer. Both would enjoy long stays with Boston.

He, with Fred Haney of the St. Louis Browns, became the first two managers to take their teams to Mexico during spring training. They played two weekend games in Monterrey, but few fans turned out on Sunday, which was bullfight day in Mexico. (Haney later managed Milwaukee against Casey in the 1957 and 1958 World Series.)

EARLY IN THE 1940 season, Casey sent a handwritten letter back to his sister, Louise, in Kansas City, on hotel letterhead from Cincinnati:

Dear Louise. I have been very slow to answer your letters' reason is that Edna + I have been so busy and she returned home today by way of Chicago + then on the Union Pacific so won't stop at K.C. She had a nice trip but did not see us win many games.

Every club is after my ["pitchers" written with a line through it]
*players for a trade but will not give any good players in return
and our club needs the money badly + expect the owners to
make a deal by June 15th. My pitchers are terrible but my young
men in the field have been doing well. I am mailing you 100.00
for your account at the bank and will positively send you another
hundred at the first of July. Hope all are well and doing O.K.
With love to all your loving brother C.D. Stengel.*

Money would always be an issue with the Bees, even more so than in
Brooklyn. They drew fewer than four thousand fans a game during Casey's
time there, and never had enough to contend seriously. Casey's effort was
recognized by the respected H. G. Salsinger of *The Detroit News,* who
wrote: "Stengel has one of the least desirable jobs in baseball. The Boston
club controls so little money that it cannot even afford to pay the waiver
price and they say that only Bob Quinn's personal popularity has kept the
sheriff from taking over. Unable to buy players, Stengel has been limited to
such material as he could get for nothing, and when you think how thoroughly the minor leagues and sandlots are scouted today for material, you
can realize what a limited field was left for Stengel to choose from."

There was one Boston owner, Charles Adams, who had lots of money
to invest. He also owned the Suffolk Downs racetrack and the Boston
Bruins hockey team. But because Commissioner Landis wanted no inter-
mingling of racetrack money and baseball teams, Adams was unable to
help out.

In April 1941, Adams sold his share to about a dozen investors,
including Lou and Joe Perini, Joe Maney, Guido Rugo, golf star Fran-
cis Ouimet, Casey's friend Max Meyer (a Brooklyn jeweler, who tried
several times to buy the Dodgers—with Casey as part of the investment
team), Bob Quinn and his son John, and Casey, who put in twenty-five
thousand dollars and became a team owner. Johnny Cooney wanted in,
but was rejected because he was an active player. Bing Crosby wanted in,
but was rejected for his racetrack connections.[*]

The annual results were disappointing, and attendance was horrid.
But Casey loved Boston, loved walking down Commonwealth Avenue

---

[*] Lou Perini, Rugo, and Maney—"The Three Little Steam Shovels"— bought the others
out in 1944. Perini moved the team to Milwaukee in 1953.

to the ballpark and talking baseball with the fans. Braves Field (fans still called it that, even though the team was now the Bees) was about a mile and a half from Casey's hotel. The breeze from the Charles River played a role in his games, but also provided a nice summer climate. (The field still stands, as well as the right-field bleachers, as Nickerson Field, on the campus of Boston University.)

Casey traded Al Lopez, again, this time to the Pirates, during the 1940 season. "Sailor Bill" Posedel tied for the team pitching lead, with a dozen victories (he would later be pitching coach for the great Oakland A's teams of the early 1970s).

The '41 team included Babe Dahlgren, the first baseman who replaced Lou Gehrig on the Yankees, only to be "banished" by Joe McCarthy, who described him as having "short arms." As eventually came to light, McCarthy never forgave Babe for an error in September 1940 that led to a loss that knocked the Yankees out of first. Off-handedly (and strangely), he suggested to a small gathering of writers, "If Dahlgren doesn't smoke marijuana, he catches that ball." (None printed it.) So this first baseman on the '39 Yankees—one of the great teams in baseball history—found himself on the Braves, where he hit .235, and was essentially blackballed out of the game. Yes, being on the Braves was like being out of the game.

The Braves (their name had been changed back by now) trained in San Antonio in 1941, removed from most other teams. (At one exhibition in Fort Smith, Arkansas, Casey was presented with an active beehive, containing, it was said, 1,296 living bees). The Braves picked up the great American Leaguer Earl Averill that spring, but the short experiment was yet another failure, and after eight games, he was released.

Cooney, meanwhile, hit .318 in 1940 as a player/coach, and .319 in 1941—at age forty. The Boston baseball writers gave him their player-of-the-year honors (the Walter Barnes Memorial Award) in the former year, over Ted Williams' .344 season for the Red Sox.

In 1941, of course, the Braves were more of an afterthought than usual; across town, Williams was hitting .406.

The "off-season" of 1941–42 was anything but quiet. The bombing of Pearl Harbor on December 7 put the United States at war. Until Franklin Roosevelt gave baseball the green light to keep going, largely to provide factory workers with a form of recreation, there was uncertainty over whether the national pastime would be put "on hold."

"Maybe I'll go back in the Navy and paint ships," Casey told Edna, recalling his World War I service.

Given the relative speed with which World War I ended for the United States—which was actively engaged for only nineteen months—most did not anticipate that this new war would last nearly four more years. The depletion of baseball's rosters was mighty, but for the Boston Braves it was hardly noticeable. The replacement players, mostly classified 4-F, were nearly as bad as the ones who went to serve.

In 1942, the Braves trained in Sanford, Florida. One afternoon, the team had an exhibition game in Sebring, against the Yankees' powerful farm club, the Newark Bears. Casey did not suit up that day. He left his number-31 uniform back in Sanford and let his coaches manage. He decided to sit in the stands with his old friend from the Eastern League days, George Weiss. Weiss, director of the Yankees farm system, was there to watch his Newark players in action. The Bears were probably a better club than Casey's major-league team—an observation that must have been shared by Casey and Weiss as the afternoon unfolded.

Ernie Lombardi came in to do the catching in 1942 and hit .330 despite being woefully slow afoot. A pitcher named Tom Earley was suspended by Stengel for "indifferent pitching." Meanwhile, the Boston press showed signs of turning on Casey, getting tired of the team's annual plunge to the lower recesses of the league standings. Only a more awful club in Philadelphia kept the Braves from last place in these seasons.

In 1942, a couple of pitchers, Warren Spahn and Johnny Sain, made their debuts; they would lead the franchise to a pennant six years later. Sain, who later pitched for Casey at the Yankees, in his forty appearances as a rookie, made a nice impression before going off for three years in the service. Spahn, who would also pitch for Casey but with the Mets, was only twenty-one in 1942, and made less of an impression. He, too, went off for three years of military service.

On April 20, in a game at Ebbets Field, Casey ordered Spahn, pitching in relief, to fire a brushback pitch at the Dodgers' Pee Wee Reese. Three times Spahn threw inside—but not enough to satisfy Casey's definition of a brushback.

"Young man, you've got no guts," Stengel told him when he reached the dugout. "Go pick up your railroad ticket to Hartford."

And Spahn was gone, though he would return for two games in September before heading off for his three years of combat service. Eventually, Spahn became the winningest left-handed pitcher in baseball history.

"Yes," Casey later reflected. "I said 'no guts' to a kid who wound up being a war hero and one of the best pitchers anybody ever saw. You can't say I don't miss 'em when I miss 'em."

Spahn would later tell people, "I'm the only guy to play for Casey Stengel before and after he was a genius."

17

CROSSING KENMORE SQUARE

WARTIME TRAVEL RESTRICTIONS FORCED spring training north in 1943, and the elite, private Choate School in Wallingford, Connecticut, 125 miles southwest of Boston, would be the Braves' training site.

As with most teams working out in cold climates, a lot of time was spent indoors, practicing throwing and exercising, and few exhibition games were actually played. (They did play one against the Yankees in Yankee Stadium.)

The most interesting new face in camp was the veteran Lefty Gomez, who had been sold by the Yankees in January. Now thirty-four, he was as funny as Casey and great copy for the writers. But alas, he would be on the team until May 19 without ever getting into a game.

Opening day was Saturday, April 24, in Boston. This would be Casey's sixth year as the Braves' manager, and his thirty-fourth year in the game. He was soon to turn fifty-three.

On the 19th, Patriots' Day, the Braves beat the Red Sox in the last exhibition game of the spring. Late that night, a stormy night made all the gloomier because of World War II blackout rules, Casey was crossing the difficult intersection at Kenmore Square, walking across Commonwealth Avenue; he was heading, he later said, for a lunchroom, probably Charlie's, on the south side of the busy street. He had left his hotel, the Sheraton, around midnight.

As part of the wartime blackout rules, the top halves of auto headlights were taped over. Casey held his raincoat high so it shielded his face. The moment must have had the look of a black-and-white film noir.

Suddenly he was struck hard by a car. Imagine the sound of impact mixed with the driving rain and the screams of other pedestrians. Casey was laid out on the pavement as a crowd gathered in horror. Few if any recognized him in the rain and the darkness. The impact caused severe fractures to his right leg. Both the tibia and the fibula were shattered. Thomas Hastings, the driver of the car, got Casey to St. Elizabeth's Hospital in Brighton, which was so crowded that he was placed in the maternity ward. His shattered leg was raised by hanging weights.

It was bad. His shortstop Whitey Wietelmann said, "That leg was snapped off clean in two. They did a tremendous job just to save it." Fortunately, Wietelmann was exaggerating.

For the first minutes in the hospital, amputation was considered. The Braves' team doctor, Edward O'Brien, Jr., said the leg was so severely swollen it could not be set for a week. Then the surgeons went to work and did their jobs. Saving the shattered leg was a very complicated procedure. The surgeons put nearly twenty-five pounds of metal into his leg, all dangling from a spike through his heel to draw the bones into place. The limb would be saved—there would be no amputation—but the effects of the injury would be with Casey for the rest of his life.

FRANKIE FRISCH, MANAGING THE Pirates, visited him in the hospital when that team came to Boston and brought him roses—and diaper pins (given that he was in the maternity ward). He had earlier sent a telegram stating: THIS IS NO TIME OF YEAR TO TRY TO COMMIT SUICIDE.

Players old and new sent him get-well wishes, playfully addressed to the hospital's psychiatric ward. The New York writers visited him, en masse, on May 5, bringing a huge ice cream cake and a travel clock, not that he was going anywhere soon. Braves players visited him, one at a time or in small groups.

But make no mistake: When he looked up at his leg suspended above him, Casey felt depressed. He was older now, but he was still an athlete, and such a setback does not play well for anyone, least of all an athlete. "He brooded about it and finally decided that if he was going to be a cripple, he would never again appear before the public," wrote Edna. "For the first time in his life, he talked about quitting baseball."

Bob Coleman, a coach, would be acting manager, assisted by High Pockets Kelly. The best Casey could do was listen to the games on WNAC on his bedside radio.

On May 22, just over a month after the accident, he got out of bed for the first time, and stayed out ever so briefly. The leg was finally put into a cast on June 5; three days later, he began to walk on crutches.

EDNA INTERRUPTED HER CARE for her dying mother to fly to Boston on June 12, in time to accompany Casey to the Myles Standish Hotel after fifty-three days in the hospital. Casey had understood her absence before then, and wired her, "Don't come unless you can set a broken leg."

On June 18, still on those crutches, Casey returned to Braves Field for the first time to resume managing. In his first game back, he sent Chet Ross up to pinch-hit in the ninth, and Ross delivered a three-run homer, to beat the Giants 8–6.

The Bees had been 21-25 under Coleman, in sixth place (which is where they would finish). Casey had missed forty-six games.

On June 19, Edna's mother, Margaret, died in Glendale; back Edna went, although Casey wasn't able to accompany her.

In September, Casey had improved enough to come out of his cast and discard his crutches, but he now walked with a pair of mahogany canes, his leg in a brace. Despite the compliments Casey paid to the hospital staff, his leg never healed perfectly.

The sportswriter Harold Rosenthal would write in 1961: "Ever notice the way Stengel used to walk out to the mound, one leg seemingly shorter than the other and a definite bow to the shorter one down around the ankle? Well, it was shorter and there was a definite bow to it, tracing to a wet-night accident in Boston. A fellow driving an uninsured car knocked Casey down, and the accident put Stengel in the hospital for a couple of months. The leg healed with an unsightly burl-like knot, and the doctors cautioned him not to get any severe blows on the part where the healed bone seemed to be struggling to burst through the pale skin."

The acerbic and sometimes cruel *Boston Record* sportswriter Dave "the Colonel" Egan wrote that the prize given by the local chapter of the Baseball Writers' Association for the man who had done the most for baseball in Boston in 1943 should go to "the taxi-driver who knocked Stengel down and put him out of commission from April 20 until July." (News accounts vary on whether it was a car or a taxi.) Casey never publicly responded to this, though he did go on to tell some people that Egan had a drinking problem.

—

EVEN THOUGH THE SEASON ended with the Braves up a notch to sixth, it was over for Casey. Perini had grown tired of hearing explanations doled out in Stengelese. He wanted answers and he got double-talk. It may have been charming for the press, but it wasn't working with the boss. "I decided that at the first opportunity I was going to give Stengel some of his own double talk as well as a pink slip," said Perini. "But I never got the chance. Casey resigned before I could fire him."

On January 28, 1944, Casey resigned in a letter, sent airmail to Perini from Chicago. "Whenever a new group purchases control of a corporation they have the right to dictate the policy. And in order that there be no embarrassment on the part of this group I hereby tender my resignation. Casey Stengel."

To Bob Quinn, he wrote a longer and more personal letter:

> I am sure the city of Boston, with the Braves, will profit by the young players who I have developed since I have been there. Many of the players are now in the service.
>
> No one realizes more than you, the interest and faith I have in the city of Boston. You are familiar with the substantial amount of my personal cash which I invested in the club. You also know that whenever the directors asked for more cash I put up as much as any other director.
>
> I want to thank you and believe it or not, my many friends in Boston, my able coaches, and particularly the newspapermen who were kind to me while I was trying to win and also develop young players for the future of the Boston club.
>
> I sincerely hope the new owners have every success and that Boston will have a first division team.

And so he went home to Glendale, probably assuming that his baseball career was over. He had no job for 1944 and would have to count on his oil money, never a sure thing. But he was not willing to admit he was done. In February 1944, Casey told friends, "I have a few irons in the fire. I won't be out of baseball this year." He had hoped to be part of a group buying the Dodgers with Max Meyer, but it didn't happen. One newspaper report had him succeeding the retiring Earle Combs as a

Yankee coach, but the job went to Johnny Neun. Ed Barrow, running the Yankees, was said to have recoiled at the thought of hiring Casey.

EDNA WROTE: "HE WAS on crutches, he was inconsolable. 'If I gotta walk out on that coaches box with a old man's limp,' he repeated over and over, 'I just don't belong in baseball.'"

Edna reflected on those first weeks of spring training in 1944:

I had my man around the house at last, that nine-to-five guy, but (I hate to confess) he was a nuisance. After he finished reading the ups and downs of both baseball and stocks, he didn't know what to do with himself. He'd grumble aloud about the trades, the choice of starting pitchers, and to anyone he met—the mailman, the gardener, the delivery boy, my father—he'd grab the chance to talk, talk, talk baseball.

Lonesome? He was dying.

This was different than his 1937 "vacation"—then he had been bustling with plans for going back.

As the winter went on and his leg showed little improvement he convinced himself he was through.

18

MILWAUKEE
AND K.C.

CASEY WAS OUT OF work and sitting at home as the 1944 season opened. No spring training, no phone calls.

At last, the American Association, where he had managed Toledo for six years, came calling.

The Milwaukee Brewers (the minor-league team from which today's major-league team took its name) had been purchased by twenty-seven-year-old Bill Veeck in 1941. Veeck's father had been president of the Cubs, and, together with some friends of his father's, he found enough cash to buy the Brewers. It was the start of a career that would lead "Sports Shirt Bill" to the Hall of Fame.

He was called "Sports Shirt Bill" because his practice of disdaining ties and wearing open-collared shirts was so attention-getting at the time; he seemed to be the only person in baseball besides Ted Williams who shed accepted standards and practices.

His reputation for showmanship began in Milwaukee, where he thought every game was a promotion opportunity, even if it meant having a fruit-and-vegetable night, when some lucky fan would go home with a basket of peaches.

His manager in Milwaukee was the Chicago Cubs legend Charlie ("Jolly Cholly") Grimm, Casey's teammate on the 1919 Pirates. Grimm was a banjo-playing former infielder turned broadcaster. He had many friends in the game and was a delight on the baseball scene for decades.

Grimm won the American Association pennant with the Brewers in 1943, and got off to an 11-2 start in 1944. At that point, the Cubs decided to change managers; they fired Jimmy Wilson and asked Grimm to leave Milwaukee and take the job. As Grimm would remember it:

Before I could accept this chance to come back to the Cubs, I told them I'd first have to get a replacement for the Milwaukee job, one who was acceptable to Bill Veeck.

My choice was Casey Stengel, who had announced his retirement after a somewhat dismal experience in Boston. . . . I never thought of anyone except Casey as the man to free me so I could return to the Cubs. . . . I put in a call for him in California. He was glad to chat with me but manage the Brewers—never!

"I've had enough," he told me from Glendale. I didn't take it for a final answer. I sent a cable to Guadalcanal, hoping it would reach Veeck [who was stationed there with the Marines].

It did.

"Oh no, not Casey Stengel," was the gist of his first message.

Another one brought a half-hearted okay. I called Stengel, being careful not to tell him of Veeck's first reaction. "For you and Bill I'll do it," Casey finally conceded.

Actually, Grimm's portrayal of Veeck's reaction was mild, perhaps given his continuing role as a stockholder in the team. In actuality, Veeck thought very little of Stengel, and let it be known in letters to his front office after his hiring, letters that found their way into the newspapers. For instance: "I'd like to have a complete explanation of where Stengel comes from. Who hired him? Who suggested him? For how much and how long? I don't want anything to do with Stengel nor do I want him to have anything to do with anything I have a voice in." He then cited seven reasons why he hated the selection of Casey:

First, Stengel has never managed a winner. In my humble opinion, he is a very poor manager.

Second, he has been closely connected with Bob Quinn and the operation of the Boston Braves. This in itself is enough to damn him.

Third, I don't believe Stengel is a good judge of players and so can be of no value in amassing future clubs.

Fourth, from what I know of Stengel he is tight-fisted and this will not prove acceptable.

Fifth, from my observation, Stengel is mentally a second-division major leaguer. That is, he is entirely satisfied with a mediocre ball club as long as Stengel and his alleged wit are appreciated.

Sixth, I have no confidence in his ability and rather than be continuously worried I'd rather dispose of the whole damn thing.

Seventh, Stengel doesn't fit in at all with the future—and I'm looking as usual, for the long haul.

If these aren't reasons enough, I don't like him and I want no part of him. If Stengel has an ironclad contract and it will be expensive to break, I guess we'll have to be stuck with him. If not, replace him immediately with Ivy Griffin.

For his 1967 biography of Casey, Joe Durso got Veeck to write an introduction. He wrote, "Although I had known Casey casually since early childhood, I still thought of him as a clown . . . a guy who didn't win. I had bought the then 'public image.' "

And so Casey packed his bags and headed for Milwaukee to rejoin the American Association, after nine years managing in the National League.

It was a comedown for sure, but this was May, and he was tired of the home life. He was off his crutches. He was only fifty-three. It was time to go back to work.

And it would be fun! He was hailed as a hero when he returned to Toledo (he made two speeches in one day at local functions there on May 22), and he was hailed as a hometown boy when he returned to Kansas City. In Kansas City, he could visit with his brother and sister and visit his old house. He had seen them only occasionally since 1931.

PFC VEECK, JUST THIRTY-ONE, was not a factor; he was at war. He always blew hot and cold on Casey. He barely mentioned him in his own best-selling memoir, *Veeck—As in Wreck*. By the end of May, conceding that Casey had won over the press, Veeck wrote that he "should be OK until the season ends."

Casey arrived at Borchert Field, the Brewers' home park, on May 6, where an overflow crowd of 10,044 saw Milwaukee take a doubleheader from Columbus. Grimm had handed Casey a terrific ball club. He discarded his brace and coached third again.

Borchert was built in 1887, and showed it. On June 14, a month into Casey's term, a storm literally tore the roof off the first-base side of the ballpark; thirty-five people were injured in a mad scramble to get to the field.

The Brewers had no major-league affiliation, although they had a close "friendship" with the nearby Cubs—because of Grimm, who still was a stockholder in the team, and because Phil Wrigley, the Cubs' owner, also put some of his own money into the purchase of the Brewers. Casey got to juggle ten .300 hitters in and out of the lineup, and the team led the league with 135 home runs and a .307 team average. They scored a hundred runs more than their nearest rival.

Twenty-two of the twenty-eight players on the team that year saw major-league experience at some point, including Dale Long, who played for Casey on his last Yankee team, sixteen years later. Frank Secory, who would umpire games when Casey managed the Mets, was one of his outfielders on the Brewers. The Brewers went 91-49 and won the American Association pennant by seven games. Casey had managed his first championship team since Toledo in 1927.

Alas, Milwaukee lost the playoff series, held among first-division teams, to third-place Louisville, dropping the last three games.

CASEY WAS NOT INVITED back for 1945; he resigned after the season rather than get fired. Veeck, seriously injured in the war (he lost a leg), would be home to run the team and did not want to deal with Casey on a daily basis.

Stengel learned that he was on the way out when informed by *The Milwaukee Journal*'s sports editor. "I took this job to help out my friend Charlie Grimm, because he said he could not take the job with the Chicago Cubs unless I did. The understanding was that I would just finish up the season, and that would give them time to find a manager for 1945."

The Milwaukee press loved Casey, as did the press wherever he played or managed. At season's end, he threw dinners for his players and for the writers. A few fans started a "Bring Back Casey" movement, but Casey knew that he and Veeck were not intended to work together. He departed without a fuss. Veeck and Stengel met quietly over the winter in California, and a small attempt was made to mend fences. Veeck now offered to have Casey return in 1945. (In fact, about a year later, he invited Casey to join his group in buying the Cleveland Indians.) But in his own mind, Casey had already moved on.

At the Winter Meetings in December, George Weiss asked him if he would like to manage the Yankees' farm team in Kansas City in 1945—

not only his hometown team, but the team that had first signed him, out of Central High in 1910.

This was one of the most significant career moves he would make, for it would formally put him in the Yankee organization. He knew Weiss, but now he would come to know everyone in the Yankee operation involved in player development and minor-league administration. It was a good path for him to be on.

Who knew where this would lead? It would be his first assignment in the Yankees' organization, and in fact, the first time he would work for a team affiliated with the American League. New doors were opening. Maybe—did he dare to think it?—it would put him on a path to succeed Joe McCarthy as manager one day in New York.

However, he came to see it in smaller terms, "I took over a weak Yankee farm team as a favor to George Weiss, who had sold me players on the installment plan when I was with clubs that couldn't afford to pay for them outright," Casey reflected in later years.

The Kansas City press loved this story. A testimonial dinner to welcome Casey was held at Kansas City's Muehlebach Hotel, attended by Weiss and one of the new Yankee co-owners, Del Webb (he, Dan Topping, and Larry MacPhail had just purchased the team from the Jacob Ruppert estate). "So much fan enthusiasm has been kindled here that the smile on Business Manager Roy Hamey's face is real for the first time in a couple of seasons. Fans are asking for opening day tickets and the sun shines again," reported *The Sporting News*.

The Blues weren't much of a team, despite their eight-year Yankee affiliation, and the pay wasn't much, but Casey could see his brother and sister, sleep in his old house if he chose to, and visit with old friends whenever he wanted. They played in Blues Stadium (where the Athletics and later the Royals played), which then had a capacity of 17,476.

The Blues finished seventh in 1945. They hit only thirty-five home runs as a team and didn't give the fans much to cheer for, although season attendance tripled—to just around a hundred thousand. Milwaukee won the pennant again. Late in the summer, a free-for-all took place on the field during a 17–7 romp by the Blues over the Brewers, and when the dust cleared, Casey was found at the bottom of the pile of players. He was fifty-five years old.

There were not many notable names on his team, but he had his oil partner Johnny Cooney, age forty-four, back for one last year as a player/

coach. It was Cooney's twenty-fifth season as a player, and it felt like most of them were with or for Casey. Clarence "Cuddles" Marshall, a right-hander, was the only player on the team who would later play for Casey in New York.

It had been quite a year. The death of President Roosevelt, the ascension of Casey's Kansas City "neighbor" Harry Truman to the presidency, the dropping of the atomic bombs over Japan, the end of the wars in both Japan and Europe—and, it was hoped, the end of baseball's wartime slumber.

Just days after the season ended, the Oakland Oaks of the Pacific Coast League fired their manager, Billy Raimondi, and Casey's name appeared in stories as a possible successor.

The owners, Brick Laws and Joe Blumenfeld, along with Cookie DeVincenzi, the team's general manager, reached out to Casey, De-Vincenzi taking the lead in the negotiations. They brought him up from Glendale but couldn't nail down a deal right there. The next morning, with Casey already back home, they received a wire: I'LL TRY IT FOR A YEAR. STENGEL.

He resigned his Kansas City post.

ON OCTOBER 17, HE was signed to a twelve-thousand-dollar contract. George Weiss actually made the announcement, noting that the Yankees had "friendly relations" with Oakland, even if not a direct affiliation. "We are sorry to lose Casey," said Weiss, "but it has always been our policy never to stand in the way of a manager who wants to move on. We thought Casey did a fine job for the Blues and I'm sure he will prove a popular manager at Oakland."

Oakland had gotten consistently good reports on him from the local Yankee scouts, Bill Essick (based in Los Angeles) and Joe Devine (in San Francisco), the two who had signed Joe DiMaggio a decade earlier. Brick Laws frequently played golf with Del Webb. Relationships were building.

19

OAKLAND

CASEY ATTENDED THE PACIFIC Coast League meetings in Los
Angeles on October 26, which were called largely to talk about
trying to turn the league into a major league by 1949.

With the war over, anticipating boosts in attendance and revenue
(which came to be), the PCL was thinking big. Although the league's
ballparks were inferior to major-league facilities, it occupied strong markets, and had loyal fans and a great history. The West Coast was growing
rapidly in population.

In 1946, baseball officials reclassified the minor leagues and created
"Triple-A" ball. This moved the International and Pacific Coast Leagues,
plus the American Association, up to a newly created grade. They were
still the highest minor-league level.

To West Coast fans, before the Dodgers and Giants moved west in
1958, the PCL really felt like a major league. This was their baseball. The
East Coast games were over by lunchtime; following them before television was difficult. The quality of play in the PCL was always high, the
competition keen, and the media attention strong. For Casey and Edna,
one of the benefits of being in the league was that they could be "home"
in southern California to play Los Angeles, Hollywood, and San Diego
in two trips each season, a total of thirty-three days. That gave them a
chance to be in their Glendale home more than ever before. They had
cookouts for the team at their home.

"I went up to Oakland with Casey," wrote Edna. "It was so close I
could fly home in an hour and a half. We had a marvelous time. Oakland
is a gay town. To Casey and me the associations were like Toledo all over
again. Casey was an intimate friend of colorful Brick Laws and Cookie

DeVincenzi, owners of the team, and we were one of the gang with the players."

OAKS PARK WAS ACTUALLY located in Emeryville, between Oakland and Berkeley. It was built in 1913, seated eleven thousand people, and was in an active business district with fan-friendly eating establishments just outside. There was also the California Packing Company plant across the street, which produced the scent of cooked tomatoes in the air around the park. Visitors developed a hunger for pasta almost daily.

Laws put $250,000 into park renovations after the war in anticipation of a big attendance boost.

The franchise, like the city of Oakland itself, was a weak stepsister to the San Francisco team, and had won only one pennant, in 1927, in its PCL history. Brick Laws bought control of the Oaks in 1943, and the '44 team made the playoffs. He saw in Casey a man who could motivate players to success.

The team's home opener on April 2 drew 15,189, a home attendance record. Governor Earl Warren (later chief justice of the Supreme Court) came from Sacramento to throw out the ceremonial first pitch. Casey coached third base and wore uniform number 1.

The Yankees sent Spec Shea to Oakland (he who would later pitch for Casey in New York), and he had a 15-5 season, tying Gene Bearden (who would star for Cleveland in 1948) and Rugger Ardizoia for most victories on the staff. Ardizoia, who played one game for the '47 Yankees, called Casey "the nuttiest guy I ever met" in a 2015 interview for *The New York Times,* when, at ninety-five, he was the oldest living Yankee.

"I came under the wing of Casey Stengel, a great guy, a remarkable student of baseball, a smart analyst of pitching," said Shea. "He showed me plenty. He instructed me in such matters as holding a man on base, moves with runners threatening you, and the desirability of pitching that ball low."

Casey wrote about this:

We used to get in fights with the San Francisco club. The rivalry there . . . was so great. It was like Brooklyn and the Giants used to be. A free-for-all would break out during a game, and our tough players would run on the field, and their tough players. It would look pretty good, so I'd run out and get into it too.

I was in my late fifties then. And every time you looked at a picture of the fight afterward, you'd see maybe fifteen or eighteen men standing up and fighting with each other, but you couldn't see me. There'd be a long arrow pointing down at the ground at the bottom of everything, and there'd be a line on it that said, "Stengel." So I found out that I was slipping.

Jimmy Dykes was managing the Hollywood team . . . and he said to me, "Don't you think you're getting a little old to be doing all that fighting?" And I commenced thinking, "Well, he's probably right." After that I decided to become a bench manager and let the players do the fighting.

CASEY WAS NAMED TO manage the PCL "All-Stars" in a game against Lefty O'Doul's San Francisco Seals in August. The entire net proceeds went to the Association of Professional Baseball Players of America, a charitable organization for which Casey served on the board for many years.

The '46 Oaks got into the playoffs, winning 111 of their 183 decisions (yes, the PCL played very long seasons), and finished second, four games behind San Francisco. They then swept the Los Angeles Angels in the first round of playoffs, before losing in six games to the Seals in the championship round. (The Oaks had been up, 2–1, before dropping three straight games.)

CASEY HELD OFF ON signing a 1947 contract because his name was being floated in the press as a manager for either Pittsburgh or the Yankees. But in October, he signed to return to Oakland. The Oaks finished fourth in 1947, with Vince DiMaggio, released by the Seals, reuniting with Casey. Nick Etten, the 1944 American League home run champion with the Yankees joined the team, and a nineteen-year-old local kid from Berkeley came up late in the season. His name was Billy Martin.

Casey first saw Martin when he was sixteen. The Oakland trainer persuaded Martin to take some ground balls for Casey, and Casey himself hit to him at third base. Casey didn't hit any past him. "I hit that kid everything I had and he took them all," he said. "I'll say he's got the stuff it takes, even though he's a little shrimp."

Billy had broken in in 1946 with the Class C Idaho Falls Russets, and started '47 with the Phoenix Senators of the Class C Arizona–Texas League. A .392 average there got him a late-season promotion, all the way up to Oakland. He got into fifteen games and hit .226.

The Oaks won the first round of the 1947 Governor's Cup, four games to one over the Seals, before losing in five games to Los Angeles in the championship round.

Johnny Babich, who had pitched for Casey in Brooklyn in 1934–35 and coached for him in '46, came back in 1948 to coach again. Casey was still coaching third base at this time, but he was spending so much time in conversation with the nearby fans along the third-base line (including a lot of "regulars" he had come to know) that Babich finally suggested Casey manage from the dugout, and he would coach third. The shift happened in midseason.

The '48 Oaks had forty players who came and went (about half of them former major leaguers), and many of them were up there in years and in experience. If an older player is "on his way down" in the minor leagues, it can be a time of discontent. But when surrounded by a roster of people in a similar situation, a good manager can bring them together to have a lot of fun. That is what happened for the Oaks in 1948, even with the long season of nearly 190 games.

Among the "elders," he brought in pitcher Jim Tobin and catcher Ernie Lombardi, thirty-five and forty, respectively. Lombardi was a big local hero, who had played for the Oaks in 1928–30. His slow speed and big nose made him the object of some ridicule over his career (including from Casey), but he eventually went into the Hall of Fame, with a lifetime .306 average, two batting titles—and no infield hits that anyone remembered. Casey had managed Lombardi in Boston in 1942, when he won his second batting title, and he also had Tobin there (a twenty-one-game loser). The pitcher Lou Tost, now thirty-seven, had been on that club as well, and Casey brought him back.

Also on the club were Ralph Buxton (37), Nick Etten (34), Brooks Holder (33), Cookie Lavagetto (35), Dario Lodigiani (32), Billy Raimondi (35), Les Scarsella (34) Maurice Van Robays (33), Thornton Lee (41), Jack Salveson (34), and Floyd Speer (35). Billy Martin, who turned 20 in May, stood out for his youth. Merl Combs, 28, was his double-play partner at short. Catfish Metkovich, 27, was a rare young outfielder.

"We look better on paper than we really are," Casey told Taylor Spink of *The Sporting News*. "Fellows who should be pitching well by now have sore arms, and my team is riddled with injuries. And one of the damnedest things you ever heard of happened to one of my young outfielders who can also play first base, George Metkovich. A catfish chawed off a hunk of his foot." It was true, a freak fishing accident; George would forever be known as Catfish Metkovich.

Lavagetto, an Oakland native, had been a hero of the 1947 World Series for Brooklyn, coming through in the clutch to break up a no-hitter of Bill Bevens. Casey appointed him as a roommate and "mentor" to Billy Martin, who had his nose surgically trimmed down in May and wore bandages on the field. (Cookie would later be a coach for Casey on the Mets.)

What a time this club had, winning 114, and losing 74. There wasn't a single "league leader" in any category among them, but Etten clubbed forty-three home runs and drove in 155, Metkovich hit .336, and Martin hit a very creditable .277.

"Casey let me handle the pitching rotation," said Babich. "But he liked to play hunches. He would ask me for my starting pitchers for the week—but to leave Thursday blank. And he would pick the Thursday pitcher. No special reason he picked Thursday, he just wanted one day to pick the guy. And he was usually right."

Someone called the Oaks "the Nine Old Men" (a frequently used term for the U.S. Supreme Court judges). When Billy Martin assumed an everyday role in the infield after a slow start, some took to saying "The Eight Old Men and the Kid."

There was no doubt that Casey was taken by Billy's scrappy brand of baseball and self-confidence. And Billy had never seen a manager like Casey, someone who could pick out the smallest things on the diamond. He could tell if a fastball was coming by how quickly the pitcher was chewing his tobacco, or by how wide the third baseman opened his eyes. Billy never knew there was this much to learn about "inside baseball."

When Billy wasn't on the field, he was serving as a profane bench-jockey, and was egged on by Stengel to do even more. He got into his first on-field fight in a game at Portland that summer, a fight made notable when Casey, at age fifty-eight, joined in the fray and had his uniform torn and his arms scratched, despite his earlier promise.

There were rumors in *The Sporting News* during the summer that Casey and DeVincenzi (who was now operating Sacramento) were trying to buy a PCL team. "Stengel," said the paper, "owner of several oil wells and apartment houses, is said to be a millionaire."

"I might have gone to Sacramento but only as a part owner," Casey later said. "I was too happy in Oakland to move just for another job."

THE OAKS WENT 24-6 in the final month, and were tied for first with the Seals on September 20, with a week to go. The local press called Casey's lineup juggling, which he applied instead of platooning, the "revolving door technique."

On the 26th, they hosted Sacramento in a doubleheader—except that Sacramento batted last, as the home team, their own ballpark having burned down. Oakland rallied late in the game to win the first game 10–8. With that, the Oaks had won their first pennant in twenty-one years.

Oakland fans went crazy and stormed the field.

The pennant meant more than the Governor's Cup, but they sure didn't want to lose the cup after such a great year. And they won it, beating first Los Angeles in six, and then Seattle in five, to leave no doubt as to the champions of 1948.

"These are the finest, strongest, and best men in a pinch I've ever managed or played with in my long years of baseball," Casey said at the banquet saluting the team.

Everyone got a ring, a parade ran through downtown Oakland, and Casey was given a new five-thousand-dollar Cadillac Fleetwood. A full championship share of $1,007.93 also went to each player, including Casey. *The Sporting News* named him Minor League Manager of the Year.

"It was the biggest thing that had happened in that city since the Bay Bridge was built," said Edna. "Oakland went wild. . . . His fame spread, his antics became legend. All these years, Casey had lived in California, but the fans and press had never known him. Now they took the prodigal to their heart. It's ironic that he had to come home to find great success, because Oakland was the turning point of his baseball career. Casey was a little too famous for the Coast League to keep to itself any longer."

PART TWO

20

THE YANKEES
BECKON

WHILE OAKLAND WAS WINNING the Governor's Cup and Cleveland was winning the World Series, the New York Yankees were firing their manager, Bucky Harris.

Harris had managed the team for only two seasons, winning the world championship in the first of them, and then finishing third in 1948. The move made fans, and even some of the press, angry. It didn't seem right.

But what did Harris in was his somewhat casual approach to management. He wouldn't, for instance, provide his home telephone number to his boss, the general manager, George Weiss. He left quickly after games and wasn't one for long conversations with Weiss or Dan Topping.

Harris had been hired by the now departed Larry MacPhail, the most active of the three men who bought the team in 1945. His remaining bosses were frustrated by his approach to his work. They took the heat, let him go, and began a quick search for a new man.

"Have you ever been hit with a piece of lead pipe?" said Harris. "I had a date to meet Weiss and Topping and had a 15-minute talk with Weiss first. I came out of that feeling that everything was fine. Weiss led me to believe that I would get a new contract. Ten minutes later I was hit with that lead pipe. I went into Topping's office and got fired."

So the New York Yankees needed a manager.

THE YEAR 1948 HAD been a long one for Casey, who spent part of it ill with the flu, and part of it with his eyelids painted with a black antiseptic, thought to be a cure for the illness. He looked forward to a well-deserved rest at home for the winter. He was fully expecting to be back in Oakland for 1949, and had even used his influence to contact Verdugo Park in Glendale as a spring-training base for the Oaks in 1949.

Within days, the rewards of the championship would be felt. It wasn't the $1,007.93, it wasn't the ring, and it wasn't the Cadillac Fleetwood.

It was the long-distance call to his home from the Yankees' other co-owner, Del Webb, who was attending the World Series in Cleveland—the most important phone call of his life.

"Fly right to New York; we want you to manage the Yankees," said Webb.

THE LIFE OF CHARLES Dillon Stengel, entering his sixtieth year, and his fortieth in baseball, was about to change forever.

So, too, would the New York Yankees franchise move into one of the most successful eras in its storied history.

21

"I OWE IT TO MYSELF"

WE WERE AT AN age where I, at least, wanted to take it easy," wrote Edna in her unpublished 1958 memoir, as though sighing and accepting the inevitable.

He was happy at Oakland. We were happy with our life in California and were looking forward to fully enjoying our home for the first time.

My parents were gone, and we were alone. Casey had convinced me that I should retire as full-time business manager of the Lawson Estate and let my brother John take over. Now I was trying to convince him that he should retire.

So when I knew he was meeting the co-owner of the New York Yankees, I couldn't sleep. I sat up in bed waiting for him.

Casey came in late, and went straight into the den. I sneaked downstairs, and found him sitting in a large old brown leather chair by the window. He was speechless. He raised his head slowly and looked at me. Neither of us spoke. His eyes told me everything.

"You didn't sign," I began, falteringly. "Tell me you didn't."

"I had to, Edna," he replied in a voice so low I had to bend to catch his words. "I'll only take it for one year, I promise."

That had a familiar ring—I had a strange premonition that his "one year" would be like his promise to return to dentistry—it would go on and on.

"Oh Casey," I wailed. I was speechless, too.

Finally he said, "Edna, I had to. I owe it to myself to prove that I'm a better manager than they've given me credit for. I have to prove that I can win in the majors. I have that confidence in myself. But I have to prove it to others."

Ironically, Edna had employed Del Webb before Webb employed Casey. In 1947, a Lawson property in Glendale, the Maryland Hotel, needed expansion. Webb dined with Casey and Edna, and Edna had hired his construction company to do the job.

"I FLEW EAST AND met Topping, Webb, and Weiss on the night of October 11, signed my contract for two years, and here I am," said Casey.

Casey's name was thrown about on the West Coast as soon as Harris was dismissed. After three years in the PCL and residence in Glendale, he attracted more press attention there than in the east. He took a call from Weiss even before the call from Webb asking him to come to New York.

In another version, Casey said he was invited to discuss and perhaps recommend for the position Billy Meyer, who had managed the Yankees' farm club in Newark. "What I didn't know was Meyer had a conference with the Yankee owners the day before. . . . One thing led to another and Meyer told off the owners and they are men with a lot of money and they don't like to be told off and Meyer loses the job before he has it. . . . But I go into the meeting and I start talking up Meyer as manager and they say to me: 'We ain't interested in Meyer. We're interested in you.' So there I was—and here I am."

"I knew Weiss," he added. "I had worked for him in Kansas City. I had been associated with him back in the days when I ran the Worcester club for the Braves and he had the New Haven club, in the Eastern League." And Weiss had maintained that friendship, always inviting the Stengels to World Series games at Yankee Stadium after he joined the Yankee organization.

Casey, of course, was not the only candidate, and Topping was not sold on him at first, but he had a big endorsement from Joe Devine, the trusted Yankee scout based in northern California. Also thought to be candidates were Jim Turner, who had managed in the PCL against Casey in Portland, Luke Sewell, Bill Terry, Tommy Henrich, Bill McKechnie, and the great Joe DiMaggio himself.

—

"I HAD KNOWN DEL Webb for some years, but we never had discussed the Yankees," added Casey. "Doubtless Del brought up the subject of wanting a new manager for the Yankees, and doubtless [Brick] Laws [who accompanied Casey on this trip] brought up the subject of Stengel being the right man for the job."

"I first became acquainted with Casey right after World War I," said Webb. "He struck me immediately as quite a character, but quite frankly I never looked on him then as the type to become a manager.

"Later, in 1945, when I was president of the Kansas City Blues, Stengel was manager. He later went to Oakland, at his own request, but I always had him in mind."

"Brick said to me one day," recalled Casey, "'I hear the Yankees want you.' I also hear that other clubs would like to get you. Now, if you don't land the Yankee job, we will bid against any other outfit, even in the majors, to keep you.'"

Responding to critics who suggested his hiring was all about friendship, he told the Associated Press, "Personally I don't think they're going around handing out jobs like that just because they know a fellow by his first name. I was in the organization in 1945, managing Kansas City, but I had to go out and work my way back to the majors, just like a player."

THE YANKEES QUICKLY SCHEDULED a press luncheon at the posh 21 Club for Columbus Day, October 12. This was half a block away from the big parade going up Fifth Avenue. It was also the twenty-fifth anniversary of his World Series home run against the Yankees, when he had thumbed his nose at the team as he circled the bases, enticing Colonel Ruppert to complain to Judge Landis. Casey knew most of the writers; he had always made it his business to know everybody in the game. Even though he'd been away from the major-league scene for five years, he had always shown up at the Winter Meetings and other baseball functions.

Casey, his blond hair having fully given way to gray (except when Edna dyed it darker), wore a dark-blue business suit and spoke in a low, serious voice. The austere nature of the establishment as well as the "Yankees culture" may have gotten to him that day. He was given a two-year deal at forty-five thousand dollars a year, and would be paid monthly over twelve months, not over six. The two years, of course, flew in the face of his pledge to Edna, but managers always want that extra year, to maintain the concept of permanence and credibility for their players.

As a show of continuity and acceptance, Joe DiMaggio attended the press conference. The great DiMaggio was about to sign his first hundred-thousand-dollar contract—a rarity, that a player would make more than his manager—and he was also beginning to deal with a troubling heel spur, which would eventually bring down his career. Casey did not really know Joe (they had met once before, at a boxing match), though he had of course managed his brother Vince in Boston and Oakland.

If Casey was at all awestruck at being with DiMaggio, it did not show, nor should one think he was. Casey Stengel was not easily intimidated.

Asked how he would "manage" Joe, Casey said, "I can't tell you much about that, being as since I have not been in the American League so I ain't seen the gentleman play, except once in a very great while."

It was moderate Stengelese, in that one could interpret it at once. Understanding of the more classic Stengelese usually didn't happen until he spoke several minutes—and that was, of course, the whole point. But there was no television in those days, and Casey's response was accurate. He had not seen Joe DiMaggio play very much, and since he didn't go to the movies, he probably never saw the newsreel highlights during Joe's career.

Some writers wondered about how Casey would adjust to the American League after thirty-nine seasons in baseball without ever being part of it. There were ballparks he had never even seen the inside of, notably Detroit, Cleveland, and Washington. He may have been to Comiskey Park in Chicago on an off-day while in town to play the Cubs, but he couldn't remember. He'd been to Fenway with his Boston Bees for pre-season exhibitions, and the parks in St. Louis and Philadelphia were used by both leagues. Yankee Stadium, of course. There was something about the first World Series home run ever hit there that would be mentioned in all the stories about his hiring.

Casey's one screwup at the press conference was to call Dan Topping "Bob." Dan was one of the three who had bought the Yankees in 1945 (along with Del Webb and Larry MacPhail) from the Jacob Ruppert estate. Among his six wives had been the Olympic figure skater Sonja Henie, although he was now married to the actress Kay Sutton. His brother Bob was best known to the public as having been married to actress Lana Turner. It was not a good idea to call your new boss by the wrong name, especially the boss who wasn't so keen on you in the first place, but the matter passed.

There was not universal rejoicing over this signing. Though Casey was well liked and his baseball knowledge well respected, he seemed, well, un-Yankee-like. It was hard to separate Casey from the "c" word—"clown." The team of McCarthy-Gehrig-Dickey-DiMaggio was so buttoned up, so corporate, they were, as the expression went, like U.S. Steel. How was Casey, with his style, going to be the "boss" to DiMaggio, to Charlie Keller, to Tommy Henrich, to Phil Rizzuto—ultimate professionals who knew how to win?

Immediately, Dave "the Colonel" Egan in Boston let his poison pen express his disdain for this move:

> Well, sirs and ladies, the Yankees now have been mathematically eliminated from the 1949 pennant race.
>
> They eliminated themselves, October 12, when they engaged Perfesser Casey Stengel to mismanage them for the next two years, and you may be sure that the Perfesser will oblige to the best of his unique ability. From McCarthy to Harris to Stengel hardly can be considered an onward and upward movement, and to paraphrase the remark of Winston Churchill on another occasion, here is a man who has been brought in to supervise at the dissolution of the Yankee empire.
>
> There was some grumbling in New York, during the long and spectacularly successful regime of Joe McCarthy, that he was no good copy. He won pennants, of course, but he won them gnawing on a cigar and keeping his thoughts to himself and giving infrequent interviews, which were as unspectacular as his teams were spectacular. He let his performance do all the talking for him and some of the gentlemen of the press did not like this a little bit. They'll love Stengel. If it's stories and mimicry and home-spun humor and conversation they want, they'll get it from Stengel by day and by night, each day and each night. They'll get everything from him, indeed, with the exception of the pennant to which they have become accustomed.
>
> This department keeps running across ball players who formerly worked for Stengel, and three different ones have told me that they still keep and cherish one of my old columns. On each occasion, I naturally think it is a story in which I lauded them as idols of the youth of America or hailed them as super-stars of the grand old game, but it never is. It's always the one I wrote in which I named as the man who did the most for Boston baseball,

the truck driver who ran over Stengel and broke his leg, thus putting him out of action for the balance of the season. It is a fact that the entire team felt so good about the incident that it immediately went out and won a ball game.

He's a great guy, in other words, except to those who work for him. He's a funny guy, too; he's always funny at somebody else's expense, and the somebody else usually is within hearing distance. So he wound up with a sullen ball club, here in Boston, and the majority of the members of that club hated him then and hate him now, so that I laugh a sour laugh each time I read in the papers that Stengel is a great man in developing young ball players. He set Sibby Sisti back fully half a dozen years, and ruined Arthur Johnson and Alva Javery, yet he always remained funny in his cruel and malicious way, so now, at a cut price, he holds what once was the most important position in all baseball. . . .

[Jack Onslow, the White Sox manager] you see, was chosen because of what he knows. The Perfessor on the other hand, was chosen because of whom he knows, the whom being George Weiss of the Yankee organization. He received the job after Joe DiMaggio had declined it, and it's wonderful news for the Red Sox fans. They can stop worrying about the Yankees.

Fact of the matter is that Stengel is not a baseball manager at all. He is purely a baseball politician, which explains why he keeps cavorting into good jobs while his betters stand on the outside looking hungrily in.

Egan died in 1958, eight Casey pennants later.

STENGEL QUICKLY ASSUMED HIS duties. He was part of the Yankees contingent at the minor-league meetings in Minneapolis before Thanksgiving, and the major-league meetings in Chicago in early December. Everyone wished him well, but surely a lot of people wondered how he was going to pull this off. At Brooklyn and Boston, he had managed for nine years and had never finished in the first division. Obviously, this was a better team, but many still wondered where the justification was.

A first order of business was selecting a coaching staff. Red Corriden and Chuck Dressen were out—Dressen, in fact, on Casey's recommendation to Brick Laws, took Casey's old job as Oakland manager, where he would inherit Billy Martin.

Because of Casey's association with George "High Pockets" Kelly, who had coached for him in Boston, many thought Kelly would be named as Dressen's successor. But Weiss wanted Frank Crosetti elevated. The longtime Yankee shortstop, who had never beefed when Phil Rizzuto replaced him, who was always a good and loyal company man, would be the third-base and infield coach. Casey's days of managing from the third-base coaching box were done, although he did time in the coaching box during spring training, since he was accustomed to viewing his hitters from there.

Replacing Corriden would be Jim Turner. This was a Casey pick. He had managed Turner in Boston, and had managed against him in the Coast League. At Portland, Turner had managed Vic Raschi and Charlie Silvera, both of whom went to the Yankees. Turner knew pitching, was organized, dependable, set in his ways, and would be a fine lieutenant to keep the pitching staff organized. He was "old school" before that was even a commonly used term in baseball.

In fact, he would be one of the first pitching coaches in major-league history. Some historians, reviewing Wilbert Robinson's role with the New York Giants, believe he was, at least in part, a pitching coach under McGraw. But before Turner's appointment, there were few; Frank Shellenback with the Browns, Red Sox, and Tigers during the 1940s was the best known. In 1948, the Indians made Mel Harder pitching coach (and the team won the World Series), thus pushing the necessity of having a pitching coach forward a peg. In '49, the Yankees added Turner, and the White Sox added Ray Berres.

Not many teams employed three coaches, but for 1949 the Yankees were going to break that barrier. They added Bill Dickey, who would coach at first, be a batting coach, and take a special interest in making Yogi Berra a better catcher.

This was happy news for Yankee fans, who had loved Dickey ever since his arrival in 1928. Although remembered for punching out the Washington catcher Carl Reynolds in a home-plate fracas, Dickey was actually the strong, silent type—the perfect Yankee image. He would likely have been the team captain after Lou Gehrig died, had not Joe McCarthy declared the position "retired."

When McCarthy stepped down as manager in 1946, Dickey was

named to succeed him, but only for the remainder of the season. Bill wanted a contract for 1947, and when none seemed to be forthcoming, he quit, too. Johnny Neun finished the season, and Dickey went home, his Yankee career seemingly over.

But now, with the passage of two years, he was ready to return, and this was a feel-good announcement for the organization that had, after all, released Babe Ruth and never considered him for a position with the team short of offering him a minor-league team to manage (which he refused)—and that had had nothing to offer the dying Lou Gehrig. The New York City Parole Board had hired him.

Weiss had Casey make the call to Little Rock to invite Dickey back. Dickey may have felt insulted that "this clown" was calling about a coaching job, when in fact he should rightly be the manager, but he accepted, and became a loyal, long-term, and much-admired member of the staff.

22

DIMAGGIO AND
MR. BERRA

SPRING TRAINING WAS TO open on March 1, 1949, in St. Petersburg; Casey and his coaches arrived about five days early. Some extra coaches were brought in—Bill Skiff, Buddy Hassett, Johnny Neun, and High Pockets Kelly. (Hassett, the Newark manager, had played for Casey in Brooklyn.)

Casey had trained in St. Pete when he played for the Boston Braves in 1924–25. Crescent Lake Field, now called Miller Huggins Field, was the site of the team's workouts; games would be played at Al Lang Field, which had opened in 1947. Both fields were needed, because the Yankees and the Cardinals shared the city, and before games began, both teams needed a place to work out at the same time.

On the first day, with photographers present, Casey gathered his team around the potbellied stove in the middle of the clubhouse and laid out his rules. He was in uniform for the first time, number 37 on the back of his three-quarter-sleeve jersey. The number had previously been worn by Bucky Harris. (Why 37? Edna said it represented the only year he was out of baseball, but, more likely, the jersey with number 37 was the right size and had the prerequisite sleeve length. Why the longer sleeves? It was what McCarthy had worn, but it would be replaced by the traditional short sleeves in 1951.)

"Stengel was a very good teacher," wrote Frank Crosetti in an unpublished memoir. "He knew baseball inside and out. He lived baseball all the 12 months of the year. He would teach players all the fine points of the game, things that never show up in the box scores."

Crosetti had that right. The man lived and breathed baseball, and put a lifetime of knowledge and insight into every game.

—

ON MARCH 1, CASEY would formally greet the team's young catcher, Lawrence Peter Berra. He was still more popularly known as Larry, rather than as Yogi.

Yogi was not a "Joe McCarthy Yankee." He was ready to be a "Casey Stengel Yankee," and the tutoring he would receive from Dickey would rapidly make him one of the game's elite players. This would be one of the monumental meetings in baseball history—two great baseball minds, two future American cultural icons, one noted for Stengelese, the other for Yogi-isms, were about to carve out their own history together.

"I wanted Berra to be the catcher because of his hitting," Casey later reflected. "The club didn't have that much punch in the infield or the outfield. . . . Berra had been awkward behind the plate against Brooklyn in the 1947 World Series and in 1948 they tried making him into an outfielder. But I found that he could go back and become a first string catcher with coaching by Bill Dickey. Later on I platooned Berra at other positions, but in his first seven years for me he caught practically all our games."

Platooning (which had been called the "revolving door technique" when he managed at Oakland) was part of the general plan of Casey to move players in and out of the lineup, and even into unaccustomed defensive positions, to maximize each day's offense and defense. He didn't quite invent the concept—he himself had been platooned by McGraw—and he needed an abundance of talent to make it work, but it would become his trademark as a manager.

Turning over daily catching to Yogi wasn't all that Casey did for him. By 1949, the writers were having their way with Yogi's looks and intelligence. They had, fun-loving though they may have intended it to be, presented the public with a bit of a laughingstock. His modest education (seventh grade) was often mentioned, and his looks were lambasted in cartoons and in jokes. Casey took to calling him "Mr. Berra," and always spoke of him with respect. From time to time, he would credit Yogi with some on-field decision that played a part in a victory. He never gave in to the sport of ridiculing him, even though the writers seemed to encourage it, and certainly did it among themselves.

"What Casey did, in terms of respecting Yogi, carried over for his entire career," said Dave Kaplan, director of programs at the Yogi Berra

Museum and Learning Center. "People still had fun with Yogi, but with it came great respect for his baseball knowledge and instincts."

Casey quickly put some unpopular rules in place.

The team would work out not once a day but twice, which they hadn't had to do since Huggins imposed it in 1922. This did not play well with the McCarthy men—including DiMaggio, Keller, Rizzuto, and Henrich—though Casey did give his regulars Sundays off. (It did also mean that the Yankees scheduled few road games in spring training that they couldn't get to in less than an hour, so they wouldn't miss their morning workout.)

"I like two-a-day practicing," Casey said, "and while I'm willin' to concede that some of the old Yankee clubs was winning under the old method, I like my way now and if my guys can't get in shape we turn 'em loose quick. They gotta be in shape on account games are longer and I notice where some them clubs seems to tire out in September, when the pennant race is getting hot."

"The Yankees had so many players, they were probably unique in this," says Ralph Branca, who was with Brooklyn then. "We were just once a day. Probably everyone else was too."

Casey also established a midnight curfew and 7:30 a.m. wakeup calls. This struck the veterans as condescending.

Then he banned attendance at the local dog track, Derby Lane, which had long been a popular form of relaxation for the team. There were publicity photos of Babe Ruth and Lou Gehrig in attendance at the track; Bucky Harris had gone with the players to the track; a young Yogi Berra once borrowed two dollars from the sportswriter Grantland Rice to place a bet there, and the two became friends.

But Casey didn't like having the players gamble, which was, of course, what the track was all about. After all, his first manager in Brooklyn had told him to stop playing dice games.

This was an early test of his relationship with DiMaggio. Stengel knew that Joe liked to go to the track in the evenings. The rule was for everyone, of course, but—given all his accomplishments, all he had meant to the Yankees, and his World War II service—to be told "no dog track" was a big line in the sand.

This was really a bigger story than the press made it out to be. DiMaggio had long before become royalty in American sports. There were no gossip-type tabloids to follow athletes in the late 1940s, and Joe lived a privileged life; moreover, the idea of his going to the dog track on a hot Florida evening would have seemed perfectly appropriate to most people. Casey, who did not frequent tracks or do much of anything aside from staying in the hotel and lobby-talking baseball with anyone, did not relate to this.

When DiMaggio expressed displeasure at the rule, Casey relented—a little. He said one night a week—Thursdays—players could go to the track.

DiMaggio still went more than once a week, an act of defiance the great star felt entitled to make. He was just doing as he pleased, feeling he had earned the right to do so. When told that DiMaggio had been sighted at the track, Casey chose to look the other way. "I have no first-hand information about this" was all he said. And as long as he himself wasn't at the track to see which players were there, it was all secondhand.

Some who watched this conflict develop considered it a victory for Joe, and were surprised that Casey would put his leadership on the line so early in his Yankee career. It was to the advantage of both of them that there were no paparazzi looking to cough up a scandal by publishing photos of Joe defying the rule. Today the *Daily News* and the *New York Post* would have posted photos on page one of Joe at the track, with the headline WHAT NOW, CASEY?

This was a real test for Casey, who had never led a team with such stars, or been in a position to feel challenged by a senior, star player. As it happened, the ban was quietly dropped, or at least not enforced. After 1949, it was never mentioned again. A quiet defeat for Stengel.

ON MARCH 12, CASEY managed his first Yankees spring-training game, a 10–3 win over the Cardinals at Lang Field, with Ralph Houk and Bobby Brown[*] each collecting four hits. A record crowd of 6,854 turned out.

"It looked at the beginning like I should take it easy and not do too much managing, because we had so many experienced men that didn't need any instruction," said Casey. "I think one of the first times I really started managing that ball team was when the Brooklyn club showed

---

[*] Brown, a medical student, had reported late for spring camp after his semester ended, and when he met Casey, the manager said, "We have something in common. We're both professional men. I studied dentistry; but then I found out there were no left-handed tools."

us up in some spring exhibition games. I got our men together and I said, 'There's one thing I can tell you you're weak on. There haven't been any base-running teams to test you.' So that gave us something to practice on all year, and things were pretty well ironed out by the World Series. . . ."

There came the day in spring training when the Red Sox came to town to play the Yankees. Joe McCarthy was now the Boston manager. Sitting in his dugout, he said to the Boston beat writers, "Should I go over to see Casey or should he come over to see me?" Told there was no real answer, McCarthy said, "Has he got any good stories? If he has, I'll go over and listen to them."

And he did, to be greeted cordially, of course, by his old players. The moment was not at all awkward.

Casey would now begin a bonding with "my writers," the daily scribes who would cover his every word. Covering his first Yankee training camp were some giants in the field—Grantland Rice, Dan Daniel, Red Smith, Tom Meany, John Drebinger, Arthur Daley, Joe Williams, Lou Effrat, Hy Goldberg, Milton Gross, Ben Epstein, Frank Graham, and Joe Trimble. He was most comfortable with Daniel and Drebinger, who were his age.

With "my writers," whoever happened to be on the scene on a given day, Casey could be forthright and disarming, perhaps even jabbing DiMaggio a bit, confident the writers wouldn't quote him. If a new writer arrived, there would be a waiting period before Casey accepted him, welcomed him in. This practice was largely encouraged by the veteran writers, who could make a rookie's arrival awkward, treating him as an ignoramus for asking a dumb question or not understanding protocols. Still, the informality of relations that had evolved under Harris was taken back a step when the door from the pressroom to the manager's office in St. Petersburg was boarded up, and the press had to go through the clubhouse to see the manager.

FOR EDNA, BORN INTO wealth, the doors were about to open to high style.

Just before the season opened, we came up to New York. Casey had been around New York all his life—first as a player, later as a National League manager—but this time, in the spring of 1949, he returned in style. Believe me, there is such a difference between managing a lowly Dodger club, and moving with the magnificent Yankees. The whole city looks different—the lights go on!

We took a suite at the New Yorker Hotel—a far cry from that $5 a day shoebox we'd shared 13 years before—and I started looking for a place to live.

Hazel Weiss went apartment hunting with me. Those first few years, I leaned heavily on the help and advice of Hazel and George Weiss. From them I learned the lay of the land and what was expected. It is not by accident that the Yankees are known as the "royalty" of baseball. Dignity and position have always been the Yankee way of doing things.

She would soon be seen as the First Lady of the Yankees, and would wear the crown well, with a dignified presence.

EVERYTHING ABOUT 1949 WAS a "first time" for Casey with the Yankees, and the importance of the season can barely be overstated. All eyes were on him, and on whether this longtime second-division clown really had the smarts to lead such a team. His ultimate success record with the Yankees took root in 1949 in what was probably his most challenging season.

Not only would he have to establish his leadership over veteran star players, and manage in a league that was wholly new to him, but he would have to manage a team that wound up enduring seventy-one player injuries along the way. On opening day alone, DiMaggio was out with a bad heel, Berra with a bad cold, Keller with a pulled side muscle, Bob Porterfield with a pulled arm muscle, Spec Shea with an ailing neck, Johnny Lindell with a sprained ankle, and Cuddles Marshall with a fever. That was seven right there for the new team doctor, Sidney Gaynor, to work with.

If Casey was at all hesitant about platooning, he had no choice. He was constantly bombarded by ailments large and small. Berra alone:

April 19—upper respiratory infection.
April 20—hit by pitch, sidelined.
April 22—collision with first baseman Dick Kryhoski.
April 27—hit on arm by a foul.

April 30—spiked on leg.

May 10—hit over eye by ball.

June 20—sore hand, stiff neck.

June 29—split little finger.

July 22—bruised side.

August 7—fractured thumb.

If Dickey really wanted to give Berra advice, it should have been to forget catching. But Yogi caught 109 games in 1949, thirty-eight more than in the previous season.

Appreciating the importance of his new position, Casey was a little less the jokester, and much more the serious evaluator of his injury-and-roster situation in dealing with the press. Those who had followed him for a long time could tell the difference. This was a job he had to take very seriously. Success was expected.

Charlie Keller was not on the opening-day roster. Just thirty-two, he had been sent to Newark at his full salary, $20,625, a cut of seven thousand from 1948. A torn muscle in his side, after he had missed much of the previous two seasons, had forced the move. But Keller had no complaints, at least publicly, and would return on June 16.

The season opened at home against Washington on April 19. Casey sat at his rolltop desk on a big swivel chair, his office to the left of the massive clubhouse as one entered from the field. He wrote in Stirnweiss (2B), Rizzuto (SS), Woodling (CF), Henrich (RF), Bauer (LF), Brown (3B), Kryhoski (1B), Niarhos (C), Lopat (P). Lopat rewarded him with a 3–2 victory on a walk-off home run by Henrich (though the term "walk-off" wasn't actually used in baseball at the time). It was the first of eight such walk-offs the team would enjoy in '49. If Casey failed to remind himself that this wasn't Brooklyn or Boston he was managing, winning his first four might have done it. This was going to be fun.

Casey sometimes called Henrich "Medwick" or "Handricks," and sometimes called DiMaggio "Vince" if he wasn't calling him "the Dago." The players laughed behind Casey's back, thinking he was occasionally off his game, but most came to realize he very much knew what he was doing.

Henrich was among the veterans who had a problem adjusting. "I'm afraid I'm a McCarthy man myself," he reflected some years later. "He ran a better show. He did it without ever sacrificing self-respect. Stengel started out as a clown. When he won, he became a genius."

Gene Woodling hated being platooned, especially after winning four batting championships in the minors. But, grudgingly, he came around. "Sure, Stengel and I had words . . . but Casey could take it. After all, I didn't like being platooned . . . but I'm glad [he] needled me. It made me play my best."

One day, Casey even overshifted, sending his shortstop Rizzuto to the right side of second base to defense Pat Mullin of Detroit, who had been hitting the Yankees well. The Indians manager Lou Boudreau had done this against Ted Williams, but it was still considered radical.

He occasionally had his traveling secretary, Frank Scott, hand out his own ten-dollar bills to the players on train rides, so they could have dinner "on the manager." He put the players on the honor system for rules and curfews and disdained using any detectives (as the Yankees had done in the past; Weiss would reinstate the use of detectives while Casey was managing).

Scott, who sometimes shared a suite with Casey on the road, was fired in October 1950, after a long running feud with George Weiss. Weiss had wanted Scott to spy on Bucky Harris in 1948, and Scott refused. The act of disloyalty finally came to roost after the 1950 World Series, despite pleas by Casey, by sportswriters, and even by Topping. Webb sided with Weiss; Scott was gone. He would go on to open an athlete agency with many Yankees, including Casey, as clients. No longer would players get wristwatches for off-field appearances. Scott turned it into a cash business for everyone, essentially the first time anyone had done so since Christy Walsh served as an agent to Babe Ruth.

THE YANKS WON THEIR first four and grabbed hold of first place, but a test came on Sunday, May 15, when they dropped a doubleheader in Philadelphia to Connie Mack's hapless Athletics, twice blowing leads. It was their fourth straight loss, and although they were still in first, and were 16-9, Casey felt it might be time for the first clubhouse "talk" of the young season.

This was the first year in which the Yankees games were televised, and the sportscasters Mel Allen and Curt Gowdy were in the clubhouse for the talk, standing quietly in the back of the small Shibe Park visitors' clubhouse. Some players were sobbing, including tough-guy Bauer and Coleman, who had made a crucial error. The team was stunned.

Gowdy later remembered the meeting:

At the end of the clubhouse the manager's door swung open and Casey walked in. He was wearing nothing but his shorts. He's a funny looking guy anyway, but this time he looked funnier than ever. He sauntered to the center of the room and then began talking. He said, "Listen you guys, we got thirty two or three hits today. Why those Dodgers and Braves teams that I had couldn't get 35 hits in a month. You, Coleman. Yeah you blew a game for us today. But let me tell you something. You're going to be a great second baseman. I've seen a lot of 'em come and go. I'm telling you, you're gonna be one of the best.

"You, Bauer. Yeah you looked bad at this plate, but you're gonna hit for me before the year is over. And you, Henrich, you're supposed to be my clutch hitter. Today you didn't hit in the clutch. But you're gonna hit for me. And I'm saying that you're gonna be one of the great clutch hitters. . . . Woodling, the writers tell me you're not a major league hitter. I say you are and I say you're gonna help us win this pennant. And I'm tellin' all you guys that despite what happened to us today, that we're gonna win this pennant. There's nothing gonna keep us from it."

After saying that the Yanks are going to win, he turned and walked to his room and shut the door. As soon as he left the players chirped. They began talking to one another. They showered and left. That night the team went on a western trip and won 13 or 14 games and went on to win the pennant, like Casey said they would. That speech in Philadelphia was the turning point of the season. And it's about the only speech of Stengel's which has never been published.

Said Coleman: "I played for Casey for eight years and he only said 'Nice goin' once. He wasn't the kind of man who applauded, patted people on the back, or even shook hands. He was never close to the players and exuded very little warmth. At first, especially during the months he never talked to me, I resented his gruffness and blamed all my own shortcomings on him. But I finally realized that big league players don't play for compliments. They play to win."

DiMaggio, heroically, came back on June 28, grabbing a flight to Boston and telling Casey he was ready to go. This would, at last, be his first game for Stengel, and of course it was his call when he was ready to play. Casey was delighted to finally scribble his name on a lineup card.

He homered that night in a 5–4 Yankee win, then homered twice more the next day, and once again in the series finale, for such a dramatic return that it became the talk of the nation.

So this was what managing a team with Joe DiMaggio felt like.

ON AUGUST 22, THE Yankees bought Johnny Mize from the Giants for forty thousand dollars. One of the great sluggers of National League history, Mize was thought to be near the end, but he might be valuable off the bench in the final weeks of the season. Before the purchase, Casey had called his pal Johnny Cooney, acting manager of the Braves, for a scouting report. Cooney advised getting Mize, and Casey shared that with Weiss.*

Mize was "an old thirty-six," slow afoot, somewhat of a defensive liability at first, and he had hit only eighteen home runs for the Giants so far that year, after hitting ninety-one in 1947–48.

With the Yankees, Casey would get him into thirteen games, in which he would contribute one home run among his six hits. But he got two pinch hits in the World Series and would go on to earn five series rings for the Yankees. He became the poster boy for smart late-season pickups by the already talent-rich Yankees.

ON SEPTEMBER 18, DIMAGGIO came down with pneumonia, and was still quite ill on Joe DiMaggio Day on October 1, when he said, "I'd like to thank the good Lord for making me a Yankee." Casey, standing on the field with all the celebrities and dignitaries (including Boston manager Joe McCarthy) could surely nod his approval of that.

The Yankees held on to first place until September 26, when they dropped a third straight to the Red Sox, falling a game behind Boston with five games remaining.

This was a very dramatic moment in the season. Stengel had done a remarkable job, but now it was Joe McCarthy's Red Sox who had moved

---

* The Yankees, in the Stengel years, were thought to be the first team to employ advance scouts to watch the upcoming competition.

in front. Some believed that the experienced, proven McCarthy, knowing what to do in the final days, would therefore have the edge over Stengel.

But when the Yankees got a 5–4 win on DiMaggio Day, before 69,551, they were tied for first with the Red Sox, with only the final game remaining. One team was going to go to the World Series, and the other one would go home.

A total of 68,055 turned out for the historic game, which found the Yankees taking a 5–0 lead, helped in part by a Henrich home run. But the Sox narrowed it to 5–3 in the ninth, when DiMaggio, playing despite illness, couldn't run down a long drive by Bobby Doerr. At that point, DiMaggio waved to Stengel to take him out, and Casey sent Woodling to center.

Raschi held on to stop Boston, and the Yankees won their sixteenth pennant. Casey, in his tenth season as a major-league manager, had his first pennant. This was what it was all about—this was why he left Oakland.

Topping, Webb, and Weiss joined Casey in the clubhouse celebration—the only times they would ever enter the clubhouse was for these pennant or World Series celebrations. The Yankees had drawn 2,283,676, to lead the league (they had been second to Cleveland the year before).

Although his starting lineup was constantly in flux, Raschi, Allie Reynolds, Lopat, and Tommy Byrne had started 128 of the team's 154 games, going 68-33. Joe Page made a spectacular comeback as a relief pitcher, appearing in 60 games, with 27 saves and 13 wins, after a very disappointing fall from grace in 1948.

"I didn't catch a fly ball, make a base hit or strike a guy out all season," said Casey. "So why should I take any credit?" But, of course, he loved it.

The World Series opened at Yankee Stadium on October 5. This was Casey's first World Series in uniform since his heroic 1923 star turn as a player, when he hit the first World Series home run in Yankee Stadium history while playing for the Giants. What a grand moment this was for him—and for Edna, who had met him around the time of that milestone, and was now in full embrace of the glamour of the Fall Classic. And, of course, Casey would be in Ebbets Field for Games Three, Four, and Five, where, it was recalled, he had played in the first game ever in that ballpark.

The Dodgers had also won their pennant on the final day of the season, and in Jackie Robinson (the league's MVP), Roy Campanella, and

Don Newcombe they had black players—something years away for the Yankees.

Casey being Casey, he seemed to know everyone who showed up for the series. There was Ty Cobb, who participated in first-ball ceremonies for Game One, a game won 1–0 by a Henrich walk-off home run, just like opening day of the regular season. This was the first 1–0 World Series game decided by a home run since Stengel, Charles D., had done it himself.

And who was coaching at first for Brooklyn but old Jake Pitler—a teammate of Casey's on the 1918 Pirates.

Game Two, the only Dodgers win, featured a play that would today surprise DiMaggio fans, who have come to think of him as a flawless and graceful center fielder who never made a mistake and never looked bad lunging unsuccessfully for a ball. In the fourth inning the Dodgers' Gene Hermanski singled to center, where DiMaggio awkwardly fell while moving to his left, allowing the ball to skip past him for a triple. This wasn't the play that cost the Yankees the game, and perhaps Joe was still feeling the effects of his late-season pneumonia.

Now the series shifted to Brooklyn. Before Game Three, living members of the 1916 Brooklyn Robins—National League champions—were introduced on the field by Casey himself. They weren't exactly elderly old men—they were in their fifties and sixties. His hands shaking a bit, his voice quivering, Casey was clearly filled with emotion as he called out Zack Wheat, Otto Miller, Jeff Pfeffer, Chief Meyers, Rube Marquard, George Cutshaw, Ivy Olson, Nap Rucker, and others. That night, after fine relief work by Page helped the Yankees to a 4–3 win, Branch Rickey hosted them all for a dinner at Brooklyn's St. George Hotel, and Casey was, of course, the man of the hour.

The Yankees won the fourth game 6–4, with Bobby Brown unloading a big bases-loaded triple (Brown hit .500 for the series). During the game, Casey came out of the dugout (which was against the rules), cupped his hands to his mouth, and shouted to Berra, "Throw to second, throw to second." Yogi's throw nailed Pee Wee Reese, who was trying to advance to second, and Casey took a reprimand from Commissioner Happy Chandler after the game.

There was, it seemed, an air of resignation hovering over Ebbets Field for Game Five, as the Yankees again won and captured the world championship for their first-year manager. When Joe Page struck out Gil

Hodges for the final out, Berra gave the ball to him, but Page gave it to Casey.

"Just as I told you," gloated Del Webb after the game. "I knew he would win, whether we got some more players for him or not. . . . I am not kicking Stanley [Bucky] Harris. He happens to be a friend of mine, too. But I knew Casey would work harder at the job."

Jerry Coleman was among the players who sought a one-to-one moment with Casey during the celebration. "Thanks for giving me a chance to play," he said. "I hope I never disappoint you."

"You're thanking me?" said Casey. "I gotta thank you. You made me a manager of the world champions. Nobody ever did that kind of a favor for me before."

The Yankees held a big victory party at the Biltmore Hotel, the site of the famous victory party of 1947 at which the drunken co-owner Larry MacPhail slugged and fired George Weiss; he sold his one-third share to Topping and Webb the next morning. (Weiss was "rehired.") But the Yankees did not hold "the Battle of the Biltmore" against the hotel, and celebrated into the morning at the Midtown Manhattan venue.

When Casey and Edna had taken their trip home, the city of Glendale sent the police to the train station in Pasadena to meet them and held a Casey Stengel Day parade, gave him the key to the city on the steps of City Hall, and escorted the couple in an open car on the two-block-long parade, accompanied by two bands and drum majorettes.

"Most of the credit for my being here today belongs to my wife," said Casey. "She persuaded me to live here 25 years ago when we got married—and then, she won quite a few games for us this summer!"

The next night, a banquet was held in Casey's honor at the posh Oakmont Country Club; the actor Pat O'Brien served as emcee, and Del Webb attended with his parents.

Edna weighed in with her own words in her memoir.

"No thrill in our entire lives will ever equal that first World Series win," wrote Edna, now herself a celebrity in the New York tabloids, and a classy complement to her rough-around-the-edges husband.

I was selfish about it; I wanted him to finish the job in the blaze of glory and clean-sweep the Series. He'd waited so long and so patiently for this, hoping that someday he'd have a team like this—and now he had it.

I waited patiently that winter for him to say something about, "Well, Edna, I guess that's it. I showed 'em I could do it."

Instead, he was talking about, "Now if Coleman comes through, and this fellow Whitey Ford is in good shape, we oughta win this thing easy next year."

So I bought a new suit for opening game, shipped a few more personal belongings to the Essex House, and prepared to sit it out.

Casey was named Manager of the Year by 101 out of 116 votes cast in the Associated Press election, and then "my writers" gave him the William J. Slocum Award for long and meritorious service to baseball.

To some, he was just starting out!

23

WHITEY AND BILLY

THERE WAS A MARKED change in Casey in 1950. The world championship of 1949 won him more credibility than he'd ever had in the game. He had gone from clown to genius "overnight," and suddenly he was baseball nobility.

If DiMaggio, Keller, Rizzuto, and Henrich preferred McCarthy, they still had to respect Casey's accomplishment of overcoming seventy-one injuries and winning.

Though even Casey had been cautious in 1949, reining in his supersize personality while he settled in, by 1950 he was his old, relaxed, self-confident self again, pouring on the Stengelese at will. Television was becoming a more daily presence in the lives of Americans, and Casey took naturally to interviews, which could be informative and confounding at the same time. The camera loved his face.

As a first order of business, the Yankees decided to hold an early spring camp for prospects. They had to tinker with major-league rules to pull this off, because it was quickly seen as a Yankee advantage, the Yankees being the team of "haves." The players who were invited received only a per diem for expenses, no pay, but this still gave the Yankees an edge: a spring camp before camps could legally open on March 1. It was conceived by Stengel and Weiss.

Branch Rickey, as general manager, had done something like this with the Cardinals in the 1930s.

To get around the rule, they called it an "instructional school," as if it were not part of spring training, and further flouted the rules by designating some of the players as "instructors," when in fact they had never even played a single major-league game.

Included among the forty-four Yankee farmhand invitees were Jackie

Jensen, Billy Martin, Gil McDougald, Tom Morgan, and Tom Sturdi-vant, all of whom would play big roles in future pennants; both Jensen and Martin were called "instructors," as were such veterans as Hank Bauer and Cliff Mapes.

The players who like most players in all organizations, held winter jobs (such as pumping gas, stocking shelves, or selling shoes), had to decide whether to keep earning that money or go to camp for no pay. Few declined.

The school, based on fundamental drills, lasted only a short time: complaints from other teams led to an early closure. Still, the concept of this school would be renewed in 1951 and go on for eight seasons before the Florida Winter Instructional League—with more teams participat-ing, and games actually played—kicked in.

As spring training started (Casey interceded in holdouts by Berra and Raschi to help get them signed), Edna was back home in Glendale, recov-ering from a surgical procedure. She placed a framed photo in the den, of Casey and Rizzuto, in their handsome tuxedos, receiving their respective awards from the New York chapter of the Baseball Writers' Association. (Rizzuto had been voted Player of the Year for 1949.) The irony of the photo, of course, was that thirteen years earlier Casey had pretty much kicked Rizzuto out of a Dodgers tryout session. The story took on a life of its own after Rizzuto became a star for him with the Yankees.

Whitey Ford was not among the forty-four players invited to the early camp, nor was he on the forty-man roster, but he was invited to spring training. And why not? He had put in three minor-league seasons, mov-ing from Class C to Class B to Class A, with forty-five wins against sev-enteen losses, and all the poise one might hope for from a slick kid who lived in Queens and went to high school in Manhattan. George Selkirk, who had been Babe Ruth's right-field successor on the Yankees, had managed Ford at Binghamton in 1949, raved about his maturity. The Yankees' trustworthy scout Paul Krichell, who had signed Lou Gehrig and Ford, was still touting him highly. He was going to open the season at Kansas City in 1950.

Casey described him as a "quiet, well-behaved, good living, earnest unspoiled kid from a quiet unspoiled lower financial bracket family, and that girl of Whitey's isn't going to hurt him either. I have met her."

He also called him "whiskey slick," which was his term for guys who could hold their liquor.

Jackie Jensen was a "golden boy," blond, handsome, strong—he was

Mickey Mantle without the switch-hitting and without the speed, but he had star quality. He had been an All-American football hero, played in the Rose Bowl, and married an Olympic diving champion. He was raw, with only one season in the minors after playing at the University of California, Berkeley, but at twenty-three he was considered nearly ready for the majors. Because he was a bonus player,* the Yankees had to keep him anyway, or risk losing him to another organization.

Then there was Billy Martin, who at twenty-one already had four minor-league seasons behind him, including two with Casey at Oakland, and an additional one at Oakland in 1949 under Dressen. Early on, he was thought of as "Casey's Boy," not only because he had played for him in the minors, but for having the kind of personality and drive that Casey loved in ballplayers. Martin was an infielder who played at such a high level of intensity that he could take command on a diamond no matter where he was playing. Like Casey, he could live hard—he drank, he smoked, he got into fights, he battled umpires, he developed animosities. Casey was better at holding his liquor; Billy let it get the better of him. But as a ballplayer—and that is really all Casey cared about—Billy was the real deal.

In Ford, Jensen, and Martin, Casey was going to have "Stengel Yankees" continue to emerge, and make it even more his team. They were not McCarthy Yankees or Bucky Harris holdovers. They were his.

Martin made the opening-day roster, and had a memorable debut in Fenway Park on April 18, getting two hits and driving in three runs in one inning, when he replaced Coleman at second late in the game. He got into only five other games before being sent back down in May, when rosters had to be trimmed to twenty-five players, but he returned in late June, made some sporadic starts, hit .250 for the season, and sat next to Casey on the bench, listening and learning.

Jensen made the team, debuting the same day as Martin, but he stuck around all season; he played in forty-five games, though he started in just twelve of them, and hit .171 with one home run. Though he wasn't quite ready, he, too, was learning from the experience of being in the majors. One thing he couldn't handle—and never would—was his anxiety over

---

* The bonus rule, in effect from 1947 to 1957, said that a player receiving a bonus of $4,000 or more had to stay on the major-league team and could not be farmed out. The rule was designed to keep the best teams from hoarding the best prospects and to discourage big bonuses.

airplane travel. The Yankees still traveled mostly by train, but if he knew a flight was coming up in a few weeks, he'd let it bother him all that time.

OPENING DAY AT YANKEE Stadium, April 21, 1950, included the raising of the 1949 world-championship flag (along with the American flag), at the pole in deep center field by the monuments. Casey did the honors, as he would many times over coming years, hoisting the huge flag with gusto as the crowd cheered. After a winter of banquets, awards, and accolades, this was the final cap to a wonderful first season with the Yankees. And now all that mattered was how things would go in 1950.

WHITEY FORD HAD GONE 6-3 in twelve starts at Kansas City. He was ready, perhaps overripe—he had even stopped at a pay phone one day to call the Yankee minor-league offices in the Bronx to say he was ready, and to ask when he was being called up.

It happened on June 29, with the Yankees in second place, four and a half games out of first. He made a relief appearance on July 1 and then made his first of 12 starts on July 6, beating the Philadelphia Athletics 5–4.

For Ford and Stengel, and of course for everyone else, playing the Athletics meant that Connie Mack was in the opposing dugout, in his final weeks as manager. Mr. Mack was eighty-seven. He had begun his pro career in 1884, and his managing career in 1894. He had been managing the Athletics since 1901. And this was going to be it. Maybe it wasn't that big a deal to Casey, who went back to 1910 as a player, but to Ford and Jensen, and to Martin and all the other young players on the team, it was an amazing thing to ponder.

While Martin and Jensen sat and watched, Yogi Berra was doing the heavy lifting. Little thought was given to days off back then, partly because there were more off-days in the schedule (doubleheaders being more common), and partly because you were being paid to play, so stop whining.

The Yankees played twenty-two doubleheaders in 1950, and Yogi caught both games in nineteen of them, including back-to-back doubleheaders on September 25 and 26. And nary a complaint. This would come to be the norm. He pretty much did the same thing every year, peaking in 1954, when they played eighteen and he caught them all. He caught eighteen out of twenty in 1951, and in one, the first game went fifteen innings. Didn't matter.

"Casey would walk by my locker before the doubleheaders and tell me, 'You're catching the second game,'" said Charlie Silvera, the backup catcher. "I was always sitting there to make sure no one took my uniform away. But if Yogi was feeling okay after one, he'd play the nightcap. I hardly ever got in."

Yogi's intelligence in calling ball games was unquestioned. "He calls his own games except for some occasional advice in a tight spot when a manager might give the pitch to any catcher," said Casey.

If all the work behind the plate took a toll on his hitting, no one could detect it. In 1950, Yogi batted .322 in 151 games with 28 home runs and 124 RBIs. Though Casey occasionally complained that Berra swung at a lot of bad pitches and could have walked more, he struck out only twelve times in 656 plate appearances.

"One day he struck out," recalled the batboy Joe Carrieri in a 2014 interview, "and when he came back to the dugout, Casey muttered something like 'I told you.' And Yogi, adopting an immigrant Italian accent, said, 'Eh, Casey, go take a good crap for yourself.'"

For all of this, Yogi finished only third in MVP voting (Billy Goodman, .354 with Boston, was second), with the ultimate honor going to his pal Rizzuto, who played 155 games and batted a career high of .324 with sterling defense, an on-base percentage of .418, nineteen sacrifice bunts, and two hundred hits, which was rarefied air back then. (No one on the Yankees accomplished it again for another twelve years.)

Casey's pitchers were reliable and often overpowering. Working through the season with virtually no bullpen to turn to (Page fell off to a 5.04 ERA in what would be his final season), Casey got 134 starts and fifty-six complete games from Raschi, Reynolds, Lopat, and Byrne, and then added Ford for a dozen more starts and seven more complete games.

In July, Casey got to serve as manager in an All-Star game for the first time, and promptly named six Yankees to Rizzuto and Berra, whom the fans had already picked; Casey added Raschi, Reynolds, Byrne, Coleman, Henrich, and DiMaggio. He also named his three coaches, Dickey, Turner, and Crosetti, to assist him, thus putting twelve Yankee uniforms along the baseline for introductions, plus the trainer, Gus Mauch. Call it executive privilege.

Ford won his first nine decisions as a starting pitcher, although he was rescued a few times on bad starts that might have turned into losses. But each start produced more maturity, more command, and more respect from the league's hitters. He did not lose a game until he relieved Lopat in the seventh inning on September 27 in Shibe Park. There, Sam Chapman hit a two run homer off him with one out in the ninth to send the Yankees—and Ford—to an 8–7 defeat. It was the next-to-last win of Connie Mack's career.

Whitey's regular season would thus end 9-1 with a 2.81 ERA.

"I knew Whitey could pitch," boasted Casey. "I told you that as far back as March, but I did not look for the amazing poise and the veteran's know how which he showed me right from the start in July. It's the thrill of a lifetime in a manager's career."

A controversial point in the season came on July 3, when Casey decided to try DiMaggio at first base. Perhaps this was his way of reminding Joe who was the boss, maybe motivated by some small unreported incident in the days leading up to this. Stengel knew the move was not going to please "the Dago," who never wanted to be in a situation where he might look bad. In fact, Casey didn't even tell DiMaggio about it. They spoke only on occasion—theirs was an uneasy relationship. Casey told Weiss; Weiss told Topping; Topping told DiMaggio. The game got a lot of publicity, and Joe handled thirteen chances successfully. Two were unassisted groundouts to first; the other eleven were routine throws to first. No errors, no embarrassment.

"The time for me to learn to play first base is in spring training, not when we're trying to win a pennant," Joe said after the game.

He never played there again.

As for the season itself, the Yankees abandoned first place in mid-June and hovered in second or third for most of the summer without reclaiming first—to stay—until September 16, when Ford beat Detroit 8–1. The actual pennant clinching came on an off-day, September 29, with two games left. The team gathered in the Kenmore Hotel in Boston as Mel Allen read reports from a ticker and the players found the critical Indians–Tigers game on the radio. Red Rolfe's Tigers lost 12–2, and the Yankees won the pennant. With the team dressed in suits and ties, the PR director, Red Patterson, summoned news photographers to capture their celebration at the hotel, as they tossed Casey up and down into the air.

"Hey, be careful," he said, laughing, "you know I broke my leg in this town!"

THE PHILADELPHIA PHILLIES "WHIZ KIDS" won the National League pennant in 1950, edging Brooklyn on the last day. The Phils had not won a pennant since 1915, five years before Casey played for them. This would in fact be their only pennant between 1915 and 1980.

The Phillies had long been a sad-sack team. Just seven years earlier, the club had been sold for eighty thousand dollars to a New York businessman, William Cox. Cox was gone in just eight months, charged with betting on baseball games, and the team was then owned by Bob Carpenter, Jr., whose mother was a member of the DuPont Chemical family. (His father, Bob Sr., had died the year before.)

Beyond Robin Roberts and Curt Simmons, who won thirty-seven games between them, the Phillies' best pitcher in 1950 was the reliever Jim Konstanty, who was 16-7 with twenty-two saves in a record seventy-four appearances. The manager, Eddie Sawyer, named him as starting pitcher in Game One at Shibe Park, but Raschi beat him 1–0 on a sacrifice fly by Coleman in the fourth inning.

Reynolds won Game Two in ten innings on a DiMaggio homer in the top of the tenth, and Lopat won Game Three, at Yankee Stadium, 3–2, on a walk-off single by Coleman that scored Woodling.

Casey turned Game Four over to his rookie, Whitey Ford. He hadn't intended this to be the deciding game, but now it was, and a rather pressure-less one at that. It was pretty clear that the Yankees were going to repeat as series champs.

Ford, wearing his rookie number 19, put eight zeros on the scoreboard, and the Yankees led 5–0. Out to the mound he went for the ninth. He gave up a single to Willie Jones and hit Del Ennis with a pitch. Dick Sisler grounded into a force play to put runners at first and third with one out. Ford struck out Granny Hamner for the second out, and the catcher, Andy Seminick, came up.

Seminick lifted one to deep left that got the better of Woodling, left field being a particularly difficult sun field in October. Two runs scored.

Mike Goliat singled, and suddenly the tying run was at bat, in the person of Stan Lopata, pinch-hitting for Roberts.

Casey briefly talked to Jim Turner on the bench and headed for the mound, his hands characteristically tucked into his back pockets. He signaled for Reynolds, who had relieved six times during the season.

The fans cheered Ford as he departed, and then booed Casey as he followed Whitey off the mound. They wanted Whitey to get the complete-game win.

Lopata fanned on three pitches.

Stengel fulfilled his two-year contract with his second consecutive world championship. And he got bonus money, estimated to be ten thousand dollars, each year he won, on top of his World Series shares.

Earliest known photo of Charles Dillon Stengel. He was born in 1890, four and a half years before Babe Ruth. *(National Baseball Hall of Fame Library, Cooperstown, N.Y.)*

The Central High Eagles baseball team, with "Dutch" Stengel, top left. As a senior, he pitched a fifteen-inning complete game to take the Eagles to the Missouri State Championship.

Stengel played for a traveling amateur team, the Kansas City Red Sox, as his high school days were coming to a close. The initials on his jersey—"K.C."—would lead to his eventual nickname, "Casey." *(National Baseball Hall of Fame Library, Cooperstown, N.Y.)*

After his first pro season in 1910, Stengel enrolled in Western Dental College, a career detour that did not pan out due to the difficulty in getting left-handed dental equipment.

Casey rejoiced at being traded to the New York Giants in 1921, where he got to play for—and learn from—John McGraw. *(National Baseball Hall of Fame Library, Cooperstown, N.Y.)*

NEWS OF SPORTS

LOSE THE GAME; LOSE THEIR JOBS

Decatur Pitchers Go Comet Chasing.

LUNATICS WIN FIRST

Making Commies the Cellar Champs.

Two Commodore pitchers lost their jobs as a result of one awful inning in the game against Kankakee at the local league park Friday afternoon. The unfortunate ones are Twirlers Lacey and Dashner. The Lunatics found them for nine safe hits in the sixth round, winning the game, 7 to 6.

ROUGH ON ALL.

It took all the courage and pepper out of the rest of the team to see the Kays race around the sacks like mad in that lamentable sixth. And it took all the starch out of the small crowd of fans to see their pets used so roughly by the bugs from up north. But it was hardest of all on Doc Childs, who was forced to sit with folded arms and watch the slaughter.

STARTED WITH RUSH.

Decatur made a brilliant start, shoving across four runs off McTighe in the first inning. In No. 2, Twirler Williams was sent to the mound by Manager Collins. He was clouted freely also, and with the score 5 to 0 up until the

League Standing.

NORTHERN ASSOCIATION.

	Won.	Lost.	Pct.
Muscatine	7	2	700
Elgin	7	2	778
Joliet	6	3	667
Jacksonville	6	4	600
Kankakee	5	5	500
Clinton	5	6	353
Decatur	3	7	300
Freeport	2	8	200

NATIONAL.	W.	L.	Pct.	AMERICAN.	W.	L.	Pct.
Pittsburg	16	8	667	Philadelp'a	19	5	792
Chicago	15	11	577	New York	17	8	680
New York	16	13	552	Detroit	16	12	571
Cincinnati	13	11	542	Boston	15	12	556
Philadelp'a	12	12	500	Cleveland	15	15	500
St. Louis	14	14	500	Washington	11	17	393
Boston	9	17	346	Chicago	8	16	333
Brooklyn	9	19	321	St. Louis	4	20	167

KANKAKEE—	AB.	R.	H.	PO.	A.	E.
Gilligan, rf.	5	1	1	0	0	0
Locke, 3b.	3	1	1	0	2	1
Uhl, 1b.	4	0	1	14	0	0
Stengel, cf.	4	1	3	2	1	0
Collins, ss.	5	1	2	1	4	0
Ruhland, 2b.	4	1	1	2	3	0
Ash, lf.	5	0	3	1	0	1
Boyle, c.	5	1	1	6	1	0
McTighe, p.	0	0	0	0	1	0
Williams, p.	3	1	1	0	2	0
Totals	38	7	14	27	14	2

DECATUR—	AB.	R.	H.	PO.	A.	E.
McGrew, 2b.	5	2	2	2	3	0
Jenkins, rf.	5	1	0	1	0	0
Lewis, 1b.	4	0	3	10	0	1
Lane, 3b.	4	1	1	3	1	0
Redding, lf.	4	0	0	4	1	0
Hartley, c.	4	2	1	3	2	0
Beck, ss.	3	0	1	1	3	0
Schissel, cf.	4	0	1	2	0	0
Lacey, p.	2	0	0	0	2	0
Dashner, p.	1	0	1	1	1	0
Cowell, p.	0	0	0	0	1	0
*Houser	1	0	0	0	0	0
Totals	37	6	10	27	14	1

Score by innings:
Kankakee ....0 0 0 0 0 7 0 0 0—7
Decatur ....4 1 0 0 0 1 0 0 0—6

Hits by innings:
Kankakee ....1 1 0 1 1 0 1 0 0—14
Decatur ....4 2 0 0 1 2 1 0 0—10

Summary:
Bases stolen—Lane.
Two base hits—Locke, Uhl, Beck.
Sacrifice hits—Beck.
Bases on balls—Off Lacey, 1; off Dashner, 3.
Hit by pitched ball—Locke by Dashner.
Struck out—By Williams, 5; by Lacey, 2; by Cowell, 1.
Time of game—2:10.
Umpire—LaRoque.

The Kankakee Kays were called the Lunatics in the local press, their park being located next to an asylum. So, yes, Stengel began his pro career as a Lunatic. (Decatur [IL] *Daily Review*)

On May 7, 1923, police had to come onto the field at the Polo Grounds to escort Casey off. He had thrown his bat at Philadelphia pitcher Lefty Weinert after being hit by a pitch. *(National Baseball Hall of Fame Library, Cooperstown, N.Y.)*

October 10, 1923: Casey sliding with an inside-the-park home run—the first World Series home run ever hit in newly opened Yankee Stadium. Hughie Jennings is the third-base coach who followed him home; Bill Evans is the umpire; Wally Schang is the catcher. Casey thought he lost a shoe running the bases. *(New York Times)*

Casey's time in Pittsburgh produced this 1919 artist's sketch for an early trading card, part of the so-called W514 set, which was sold in strips.

CASEY STENGEL
RIGHT FIELD
PITTSBURGH "PIRATES" N. L.

After the 1924 season, Casey was invited on a European tour, donning his New York Giants uniform despite being property of the Boston Braves. Here he meets King George V of England as the players lined up after a game.

A contemporary photo of the complicated crossing at Kenmore Square in Boston, where Casey was struck by a car late at night, just before opening day in 1943. He spent fifty-three days in the hospital, and the accident left him with a permanent limp. (*Marty Appel*)

Casey's days as manager of the Boston Bees, 1938–43, were not successful. They ran to nine, his consecutive second-division finishes, which began with Brooklyn, 1934–36. (*National Baseball Hall of Fame Library, Cooperstown, N.Y.*)

A much happier time for Casey as manager came with the Oakland Oaks of the Pacific Coast League. And a championship in 1948 propelled him to the New York Yankees manager job. (*National Baseball Hall of Fame Library, Cooperstown, N.Y.*)

Casey was a commanding figure in the Yankees dugout, and his Yankee success was historically unrivaled. Still clownish when he chose to be, he was generally all business during the games. *(National Baseball Hall of Fame Library, Cooperstown, N.Y.)*

A 1949 Yankee Stadium photo of Casey, the rookie manager of the Yankees. He wore a long-sleeve #37 jersey, inherited from his predecessor, Bucky Harris. *(National Baseball Hall of Fame Library, Cooperstown, N.Y.)*

Casey had Billy Martin at Oakland, and then with the Yankees. The 1957 trade of Billy to Kansas City broke the infielder's heart, but not Casey's. "[Billy] took it too personally. It was the business he was in. Trades happen." *(National Baseball Hall of Fame Library, Cooperstown, N.Y.)*

Hired by George Weiss to manage the expansion New York Mets in their first season, Casey got to return to the Polo Grounds, where he had played for the Giants forty years earlier. *(Lew Lipset/Fantography.com)*

Casey and his beloved Edna on the field at Shea Stadium, where they were presented with original Polo Grounds seats. That was where Edna was seated the day she and Casey first met in 1923. *(Courtesy New York Mets)*

Casey and Yogi Berra were reunited on the Mets in 1965, after twelve years together on the Yankees. Stengelese and Yogisms had by then become part of the nation's language. *(National Baseball Hall of Fame Library, Cooperstown, N.Y.)*

Casey is escorted onto the field at a Mets Old-Timers' Day by club owner Joan Payson. The two of them died five days apart in 1975. *(George Kalinsky)*

Casey was forced to retire as Mets manager in 1965 following a broken hip. In a press-only ceremony at Shea Stadium, Casey's longtime partner George Weiss presented him with his now-retired #37. *(Courtesy New York Mets)*

Casey went into the Baseball Hall of Fame with Ted Williams in 1966. The five-year waiting period was waived for Casey. *(National Baseball Hall of Fame Library, Cooperstown, N.Y.)*

This casting of the sculpture of Casey Stengel by Rhoda Sherbell, originally completed in 1965, stands in the National Portrait Gallery of the Smithsonian Institution. *(Rhoda Sherbell, National Portrait Gallery, Smithsonian Institution)*

During a "team photo" at the Yankees' 1973 Old-Timers' Day, Joe DiMaggio (left) and Mickey Mantle reach across Casey and his successor, Ralph Houk, to shake hands. Long-time pitching coach Jim Turner is behind Casey; Phil Rizzuto is to Mantle's left. *(Irv Welzer)*

Yankees president Michael Burke welcomes Casey to his first Old-Timers' Day return in 1970, ten years after the previous ownership had fired him. On the right, Whitey Ford and Yogi Berra prepare to present Casey with his retired #37 uniform. The author is on the left. *(Louis Requena)*

Casey reenacts his "bird flying out of his hat" moment (originally done at Ebbets Field in 1918) during an Old-Timers' Day appearance at Dodgers Stadium. It was one of his final public appearances. *(Los Angeles Dodgers)*

Casey and Edna Stengel's "splendid" home on Grand-view Avenue in Glendale, California, where they resided from 1924 to 1975.

Casey's den in the Grand-view Avenue home was filled with memories of sixty-five years in baseball—even more if you count the school bell from Central High School. *(Janet Allen, estate of Maury Allen)*

Bobby Case with Casey on his and Edna's Polo Grounds seats, poolside, at the Grandview Avenue home, late in Casey's life. Bobby was hired as a general assistant by Casey and "did what needed to be done" for the last ten years of Casey's life. *(Bob Case)*

The Stengel gravesite and adjacent wall plaque at Forest Lawn Memorial Park in Glendale, California. *(Courtesy of Dr. Fred Worth)*

24

THE MICK

O N October 10, three days after the World Series ended, Casey walked over to the Yankee offices at 745 Fifth Avenue— the Squibb Building—took the elevator to the twenty-ninth floor, and signed a new two-year contract for what was reported to be between sixty-five and eighty thousand dollars a year, plus bonuses for "doing a good job," not necessarily for winning the World Series. Again, he would be paid over twelve months, not six, with responsibility for running the instructional camp included.

Red Patterson summoned the press to watch as Casey sat at George Weiss's desk and signed the contract with his right hand. (If he'd been able to operate dental equipment that way, would he have been there that day?) He was to be the highest-paid manager in the game and, probably, all time. It's possible, though unlikely, that Lou Boudreau of Cleveland made more, but that was as a player/manager.

There had been whispers of Casey's considering retirement, somewhat fueled by Casey himself, and probably encouraged by Edna. But this announcement put that to rest.

Only a couple of weeks later, Whitey Ford was drafted into the army for twenty-one months. Just like that, he was out of the picture for the next two seasons.

"Anytime you lose a man like that it's going to hurt your ball club," said Casey from his Glendale home. Suddenly speaking of Ford in the past tense, he continued: "Whitey had uncanny control for his age, showed splendid nerve on the mound and good judgment. He was a very good player from the time he came up last year."

The Yankees trained in Phoenix, Arizona, in 1951. It was Del Webb's hometown, and he made arrangements with the New York Giants' owner, Horace Stoneham, to swap sites for one year, so that the Giants—and their prized rookie, Willie Mays—would go to St. Petersburg. The Yankees made the Adams Hotel their headquarters, but the rookies lived at the Continental Motel.

One attractive result of the swap was that the Yankees would play twelve exhibition games in southern California, including one against the White Sox on March 20 at Verdugo Park Municipal Baseball Field in Glendale. The park was built in 1949, and would be renamed Stengel Field in 1952 in honor of its favorite local citizen. (It had a long run; it was condemned in 2011 and torn down in 2015, but there is an ongoing effort to rebuild it.) The Yankees lost to Chicago 5–0, but a banquet at the Verdugo Club (founded in part by Edna's brother John M. "Jack" Lawson, after the game was attended by writers and dignitaries from New York, Chicago, and Los Angeles. This was a very high-profile event for the small city of Glendale.

The Yankees' early camp opened on February 15. Twenty nonroster players were invited, including Mickey Mantle, who was on the Binghamton roster, and who would be moved to the Kansas City roster during camp. Others included the catcher Clint Courtney, the pitcher Lew Burdette, and the third baseman Bill Skowron (who would be shifted to first). Casey would run the school, assisted by Neun, Dickey, Turner, Crosetti, and Henrich, who had just retired as a player. Henrich would take charge of Mantle, and of his conversion from a Class C shortstop to a major-league outfielder. In his unpublished memoir, Crosetti wrote:

> Casey brought out and taught these kids an "Offensive Routine." I had been in the game for 23 years and I had never heard of anything like this, and never saw anyone teach anything like this before. He no doubt learned this from McGraw.
>
> I believe that Stengel would have been a success at anything that he wanted to do. He was very talented. I believe also that he would have made a good comedian, as he was a natural. In fact, he was even funny to look at with his big floppy ears. The expressions that he would go through were unbelievable.

The parent roster would include rookies Gil McDougald, an infielder, and Tom "Plowboy" Morgan, a pitcher. McDougald did so well in camp that he beat Billy Johnson out of a job at third base. Johnson was soon sold to the St. Louis Cardinals.

Johnson was not a fan of Stengel. "He always wanted to make himself look good. By shifting a guy in there one day and out the next, he thought he was making himself look good in the newspapers and in the front office." This was a rough comment, open to the interpretation that all the players hated the way Casey used them, keeping them unsure of what their role was. But Casey responded with a great deal of class and dignity, two characteristics some may have felt he had been lacking in the past: "I thank him for all the hard work he did for me," he said to his writers about Johnson, from his perch on the Yankees bench. "He was a true Yankee and always played like one, hustlin' every minute and never givin' anything less than his best. He's one guy I never had to worry about. I always knew he'd be in bed at the right time and ready for work the next day. But he told me he needed to play every day in order to be a top-grade performer. And I just couldn't give it to him. Now he'll have it and I hope he's a success. I truly hated to see him go."

MOLDING MANTLE AS AN outfielder was a wonderful pet project for Stengel, a former right fielder himself. "The first thing I had to teach was to run in the outfield, looking back over his shoulder, which DiMaggio was so great at, and not run looking down at the ground. 'They have no plowed fields up here, boy,' I tell him, 'and you don't have to run and watch out for furrows at the same time because this is the big leagues and the fields are all level and they have groundskeepers and everything.'"

But it wasn't a perfect transition. In an exhibition game against the Indians on March 11, Mantle had trouble with his sunglasses, and a fly ball hit by Ray Boone hit him over his left eye. Fortunately, he sustained no injury of significance.

Casey knew sunglasses could be dangerous and awkward, since he had been among the first to wear sunglasses in the outfield himself, going back to his Brooklyn days.

If there was a moment when it seemed Mantle needed to be considered for the opening-day roster, it came on March 26, 1951, during the Yankees' spring-training trip through southern California. As a favor to Casey's old Dodger player Rod Dedeaux, now the baseball coach at USC, the Yankees were to play the Trojans at the university's Bovard Field.

Mantle connected for two home runs that day—one from each side of the plate. No measurements were taken, but each was said to have traveled about five hundred feet. (James Dawson, writing in *The New*

York Times, said nothing about their distance, which makes one skeptical. However, distances were not routinely reported then.)

There were still three weeks to go before opening day, but attention was now clearly focused on this muscled-up teen from Oklahoma who might one day—was it possible?—be the successor to DiMaggio. Comparisons were made with Mel Ott, who broke in with the Giants at seventeen under John McGraw. Ott went on to hit 511 home runs, a National League record, and, remarkably, led his team in home runs in eighteen consecutive seasons. No one else has ever come close to that.

But Mantle offered more. In the first place, he was a switch-hitter. Today there are many switch-hitters in the game, and it could be said that Mantle influenced their fathers to teach them switch-hitting. But in the early 1950s, switch-hitting was really quite rare. The only other switch-hitters in the majors at that point were Dave Philley (the only American Leaguer), Red Schoendienst, Pete Reiser, and Sam Jethroe. Mantle, if he made the grade, would be the first significant switch-hitter on the Yankees since the shortstop Mark Koenig, from the Murderers' Row era of the 1920s. Mantle also had tremendous speed, which made his bunting—especially from the left side—a big weapon. Rizzuto, the best bunter in the game, worked with him at that skill.

ON APRIL 14, WHITEY Ford was set to marry his sweetheart, Joan Foran, right after the Yankees played a pre-season exhibition game at Ebbets Field. He was on a weekend leave from the army. They had a small ceremony planned in Queens. Probably just as an announcement to let the front office know, Whitey had sent an invitation to Red Patterson, the team's public-relations director. Maybe he thought he'd get a nice gift basket out of it; no attendance was expected.

But Red told Casey about it, and Casey had Bill McCorry (the new traveling secretary) order a bus and take the whole team to Donohue's Bar in Astoria, Queens, for the evening reception. Whitey could not believe it when the team entered. Mantle, who didn't know Ford, shyly stayed in the bus until the Fords came out to greet him. That was the first time Mantle and Ford met—on a bus parked outside of Donohue's.

It was, to quote from *Casablanca,* "the beginning of a beautiful friendship."

Mantle made the team without going to Triple-A. On opening day, his name was announced by the new public-address announcer, Bob

Sheppard. It was a perfect-sounding name for someone with a perfectly sculptured body. And read by a PA announcer with perfect diction, to boot.

"We were in the lobby of the Concourse Plaza Hotel waiting for our husbands to come downstairs for the Welcome Home Luncheon," recalled Yogi's wife, Carmen. "We had been hearing about this very handsome boy named Mickey Mantle, which sounded like a made-up name. Was it a nickname for Michael Mantle, or something like that?

"Suddenly, the elevator door opened and out he stepped."

"Oh my God," she thought. "Look at this boy!"

AT THE WASHINGTON SENATORS' home opener Vice President Alben Barkley did the first-pitch honors, and a photograph showed Casey, Bucky Harris (now the Senators' manager), and the "Old Fox," Clark Griffith, owner of the Senators, alongside the vice president. That made three Yankee managers in the picture, Griffith having managed the original team, the New York Highlanders. But the photo would be bested on Old-Timers' Day that summer, when the same three were grouped with Joe McCarthy, Bob Shawkey, and Roger Peckinpaugh—six Yankee managers in one shot. Somehow, Red Patterson missed getting Dickey into the photo, too. Or perhaps Dickey refused, given his unpleasant experience as manager.

Future managers Yogi Berra, Ralph Houk, and Billy Martin were also "in the house."

THERE WAS MUCH SPECULATION on the future of DiMaggio, and whether 1951 would be his final season. He seemed to have no qualms about saying it was, as early as spring training, but, still, people felt his mind could change.

Whenever he was discussed (more often in magazine pieces than in the daily press), so was his strained relationship with Stengel. The only difference between 1949 and 1951 was that now Casey had established strong credentials on his own, and was more of a significant figure in the discussion.

On July 7 in Fenway Park, with DiMaggio in center in the second inning, Casey saw something in Joe's movement that suggested leg or heel pain. After Joe ran to center in the third, Casey sent Jensen out to replace him. DiMaggio stood still for a few moments before he jogged off. He didn't show Casey up, he didn't shake his head or make any gesture, but his teammates knew "Oh boy, you don't embarrass Joe DiMaggio." Joe was, of course, seething, and told the press afterward, "You'd better talk to Stengel about that." He called him Stengel, not "Casey," not "the manager."

Casey explained to the press that Joe had a sore leg and the rest would help him.

Joe did have a sore leg muscle, and he and Casey had a controlled conversation at his locker. It did not deal with the drama on the field, just with the condition of his leg. "I don't want to take a chance on hurting it more, so I got out," he finally said, standing at his locker. The injury was confirmed by Gus Mauch.

"He'll go to the All-Star Game, and maybe I can use him as a pinch-hitter," said Stengel in his office, and then turned attention to how hard Joe slid into second base.

Joe DiMaggio was famously thin-skinned and easily insulted, but Casey lacked the proper skills—or didn't care if he hurt Joe's feelings. "Insensitive" would be the best way to describe his current relationship with Joe.

But, for all Casey's such actions, he was still beloved by the press, who had their own moments of insensitivity with DiMaggio. "He kids his players, he mocks them on the bench, and [the writers] think he's a funny man, a fine ribber," noted the *Cleveland Press* writer Franklin Lewis.

Casey was effective at charming umpires, too. He didn't get tossed from a game (as a Yankee) until April 7, 1951, during an exhibition, and that was by a National League umpire, Augie Donatelli. (He wasn't ejected from a regular season game until July 6, 1952.) Of course, many who rooted hard against the Yankees' success felt it was all a big plot to keep awarding championships to the Yankees, since that was thought to be good for baseball.

A moment that particularly played into the hands of the anti-Yankee crowd came on July 27. The Yankees led this home game 3–1 after eight, but the White Sox scored three in the top of the ninth to take a 4–3 lead. Rain clouds were approaching, and Casey sent McDougald to the mound to stall for time. It was so blatant that McDougald was ejected. The rains came in torrents, and after a ninety-minute delay—it was now twelve-thirty in the morning—the umpires called the game, and the score reverted to the last full inning, to make it a 3–1 Yankee victory. Chicago's three in the ninth didn't count.

"It wasn't impossible to play," stormed the Sox manager, Paul Richards. "They told us we could stay until dawn, that there was no time limit. Why such a hurry? If they want a time limit let the league put one on. Somebody should have the authority to order the game played from the point it was stopped."

It was moments like this—the win broke a first-place tie and put the Yankees up by a game over Boston and Cleveland—that could really rile fans. Feuding with the White Sox seemed to take on a life of its own. There was never a rivalry between New York and Chicago as storied as the one with Boston, but the White Sox always seemed to have it in for Casey. When Hank Greenberg and Bill Veeck took over the Chicago club, it grew even stronger.

One day in Chicago in 1951, Casey criticized Chicago fans, and indirectly the management, for allowing firecrackers and paper debris to be thrown on the field. The general manager, Frank Lane, another long-running Casey critic, said, "I believe Stengel has enough of a job just managing the Yankees without trying to tell us how to run our ballpark."

Richards called Casey a clown—an insult that was tossed out less and less with each pennant—and other disparaging things. However, this enmity didn't prevent him from later becoming partners with Stengel on an oil deal.

CASEY'S SCHEDULE HAD BY now fallen into a predictable pattern.

The calendar year would begin with the sportswriter dinners in Los Angeles, New York, and Boston, with an occasional smaller one thrown in, such as the annual "Dapper Dan" awards dinner in Pittsburgh. Then would come the instructional camp followed by spring training. The team would barnstorm north, make it to the Bronx, have the Welcome Home Luncheon (or Dinner), and then raise the pennant on opening day. The season would roll on until the All-Star Game, which he usually managed, and then the summer months would give way to the World Series. Then came the World Series party. There would be a visit to the team offices to sign a new contract every other October, the Winter Meetings, and the holiday break. And then it was time to crank it all up again. Always, it seemed, the familiar face of Charles Dillon Stengel was a presence.

One thing not in the schedule was a health interruption.

In 1951, a kidney stone put Casey in the hospital for several days. He recovered without surgery, but a second flare-up landed him back in bed at the Essex House. Oddly, a car trip that the Stengels and the Weisses took to upstate New York somehow cured his kidney-stone issue for good. Or maybe it was a coincidence. Casey felt great after the trip and had no further episodes.

Edna thought her husband's energy was remarkable. Yes, she was always trying to get him to retire, but she had to admit, his stamina was awesome. "Casey is a physical marvel," she said. "He'd come home after a hard game, eat a big meal, entertain a gang of people, go to bed, and be snoring in ten minutes."

The kidney stone did have one other result: for some time, he gave up drinking, although eventually he resumed.

MEANWHILE, THE MANTLE EXPERIMENT (jumping him up to the majors so quickly) was hitting some bumps. He seemed overmatched at times. There were those traces of power and moments of great speed, but after a 1-for-5 game with three strikeouts on July 13, he was hitting just .260. His timing was off—he had hit only one home run in his last fourteen games and had seven for the season thus far. This was a pennant race, and Stengel needed more reliable bats in the outfield.

In his autobiography, *The Mick,* Mantle wrote that Casey called him into his office to tell him he was being sent down to Kansas City for additional seasoning.

"He had tears in his eyes," Mantle wrote. "He says, 'This is going to hurt me more than you, but—'

"No, skip. It was my own fault."

If Casey did have tears, it would have been an uncommon moment. His history with teenage players in the majors was limited, and though he could be an emotional man, he also saw baseball as a profession in which things like this happen. A lot of players get sent down, and for many it is often seen as the last call.

"He's just a green pea out there," Casey told reporters. "But he'll be back soon, and you'll see something.

"I am not disposed to quit on the boy. I just want to make his task easier. I was an outfielder myself, and I know what he is up against."

There was talk of abandoning his switch-hitting, but Mantle continued to hit from both sides at Kansas City. In the forty games he played for George Selkirk with the Blues, he batted .361, with eleven homers and fifty RBIs.

He returned August 24, and though he only raised his average to .267 and hit six more homers, people agreed he'd had a good rookie season, given that he was still nineteen and playing under such a spotlight, even if it wasn't brilliant. McDougald would win the Rookie of the Year Award.

Then there was the Jackie Jensen saga. The prized All-American boy was seeing only limited action—fifty-six games in 1951—and he, too, would be sent to Kansas City; the following May, he would be traded to Washington. "I was fed up," he said after the season. "I felt so badly about the treatment, that although I was in New York at the end of the season, I didn't feel like sticking around to even watch the club play in the World Series." (He was not selected for the World Series roster.)

As for Stengel, Jensen later looked back with kindness. "Casey is a wonderful, sweet old guy. I think he is the smartest manager in baseball. I know he taught me more in two years than anybody before or since."

By 1960, after Jensen had won an MVP award and blossomed into a star at Boston, Casey was calling the trade of Jensen "my worst mistake as Yankees manager." Casey even named him to the 1952 All-Star team, just weeks after trading him away.

THE YANKEES HAD PICKED up Mize in 1949 and Johnny Hopp in 1950; their mid-season surprise in 1951 turned out to be Johnny Sain, acquired in a trade for the farmhand Lew Burdette on August 29. Sain, of course, had pitched for Stengel in Boston in 1942, so this would be a reunion after nearly a decade. With the Braves, he and Warren Spahn had become pitching stars ("Spahn and Sain and pray for rain"). It was Stengel who made him a pitcher in Boston, when there was some question whether he was a pitcher or an outfielder.

Now he would earn three World Series rings under Casey in New York.

Sain could immediately see Stengel's organizational abilities. "His willingness to delegate responsibility to his coaching staff is one of the reasons for the Yankees' domination of the American League," he said.

As for Burdette—more would be heard from him before the 1950s were over.

By Yankee standards, the 1951 team struggled. They were still tied for first in mid-September and unable to break free. In the end, they won their last five games—all against Boston—on the last three days of the season, to win the pennant. They actually clinched with three games left after a doubleheader sweep on Friday, the twenty-eighth, as Reynolds threw his second no-hitter of the season in the clincher, inducing a second pop foul by Ted Williams after Berra dropped the first one. (His earlier one had been on July 12, and the two would be the only major-league regular-season no-hitters Casey ever managed—or played in. As a minor-league manager, he had been on the losing end three times.)

After the clinching no-hitter, the clubhouse was quiet, and more restrained than in previous seasons.

Casey walked over to DiMaggio's locker and said, "I want to thank you for everything you did." Joe accepted this politely. When asked about retirement, he only told reporters, "I don't know, this isn't the time to talk about it." Despite his spring announcement that this would be his last season, which would make this his final championship, the time was not right for a grand pronouncement.

There was always talk of Joe's becoming manager, or perhaps Tommy Henrich. But Henrich, seeing a better financial future in a beer distributorship he invested in with his former teammate Snuffy Stirnweiss, resigned as a coach after the season and pretty much left baseball for good. George Selkirk's name was also mentioned, in case Casey retired.

The Yankees won ninety-eight games, a solid showing, but, as Shirley Povich wrote in *The Washington Post,* "This is the year when the worst Yankee team in a generation won the pennant, and it is Casey Stengel's greatest triumph."

Added Arthur Daley in the *Times,* "The Yankees are not a great team. They barely qualify as a good team. Their pitching couldn't begin to compare with Cleveland's or their hitting to Boston's. This was a triumph for their manager."

Casey would win Manager of the Year honors from United Press International.

The focus of the final days of the season was not on the Yankees—their winning was all too familiar—but, rather, on the spectacular comeback made by the New York Giants in catching the Brooklyn Dodgers and tying for first place in the National League.

So New York City had three first-place teams. The Giants had their own version of Mantle in their center fielder Willie Mays, who, like Mantle, needed a stint in the minors before he got going.

But it was another Giants outfielder, Bobby Thomson, who would become a household word that fall, when his pennant-clinching, walk-off home run off Ralph Branca, "The Shot Heard 'Round the World," concluded "The Miracle of Coogan's Bluff" as the broadcaster Russ Hodges screamed, "The Giants win the pennant! The Giants win the pennant! The Giants win the pennant!"

The World Series opened at Yankee Stadium on October 4, with Mays in center for the Giants, and Mantle in right for the Yankees. Maintaining their late-season momentum, the Giants won the opener 5–1.

The next day, on a fifth-inning drive to right-center by Mays, Mantle moved to his right and DiMaggio to his left, to converge on the ball. Mantle felt he would catch it, but at the last moment, DiMaggio called him off. "It was the first time he spoke to me all season," Mick later said, half-seriously. Mantle put on the brakes, but his spikes caught a drainage pipe in the vastness of the outfield grass, and he collapsed to the ground as DiMaggio made the catch.

He was carried off on a stretcher as Bauer replaced him in right. The injured knee would affect Mantle's play for the rest of his career. Never again would he be as healthy as he had been as a rookie, even though he had been diagnosed with osteomyelitis (a serious bone infection) while still playing high school football. (It had also kept him out of the army.)

The Yankees won the game behind Eddie Lopat, and then the action moved across the Harlem River to the Polo Grounds, where the Yankees took two of three, Lopat again winning Game Five. In the fourth game, DiMaggio hit what would be his final home run, and in the fifth game, McDougald, with his odd, wide-open batting stance, became the first rookie ever to hit a grand slam in a World Series game.

Then, back in Yankee Stadium, they won Game Six, to capture their third straight world championship, with Bauer the hitting hero. The most talked-about managerial moment came in the ninth inning of that game, when Stengel summoned the southpaw Bob Kuzava, an otherwise ordinary pitcher, to face the right-hand-hitting Monte Irvin, who had eleven hits in the series, not to mention a steal of home and a spectacular catch. Kuzava retired three in a row and closed out the game, to walk off a hero.

"I am not too interested in which arm a pitcher uses," said Casey, surprising some, who felt his platooning—now widely considered the trademark Stengel move—was usually lefty-righty based. "To me, a pitcher is a pitcher, and if he is worthy of a locker in Yankee Stadium, I don't care if he has two heads and pitches with two left arms. Performance is what counts. I don't belong to that old-fashioned school which is too taken up with the percentages in alleged favor of one scheme over another. When I called on Kuzava, the press box gasped. I could feel the draft in our dugout. Well, you know what Kuzava did to those right-hand batters."

The party that night, again at the Biltmore, lasted until four in the morning. There were no speeches (always a setback for Casey, who loved making them), but a lot of satisfying merriment through the night.

Mantle wasn't there. He was in the hospital, recovering from the terrible knee injury, and was sharing a room with his father, Mutt, who, along with his grandfather, had taught Mickey to switch-hit. Mutt was ill with cancer, and would die the following May. It was Casey who called Mickey at the Concourse Plaza Hotel, near Yankee Stadium, to break the news of his father's death. Casey kept him out of the lineup that night, and then Mickey flew home to Oklahoma the next day for the funeral.

Losing his dad at twenty was a deep emotional setback for Mantle. His father could "talk sense" to him like no one else. He'd talked him into playing hard at Kansas City instead of quitting. "After my dad died, Casey treated me as a son and taught me a lot off the field too," Mantle would recall.

Since Edna and Casey were childless, having an "adopted son" in Mantle was significant in both of their lives. Neither man was sentimental, but the bond between them was genuine and meaningful. Many people saw their relationship as each man filling a gap in the other's life. Mutt's death during the baseball season left a large void for Mickey, and there was the sixty-year-old Stengel to play the role of surrogate.

AFTER THE SEASON, CASEY and Edna stopped in Oklahoma on their way home, where Casey broadened his oil holdings by investing in a new oil well with a fellow named Bob Jordan. He further broadened them the following year with the "Casey Stengel No. 1" well in Magnolia, Arkansas, where his partners included Charlie Grimm, Steve O'Neill, Jimmie Dykes, Phil Cavarretta, Carl Hubbell, Pinky Higgins, Fred Haney, Eddie Stanky, Marty Marion, Rogers Hornsby, Al Lopez, Hank Greenberg, Dizzy Dean, J. G. Taylor Spink of *The Sporting News,* Gabe Paul, and Paul Richards. The deal was put together by R. W. "Dick" Burnett, owner of the Texas League's Dallas franchise and himself an oilman from Gladewater, Texas. Casey's oil empire was expanding.

It wasn't until late 1953, and seven dry wells, that oil was struck in Oil City, Louisiana, which enabled the partners to get their money back and show a small profit.

But when they returned home, tragedy struck the family. On October 27, Edna's brother Brigadier General Larry Lawson was found dead in a car parked in his garage in Glendale. He was only fifty-three, and the death was ruled a suicide. He had served as base commander for the U.S. Army Air Corps base in Okinawa, Japan, after the Japanese surrender.

The Lawson family gathered in Glendale for the somber funeral. Larry was the brother who had helped bring Casey and Edna together in marriage. Edna's sister, Mae Hunter, and her baby brother (by ten years), John, lent support to her. (John Lawson was a formidable figure in Glendale—he was, at various times, the city's mayor, city councilman, and head of Valley National Bank, which opened in 1957.) This was a difficult time for this prominent family.

Casey flew back from Glendale to New York and reported to the Yankees' Fifth Avenue offices for a press conference on December 11. Joe DiMaggio was announcing his retirement. It was important that Stengel be there, especially to show that there were no bad feelings between the two.

"I've played my last game of ball," said Joe. Casey said:

> What is there to say? I just gave the Big Guy's glove away and it is going to the Hall of Fame, where Joe himself is certain to go. He was the greatest player I ever managed and right now I still say there isn't another centerfielder in baseball his equal.
>
> When they played the Star Spangled Banner, every player would stand in the dugout and they'd look at Joe. When the music stopped, Joe would charge out on the field and they'd charge after him and I knew I had a leader.
>
> And when the game was over, 10,000 people would be waiting to look at him and I knew I had something.

But Casey was probably relieved. Joe had slumped to a .263 average in 1951, the lowest of his career. His twelve home runs were embarrassing by DiMaggio standards, and his selection to the All-Star team was a Stengel courtesy.* He had not earned it, but it gave him the record of having made the All-Star team in every one of his thirteen seasons.

Casey would no longer have to concern himself with Joe's hurt feelings about being in and out of the lineup, when Casey knew he wasn't the DiMaggio of old. He would now move Mantle to center, and have greater control over his daily lineup.

The DiMaggio-Stengel relationship had been tense at times. To close observers, Casey was not very sensitive to Joe's declining skills and strong ego. He could talk to "my writers" about "the Dago" and know they would respect his late-night meanderings and not quote him or write about it. Similarly, DiMaggio could never bring himself to respect Casey, not even after three straight world championships. This he would not tell the press, but he did share it with Toots Shor and all of his nonbaseball friends. Publicly, both would always be properly respectful toward each other. Both understood the consequences of doing any less.

---

* This was still a time when most of the player selections for the All-Star Game were made by the manager.

25

TAKING ON
JACKIE ROBINSON

BEFORE THE YANKEES' 1952 instructional camp at Lake Worth,
Florida, marking what would be the franchise's fiftieth season,
Casey and Edna took a vacation to Puerto Rico. All Stengel
vacations were arranged by Edna. Casey, who had no hobbies, would
have been perfectly fine sitting at home and reading *The Sporting News*.
Edna would write about this:

> The first night we are [in Puerto Rico], he can't go to sleep. Not
> too far off there is a familiar muffled roar. "Sounds like a baseball
> game," Casey said, peeping over the covers. I urged him to go to
> sleep. "It's probably some sort of festival," I said. "These people
> are great for festivals. They have them every night. Now turn over
> and get some rest." Well, three hours later he's back in the room
> and telling me about a pitcher and shortstop he saw and cussing
> out George Weiss. "We have both of these guys signed up as pros-
> pects," he says, "and Weiss don't tell me nothing about 'em and he
> knows I'm coming down here." Of course George knew nothing
> about our plans. I had purposely kept them secret. That was the
> end of our baseball sabbatical.

Edna followed her Puerto Rican vacation with a two-week vacation,
without Casey, to Hawaii. This could be seen as a vacation from vaca-
tioning, or a truly relaxing one without her husband.

WHEN SPRING TRAINING OPENED in St. Pete, Mantle would again be
the big news: he was competing to take over DiMaggio's center-field post.

DiMaggio was not about to disappear; he signed two television contracts for over a hundred thousand dollars to work on NBC and WPIX, the Yankees' local station in New York.

Casey was looking for more maturity from Mantle. "[He's] not just any player. He is a definite type," he said. "He stands out in a lobby, he stands out on a field."

Mantle would earn the center-field job that everyone had been predicting for him, and would, in fact, finish third in 1952 MVP voting, his first full season in the majors. (Allie Reynolds was second to the winner, Bobby Shantz, a slight Philadelphia Athletics pitcher for whom Casey had great respect. Berra finished fourth.) Still, Stengel was concerned— and thus the press and the fans were concerned—over his propensity to strike out, even if the numbers pale by today's standards. His 111 strikeouts broke the team record of 105 set by Crosetti in 1937. Not even Babe Ruth, baseball's all-time leader at that point, ever topped a hundred during his Yankee career.

"I cut down noticeably on my fanning in the final six weeks," Mantle reflected. "I began to pay attention to instructions from Casey and Bill Dickey. They had been warning me that I swung too hard and went after too many bad pitches. I cut down on the swing; I waited for better deliveries."

Stengel loved sitting in his hotel lobby, observing his players as they returned at night (noting those who were breaking curfew), and making his keen observations from a stool in the hotel bar. That was where the writers knew they could find him and get good quotes from him—some even usable.

He would pay for everyone's drinks by signing a tab to his room, and the team would cover the cost. The generosity was never questioned; it was great PR for the Yankees to have the manager entertaining the press on overtime, long into the nights. And that wasn't all. The gossip columnist Leonard Lyons reported that the team also paid for various club memberships for Casey, such as the Elks Club, which Casey explained thus: "That's a business office expense; it comes under the heading of promotion."

As comfortable as Casey felt in this routine, it was not to Edna's liking, since she stayed in their room while Casey entertained downstairs. "If he does not quit baseball this year, I'm going to leave him, and I want you to put that in the paper, too," she said to a beat reporter, probably playfully. But he used it.

This was just Edna going back and forth on the subject. She never really objected, and in fact loved the glamour and the glory. Still, Casey had promised her "just one year." She was a strong woman, not the shy, retiring type, and her encounters with the press and the public complemented Casey's.

The Yankees did not get off to a strong start in 1952. Their 18-17 record as of May 30 (fifth place) did not cause panic, but it looked as if this season would be Casey's toughest challenge. He lost Jerry Coleman to military service in April, Bobby Brown in July, and Whitey Ford was gone for the season. The team picked up the outfielder Irv Noren, whose .235 for the year was a disappointment, and Lopat won only ten games. But the Yankees would lead the league in batting average and in ERA and, even in a so-called off-year, had the most talent in the league. Berra, replacing DiMaggio as cleanup hitter, belted thirty home runs, a record for catchers.

The season progressed. On June 3, Casey worked out an eighteen-year-old bonus kid from Memphis named Marv Throneberry. He'd make the majors a few years later, and a decade from his workout, would become a legend with Casey's Mets.

When the umpire Jim Honochick ejected Casey on July 6 (his first regular season ejection as a Yankee), Casey claimed he said, "Jim, we all know you're entitled to blow a few, but this is getting to be ridiculous." He told the press after the game, "I had a hunch I was about to leave the premises."

When it came time for the All-Star Game, Casey picked his oil partner and onetime player Al Lopez (now manager of Cleveland) as a coach, and picked the Negro League legend Satchel Paige as one of just six pitchers on his staff. (He would pick him again in 1953.) Paige was now pitching for the St. Louis Browns, owned by Bill Veeck, who had also employed him earlier with Cleveland, when he owned that team.

On Old-Timers' Day, at the evening party held at the Ruppert Brewery, on the Upper East Side, Casey got to converse with five members of the 1903 Highlanders, the very first Yankee team. Jesse Tannehill, Clark Griffith, Dave Fultz, John Ganzel and Wid Conroy were all there. Casey knew Griffith (owner of the Washington Senators) from his regular attendance at Winter Meetings, banquets, and so forth, but the other four were actually out of the game by the time Casey broke in with Brooklyn in 1912. It was rare for him to encounter anyone he hadn't played with or against.

—

CASEY JUGGLED NINETY-FIVE DIFFERENT batting orders in 1952. On September 5, after the team lost two of three in Philadelphia, there was too much frolic over steaks on the short train ride to Washington for his taste. "You men amaze me," he said to the team, in the presence of the newspapermen. He then proceeded to berate the "fun makers" and to give the season much more serious thought. "Stop counting on the Browns to win this pennant for you."

The story got reported. The newspaper guys always traveled on the train with the team; they heard and saw everything, but their discretion was counted on. This time, however, Casey's verbal thrashing of the full team seemed like appropriate fodder for print.

The Yankees went 15-4 after that dressing down to take them to the final days of the regular season.

More controversy arose near the end of the season, when Clay Felker and Ernest Havemann wrote a major feature story about Casey for *Life* magazine. *Life* was the nation's most important cultural weekly at the time, and even though chorus girls in tight sweaters danced on the cover, the Casey story dominated the conversation among those in the sports world.

"Lend an Ear to Old Case" was the name of the piece, which playfully described his pantomime gifts while telling stories and his lobby-sitting habits, at least those observed at the Sheraton-Cadillac in Detroit by the authors.

"Frequently," they wrote, "Stengel begins to tell a story at the start of an evening but gets so sidetracked in footnotes or reminiscences he is still approaching the point five or six hours later, and the bartender will step up, point to the clock and say 'the bar is closing.' Then Casey will rise, smooth his plaid coat and say, 'Gentlemen, there is much more which could be said, but my man here in the white jacket has said it all. Goodnight.'"

Casey was not happy about the story, and claimed to have been fooled into thinking it was about the team, not just him. He took exception to such literary flourishes as the authors' suggestion that if the Yankees happened to be on a losing streak, he could be found in a "nearby saloon."

"That's what I get for being nice to people. I have refused permission to many writers, some of them friends of long standing, to do the story of my life. I would like to do that leisurely," he told Dan Daniel in *The Sporting News*.

He also resented the claim that he dressed "like a burlesque actor."

"I would not know, and I don't care how a burlesque actor dresses. That's the actor's business. I buy my clothes in Los Angeles from a place which really is more expensive than I can afford.

"I've had a lot of nice offers to do my book, but the time isn't ripe. I don't want people to think I am important, that I am the great man I am. When I quit, I might do a movie about Casey."

(Undaunted by Casey's reaction, Felker would produce a heavily illustrated book about Casey, *Casey Stengel's Secret,* in 1961, several years before founding *New York* magazine.)

Dan Daniel, Casey's "senior" writer, took the occasion to write glowingly about Stengel and, not surprisingly, Casey's respect for the press: "If he isn't sure about something, he will say so. . . . He will never equivocate and he is one manager who has a sense of news and loyalty to the writers covering the club. When the picture men charged into the Shibe Park clubhouse and began to take over, Casey said, 'Gentlemen, in your time and turn. I am talking with the writers covering my club and with me they come first."

They clinched their fourth straight pennant on September 27 in Philly. Now it was party time, and the club returned to New York and celebrated with a big one at the Warwick Hotel on Sixth Avenue.

AND NOW, AS THREE years prior in 1949, the New York Yankees would face the Brooklyn Dodgers in the World Series. As more and more Americans were owning televisions, the World Series was taking on a look and sound that a generation of baby boomers would come to know. The musical theme of the *Gillette Cavalcade of Sports* would play as their animated parrot, Sharpie, appeared on the screen. A commanding baritone would come in to introduce the venue—"From Ebbets Field in Brooklyn, New York, it's the first game of the 1952 World Series . . . featuring the Brooklyn Dodgers, seeking their first world championship, and the New York Yankees of Casey Stengel, going after a fourth straight. . . . Hello there, everybody, this is Mel Allen, along with Red Barber, on a beautiful autumn day in Brooklyn. . . . We'll be back after this word from Gillette Foamy shave cream and join public address announcer Tex Rickard for the introduction of the teams. . . ."

And onto the field would come some of the great names of postwar baseball—Robinson, Hodges, Snider, Reese, Campanella, Mantle, Berra,

Rizzuto, Martin, Reynolds, Raschi, Lopat, Mize. . . . What a time it was to be a baseball fan, especially in New York.

Before Game One, Casey took Mantle to right field in Ebbets Field to show him the concrete wall and the unusual way balls caromed off it. The Yankees had played in pre-season exhibitions there before with Mantle, but this time Casey felt a short tutorial was in order.

"The boy never saw concrete before," Casey told people. "So I told him not to worry about the angles. I told him I played that wall myself for eight years.

"Know what he said when I told him that? 'The hell ya say?' and looked at me as if I was screwy. Guess he thinks I was born at age 50 and started managing immediately."

Among the Mantle-Stengel stories that people loved to tell, this one was usually high on the list.

This was a terrific series; it would go seven games. In Game Five, with the series tied 2–2, Casey had a tough call to make—selecting a starting pitcher to oppose Carl Erskine. Reynolds, Raschi, and Lopat were not rested. And when the players entered the big clubhouse in Yankee Stadium, their pitching coach, Jim Turner, had placed a baseball in the shoe of Ewell Blackwell. The job was his.

Blackwell, who had been so devastating in the National League, was nursing a sore arm and had made only five appearances since coming over from Cincinnati on August 28. But in those five appearances, he had allowed only one earned run in sixteen innings. This six-time All-Star, whom most National League hitters saw as one of the top pitchers in the league, was widely perceived to be the Yankees' annual late-season surprise, but there wasn't much gas left in his tank.

Blackwell gave the Yankees five innings that afternoon, allowing four runs including a two-run homer by Snider. The Yankees scored five times in the last of the fifth, but Johnny Sain, hurling six innings in relief, lost the game 6–5 in eleven innings, with Erskine going all the way on a five-hitter.

Now the Yankees needed to win two straight.

The Yanks won 3–2 in Game Six, with Reynolds relieving Raschi to save the victory.

The final game was also a thriller.

Lopat learned he was getting the start at 11:25 a.m., ninety minutes before game time. Stengel used a combination of Lopat, Reynolds, and Raschi over six and a third innings, and the Yankees built a 4–2 lead.

With the bases loaded and one out in the seventh, he again turned to Kuzava, an otherwise ordinary pitcher who had been a hero the year before.

Kuzava got Snider to pop out to third. Then Robinson hit a pop to the southpaw side of the pitcher's mound—an unusual place for a ball to be put in play. It was a no-man's-land just thirty feet from home plate, requiring a play one seldom sees in baseball. There was some confusion over whose ball it was, but Billy Martin raced in from second at full speed and caught the ball at his shins. It was a game saver, and a series saver. The runners were going, and, almost certainly, two would have scored.

The final pitch of the series was a curve ball thrown to Reese, who flied out to left. Up to that point, Kuzava had thrown only fastballs. Suddenly Stengel signaled curve ball to Berra (perhaps on Jim Turner's suggestion), and again Kuzava rose to the occasion. He hurled two and two-thirds hitless, scoreless innings, facing nine batters, of whom only one reached—Hodges, on a throwing error by McDougald. (Hodges was 0-for-21 in the series.)

The series was over. The Yankees had their fourth straight world championship, and Stengel tied Joe McCarthy for performing such a feat as manager. (McCarthy had won in 1936–39, Joe DiMaggio's first four seasons.)

Within hours, the team was back at the Biltmore Hotel, which was standing ready. They knew the drill. And another great party celebrated the victory.

CASEY'S POST-SEASON SCHEDULE WAS fast and furious.

Six days after the series ended, he signed a new two-year contract, worth as much as two hundred thousand dollars with bonuses. Again there was a "good job bonus" clause, not requiring a championship season. Certainly, with DiMaggio retired, Casey was making more than any of his players. He also was accruing money annually in the team's profit-sharing plan, which was to be given to him at such time as he left the organization.

The very next day, he flew to Oklahoma City, partly to check on his oil wells, but specifically to be the main speaker at a dinner honoring Oklahoma sons Allie Reynolds and Mickey Mantle. The event took place on Mantle's twenty-first birthday.

On October 29, when they had gotten back home, the Los Angeles sportswriter Braven Dyer tricked Casey into going with him downtown to accept an award. Surprise! There was no award, but a live appearance on the hit TV show *This Is Your Life*, hosted by Ralph Edwards. The production staff managed to recruit Zack Wheat, Bob Meusel, Chuck Dressen, Duke Snider, Billy Martin, and Casey's boyhood pal Harold Lederman to appear on the show, and the surprise worked out perfectly. The people at Central High School in Kansas City even shipped two bricks from the school to be used as bookends.

To appear on *This Is Your Life* was a very big deal in the 1950s, and for those regular viewers unfamiliar with Casey, his story, and his speech patterns, the broadcast was a wide introduction to this increasingly famous character. (This was the fifth episode after it moved from radio to TV.) If there were any Americans left after *Life* magazine and *This Is Your Life* who didn't know Casey Stengel, they were few in number.

On November 3, he was honored at the Verdugo Country Club in Glendale, and then, on November 12, the ballpark in his town was renamed Casey Stengel Field. "I've been thrown out of a lot of baseball parks," he said, "but this is the first one named for me."

At the end of the year, "Casey Stengel No. 1," the oil well near Magnolia, Arkansas, came in, and Casey, Grimm, O'Neill, Dykes, Cavarretta, and Richards were present when it gushed. "[Stengel and Grimm] washed their hands and face in the black gold and were smeared from head to foot," reported the Associated Press. This was Dick Burnett's well in which eleven major-league managers were said to have invested.

On Sunday morning, November 30, just as things were quieting down, Jackie Robinson was the guest on the local New York TV show *Youth Wants to Know*, on WNBT (later known as WNBC). A youngster in the audience asked Robinson if he thought the Yankees were prejudiced against Negro players. By now, six years into his Dodgers' career, Jackie was freely expressing his thoughts on whatever was asked of him. "You've asked me the question and I'll answer it as honestly as I can. Yes, I think they are. I don't mean the players are—but I think the Yankee management is prejudiced. They haven't a single Negro on the team and very few in the organization. You asked the question and I've answered it honestly. That's my opinion."

Since Jackie Robinson's entry into the major leagues in 1947, only three of the eight American League teams had promoted a black player. The topic would come up especially among teams that failed to do so.

For the most part, the national news and sports media were not openly discussing the lack of Negroes in corporate management positions, on boards of directors, holding political office, on police and fire departments, at law firms, or even on television commercials. It was just business as usual, with little scrutiny applied. The civil rights movement had yet to take center stage on the national agenda. Old attitudes were accepted as long as they seemed to be applied without prejudice.

Jackie was now venturing into how another team conducted its business and he didn't hold back: prejudiced.

Asked to respond to Robinson's charge, George Weiss said, "Our attitude always has been that when a Negro comes along who can play good enough ball to win a place on the Yankees we will be glad to have him—but not just for exploitation. Our scouts have been instructed to make every effort to land good prospects."

It was basically the same argument Judge Landis had used as far back as 1920, when he became the game's first commissioner.

Stengel had a shorter answer for Robinson: "Tell Robi'son he's Chock full o'Nuts," referring to the local coffee brand that Robinson did commercials for.

Ruben Gomez, a dark-skinned Puerto Rican (the "ban" extended beyond American Negroes to include dark-skinned Latino players as well), pitched just five games at Kansas City in 1952 and got away from the Yankee organization that summer by buying his own release, to pitch in a summer league in the Dominican Republic. Gomez was one of those Casey had seen pitch when he slipped away during his and Edna's Puerto Rican vacation. He told the front office it was a mistake to let Ruben go, and he was right. Gomez was signed by the Giants, made the major-league club in 1953, and went 30-20 in his first two seasons, hurling 425 innings.

Vic Power, another dark-skinned Puerto Rican, was the organization's best prospect; he had just completed his second year in Triple-A, batting .331 with 109 RBIs at Kansas City.

But Power was a bit of a showboat—cocky, even—by the staid Yankee traditional standards, and whether he was black or white, he didn't seem to be in the right organization to advance. Cocky white players didn't make it, either, although a case could be made for Billy Martin. And, of course, the Yankee manager was pretty cocky himself!

Two days after Robinson's remarks, at a dinner in Phoenix, Stengel addressed the matter again. He didn't avoid the controversy. "I don't care who you are in this organization, you're going to get along and make the big team if you've got the ability. We've got some good coaches, a good front office, good scouts and good minor league managers, and we're not going to play a sap at second base just because [he's black]."

Casey didn't like Robinson, and it was mutual. A lot of it was competitive, a Yankees–Dodgers thing, when that rivalry was very strong. But some of it was surely subtle racism.

The door had opened a bit. It would be another couple of years before there was a black face on a Yankees team photo, but Robinson had stirred the pot and perhaps caused the Yankees to consider the possibility. Though some in the management would never budge, attention would be paid.

Power was not invited to the Yankees' spring training in 1953; he would hit .349 that year at Kansas City. It was whispered that he "dated white women."

"Our manager in Kansas City recently benched Power for lack of hustle, and our scouting reports rate him a good hitter, but a poor fielder," said the co-owner Topping. "My information is that Elston Howard, at Kansas City, has a better chance to come up than Power.[*]

"Who brought up the first Negro football player into the All-America Conference? I did," continued Topping. "I signed Buddy Young. How can anybody accuse any organization of which I am the head of Jim Crowism? We are eager to get a Negro player on the Yankees, but we aren't going to bring up a Negro just to meet the demands of pressure groups."

But this issue wasn't going away.

---

[*] Power would win six Gold Gloves for fielding excellence in the American League.

26

FIVE STRAIGHT

THE YANKEES ADDED A second, even earlier instructional camp that began on February 1, 1953, right in Casey's backyard. Casey Stengel Field in Glendale was good enough for professionals to work out there (later, the Portland Beavers of the PCL made it their spring training home). But the added two weeks of drills, which included Casey's neighbor and pal Babe Herman as an instructor, proved to be simply too much, and this was the only year this early Glendale camp was run.

Beginning with that camp, and, of course, in all of the pre-season baseball magazines that were published, attention was drawn to the possibility of an unprecedented five straight world championships. If ever winning a pennant but losing a World Series would seem like failure, this was the time. It had to be all or nothing. To win five straight when no team had ever done it before, even if you turned the calendar back to nineteenth-century baseball—well, that would really be something. And that was the mission.

The spring camp of 1953 was also the first time that Mantle, Martin, and Ford were together: Whitey had been discharged from the army after two years. The friendship formed by that trio, all in their early twenties, would last their lifetimes.

Sometimes they would get into trouble; ultimately, it was thought that Martin was a "bad influence." But the reality was, they were young, had spending money, and were Yankee heroes; the world was their oyster.

Of course, they were adults and capable of making decisions on their own—even bad ones. And no one expected a manager to supervise nighttime behavior, save for curfews. Meanwhile, the writers had their backs; no improper behavior was reported.

Besides, Casey liked hard-drinking players. He did not have much use for the "milkshake drinkers," as he called them. By the same token, he preferred tobacco chewers to gum chewers (of whom Mantle was one). So, in that sense, he was an enabler, and is it fair to say that in that role he let three young lives get caught up in what we now classify as the disease of alcoholism? The three were hardly alone—it was the culture of the game to pass the nights by drinking. Casey set the example himself, spending hours in the hotel bars after games, regaling the writers. "Stengel's drinking has been overplayed," wrote Tom Meany, a regular member of "my writers." "He stays with a party, but never goes under the weather or under the table. His thirst is not for alcohol, but for an audience."

Given what we now know about the later health and behavior of Mantle, Martin, and Ford, it seems appropriate at least to bring their "father figure" (actually old enough to be a grandfather figure), Casey Stengel, into the discussion, even if there is no right or wrong conclusion to draw.

The dean of New York baseball writers, Dan Daniel, wrote: "Mickey is badly in need of guidance and so far he has not received it. He needed it very badly last season and he still needs it right now, as much as ever. But neither Stengel nor the front office has taken the young man in hand. The time has come for a change in method." Daniel was talking about Mantle's playing basketball, hiking, and hunting after knee surgery, but veiled within those sentences was the issue that couldn't quite be written about: drinking.

Meanwhile, if an owner was ever more pleased with his manager than was Dan Topping (winning four straight titles can do that), you would be hard pressed to find one. "We're keeping him as manager for as long as he wants and that has nothing to do with what happens in 1953," said Topping. "Casey is a great juggler; he is never afraid to jerk his big guns. Stars don't matter. Casey isn't afraid of kids and he likes to bring them up and put them in the lineup. He's really a hell of a manager."

These were glory days for the Topping-and-Webb ownership, and Casey was a poster boy. Even though there were handsome stars like Mantle (whom Casey sometimes called "Ignatz," a comic mouse drawn from 1913 to 1944 in the Krazy Kat comic strips), Casey was often the face of the franchise on magazine covers and in advertising. The cameras loved him, and his cooperation was great for the team. Ownership put more money into the stadium, televised more games, and added more

parking garages. Business was booming, even with the drop in attendance figures since the immediately postwar years.

On April 28, 1953, the Yankees engaged in a fairly major brawl in St.
Louis, resulting in a seventeen-minute delay. At the end of the ten-inning
Yankee victory, the team members, including Casey, grabbed bats and
held them like war clubs to fend off any attacking fans and get safely
to their clubhouse in the just-renamed Busch Stadium (formerly Sportsman's Park).

One player on the Browns that day, the shortstop Willy Miranda,
wound up going to the Yankees in June. It was long on Casey's mind
that he would need to replace Rizzuto one day—though not too soon,
he hoped. He even floated the idea of moving Mantle back to short. (On
July 24, 1954, when he ran out of infielders, Stengel did play Mantle at
short; Miranda played second, and they switched when a man got on base,
so Mantle would be the one to cover first on a bunt. And that's exactly
what happened: Mantle recorded the putout as a second baseman.)

Miranda, a five-foot-nine Cuban, whose brother was sports editor of
a Spanish-language newspaper in New York, didn't play often, but he got
a little "Casey treatment" on June 25 in a home game against Chicago,
when Casey batted him ninth in the lineup, with pitcher Johnny Sain batting eighth. This would be very embarrassing to any player, and it came
when Willy's brother, Fausto, was sitting in the press box at Yankee Stadium. Sain was batting .256, Willy .167, but many in the game would
argue, "You just don't do this to a man."

Said Casey's frequent critic Paul Richards, who was managing in the
White Sox dugout: "All those lineup changes he makes aren't necessary.
Somebody said he used more than 100 different lineup combinations last
season. My only answer to that is that there's a lot of Ringling Brothers
and Barnum and Bailey in old Casey. Don't misunderstand me, I believe
Stengel is a smart manager. However, nobody can convince me that he's
winning because of shifting his lineup around every five minutes."

It was easy for opposing managers to criticize Casey's platooning
system, largely because they simply didn't have the depth of talent to
work with that Casey did. There were few players on the Yankee roster
who wouldn't have been regulars on another team. Platooning them had
the added benefit of keeping them less grumpy about not starting every
day.

—

THE '53 YANKEES WERE in first place from beginning to end (or at least after the sixth game), and, as usual, positively cleaned up on the worst teams in the league, going 64-22 against Detroit, Philadelphia, St. Louis, and Washington. This was the pattern throughout the fifties. The Yankees' arrival in town would mean big crowds—and lots of "L"s for the home team.

People weren't necessarily surprised when the team ran up an eighteen-game winning streak—one off the team record—between May 27 and June 14, although beating a strong Cleveland club (and pitchers Early Wynn, Bob Feller, Bob Lemon, and Mike Garcia) for the final four of those games could not have been expected. What caught fans by surprise, and caused nerves to fray, was a losing streak that began just a week later. "Start looking like Yankees again!" a frustrated Casey shouted at his team in the visitors' clubhouse at Fenway.

He fretted over the late nights he knew some players kept. He watched them eat breakfast. "A boy who's putting away juice, ham and eggs, toast and milk has had a good night's sleep," he said. "The guys I looked for were those who were having a double tomato juice and black coffee. Chances are they'd gone out about 3 am to mail a letter. . . ."

He thought about the recent batting slumps and decided that, besides the late nights, this new pitch, the slider, was causing his men to fail. "The batters just haven't learned how to hit it," he mused as the losing streak grew to seven. "The averages will not rise until they can tell the difference between a slider and a curve."

Casey was not calm and cool during this un-Yankee-like slide. In fact, he shut the doors on the working press, preferring to stew in his office late in the streak. A press boycott always got a lot of attention, because the press, naturally, made a big story of it. The slammed door on the press happened in Fenway Park, where the clubhouse was small and stifling and tempers were rising.

"He can't qualify as a major league manager in the true meaning of the word until he learns how to be gracious in defeat as he has been in victory," said Bob Cooke, sports editor of the *Herald Tribune*. (Sports editors were not "my writers," and Casey really didn't know them.)

"The conduct of the lovable old man Stengel only proves you never know a guy until he's down. The Yankee action came as no surprise to this editor. They are the most arrogant outfit in baseball. This is just typical," said Ike Gellis, the sports editor of the *New York Post*.

This was a nightmare for the Yankees' publicist, Red Patterson. Was

Casey giving back all the goodwill he had built up in four and a half seasons?

Dan Daniel stepped in. He got an audience with Casey back at the Kenmore Hotel, and reminded him of all the support the writers had given him over the years, even bestowing awards on him. Casey agreed to open the doors to the press, but the writers, now stewing over the situation, decided that they would boycott Casey.

Raschi finally ended the slide at nine straight on July 2 with a ten-inning victory, and Daniel got the writers to relent and make nice. So the losing streak and the war with the press ended together, and the good ship Casey returned to calm waters.

FIVE DAYS AFTER THE losing streak ended, the team bus (not the good ship Casey), pulling into Philadelphia's 30th Street Station, hit a low-hanging structure, frightening the players as the roof and the sides of the bus accordioned. That the team trainer, Gus Mauch, was unconscious on the floor did not help matters. Charlie Silvera, Reynolds, Woodling, and Jim Turner were the most badly hurt, though none of their injuries were life-threatening. Casey was injured slightly but was said to be suffering from shock.

THE YANKEES CLINCHED THEIR fifth straight American League pennant at home on September 14, overcoming a 5–0 deficit to beat Cleveland 8–5. The team celebrated at the recently expanded Stadium Club on the mezzanine level of the stadium, a club that boasted the longest bar in New York City.

The man who had once been paid *not* to manage the Brooklyn Dodgers was going to his fifth straight World Series. (Despite the run of success with the Yankees, Casey's career won-lost record as a manager did not go over .500 until this fifth pennant season.)

Twelve members of the team—about half the roster—had played in all five seasons: Reynolds, Raschi, Lopat, Berra, Silvera, Brown, Coleman, Mize, Joe Collins, Woodling, Bauer, and Rizzuto, along with Stengel and the coaches Crosetti, Dickey, and Turner. (Coleman played only nineteen games over 1952–53, while in military service; Brown's twenty-nine games in 1952 also reflected service time, and Mize played only partial seasons in 1949 and 1950.)

But now came the pressure of winning another World Series, and again it was against the extremely talented Brooklyn Dodgers, later dubbed "The Boys of Summer" by author Roger Kahn. Also, this was the Golden Anniversary World Series, fifty years since the first one, in 1903.

Before the series began, the pitcher Johnny Sain had a private meeting with Stengel and told him he was going to retire and run an auto agency. "I wanted Casey to know about this before the Series so he would have plenty of time to go out and get a replacement," said Sain. "I knew that sometimes deals were made at the World Series." With the days running out on his career, Sain was called upon in Game One in Yankee Stadium, and he got the win in relief of Reynolds. Lopat outdueled Preacher Roe for a 4–2 win in Game Two, and it looked like clear sailing for number five. But the Dodgers won the next two in Brooklyn, before an emergency Yankee starter, Jim McDonald, got an 11–7 win in Game Five, highlighted by a Mantle grand slam.

That set the stage for a Game Six at Yankee Stadium, and, reminiscent of the series finale in 1950, Whitey Ford, who led the staff with eighteen wins, pitched brilliantly. Reynolds came on in the eighth inning for relief, with the score 3–1 Yanks.

"I was startled and didn't know what was going on," said the Dodger manager, Chuck Dressen. "We weren't hitting that Ford very good, but I guess Casey knows his players."

"I was not tired," explained Whitey after the game. "At the moment when Casey removed me I was somewhat on the angry side, but the manager knew what he was doing. He was right, as he has been the last five years."

In the ninth, Reynolds gave up a two-run homer to Carl Furillo, which tied the score, but in the last of the ninth, Martin singled home Bauer with the winning run, and the Yankees won the series.

"Bauer was actually our fastest runner after Mantle got hurt," said Berra in his ninety-first year, reflecting on those years while at an assisted-living home. "He could really run. DiMaggio had the best instincts—he knew immediately whether to go from first to third or stop at second. Rizzuto was wily on the bases. But Hank had speed that fooled you."

Five straight world championships!

Photographers captured the annual Stengel-Weiss-Topping-Webb celebratory photo in the clubhouse (the one time each year when Weiss would smile), surrounded by the jubilant players, playfully mussing each other's hair, a tradition that has since gone by the wayside.

"Someone call the Biltmore, please. We'll have the usual."

For Martin, who seemed to rise to the occasion each year, it was his twelfth hit of the series, tying a record, and it gave him a .500 batting average over the six games, including two home runs—a fabulous performance. "Martin's accomplishments are important for baseball," said Casey, taking a broad overview. "They show what a young man can do in these United States, what a game and determined kid can accomplish in our great sport of baseball."

The setback was so tough on the Dodgers that when Chuck Dressen asked for a two-year contract he was shown the door. Walter Alston would be his replacement as manager.

The idea of five straight in today's baseball seems unthinkable, because today's teams have to get past fourteen opponents in their own leagues (not seven), and then three rounds of post-season (not one).[*] (Still, the Yankees of 1996–2000 almost did it, losing in the 1997 play-offs.)

Yankee fans were happy, but few others in baseball were. People felt it was enough already.

ON OCTOBER 13, THE Yankees added Elston Howard and Vic Power to their forty-man roster. Howard would be the first black man to play for the Yankees. Living at his parents' home on the North Side of St. Louis, he heard about it on the ten o'clock news. *The Sporting News,* long a supporter of Judge Landis and the "unwritten rule" supporting segregation, published a glowing portrait of Howard, and called him "the All-American Boy." Power was traded to the Philadelphia Athletics on December 16 for Harry Byrd and Eddie Robinson. He went on to play twelve seasons in the majors.

CASEY STOPPED IN OKLAHOMA on his way home to check on his oil wells. In December, he actually went deer hunting with Randy Moore, his original patron in oil investment. This was a rare foray for him into

---

* The Montreal Canadiens, with only five opponents, would win five consecutive Stanley Cups between the 1955–56 and 1959–60 seasons in the National Hockey League, and the Boston Celtics, with only seven opponents when their streak began, would win eight straight NBA titles between 1959 and 1966.

that popular baseball player hobby, which he had long avoided. He came back empty-handed.

Otherwise, he stayed home. No one in baseball got more banquet invitations than he did, but the man who rarely said no was starting to pace himself.

The Sporting News named Casey Manager of the Year, and *Sport* magazine named him Man of the Year, a major award up against all the MVPs, Heisman Trophy winners, and champions in boxing, racing, and golf.

27

OCTOBER OFF

ONE OF THE ODDITIES of the first half-century of baseball was the players' habit of leaving their gloves on the field when they went to their dugouts. It made no sense, but it became tradition and the accepted norm. And few could ever cite a game—or even a play—that was adversely affected.

The outfielders would leave their gloves in the outfield, the middle infielders on the grass behind them, the corner-position players and the pitcher on the area between the baseline and the dugout.

Crazy.

In 1954, it was decided that a rule needed to be implemented to keep the gloves off the field.

Casey hated it. He was old-school on this one. "Suppose your center fielder makes the last out sliding into second," he said. "He has to run back to the dugout for his glove and then out to center field? That's a terrible rule." He did not immediately foresee the reality: that a teammate would pick up the glove and run it out to the field. But his outspokenness on the matter was a strong signal that he was a traditionalist in the strongest sense.

ON FEBRUARY 1, 1954, just after Casey departed for the annual instructional school in Lake Wales, burglars broke into the Stengels' Glendale home and grabbed $18,400 worth of furs while Edna was off at a restaurant with friends. A few days later, three teenage boys were arrested in Amarillo, Texas, with her mink coat, mink stole, and sable piece. They had ignored all of Casey's baseball treasures, including his World Series rings. Nobody thought these things had much value back then.

It was a bad omen, but not quite as bad as the news delivered at a press conference summoned by Red Patterson in Room 240 of St. Petersburg's Soreno Hotel on February 23: the Yankees were selling Vic Raschi to the Cardinals. Raschi had been a holdout, and Weiss pulled the switch and got rid of him. This reliable presence in the starting rotation was gone.

"I can't put the rap on Raschi," said Casey. "He certainly wasn't sold for anything he did on the field. They must have been awfully sore at him in the front office."

Said the general manager of the White Sox, Frank Lane, "It could be that the Raschi deal will cool off that Yankee spirit a bit. If so, it couldn't happen to a nicer guy than my old pal, Stengel."

Behind the scenes, Casey had agreed to the deal if Weiss would call Johnny Sain and coax him out of his brief retirement. General Motors had to agree that Sain could take a leave from his Chevy dealership in Arkansas. With that accomplished, Sain became a relief pitcher and saved twenty-six games that year. Raschi's starting spot would be taken by a rookie, Bob Grim, who won twenty games and the Rookie of the Year Award in 1954.

Privately, Casey also told people that it was a shame Raschi hadn't made some sort of gesture or statement about wanting to continue with the Yankees—he thought that could have helped. For close observers, this was a rare indicator that Weiss and Stengel were not joined at the hip on roster decisions. Casey would grumble over this one for much of the season.

Spring training featured the rarity of a black player in a Yankee uniform—two, in fact. Elston Howard was invited to camp along with a pitcher named Eddie Andrews, who had gone 11-2 in the Class D Pony League the year before. Nobody expected Andrews to move up, but, given the standards of the time, Howard needed a black roommate.

As it developed, when the Soreno Hotel wouldn't take Howard, he had to find private accommodations in the Negro section of St. Petersburg. He would not be able to dine with his teammates, share cabs with them, or sit out at the pool with them. But he was on the roster.

Casey was at once taken by Howard's natural talents, and Bill Dickey was also a help in tutoring him on catching, as he had done with Berra. "Howard is already a major league hitter," said Casey. "He has one of the greatest arms I ever saw and is fast for a catcher."

Fast for a catcher? Even Ellie was stunned by that evaluation when writers told him what Casey said. He was actually one of the slower runners on the team, but he had beaten other spring-training catchers in a foot race that Casey observed. These "other catchers" included a lot of future major leaguers who were just not going to unseat Berra to earn a roster spot. And so, over time, most of the rest of the game was populated by onetime Yankee catching prospects. But Casey told Howard, "There's no future for you as an outfielder and you will never make it big there. You have a good future as a catcher because Yogi and you are the only catchers who could hit the long ball."

Everyone in the organization took to Howard at once. His promotion was still a year away, but people could see that if he wasn't traded he was going to be the first Negro Yankee. Unlike the situation on other clubs, including the Dodgers with Jackie Robinson, there were no reported incidents of Southern players on the Yankees asking to be traded, or any slights against Howard within the confines of the field and the clubhouse. Even Elston's wife, Arlene, who could speak out as needed against injustice with the best of them, found the Yankees welcoming and supportive, or at least more so than she might have expected. Everyone knew what Jackie Robinson had gone through seven years before.

THE SPRING WAS ABUZZ with trade rumors and roster shifts. On March 5, Ewell Blackwell called from Tampa to say he was retiring because his arm hurt. Martin was called into the service. Bill Virdon, an outfield prospect, was traded to the Cardinals for Enos Slaughter, still considered a productive player.

Virdon, who would one day manage the Yankees himself, was in the outfield with Mantle, Bauer, Woodling, Noren, and others, taking fly balls and firing to the cutoff man. When it was Virdon's turn, his throw somehow nailed Casey in the back.

"Oh gosh, I got him right in the '37,'" recalled Virdon in a 2015 phone call. "And down he went. All the other guys were laughing their heads off, shouting, 'You killed Casey Stengel! You killed Casey Stengel!' When Casey got up and dusted himself off, he looked out at us and yelled, 'Who made that throw?' And everyone pointed to me. And he yelled, 'If you guys keep throwing that way, you might just throw someone out!'"

Bill "Moose" Skowron was going to make the club. Big things were hoped for from the pitcher Harry Byrd, whom the Yankees had gotten for Vic Power. Bobby Brown stayed with the team until June 30, when he left for San Francisco to take up his medical residency. "If I ever want an appendix out, Doc Brown will get my business," said Casey in a fare-well.

Casey observed, "Players today are intelligent and civilized. When I was manager in Brooklyn, if I released one of them birds, I first searched his room to make sure he didn't have a gun."

Casey was getting older, and his spring evenings were getting shorter. The pressroom at the Soreno opened at five-thirty, and Casey would be the dominant figure in the room, regaling everyone—writers, coaches, club officials, Dr. Gaynor—with his old stories. Weiss was seldom present. Then Casey would have dinner and go to bed at nine-thirty, so he could be up at six.

THE 1954 SEASON BEGAN with the presidential opener in Washington, and Casey got to meet Dwight Eisenhower. But the Yankees did not take off to the front with their usual pace, and were only 11-10 before running off a six-game winning streak. Meanwhile, Cleveland was very strong and on their way to a record year with 111 victories. The Yankees would occupy first place for barely one day in the whole season.

Tempers were quick to emerge when things weren't going well. Fans were booing more than usual, especially booing Mantle on each strike-out. Stengel and Ford had a shouting match in which Whitey walked off saying, "Go fry an egg." Casey got even. On May 21, a game scoreless through five against the Red Sox, Whitey had a bad sixth inning, allowing six runs on six hits, two walks, and a wild pitch. And Casey left him in, let him take his punishment for the rest of that inning. More than a few people thought it was payback for the show of disrespect. But they patched it up, and Casey started Ford in the All-Star Game.

Casey himself was thrown out of three games during the year, after having been ejected just once in the previous five years.

And Frank Lane continued to goad Stengel, even if his White Sox were finishing a distant third. Said Lane: "Casey is just getting too big for his britches. He thinks he's the biggest brain in baseball. The guy reminds me of an actor who has been playing the part of a clown with success and now wants to be a Hamlet."

In July, Lane sent Casey a long-winded birthday message that included, "After watching you in action here last Wednesday supervising our very efficient ground crew, because the game was stopped due to heavy rain and then one hour and eight minutes later, even though it was still raining hard, through sheer force of your commanding personality you made the umpires resume play on a field that was a quagmire until your excellent second placers had won, I am more than ever convinced that life begins at 63."

Casey gave it back. "Lane has a few failings. In the first place, he talks too much about things which he should not discuss. Now, I like to talk. But not about confidences. You discuss a possible deal with Lane and he will rush right off and spill the whole works to baseball writers. He is their biggest source. Also he is over-hungry for publicity. Notice how he times his cracks about me for the Sunday papers."

After having lost four All-Star Games in a row, Casey finally won one in 1954, beating the National League 11–9 in Cleveland when he got a pinch-hit home run from the Indians' own Larry Doby, and then a two-run single from Nellie Fox in the last of the eighth.

In August, however, after Edna returned from a trip to Europe, Casey reflected on his future to her. "I am paid by the Yankees to win, just as the players are paid to win, and if we can't do it, they should get rid of me and get someone who can."

The Yankees' last hope for the season seemed to fall on September 12, when they had a doubleheader with the Indians in front of a record 86,563 fans at Municipal Stadium. They were six and a half games out, going in. A sweep would put them at four and a half, and they would still have a pulse, with eleven games left. But the Indians swept them, and the lead was now eight and a half. It was, for all purposes, over.

Stengel shouted to the policeman at the clubhouse door, "Don't let nobody in. I don't want nobody in here."

After Casey was showered and dressed, the Cleveland sportswriter Hal Lebovitz offered him a ride up the hill to his hotel. "Nope," he grunted. "I'll walk." A hand was extended as a goodbye gesture. He took it, halted in his tracks for a moment and said, "If we don't win it, and right now it looks as though we ain't, I hope you do." Wrote Lebovitz: "He resumed his rapid gait and soon his brown suit was lost in the homeward-bound mob . . . one frustrated, bitterly disappointed soul among that happy, holiday-like crowd."

The Yankees won eight of those remaining eleven, to give them 103 wins for the season, but it was too late. The streak of five straight world championships and pennants was over. "We tumbled from four and a half to eight and a half faster than the stock market in 1929," said Casey, "which didn't do me no good either."

Bob Fishel, who had taken over for Red Patterson as PR director on August 10, prepared a four-page flyer for distribution, honoring the past champions on a hastily arranged "Salute to the Champions Day," Saturday, September 25. (Patterson and Weiss had had a falling out over complimentary tickets for an elevator operator; Patterson quit and went over to the Dodgers.)

The Yankees got .300 seasons out of Berra, Mantle, Carey, Skowron, and Noren; Casey called Noren "close to untouchable." Besides Grim's surprise twenty-win season, Ford-Lopat-Reynolds went 41-16, with Reynolds making half of his appearances in relief. Harry Byrd, of whom much was expected, was only 9-7, and was shipped off to Baltimore on November 17 in a record seventeen-player deal that brought Don Larsen and Bob Turley to the Yankees, and sent Woodling to the Orioles.

There was no statistical failure to point to—hey, it was 103 wins! It was the most wins a Yankee team managed by Stengel would ever have.

THE YEAR THE YANKEES LOST THE PENNANT was, coincidentally, the name of a book by Douglass Wallop published that year, which was made into the film and Broadway musical *Damn Yankees*. Casey met the author in person at a Senators game late in the season. "We had quite a conversation!" said Casey. "But I ain't gonna comment about a guy which made $100,000 writin' how my club lost."

ON SEPTEMBER 22, CASEY persuaded Edna to go out and buy a new hat. At least, that was his story. And while she was doing so, he signed a new two-year contract in Topping's private dining room at the stadium, with the press all invited. It called for seventy-five thousand dollars a year plus the usual bonus provisions. "We think Casey has done a truly outstanding job and at no time did we consider a change," said Topping. Casey talked to the reporters about possibly moving Mantle to short and Berra to third in 1955. As for Edna, who always wanted him to retire, he said he told her, "Now Edna, you know I just wouldn't be happy working around the yard all summer, would I?"

After the season, Casey wrote a letter to his sister Louise back in Kansas City:

Oct 11, 1954
Dear Louise:

Edna & myself had to stay over in N.Y. & Cleveland to see the World Series &then we went back to N.Y. to close out some meetings with the ownership in regards to trades & winter work for the Yankee club. We then flew home by air from N.Y.

I signed a two year contract at my former figure but should I get in physical shape not to carry on will retire.

We had Harold & Anne [Lederman, his best friend in Kansas City] *out for a visit at the end of the season.*

This morning's papers states that the Philadelphia Club will stay in Philadelphia as 10 men are to put up the money to continue. Sure thought K.C. would & [sic] *Grant or myself that he had them on deposit at the Law Firm.*

Personally suggest they make settlement & give the certificates etc. to you & Grant as I know my mother wanted the certificates to be left to you (Louise).

Since you were unmarried & live in the home 4149 Harrison St, K.C. Mo., I will not claim any of the money as am well fixed financially & will pay for any amount cost of the legal transaction.

Sincerely,
Charles D Stengel

28

ELSTON HOWARD

ELLIE HOWARD MADE THE opening-day roster in 1955, a historic marker in Yankee history, but a move that felt surprisingly natural. No player embraced his arrival more than Phil Rizzuto, but Berra, Mantle, Martin, Ford—they all accepted him as their teammate from the start. Dickey, from Little Rock, Arkansas, enjoyed working with him on catching. Turner, from Nashville, Tennessee, found him to be a perfect gentleman. (Fourteen years later, Howard would join Turner as a coach on the Yankees.)

Some writers, asked about why the Yankees were so slow to bring a black player onto the team, merely said, "They won every year; no reason to change. Why 1955? Well, they didn't win in 1954."

Casey said only positive things about Howard's abilities, but one day, he joked, "I finally get a nigger, and he can't run." For the rest of his life, this one line would be cited as an example of his racism. (Usually the "n" word was cleaned up in the telling, and it became simply "I finally get one. . . .")

But even for the young, liberal-thinking New York press emerging on the scene, his use of the "n" word was not taken harshly.

"He was a product of his times," they would say, almost to a man, and echoing Arlene Howard's comments (or perhaps she borrowed theirs). "He was born in Missouri in 1890, went to segregated schools, and middle America grew up with certain prejudices, or certain ways of speaking. Even Harry Truman used the 'N' word."

"When repeating that sentence, people lose sight of the first half of it," notes Toni Mollett Harsh, a grandniece of Edna's and former Reno city councilwoman, who today oversees Casey's legacy. (Her mother, Margaret Mollett, served as his bank secretary.) " 'I finally get one' is an important statement and says a lot. Remember, he played against Negro League teams and saw what Robinson, Mays, Irvin, Campanella, Newcombe, Black, Doby, Paige, Aaron and Banks meant to their clubs. People overlook that part of the statement and they shouldn't."

ARLENE HOWARD WROTE, IN her 2001 memoir: "There really was nothing malicious about what Casey had said. If anything, Elston was upset because Casey had referred to him as a slow runner. Hey, he ran track on the relay team when he was at Vashon High School, and he led the International League with twelve triples in 1954. Even though Casey would use the 'n' word and occasionally referred to Elston as 'Eight Ball,' Elston never really thought that Stengel was racist. Casey was just being Casey. He was sixty-five years old. That was how people of his era talked, Elston thought, and so he accepted it. Casey was always blurting out words that were unusual and embarrassing."

"Casey really liked Ellie and Arlene," said the sportswriter Steve Jacobson. "And he liked dancing with Arlene at team parties, because, like Edna, she was taller than he was and he thought they cut a good figure together."

WITH THE BENEFIT OF hindsight, promoting Howard onto the Yankees' roster was a much more significant milestone in the team's history than was presented at the time. Baseball has long been proud of ending discrimination in its ranks through the signing of Jackie Robinson by the Dodgers, seven years before the Supreme Court's landmark 1954 decision ending school segregation. For the Yankees, the change was long in coming, and happened after the *Brown v. Board of Education* decision. Whereas Yankee fans cared mostly about winning, the growing voices from social activists (and there were plenty in New York City) were putting pressure on the team to finally integrate. They were, after all, the game's most visible team. The Yankees were not the last team to integrate (that was the Red Sox, four years later), but they were the ones now drawing the greatest attention on this issue.

Casey's role was not insignificant, because he created an environment in which the event could "just happen," in which Howard's teammates could easily welcome him onto the roster. There was no clubhouse meeting in which Casey warned his players to "accept Howard." The theme was winning; if Howard helped to accomplish that, he was a Yankee all the way.[*]

Whatever Casey's upbringing may have taught him, at age sixty-four he accepted the change rather comfortably and, by easing Howard onto the roster, helped baseball into what may have been its greatest era—the mid-to-late 1950s, when the rosters were now at "maximum talent," featuring both black and white players squeezed into just sixteen teams.

Having traded Vic Power before he ever played for the Yankees, Casey had only a few dark-skinned players in his Yankee years—Harry Simpson (whom he had picked for the 1956 All-Star team while Simpson was still with Kansas City; he came to the Yankees in 1957), Hector Lopez (1959), and Jesse Gonder (1960) followed Howard—but, given that they were joining his swath of white players, ranging from the Oklahoma Dust Bowl native Mantle to South Carolina's Bobby Richardson—the transition was done with ease.[†]

BECAUSE ELSTON HAD TO live apart from most of his teammates who were housed at the Soreno Hotel, not all of Casey's spring-training rules applied to him. For those who lived there, rules were simple—and the no-dog-track rule was long gone.

1. Players are to report at Miller Huggins Field in uniform every morning before 10:30.
2. There will be an 8 o'clock call at the hotel for all player[s.]
3. Dress in the hotel in the morning: sports shirt permissible, which must be buttoned at neck, plus a jacket. Dress in the hotel for dinner; must have shirt and tie, and coat on at all times.
4. Tipping: Meals, 25 cents for breakfast, 50 cents for dinner, $1 per week for room maid.

---

* That the Howards found difficulty off the field—gaining acceptable housing in Florida, and fighting for the right to buy a home in suburban Bergen County, New Jersey—was considered more an American issue than a Yankee problem, and the Yankees chose not to wade into it.
† The southern pitcher Jim Coates was thought to be an exception to the tolerance. He and Howard were coaxed into a boxing match in the West Point gym on a Yankee exhibition visit one year, in which Howard scored a KO.

Dan Daniel wrote a column about this in the *World-Telegram,* noting that it marked the end of the dime tip, and the first time he had ever seen written rules regarding tipping.

Alas, spring training was not smooth sailing for Casey. On March 26, as the Yankees were preparing for a celebration to mark their thirtieth anniversary of moving to St. Petersburg, Casey got into a scuffle with a local photographer and was served with papers at Al Lang Field, charging him with assault and use of obscene language. The photographer charged Casey with kicking him in the leg. The story ran all over the country. "I'm in jail," Casey said to Bob Fishel, the Yankees' PR man. "Y'gotta come down and bail me out. It's fifty dollars, but bring more because they might change their mind." The mayor of St. Petersburg, knowing the importance of having the mighty Yankees connected to St. Pete, quickly jumped to Casey's defense, and even presented him with a key to the city, before the matter went to court.

"I'm sure sorry that the rhubarb developed at Al Lang Field the other day," said Casey to his writers. "I certainly didn't have anything against that photographer or any photographer. I don't even know him. They tell me he's a nice fellow. He got in our way at the Brooklyn game, and I ordered him off the field and out of the dugout. Maybe I was a little mad and I yelled at him. But I sure didn't know I was starting any great feud. The Yankees have been coming to St. Petersburg now for 30 years. We like it here. The city and people are great to us. I certainly wouldn't want to spoil that relationship in an argument with a photographer, or anybody else. Maybe I didn't say 'please' to him when I told him to get off the field, but it was a tense ball game and I didn't want anyone in our way. I sure hope this thing can be cleared up."

It was cleared up. The complaint was dropped, and Casey never had to go to court.

BY THE SPRING OF 1955, radio reporters were beginning to show up at training camps with tape recorders. They were big and bulky, reel-to-reel, and not easy to travel with or plug in. One such radio reporter was named Howard Cosell.

For whatever reason, perhaps a little too much self-confidence, Cosell did not click with the Yankee players or their manager, and he found it difficult to do his job until Bob Fishel intervened and coaxed people to talk with him. This saved Cosell from the embarrassment of a failed assignment, and helped launch his career on ABC Radio with a program called *Pennant Preview*.

Of course, what he got from Casey was a dose of Stengelese. Casey could really offer it up for these hapless radio guys, but the advent of recorders also allowed some verbatim coverage of the dialect. When *Time* magazine sent a print reporter, armed with a tape recorder, *Time* decided to run with the Stengelese. Its readers were probably as dumbfounded as the poor reporter.

Casey proceeded to praise Berra, and included Mantle ("my big fella") in the run-on sentence, acknowledging him almost in passing. Casey then tossed a big compliment at Moose Skowron, with a "Skowron, maybe" in his ranking of his best players.

Then came mention of Bob Cerv with "he can't field now," noting that perhaps someone else could use him. It was like putting a FOR SALE notice on his back.

"The other fella" (Martin) and the "Little Old Man" (Rizzuto) get mentioned when he covers the infield, where as usual, he was putting doubts in people's minds about Rizzuto's future.

When he got to Elston Howard, he said, "Good kid too. If they leave him alone and stop fighting the Civil War all over and they almost ruined him." Casey was showing sensitivity here to making an issue of Howard's race and perhaps interfering with his focus on the games.

He concluded with special attention to Eddie Robinson and his "16 home runs in his first 32 hits," noting that Joe Collins is a good player for first base but that Robinson "does me a good job." The Eddie Robinson performance to which Casey alluded was not uncommon at that time in Yankeeland, when a player might be a fill-in, perform well, and then sit back down when the regulars returned.

"I broke into the lineup in May after Collins and Skowron were hurt," said Robinson in 1957. "I stayed in there for just about a month. All I did was hit 13 home runs in that time and help the Yankees boost their lead to five and a half games. But when Collins and Skowron got better, Stengel put me on the bench and I never did get back in there. I couldn't figure it out then. I still can't." Between May 18 and June 15, 1955, he had thirteen homers, and twenty-nine RBIs in twenty-nine games. And then it was back to the bench.

Allie Reynolds retired after the 1954 season, and on July 27, 1955, "the Junkman," Ed Lopat, started against the White Sox in Yankee Stadium. His days of baffling hitters with off-speed breaking balls were coming to a close. After four consecutive singles by Chicago in the top of the second, Casey walked to the mound and signaled for Tom Sturdivant to replace him.

That marked the end of the Reynolds-Raschi-Lopat era. Lopat was traded to Baltimore three days later (Don Larsen was called up to replace him), where he finished his career with ten appearances for the Orioles.

The year when Howard arrived, 1955, was also the final year of Joe Carrieri's four-year tenure as batboy. Casey liked him a lot, and was often playful with him. "Joe! Joe! Get up and hit for DiMaggio!" he yelled when Carrieri had nodded off on the bench one evening during batting practice.

"I used to line up the bats in the bat rack based on the batting order," recalled Carrieri in 2015. "One game, I noticed Woodling taking a bat from the slot when it was supposed to be McDougald. I ran and told Casey, 'He's batting out of order, he's batting out of order!' And I was right, and I saved the day. McDougald went up to hit. After the game, Casey told the team, 'Even Joe the batboy makes us great!' and he gave me twenty-five dollars."

THIS YEAR ALSO MARKED the beginning of the widespread use of batting helmets, and Casey had an observation on that, as he had had on the gloves-off-the-field rule the year before: "If we'd had them when I was playing, John McGraw would have insisted that we go up to the plate and get hit on the head."

The first Yankee player saved by the helmet was Jerry Coleman, who was beaned in July. "The ball struck his helmet with a crack that was heard across the ball park and except for the fact that he was wearing the safety cap, he probably would have been seriously injured," reported *The Sporting News*.

APRIL 28–29, 1955, WAS the Yankees' first visit to Kansas City, the place from which Casey's own nickname was derived. This gave him a chance to visit with his brother and sister, though he stayed with the team at the Muehlebach Hotel. Fans greeted him warmly when he went to home plate with the lineup cards, as he had received them graciously in the hotel lobby, signing every piece of paper, answering questions, posing his own. He loved all this. He loved people, hotel lobbies, celebrity, train travel, old stories, and good times.

If a fan, perhaps a bit inebriated, started heckling Casey, the Ol' Professor was skilled at handling it. "I want to compliment you for being so fine a fan," he might say, "and we need more like you. Each city should have its red hots like you!"

"You can't hold yourself aloof from the customers," he would explain later. "You can't snub them and you mustn't snub them. If they feel hurt, they can jolly well tell you where to go. . . . The fans make baseball possible. Don't ever forget that."

The Yankees split the two games in Kansas City, and in losing the second one, they fell out of first place; they didn't get back to first place till over three weeks later, during a seven-game winning streak; then they stayed on top until July 31. After that, they didn't regain first until September 16—in the midst of an eight-game winning streak. During that whole time, however, they were never more than two games out.

The Yankees' annual Old-Timers' Day fell on Casey's sixty-fifth birthday, and there he was, surrounded by Ty Cobb, Tris Speaker, Connie Mack, and Bill Terry, with a cake that represented Ned of the Third Reader, that character in his elementary school textbook whom he always liked to "quote" when he felt it was appropriate for a silly question or an obvious answer.

He was doing fine financially at sixty-five. Soon he received his first Social Security check (for seventy-five dollars) to complement his baseball salary, his oil income, his investments, his Lawson Bank income, and his endorsements. But his health was problematic, and soon after Old-Timers' Day, he turned the team over to Jim Turner for a few days while he stayed at the Essex House with the flu and a bladder condition. He watched the games on television.

By now, the Essex House was truly a mid-Manhattan haven for him. He would leave by cab around 2:00 p.m. for an 8:00 p.m. night game, after an hour of pacing in his twenty-eighth-floor suite. Edna would follow later, get her ticket at the will-call window (Window 21), and sit next to the dugout, passing up the invitation to sit in the mezzanine box with other wives of team officials. Casey would pace the dugout throughout the game, and was always high-energy and quite animated with his arms. After the game, while Casey held court with his writers, Edna would wait up to two and a half hours at her seat and then by the switchboard operators for him to claim her, but she enjoyed talking to anyone who was passing by, even the cleanup crew. The Stengels would then take a cab back to the hotel from Yankee Stadium (talking about the game to the cabbie), and go to their suite. Casey would freshen up and, still wound up from the game, go back, alone, to the street. He needed to unwind, for he could recall every pitch to every batter, every nuance of a game. Should he have waved Bauer over three steps in right in the fourth inning? Did he fail to exploit a weakness somewhere in his opponent?

Unwinding for him meant exiting on Central Park South, across the street from the horse-drawn carriages, walking east, downhill toward Sixth Avenue, making a right turn at the corner and then another, one block south, on West Fifty-eighth Street, and finally uphill toward the back entrance of the Essex House. He would always be recognized, and always enjoyed bantering with the fans or the tourists. The experience seemed to relax him for the rest of the evening.

Toots Shor's notable restaurant was a short walk away, but he was not a regular. The New York Athletic Club was literally next door. No interest. As gregarious as he was, room service with Edna in the twenty-eighth-floor suite overlooking the park was often just the ticket when the team wasn't on the road.

CASEY COULD BE BOTH thoughtful and thoughtless when it came to his players. When George Weiss told him he was thinking of trading the injured Irv Noren, Casey jumped to the outfielder's defense. "He got hurt playing for you, didn't he?" said Casey. "You owe him something."

Noren stayed, and got to collect another World Series check.

But on September 9, Casey made out the lineup card for the game showing Don Larsen pitching and batting eighth, and Rizzuto batting ninth. This was a cruel and embarrassing thing to do to the aging Rizzuto; Casey had also done it with Willy Miranda, and would do it again with Bobby Richardson. Larsen hit well for a pitcher, but Rizzuto seemed to deserve more respect than this. Though Rizzuto held his tongue, his friends among the writing corps knew how hurtful this was to him. Some recalled the day at that long-ago Brooklyn tryout when Casey told him to go get a shoeshine box (though it was not actually Casey, but a coach, as reported earlier).

—

BILLY MARTIN HAD BEEN off with the army, playing and managing a team at Fort Carson, near Colorado Springs, but he used a month and some days of accumulated leave to join the Yankees on September 1. (He was in fact declared eligible for the World Series, despite missing the August 31 cutoff for the active roster.) He was a good addition in a close pennant race, batting .300 in twenty games, which no one expected from him. He then hit a stellar .320 in the World Series, again proving himself to be a terrific October hitter.

The Yankees reclaimed glory when they clinched the American League pennant—Casey's sixth in seven years—on September 23, with victory in the nightcap of a day-night doubleheader at Fenway Park, and with Ford, an 18-game winner, saving the 3–2 win for Larsen. Casey called on Whitey with one out in the seventh, and got Ted Williams to hit into a double play to hold the lead.

It was a season in which the Indians became the first team in Casey's seven years to win a season series against the Yankees, capturing thirteen of the twenty-two games between them. The Yankees still finished three games ahead of the Tribe and five ahead of the White Sox, thanks in part to their demolishing of the Orioles, winning nineteen times in twenty-two games.

It was also a season in which Berra won his third MVP award, tying DiMaggio, as he drove in 108 runs, while Mantle belted thirty-seven home runs, and Howard hit an impressive .290 in his rookie season, playing left field, right field, and catching.

BROOKLYN. AGAIN. ANOTHER SUBWAY Series. Casey seldom called them the Dodgers; he said "the Brooklyns." And here they came, trying to beat his Yankees after failing five times in five attempts, starting in 1941. For Dodger fans, it had become "Wait till next year!" after each setback.

And yet, arguably, they had the better team. The Brooklyn Dodgers of the 1950s were loaded with stars, and even had the "mystique" that Yankee fans liked to talk about. Maybe 1955 would put an end to the suffering.

Counting the managers, Walt Alston and Stengel, and coaches Dickey and Billy Herman of the Dodgers, the World Series featured thirteen future Hall of Famers, including Campanella, Reese, Robinson, and Snider of Brooklyn (Sandy Koufax didn't make an appearance), and Berra, Mantle, Rizzuto, and Ford of the Yankees, along with other stars, including Hodges, Furillo, Newcombe, Gilliam, Bauer, Howard, Martin, and Skowron. Formidable talent was abundant.

Not surprisingly, the teams split the first six games, setting up a dramatic Game Seven at Yankee Stadium before 62,465 fans.

Stengel named Tommy Byrne, who had pitched a complete-game win in Game Two, and Alston selected Johnny Podres, who had a complete-game win in Game Three. Only twenty-two years old, Podres had twenty-nine career victories in his three seasons with Brooklyn.

IN THE LAST OF the sixth, with the Yankees trailing 2–0, Martin walked and McDougald dropped down a bunt single. The tying runs were on with nobody out and Berra batting. Yogi hit a fly ball down the left field line—a very difficult catch for the left fielder, who had been shading to his left for the left-hand-hitting Berra. Amoros, in his first inning in left, ran at breakneck speed and speared the ball right by the foul pole. The unexpected catch caught both runners too far from their bases—and Amoros fired to Reese, who threw on to Hodges for a double play. Bauer grounded out to short, and the threat was over.

Now, it wasn't as if Casey had done anything wrong, but if he hadn't taken Byrne out, Alston would have kept Gilliam in left. Gilliam wore his glove on his left hand, Amoros on his right. The play was just so: Amoros was able to snare it, whereas Gilliam might not have been.

"I played the game wrong," Casey later reflected to his writers. "I had my hitters taking on Podres and I shoulda had 'em hitting. I knew the kid hadn't pitched a complete game since mid-July. I figured he couldn't last. But he did last and I was wrong—they shoulda been up there swinging from the first inning on."

Casey was wrong about this postmortem, too: Podres had gone the distance four days earlier.

The Yankees had been playing without Mantle, who was hampered by a leg injury. The best they could get from him was a pop to shortstop in the seventh as a pinch hitter. He was 2-for-10 in the series with one home run, but, obviously, missing a 100 percent Mantle from their daily lineup was a huge setback. (He had hardly played at all after September 14.)

In the ninth, an inning every Brooklyn fan came to know from verse, Skowron grounded out to Podres, and Cerv flew out to Amoros. That brought up Howard, who grounded out, Reese to Hodges.

And the Brooklyn Dodgers were at last world champions—for the first time in the history of the franchise. Oh, what a celebratory day and night that was in the borough of Brooklyn. This was a seismic event in the annals of Brooklyn, not just Brooklyn baseball. Brooklyn was only a borough, not a city, and the Dodgers (and the Brooklyn Bridge) provided their major identity in the nation; their fans among the most loyal, long-suffering, and boisterous. The effects were thunderous.

Billy Martin was near tears. "It's a shame for a great manager like that to have to lose," he said.

The experience of losing a World Series was a first for Casey.

THE SERIES ENDED ON October 4, and four days later, the Yankees gathered at Idlewild Airport (now JFK) for a trip to the Far East, with a stopover in Honolulu.

Casey was going back (along with a traveling party of sixty-four) to revisit Japan and the Philippines, which he had last visited in 1922 with McGraw's Giants.

This time, the Yankees would play twenty-five games (winning them all save for one tie), on a tour organized by a Japanese newspaper. It was a goodwill tour, and for three of the players—Eddie Robinson, Johnny Kucks, and Andy Carey—it was also a honeymoon trip. Carey led the team with thirteen homers in the twenty-five games; his bride was Lucy Marlow, a beautiful Columbia Pictures starlet who had appeared in 1954's *A Star Is Born*. They married October 6. Ellie Howard brought his home-movie camera to record the trip, and also hit .468, to lead the team.

Rizzuto was among a handful of players who did not go, but Phil insisted this was not because of a feud with Casey. Some thought they did have a feud, going back to a year earlier, when Phil suggested that half the pay cut he was being offered be borne by Casey for not playing him every day. Now he insisted he'd said this in jest. Meanwhile, on this tour, Casey took advantage of the opportunity to play McDougald at short almost every day, in preparation for the time when Rizzuto would indeed walk away.

The Stengels, the Weisses, the Dickeys, the Turners, the trainer Gus

Mauch and his wife—the "grown-ups" on the tour—had a great time with the first-class treatment they received; it began with a parade before a hundred thousand fans in Tokyo. (Casey had to fight a cold for most of the trip, but it didn't dampen his spirits.)

"The games didn't mean anything and we could have just gone through the motions," said Jim Konstanty, who had started Game One of the World Series in 1950 for the Phillies but was now a Yankee. "Not with Stengel though. 'The name Yankees stands for something all over the world' he told us. 'You'll play every game as if your job depends on it. And maybe it might.'"

"I hope some day to have a Japanese player on the Yanks so your fans over here can follow him," said Casey. "It would be good for baseball, for Japan and the New York Yankees."

The Yankees even appointed a Japanese scout, Bozo Wakabayashi, as a gesture to back Casey's words.

"Casey made a terrific hit with the Japanese," said Weiss. "But that hardly was surprising. He gave it to them straight from the shoulder. He said that the Japanese should make their baseball patterns conform to getting the most out of their physical abilities. The Japanese do not run as big and heavy as our players do."

In her memoir, Edna recounted the trip, surely the trip of a lifetime:

> This trip was our first voyage since that memorable Giant–White Sox exhibition to Europe 31 years earlier, and we had more excitement than at the World Series. The Yankees were big news in Tokyo. Crowds up to 75,000 saw our games; there were parades, dinners, and so many flowers in our hotel room that we nearly hung out a florist sign. Casey received bouquets every time he stepped up to home plate. He also received gorgeous gifts of bone china, kimonos, and valuable Satsuma vases.
>
> At one dinner, he was given a large box, and when he untied the ribbon, out popped a Geisha girl.
>
> "Say Edna," he winked, when he sat down. "Don't you think I ought to bring this back to Yankee Stadium? Ball boys are getting a little outdated."
>
> That trip, incidentally, evolved into a round-the-world tour for Casey and me. From Japan, we left the team and went on to Manila, Bangkok, Hong Kong, Cairo, Jerusalem, Beirut, Rome, Munich, Vienna, Frankfurt, Paris, London, and Iceland. We

brought back so many souvenirs we laid them end to end on our dining room floor and had to pick our way across like stumbling infielders. We had tea sets from Hong Kong, Meersham [*sic*] pipes from Turkey, and a Japanese doll as big as Phil Rizzuto.

Casey was photographed in a Geisha girl's wig, sitting cross-legged on the floor, and it's probably the most celebrated gag photo of his ever taken.

AFTER THE ASIAN JOURNEY, the Stengels stopped in New York to visit with Weiss, but they made it home to Glendale for New Year's. They had been in their Glendale home all of twenty-eight days in 1955.

29

ONE LAST
SUBWAY SERIES

D ON LARSEN, WHOSE TEAMMATES called him Gooney Bird, had
been, with Turley, the key guy in the seventeen-player Orioles-
Yankees trade in 1954. He had struggled in '55 and been sent to
the minors, but Casey liked his arm and even his bat. He also liked his
lifestyle, which was not unlike his own when he was Larsen's age: hard
to corral.

So, in the spring training of 1956, when Larsen, asleep at the wheel,
wrapped his car around a telephone pole at five-thirty in the morning
(and, no, he wasn't up early), Casey did not fine him; if he had any words
for him, they were private.

Larsen, whose only injury was a lost cap on a tooth, went to Turley's
home, and Turley advised him to turn himself in. He was later booked
for suspicion of speeding and having a faulty driver's license.

This was an important moment for Larsen and for Stengel. Casey's
maturity on the job enabled him to go against the knee-jerk managerial
rule of discipline. Larsen had, after all, broken curfew and embarrassed
the team, but Casey was able to see past those infractions.

"This was a man that liked to drink beer," Casey put in his autobiography five years later. "He could go anyplace very proper, never got in
fights or disputes, but he sometimes would get mixed up on when it was
time to go home. . . . I was told that if I didn't do something desperate
to him it would kill the morale of the club. But with a group of men who
are of age and have families, I doubt that if one man does something one
night, the other twenty-four would feel they had to go out and do the
same thing. So I stuck with Mr. Larsen after telling him that it would
cost him a lot of money if he got into any more trouble, and that his job
with the club was at stake."

"I will handle it my own way," he told his writers. "Larsen came to me right away and didn't lie. It was his first trip off the reservation this spring and he has done some fine pitching in the 23 innings in which we have used him.

"McGraw probably would have handled the situation some other way, and his way probably would have worked too," reflected Stengel.

As if Larsen wasn't going to be enough to keep things merry, Mickey McDermott, renowned even among players for being on the wild side, joined the team. Casey had earlier said he wasn't interested in McDermott, but now that McDermott was a Yankee, Casey's explanation was simple: "You newspaper fellers don't understand me so good. When I say I don't want a feller, that's vice-versa, in reverse, understand?"

McDermott could hit well for a pitcher, as could Larsen, and on May 16, Casey turned in another lineup with the pitcher (McDermott) hitting eighth, and Rizzuto ninth—another embarrassing moment for Rizzuto, as he headed toward the end of his career.

It was never far from Rizzuto's memory. He used to mention it when he became a Yankees broadcaster, and not with any newly discovered love or understanding of the move. "It was just embarrassing," he told his listeners. "Just embarrassing."

IF THERE WAS A hangover from the '55 series loss, it was not noticeable when the Yankees got into action in 1956. They won seven of their first eight and were in first place wire-to-wire save for two days in the first week.

Much of the fan and press attention shifted from the team itself to Mantle, who was making a genuine run at the sacred record of sixty home runs in one season set by Babe Ruth.

With sixteen home runs by Mantle in May, and forty-seven by August 31, heads around the nation were turning, a preview of the Mantle-Maris race that would come five years later. Casey basked in the joy of seeing a relatively healthy Mantle available every day, performing great feats. He had matured; he had aged; and his competition for best in game was now Ted Williams. As late as August 14, he was hitting .376.

He was, in fact, on his way to winning the Triple Crown—fifty-two homers, 130 RBIs, and a .353 average. (He also scored 132 times.) It was the first Triple Crown since Williams did it in 1947, and only the fifth in the lively-ball era, when home runs really mattered.

It was also his first MVP season—he was a unanimous winner—after Berra had won it the two previous seasons. (Yogi was second in 1956.)

Mantle's face, with his handsome country-boy looks, was on every general-interest magazine cover in the country, and the "NY" on his cap made him a fabulous marketing tool for the club. Of course, it was in an era before the game knew how to capitalize on such marketing, but Mantle had now moved into the conversation with Ruth, Gehrig, and DiMaggio, as "the next," and people were accepting his place of honor in team history.

He hit only five homers in September when he needed thirteen to tie, so the quest was pretty much over by mid-month, but no matter. His speed, his defense, and his emerging leadership all contributed to making him the poster boy for the sport.

THE YANKS WERE IN Kansas City the weekend before Casey's sixty-sixth birthday (a Monday), and a full schedule of celebratory events was scheduled for the hometown boy who made good.

A luncheon in his honor was held at the Muehlebach, attended by former President Truman, his fellow Kansas City celebrity and contemporary. (Truman was seventy-two.) Casey's brother, Grant, was there, too. It could not have been easy being the "brother of Casey Stengel," while making a living as a cab driver.

Truman toasted Casey at the luncheon and said, "We are all most happy to celebrate Casey's birthday with him. His ninety-fourth birthday. All of us admire top-notch people, from the time we are kids, and the way I grew up, there were two things we youngsters had as ideals. One was to become an engineer, like the famous Casey Jones. The other was to become a baseball player or pitcher, in a profession which is represented so well today by Casey Stengel. In those two Caseys I think you could wrap up a lot of the dreams of kids to this day."

Casey's Central High classmates George Goldman and Harold Lederman were on hand (the actual building had been razed a few years earlier), and they presented him with a huge bell from the school, with an accompanying inscription saying "To Charles (Casey-Dutch) Stengel, dentist, athlete, manager, raconteur. For whom the bell tolls; tolled at Central High School 1906–1910 from your many Kansas City friends."

The next day, a day before his actual birthday, five cakes were presented on the field "from your Kansas City fans." (They were sliced and passed around to the thirty-thousand fans in attendance.) Addressing the crowd, Casey wiped away a tear as he talked briefly about his happy relationship with the city, and everyone sang "Happy Birthday."

When the team got to Cleveland, their next stop, Bob Fishel hired a hall (Cleveland was his own hometown) and threw the third party in three days, long after their night game had ended. This party was attended by his coaches, club officials, and the press.

Oh, and the Yankees won all three games in Kansas City and that night game in Cleveland, to run their winning streak to six and their lead in the American League to ten. It all helped put everyone in a celebratory mood. (After that final party, they managed to drop six straight, but still emerged seven games ahead after this losing streak.)

ONE DAY, MARTIN, MANTLE, Ford, McDermott, and Bauer all missed the train that was taking the team from Boston to Washington. They had to scramble to catch a plane from Logan Airport to get to D.C., since the next train would have arrived too late. "We heard the front office was going to slap fines on us," recalled Bauer. "As the oldest, I was chosen to be a committee-of-one to go up and tell Stengel our side of the story and face the music. He didn't say a thing—just looked at me, like a father, and told me to get out there and play ball."

ON AUGUST 25, WHICH happened to be Old-Timers' Day at Yankee Stadium, sentiment and business met head-on. Sentiment lost.

Phil Rizzuto, one of the most popular players ever to wear the uniform, a scrappy little New Yorker who made his way to an MVP Award and a lot of World Series rings and checks, was now nearly thirty-nine, in his thirteenth season (he had lost three to World War II service), and was barely playing. He had twelve singles and six RBIs to show for the full season, and had played in only two games in August, once as a pinch runner. He had not played shortstop since August 2.

As Phil later told the story, he was called into George Weiss's office to "discuss the roster," perhaps as a show of respect for his seniority and wisdom (a respect Casey seldom showed him). He was told that the Yankees had a chance to again pick up Enos Slaughter (who had been traded to Kansas City the year before). Despite Slaughter's being forty,

Casey liked him a lot, and there were a number of injured outfielders. He was looking to add Enos in time to have him eligible for the World Series.

Rizzuto, thinking quickly of whom he could throw under the bus, suggested a few names, and then realized what this meeting was about. It was going to be him!

Told that he would get a full World Series share but that his Yankee days were over, Rizzuto professed to be shocked. The last of the "McCarthy Yankees," he had told many that McCarthy was his favorite manager, and none of this would have extended his stay with the Yankees under Casey—that was for sure. But Rizzuto was also embarrassed. His old teammates were gathering in the clubhouse to suit up for the Old-Timers' Day festivities. Now he was one of *them*.

Of course, all he could do was disappear quietly. Feisty and outspoken when pushed, he was tempted to speak to the press about this humiliation. But his old teammate Snuffy Stirnweiss talked him out of it, and walked him to his car in the players' lot. This was the best advice he ever got, because he went home, cooled off, said nothing, and found himself offered a broadcasting job in 1957—which lasted forty happy years.

For Casey, it was a business decision, and seldom did he let any sort of sentiment interfere with those. Besides, Rizzuto was a McCarthy guy, and Casey knew it. He knew Rizzuto had never really liked Casey for his platooning ways, for batting him ninth, for suggesting that Mantle might play short the following year. Theirs was hardly a loving father-son relationship.

Casey said almost nothing, but when pressed by a critical Boston writer, Joe Phelan of the United Press, he let it out: "You're entitled to your opinion, but I'll tell you this. I needed an outfielder which when I saw the chance to get Slaughter I took it. It was his first time around on waivers and you don't think I'd have got him the second time around, do you? Also I got four outfielders hurt, Cerv, Collins, [Norm] Siebern and Noren. If anything happens to Mantle, what happens to me then? Also you got to remember [Billy] Hunter comes through pretty good at short so I don't need Rizzuto."

"Let's get back to Rizzuto," said Phelan. "Do you think it was smart to let him go on Old Timers' Day?"

"Listen," said Casey, "You got your opinions. But that was the day we had to make up our minds. Now let me tell you this. I'm just glad that

Mr. Rizzuto has saved his money and also he's getting paid for the whole season. I wouldn't be surprised—it's up to the boys—but they're a pretty fair gang—they might not forget him in the Series divvy-up. Also Mr. Rizzuto has some offers to go on the radio and television and maybe [he pointed at Phelan] you could recommend him to Mr. Yawkey and he'd hire him as manager of his ball club."

Casey was over it by the time the Old Timers' Dinner came around that night at Toots Shor's. After regaling the gathering, he turned serious and decided to say some things about so many old-time players' having no pension. (The pension plan had only come to be in 1946 and did not include those who had played before, like him.) "You old timers have no spokesman. But I know what is in your hearts and I am saying it for you tonight. I do not benefit from the pension fund because I am the manager. So I am a disinterested witness, and I ask the players of 1956 to make some provision for the players of long ago."

The remarks were warmly received, of course, but not by most active players. One who refuted Casey almost at once was Bob Feller, playing in his final season but very active on the player pension committee. "Casey was just popping off in front of the old timers trying to make a big guy out of himself," said Feller. "He wasn't sincere in his remarks. If he is sincere why doesn't he turn over his World Series money or the profit from one of his oil wells, or hotel or investments to the old-timers."

THE YANKEES CLINCHED THE pennant while in Cleveland on September 16, with nearly two weeks to go to get their rotation in order. Ford was the ace of the staff with a 19-6 record, but Casey had also brought along Larsen (11-5), Kucks (18-9), and Sturdivant (16-8). Though Turley hadn't won a game in September, he was an available fifth starter.

Larsen had gone 4-0 since Labor Day, since experimenting with a no-windup delivery, as suggested by Turner. Casey liked what he had seen in the big guy, though the no-windup delivery was nothing new under the sun in the baseball mind of Charles Dillon Stengel. "I see that stuff early in my career," he said, "which ain't going as far back as Hoss Radbourne, but is long enough."

The World Series opened in Brooklyn on October 3, 1956, with President Eisenhower, who also happened to be running for re-election, throwing out the first pitch. Attention was equally divided between Mantle, coming off his historic season, and the defending champion Dodgers, matched for the seventh time in fifteen years against the Yanks.

The Dodgers won their first two at home, enjoying a six-run second inning in Game Two after trailing 6–0; they knocked around Larsen, Kucks, and Byrne, and then further pounded Sturdivant and Morgan, to emerge 13–8 winners. The three-hour-and-twenty-six-minute game left Casey's pitching staff in shambles. He was going to go with Ford in Game Three, at Yankee Stadium, even though his ace had had just two days' rest. And he read the team the riot act before the game, and they responded. Whitey hurled a complete game 5–3 victory, aided by a Billy Martin home run. Sturdivant followed with a complete-game win of 6–2 in Game Four, to even the Series at two wins each.

On the eve of Game Five, Larsen did what Larsen does: he was out drinking and making the rounds of Manhattan with his pal Arthur Richman of the *New York Mirror*. Larsen's season had begun with his auto wrapped around a pole in St. Petersburg. Game Five would be his final start of the year, and on the big stage.

"Don't be surprised if I pitch a no-hitter tomorrow," he told Richman—he might have said "today" if the hour was past midnight when he said it, but Richman insisted they were in by midnight, and were using taxis.

And so Larsen took the mound before 64,519 fans, including sixteen-year-old Joe Torre, a Brooklyn high school kid who managed to score tickets to the game. Larsen's mound opponent, Sal Maglie, had himself pitched a no-hitter just thirteen days earlier.

The first run did not score until the fourth, when Mantle homered near the foul pole in right—the first hit off Maglie. Fans who look for such things were probably noticing that Larsen hadn't given up a hit, either.

In the fifth, Mantle ran down a long drive by Hodges to left-center to keep Larsen's no-hitter alive, and in the sixth, Bauer drove home Carey with the Yankees' second run.

Now came the final third of the game, and the drama was intense. No Dodger had reached base through six, and the concept of a "perfect game" began to be considered. There had never been a no-hitter thrown in a World Series game, and there had not been a perfect game—no base runners—since 1922, when a White Sox pitcher named Charlie Robertson threw one against Detroit. Few remembered Charlie Robertson, except, of course, Casey, who had batted against him while with Toledo in 1929–30. If you wanted to know about Charlie Robertson—or almost anybody in baseball history—Casey was the man to see.

Larsen got Gilliam, Reese, and Snider in the seventh, then Robinson, Hodges, and Amoros in the eighth. When he came to bat himself in the last of the eighth, the crowd rewarded him with a tremendous ovation—Dodger fans and Yankee fans alike. They knew they were seeing history.

In the top of the ninth, Furillo flied to right on a 1–2 pitch. Campanella grounded out to Martin at second. That brought up a pinch hitter, Dale Mitchell, batting for Maglie. The Yankees knew him well—he had been a longtime Cleveland Indian—but the scouting report was long done; Berra saw no need to go to the mound to discuss him with Larsen.

On the fifth pitch to Mitchell, Larsen's ninety-seventh of the game, the umpire Babe Pinelli called it strike three, and history was served. (Yes, Casey had played against Pinelli in the 1920s, when Babe was an infielder with Cincinnati.)

Someone foolishly asked Larsen in the post-game questions whether it was the best game he had ever pitched. It was certainly the best game Casey Stengel had ever seen, and probably the easiest. After he wrote out the lineups he had no decisions left to make.

The Series returned to Ebbets Field the next day, and the Dodgers beat Turley in ten innings, to send it to a Game Seven.

Who would pitch? For the Dodgers, their ace, Don Newcombe, had had four days off, and although Berra had previously seemed to kill him in their World Series matchups, Walt Alston had no problem naming him to start. For the Yankees, Casey had Ford with three days' rest, but Turley, Larsen, and Sturdivant were not rested enough. So he would have to look at his Game Two bullpen guys—Kucks, Byrne, McDermott, and Morgan—to come up with his answer. He was very down on the well-touted McDermott, who drove him crazy with his erratic behavior and had won only two games for him. Del Webb, the co-owner, later said that it was Yogi who kept pestering Casey to go with Kucks: "He'll make 'em hit in the dirt and they won't get those pop-fly home runs."

The game ball was resting in Kucks's shoe when he got to the Yankee clubhouse. The Yankees knocked out Newcombe by the fourth (two home runs by Berra, and one by Howard), and went on to pile up nine runs, while Kucks came through with the win of his life, a three-hit shutout.

Another world championship for the Yankees, number six for Stengel, and the cloud of the '55 series was lifted.

A year after their loss, the Dodgers would announce their move to Los Angeles. This would turn out to be the last Subway Series played in New York until the Yankees played the Mets in 2000.

THE YANKEES HELD THEIR World Series party at the Starlight Roof of the Waldorf Astoria, where Casey and Edna danced to "The Band Played On" ("Casey would waltz with a strawberry blonde . . ."); this had become somewhat of a customary moment for them, the lyrics taken from a pop song written in 1895. Frankie Laine led a bunch of players—Mantle, Martin, Ford, McDermott, Berra, Bauer, Collins, and Silvera—in song.

Reflecting on his latest triumph, Casey said, "This is the best victory. . . . It showed the class we had after a terrible start [losing the first two games] and we got in and grabbed the ball and went the limit and I'll never forget it."

Casey signed his latest two-year contract, at the same seventy-five thousand dollars a year, two days after the Series ended. Casey and Edna returned to Glendale (no round-the-world trip this winter!), where Casey was fêted at the Verdugo Club on November 12; then they settled into a rare relaxing off-season.

He was named Manager of the Year for the fifth time (if you count the various electing bodies—*The Sporting News,* AP, UPI), and told Bob Myers of AP, "Well, I'd have to say on this award of the year that naturally the first thing you'd have to say, that is, you should be thankful for the award of that kind and you should be thankful it was not given by one man but by a number of men that are authorities on baseball because they have followed the sport so many years and because it's a voting proposition in which the majority share and therefore that's why you get the selection and feel honored because you have received the selection from the men who voted you the award, which is the writers, the sports writers."

This was Casey taking care of business—taking care to thank the writers—the men who had helped make him one of the most famous people in the land.

He then went on to his "second thing," which was thanking ownership and the scouts who found the players who made the team good. It was good politics to thank his bosses and to acknowledge others, like the scouts.

The third item on his list was thanking the players and the coaches, and he left room for a fourth item—"You got to be satisfied with yourself that you're doing a good job with the talent entrusted to you."

Ego was not one of his problems.

30

TRADING BILLY MARTIN

BILL DICKEY, A COACH under Casey since 1949, experienced headaches and dizziness during spring training of 1957, and needed to return home to Little Rock. It was said he was suffering from nervous exhaustion. A valuable member of Casey's unchanged coaching staff, dating back to his first season, was gone. Dickey's coaching place was first taken by the scout Randy Gumpert, but then Charlie Keller came out of retirement to fill the spot.

Meanwhile, the Yankees pulled off a trade with the Kansas City Athletics just before the 1957 training camp opened, obtaining the pitchers Art Ditmar and Bobby Shantz for Noren, McDermott, Morgan, and three others. The trade wasn't complete yet. On June 4, Clete Boyer came over to the Yankee organization as a finishing touch. (He reached the majors in 1959.) This would come to be seen as quite one-sided, as Yankee-Athletic trades often were.

Shantz was a player Casey had long coveted. Though he was just a five-foot-six left-hander, he had tremendous athleticism. Casey said, "I wouldn't mind playing him at shortstop, even if he throws left-handed." His teammates marveled at how good he was at everything, even Ping-Pong.

He had gone 24-7 for the second-division Philadelphia Athletics in 1952, winning the MVP Award, and Casey always went out of his way to praise him.

Shantz said:

I called him Mr. Stengel because I had been pitching for Connie Mack, who we always called Mr. Mack. Of course they were nothing alike; Mr. Mack hardly said anything, and Casey was always talking. When I got to that first training camp in '57, he said to me, "You little shit, the only reason we got you was 'cause you beat us so much," and he laughed. But that was about the only conversation we ever really had.

Every once in a while, he'd fall asleep. Of course, he had such great coaches in Crosetti, Turner and later Houk, that any of them could have managed. So it was okay if he'd nod off now and then. The one I remember most is he nodded off on Turley's shoulder. But we needed a pinch-hitter. Crosetti came running in from third, in front of Ed Hurley, the home umpire, almost to the dugout, yelling, "Casey, we need a hitter!" Casey jumped to attention and said, "Elston, go hit." But Elston had his catching gear on; and he said, "I'm already in the game, Casey!"

His clubhouse meetings could be funny; you could hear some guys snicker behind his back. He'd start off talking about the signs, and then suddenly he's talking about Ditmar's pickoff move.

Mantle wasn't happy about my coming to the Yankees. Because he hit me pretty good. But I had a good season for them; Casey picked me for the All-Star team, and I led the league in ERA. I had to fight and claw for a raise though—Weiss told me my raise was my World Series share. But eventually I got a $1500 raise.

Batting helmets, or at least liners inside the caps, were becoming more popular by 1957, and even though Casey was old-school on the matter, he thought he'd like to see Mantle wear one. But Mantle shook his head and said, "I don't like it."

"How do you know," said Casey. "You ain't wore one yet."

"Yes I have, I tried it a couple of times."

"You know when the season starts them pitchers will be plugging at you every once in a while, don't you? Do you want to get hurt?"

"No."

"Then wear a head guard."

"I can't get over him," said Casey. "He knows the pitchers will throw at him, and he won't wear a head guard because he don't like it. He says he tried a helmet a couple of times, but if he did, I didn't see him."

The Yankees did not get off to their usual quick start in 1957, and by early June were six games out. Still, there were some memorable moments in May.

On May 7, McDougald hit a line drive in Cleveland that got the Indians' young star pitcher, Herb Score, right in the eye, effectively ending a career that showed the promise of being superlative. With some irony, McDougald himself had been hit by a batting-practice line drive two years earlier, causing an injury that some felt led to his losing his hearing some years later. The liner at Score was one of the worst things Casey Stengel ever witnessed on a baseball field, though. The game was not televised, and no video exists, but for those in baseball or following baseball in 1957, it was a horrible memory.

Four days later, with the team having dropped out of first place (they were out of first from May 10 to June 22), Casey convened a team meeting in a conference room at the Hotel Emerson in Baltimore. "I told them I wanted to find out what was the matter with such a group of fine ball players. We are not helping ourselves. I told them, 'That's not the way this club is supposed to play and not the way it has played in the past.'"

The Yankees returned home from Baltimore for games with Kansas City on May 15 and 16, and won both by 3–0 shutouts. After the game on the fifteenth, Mantle, Bauer, Berra, Ford, and Kucks, with their wives, went out for a night on the town, to celebrate Martin's twenty-ninth birthday, which was on the sixteenth. They were joined by ex-Yankees Noren and Cerv, who were now with the Athletics. After dinner at Danny's Hideaway, the group proceeded to the Waldorf to catch the singer Johnny Ray. Noren and Cerv then departed, and the group of eleven—Billy Martin was solo—proceeded to the famous Copacabana nightclub on East Sixtieth Street to see Sammy Davis, Jr., perform. There was no game until the following night, the midnight curfew was ignored, and, needless to say, the drinks were flowing at all three stops.

A group of bowlers was also at the Copa, and one of them was heckling Sammy Davis.

"One thing about Yogi," said his wife, Carmen. "He never stood for hecklers. He wanted respect shown for entertainers."

Words were exchanged. Cooler heads did not prevail. Someone—probably Bauer—seemed to have slugged one of the hecklers in the men's room, but denials were abundant. The *New York Post* society columnist Leonard Lyons, one of a number of newspapermen in the room, hustled the Yankee party out of the restaurant. But this was too public an event not to make the newspapers.

This is what Dan Topping and George Weiss were reading at their desks on Fifth Avenue the next day. It didn't please them at all. Bauer was soon charged with felonious assault and released without bail.

Topping was furious, and Weiss picked up on his reaction at once. They were convinced that Martin was the troublemaker, and that he was continuing to be a bad influence on Mantle. They had discussed this often, and now they were convinced that Martin had to go.

They both knew that bringing Casey into this conversation would do them no good. Casey was loyal to Martin, was not unduly troubled by such an event, and was not likely to mete out punishment for what, one could argue, was a decent act by the Yankee players, defending Sammy Davis, Jr.

Given Casey's feelings about Martin and his possible indifference to the Copa event, he was not going to be a party to the trade talks that ensued. (He would later claim to have halted one that would have sent Martin to Washington.)

The story grew when it was revealed by an anonymous source on June 3 that the players had each been fined a thousand dollars by the Yankees, except Kucks, who earned much less and was therefore fined only five hundred. Casey in particular did not want the fines revealed, lest this influence Bauer's impending case.

These fines were described as "stunning," and were the first known to be imposed on Yankee players since Babe Ruth was hit with one for five thousand dollars by Miller Huggins in 1925. Make no mistake, a thousand dollars was a lot of money in 1957, when every thousand was hard fought for at salary negotiation time.

Because the leak of the fines further angered Topping and Weiss, Martin came forward to announce that it was he who had leaked the story, telling Til Ferdenzi of the *Journal-American,* "Take those five other guys off the hook. Put in your story I was the guy. Now that it's happened, I want the air cleared."

The clock was ticking toward the June 15 trading deadline. "I hope it doesn't happen to me, but if it does, it just does," said Martin to Ferdenzi. "It's happened before and it will happen again. I'm afraid to think how it would feel to play against the Yankees."

Billy was playing less, and twenty-one-year-old Bobby Richardson was playing more. That was the future. Weiss knew it; even Martin knew it.

On June 13, the Yankees engaged in a mêlée at Comiskey Park when Art Ditmar knocked down the White Sox slugger Larry Doby with a close pitch. The benches cleared, punches were thrown (Slaughter had his jersey ripped off), and, just when the fight seemed over, Martin yelled something more at Doby and the fisticuffs resumed. Chicago police walked Martin off the field. There were a lot of fines rendered by the league office—Martin was fined $150—and when Topping, seemingly defending his players, said he would pay all the fines. the league president, Will Harridge, threatened to fine him five thousand dollars if he did. "It seems odd," wrote Dan Daniel in the *World-Telegram*, "that Stengel, most intimately concerned in this matter of player relations, wasn't the one to handle the matter."

Daniel was correct. Casey clearly wanted no part of this.

Martin played on June 14, but wasn't in Stengel's lineup on the fifteenth, a game in Kansas City. Richardson was. Billy went to the bullpen, where, on occasion, position players would hang out during games. In the seventh inning, he got a message to see Casey in the Yankee clubhouse.

"You're gone," greeted Stengel. Just like that.

There was an emotional reason, it appeared, for the harshness of the pronouncement: Billy *was* like a son, and this was hard to do. But Stengel did not shirk from the responsibility of his job and delegate it to someone else. (Owning the good and the bad is a heavy burden, as Martin would learn. Years later, when he himself was managing, he asked his traveling secretary and public-relations man to tell the veteran infielder Ed Brinkman that he was being released.)

Casey explained that there had been a trade; Martin was moving over to the Athletics' side of the field, and the owner of the A's, Arnold Johnson, was coming to the visitors' clubhouse in a few moments. Casey said, "I'm going to tell him what a great person and player you are," but Billy cut him off with anger: "Don't you say shit; when I needed you to protect me, you let me down. So don't say shit."

When Johnson arrived, Billy shushed Casey again and said, "Mr. Johnson, don't listen to him. I'll play my best for you. That's what you want, right?"

The deal was done. Billy was in the lineup the next day, against the Yankees, playing second and batting second. He hit a home run in a 2-for-5 game—sharing the lineup, ironically, with almost all former and future Yankees.

Putting on an Athletics uniform had to hurt. No one had worn the Yankees uniform more proudly than Billy; it was like a fraternity jacket to him. An eighteen-year exile was beginning for him, and his sadness, bitterness, melancholy, resentment, and hurt never really faded. His career as a journeyman infielder—playing for six teams, none more than a year, and never to see the World Series again—had begun.

And, oh yes, there was the matter of World Series money. Though the Yankees repaid him for his thousand-dollar fine, gone was the prospect of a nice seven-thousand-dollar series share each fall, which seemed nearly automatic for the Yankees. Add that to the hurt-and-resentment column.

There were attempts by both Casey and Billy to be cordial over the years, but it was never the same. "I have nothing to say to Stengel," said Martin the following January. "The last time I spoke to him was the day I was traded. And he said 'See you later.'"

Casey, too, may have been hurt—hurt that Weiss had cut him out of the trade discussions, and created at least the appearance of the dimming of his power; it looked as if he had been told that he must now play Richardson.

Sitting in a position of weakness on the subject after being cut out of the trade talks, Casey said little more to the press than: "Arnold Johnson made some demands and he wouldn't budge. He wanted Martin, he wanted a right-handed pitcher, he wanted Woodie Held. And he got 'em. We gave up a lot to get [Harry] Simpson and I hope he helps us."

Of course, the Yankees held tremendous power over the Athletics and Arnold Johnson, and the trade did not have to turn out that way if they didn't want it. Writers always talked about the Athletics being a "farm team" for the Yankees (as the Kansas City Blues had been), but the connections went deep. Johnson did real-estate and concession business with Topping and Webb. He hired Bill MacPhail, Lee's brother (Lee was the Yankees' farm director), as PR director. He hired Parke Carroll, who had been business manager for the Yankees' minor-league clubs in Newark and Kansas City, as his general manager. The Del Webb Construction Company built Municipal Stadium, where the A's played. In other words, the Yankees and Athletics did have a "special relationship," and by no means did Arnold Johnson drive a hard bargain. Calls probably began with "What can we do for you?"

Twelve years after the Martin trade, and now retired, Casey noted that Martin had been named manager of the Minnesota Twins. When Casey saw Arthur Daley of the *Times,* he made a point of saying to him, "When you see that fresh little kid, tell him I wanna wish him the best of luck."

The Martin trade was not like other transactions, and Casey would preside over many of them in his thirty-one years as a manager. It hurt.

Not only did it compromise his easy relationship with Weiss and the chemistry of the clubhouse, where Martin was the most popular player, but there was something emotional about this one that he might not have liked to face. But he also knew that, in the end, he had bosses, and it was pointless to fight them. He lost this one, and it was time to move on.

In his 1962 autobiography, Casey said:

Now here's the situation with Martin. He was a young man that came out of a neighborhood, which we have in every city, which they try to watch. He'd had a stepfather. Martin was a small man. He thought he could whip anybody. And when anybody tells you Martin can't fight, that's a big joke. Martin can fight good.

He gave me a lot of spirit and everything else. Sometimes you have to have a noisy man on the team. You can have too many quiet players, and you need a man to jack it up. Martin could yell and yell at the other side, and he was a game player. And Martin is a skilled player. He knows all the plays, knows what's coming up, and he can catch the signs.

There was one thing that no doubt got him in a little bad with our ball club. He could not see the ideas of some of the men that were up in the front office. He was a man that was better for the players or better for the manager—if you could handle him, I could handle Billy Martin.

Did I approve of trading him? Well, the office had been after me three or four times to try to get rid of him. But I gave in only when they arranged to get me a left-handed hitter, Harry Simpson, who I thought would help us in Yankee Stadium. . . . As it worked out, Simpson didn't help us much. Anyway. I will have to say that there were very rare occasions on that ball club that they could slip around and get rid of a player if I didn't approve of the deal.

Nearly two years after the trade, when he was then playing for Cleveland, Billy was still bitter. "I needed Casey only one time in my life and he let me down. Whatever he said, I do not believe he ever tried to fight the deal. I am not speaking to Casey Stengel and I don't think I will."

—

BILLY MAY HAVE BEEN the son he never had, but many of the children of "my writers" carried wonderful recollections of Casey into their adult years.

"He loved the kids," recalled Liz Goldberg, whose father, Hy, wrote for *The Newark Evening News*. "Every Easter, in spring training, he would bring huge chocolate bunnies to the Soreno. And I remember his playfully mouthing words without sound so that John Drebinger of the *Times* would start fumbling with his hearing aid, thinking something was wrong with it."

Her brother Hank, later an ESPN broadcaster, remembered walking to the ballpark with Casey when he was about ten.

He had a funny gait, an odd walk. But he attracted kids like the Pied Piper.

He had a lot of good-natured teasing in him. He'd wink a lot, and he always seemed to be entertaining people in the lobby. He'd tell stories about McGraw and Wheat and Robinson and Babe Herman, and even strangers' kids would gather and join in. Didn't matter.

He told me I should grow up to be a banker. And he had great nicknames for his players. Tommy Byrne, who didn't fly, was his "train man."

When he learned my mother was from Worcester, where he managed in 1925, he immediately started naming all the store-keepers in town.

And one day when Bill Veeck was visiting, he did a trick where he let smoke blow through a hole in Veeck's wooden leg. Crazy times.

Michael Gross, the son of Milton Gross of the *Post,* remembered that he had lost his luggage on a flight to St. Petersburg, and Casey got it retrieved from South America. "It probably wasn't Casey, it was probably the traveling secretary, but Casey took the credit—he wanted to be the hero," said Gross. "He was slightly cartoonish, I thought. He told me, 'One day you'll grow up to be a [Bob] Cousy' because I was small."

Of course, it wasn't only children that he was good with; it was not unusual for him to leave as many as thirty tickets for friends at road games. In every town he had his connections, and there were always former players dropping by to see him.

—

THE DEPARTURE OF MARTIN opened the door for Bobby Richardson at second, although it would take him a couple of years to become an everyday player. Tony Kubek and Richardson had come up together after playing for Ralph Houk at Denver. Richardson and Kubek would go on to World Series triumphs, their names forever linked in Yankee history. Kubek made his mark right away, winning the American League Rookie of the Year Award in 1957. Richardson did not become a regular until 1959.

Kubek, shy and soft-spoken, had played right field in Denver, and was more of an outfielder than a shortstop when he arrived. His father, also named Tony, had played for his hometown Milwaukee Brewers in the American Association in 1931, the year Casey managed Toledo for the last time. The senior Kubek hit .357 in 101 games, so Casey would certainly have been aware of him.

Twenty-two years later, Kubek, Jr., signed with the Yankees (his father actually had to sign, because Tony was only seventeen), and Tony was hitting off Bob Grim during batting practice in St. Petersburg.

Suddenly I hear, *"Ku-bek!"* and it was Casey. I walked over, and he said, "I saw your dad play. He was a great runner, a good hitter, but they tried to make him a pull hitter, which he wasn't."

In an exhibition game in New Orleans in 1956, I made a really good catch in right field off Wally Post of the Reds. Casey told me he would take me north for the Yankees exhibition game against the Dodgers in Ebbets Field before the season started, and he did, even though I only sat in the bullpen.

By 1957, we were loaded with shortstops, and one day Casey yelled to [clubhouse man] Pete Sheehy to assemble all the shortstops for a group photo. There we were, Billy Hunter, Fritz Brickell, Woodie Held, Martin, McDougald, Coleman, me, it was crazy. I really wasn't thinking of myself as a shortstop yet, but there I was.

Casey had an answer for everything. We had this pitcher with us one spring, Mark Freeman, a very smart man. But in this exhibition game, he balked in the winning run. So Casey went to him about it, and Freeman says a bug flew in his eye.

"Son," said Casey, "you gotta learn to catch those bugs in your mouth."

Like Kubek, Richardson was a nondrinker, and the antithesis of Martin in terms of behavior. Nevertheless, George Weiss had them followed by a detective to make sure they were clean-living, as advertised. (Perhaps he couldn't believe it.)

"It was me and Bobby, along with Bobby Shantz and Enos Slaughter," recalled Kubek of the night in question. "It was actually like a movie scene: a guy in a hat and trench coat, smoking a cigarette, holding a newspaper, standing under a streetlight. We spotted him from the hotel. All we were doing was going to the Y to play Ping-Pong."

"I wasn't even sure that Casey knew my name," recalls Richardson.

He always called me "Kid," or "Rock." Of course my name was on the lineup card, but maybe Crosetti wrote it out.

I was just always so uncertain about whether I was playing. He used to play me at short when I first came up, filling in for Rizzuto in the late innings. The only game my father ever saw me play, I was at third. And he liked his infielders to be holler guys, like Billy was. He used to say, "Richardson doesn't say anything," which was true.

The day after the Martin trade, Billy rode the bus with us from the ballpark, and he sat with me on the bus. He said something like, "It's all yours now," and he did his best to boost my confidence. Of course, it was an awkward trip for both of us. Eventually they gave me Billy's number one to wear, and after the Yankees retired his number, he made a point of telling me to never hesitate to wear it at Old Timers Day or anywhere. Billy and I were different, but he was good to me. Casey may not have loved the transition, but eventually he picked me for the All-Star team [1959] and I hit .301 that year. So it worked out.

The Yankees clinched the 1957 pennant on September 23 when Kansas City (without Martin in the lineup), beat Chicago. The Yankee brass followed the game from Topping's private dining room at Yankee Stadium after watching a Carmen Basilio–Sugar Ray Robinson fight on the infield. The following night, the "official" pennant-clinching party was held in the Stadium Club. It was an awkward occasion: the ghost of Martin was still in the room, for he had usually been a center of attention at the pennant-clinching parties. But Yankee life went on.

And so they would play Milwaukee for the World Series. This was a homecoming of sorts for Casey, who had managed the minor-league club there thirteen years earlier.

Except for two games in Philadelphia in 1950, this was the Yankees' first World Series foray outside the New York area since Casey arrived. Six times they had played either the Dodgers or the Giants.

After splitting the first two games in New York, they were off to Kubek's hometown of Milwaukee for the first World Series games in the city's history. They had inherited the Braves from Boston in 1953, a reminder that the Boston Braves was yet another team Casey had managed.

Bad feelings were in the air as the Yankees came to town.

The team arrived in the town of Sturdevant, twenty miles southwest of Milwaukee. The Yankees were going to stay at a hotel in Burlington, and Sturdevant was the nearest train stop. Two thousand baseball fans and celebrity gawkers packed the train station, some with banners saying "Welcome Yanks." A high school band played, a Little League team was there, and the town's volunteer fire department stood guard. But the Yankees didn't get off the train. "Only wives and officials getting off here," said someone from the Yankees, perhaps Bob Fishel or the traveling secretary, Bill McCorry. "The players are going on to Milwaukee."

One man, with a Kiwanis Club pin, shouted, "C'mon, send out a couple of players." Seeing no activity, the same man yelled, "I hope you lose—and you're going to!"

Whitey Ford stepped out to greet the Little Leaguers and pose for some pictures. But the real hero was Edna Stengel. Dressed in heels, a striped suit, and a fur cape, she answered a call to milk a cow. More precisely, she sat on a milking stool and went through the motions, but declared, "Someone milked this cow before I did," and turned over an empty bucket.

Someone in the Yankee party was heard to say, "This is really bush league." That someone was generally thought to be the trainer Gus Mauch. The story got out that the Yankees had called the people of Wisconsin "bushers."

Managers are always quick to jump on some perceived slight to inspire their team, and the Braves' manager, Fred Haney, an old friend of Casey's, made sure all of his players heard about this insult. The fans of

Milwaukee, gentle and polite people as a rule, were outraged. And a lot of them let the Yankee players have it on the field of County Stadium the next day. However, as though to show the cordiality that existed on high, Casey, who didn't like what he considered a radio interviewer's unfair question about Haney's tactics, said, "Young man, you're talking about one of my friends and a damn good manager. Our interview is ended."

UPON ARRIVAL AT MILWAUKEE County Stadium, Casey was mobbed by about a hundred screaming fans, some looking for autographs, but some yelling, "You're a busher!"

One woman, clearly hoping to see some fine young players, yelled out, "It's just an old man."

The Yankees won Game Three, in which Kubek hit two home runs before his hometown fans, but then Spahn beat them the following day, to even the series at 2–2. In Game Five, the final one in Milwaukee, Lew Burdette won a 1–0 duel against Ford to give the Braves a 3–2 edge.

It was Burdette's second win of the series (he had won Game Two), and though few remembered that he had once been Yankee property, it was sweet revenge for him. He had actually pitched two games for New York in 1950 before being traded to the Braves with fifty thousand dollars for Johnny Sain. But he remembered being referred to as "hey you" by Casey in 1950. Now, although he ranked behind Spahn in the rotation, he had gone 17-9 in the regular season, his seventh with the club.

Turley went the distance to win Game Six at Yankee Stadium, and Haney, faced with Spahn having the flu, turned to Burdette again in Game Seven, trusting the right-hander (who some believed threw a spitball), to go on only two days' rest. Stengel went with Larsen.

And the Braves emerged as world champions. Burdette won 5–0, a second straight shutout, becoming the first three-game winner in a World Series since Harry Brecheen of the Cardinals did it in 1946. It gave him an ERA of 0.67 and three complete games in the series.

When the Braves went home to Milwaukee, the city closed schools, held a parade, and celebrated long and loud. The Yankees, humbled, had lost a World Series for the second time in three years and did not feel very good about it.

Asked by a reporter if his Yankees had choked, Casey cursed in his answer, so it couldn't be used on radio. "We're going to have Burditis on our minds next season," said Casey in a more thoughtful moment, churning Burdette's name into an illness.

BACK IN AUGUST, AN announcement had been made about the opening of the Valley National Bank, with Edna's brother, John (who completed his one term as mayor of Glendale in April), to serve as chairman of the board. The bank opened in November; near its front door was a carved, painted figure of Casey in his Yankee uniform, with his hands in his back pockets. He was an investor, and also served as a nonsalaried director. "My job," he told people, "is to stand in front of the vault"; he also signed photos of himself for new customers. Edna was not among those named as directors, but Casey got Al Lopez, Randy Moore, Babe Herman, and his boss Del Webb in as investors.

Casey did attend board meetings (for each of which he received twenty-five dollars), and when spotted arriving at one, said, "This will be the most overdressed and underpaid appearance in my career."

FRANK GRAHAM WAS A well-liked sports writer who covered the Yankees and wrote books about them for many years. His son, Frank Graham, Jr., became a public-relations official with the Brooklyn Dodgers, but left them in 1955 to become a sportswriter at *Sport* magazine. In 1957, Frank Jr. told Casey he was going to be writing a biography of him, and asked if he could spend some time with him for interviews and background.

Not only was Casey unhappy with this, he said no, and broke off his friendship with Graham Sr. It took a dinner arranged by George and Hazel Weiss to repair that.

Meanwhile, Frank Jr. continued on his project. Casey had been included in such books as *The Magnificent Yankees* by Tom Meany, in which a chapter was devoted to him, but there had not yet been a full-blown biography.

Graham Jr. continued on without Casey's cooperation. He came to believe that Casey was going to do an autobiography someday, and did not want something like this in the marketplace before he got there. What was not known was that Edna was doing a biography on her own, a memoir of their lives together; Casey wanted to protect her work as well.

The John Day Company published Graham Jr.'s book, *Casey Stengel: His Half-Century in Baseball,* in 1958. Hard to believe that this was the first Stengel biography, given his colorful life in baseball, but it was.

Edna's memoir was never published; she felt that the offers she received were not substantial enough. And Casey's autobiography didn't come out until 1962, a year and a half after he left the Yankees.

31

DAZZLING CONGRESS

THE 1958 YANKEES, CASEY'S tenth Yankee team, ran away from the pack; by August 2, they had built up a ridiculous seventeen-game lead. They started out 25-6 and didn't lose their tenth game until May 30. The season was very uncompetitive for them, even though the Yankees won only 92 games to wind up ten ahead of Chicago. They led the league in both ERA and runs scored, and Bob Turley wound up as the Cy Young Award winner, with a spectacular 21-7 season.

"This Turley guy is amazing," said Casey. "You sit near him on the bench and you hear the most remarkable flow of observations not only on pitching, but on batting, as well. I call him the Philosopher of the Bench, the Scientist of the Dugout." Turley and the other Yankee pitchers were told to sit at the far end of the dugout during the other team's batting practice, to see what could be learned. Like Larsen, Turley worked with no windup.

Ford went 14-7, but no one else on the staff won ten games. A lot of attention was paid to the hard-throwing, bespectacled Ryne Duren, who became the league's relief star, and whose "Coke bottle" eyeglasses caused hitters great consternation. He was the first big-time reliever the Yankees had had since Joe Page, unless you counted Allie Reynolds's occasional relief appearances. Duren went 6-4 with a 2.02 ERA, striking out eighty-seven batters in seventy-five and two-thirds innings, while recording nineteen saves.

"The ball makes a strange sound, like a small jet," marveled Stengel, "as it travels toward the catcher and lodges, *kerplunk,* in Yogi's mitt. Duren is a splendid product of the Atomic Age."

Still, there were moments of discontent despite all the winning. Bobby Richardson would remember:

One day Casey pinch-hit for me in the first inning. I was mad, and as I walked back into the dugout, I muttered, "If you're going to pinch-hit for me in the first inning, why bother to put me in the lineup at all?" I said it just loud enough for him to hear me, and he followed me into the clubhouse even while the game was going on.

"Young man," he said, "go get your little glove and warm up Duren in the bullpen today."

I was being punished, like a schoolboy. And saying "little glove" was intended to be demeaning; a reflection on my height.

He could be a tough man to play for.

WITH THE DODGERS AND Giants having left New York for California after the 1957 season, and with rumors swirling that the Washington Senators were taking a serious look at Minneapolis as a new home, congressional legislators who followed baseball's antitrust exemption were starting to take another hard look at the major leagues and how the organization operated. The Senate Judiciary Committee's Subcommittee on Anti-Trust and Monopoly, headed by Tennessee senator Estes Kefauver (who had run for vice president on the Adlai Stevenson ticket in 1956), convened a session for Wednesday, July 9. It was the morning after the All-Star Game in Baltimore (won by Casey's American Leaguers, 4–3), which made it possible for a number of witnesses to testify and still get back for their games that night.

Casey was to be the star witness, although Mantle, Ted Williams, Stan Musial, and the league player representatives Robin Roberts and Eddie Yost were also to testify. Casey, with his commanding, gravelly voice, stole the show.

Jack Walsh, writing in *The Sporting News,* said, "Casey Stengel proved one of the most entertaining witnesses ever to appear on Capitol Hill. Never cracking a smile himself, Stengel continually created guffaws among the Senators and the standing-room-only crowd in the Senate caucus room."

Casey was the first witness called. Wearing a light-colored suit and what he called his "magic glasses" (which he was now wearing in the dugout), he began with a little autobiography: "Well, I started in professional baseball in 1910. I have been in professional ball, I would say, for forty-eight years. I have been employed by numerous ball clubs in the majors and in the minor leagues. . . . I had many years I was not so successful as a ballplayer, as it is a game of skill. And then I was no doubt discharged by baseball in which I had to go back to the minor leagues as a manager, and after being in the minor leagues as a manager, I became a major league manager in several cities and was discharged, we call it discharged because there was no question I had to leave."

Laughter rose from the room, and from the senators on the committee. The tour de force was under way.

At one point, Kefauver halted the testimony in exasperation and said, "I am not sure that I made my question clear."

"Well, that is all right," Casey replied. "I am not sure if I am going to answer yours perfectly, either."

He went on for about an hour.* Other members of the committee could barely wait for their turns. By employing Stengelese in the halls of Congress, Casey was turning a complicated but serious issue into one best left undiscussed.

The testimony was filmed, shown on the network newscasts that evening, and over and over in movie theater newsreels. If Casey Stengel wasn't the most famous person in baseball before July 9, 1958, he was now.

Included in the reporting was a brilliant comment by Mantle, who followed Casey on the stand: "My views are about the same as Casey's," he said. To this Kefauver replied, "If you could define what these views were, it would be a service to this committee."

He couldn't.

"We want what the club owners want," said Roberts when it was his turn to testify, pretty much summarizing most players' views on the Reserve Clause, which bound players to their teams in perpetuity. Ironically, eight years later, Roberts was involved in the search for a head of the players' union, which resulted in the hiring of Marvin Miller, whose work led to the end of the Reserve Clause a decade later. But at the time, most players agreed with management that the Reserve Clause was good for the game.

After his testimony, Casey headed back to New York for the team's eight o'clock game. All in a day's work.

THE SEASON PROGRESSED WITH what some felt was a lack of discipline—such as when Mantle and Ford missed a train to Detroit and

---

* For the full transcript, see Appendix 1.

were made to buy their own tickets for a later train, or the day Art Dit-mar failed to cover first on a routine play, and Casey left him in to absorb a six-run pounding.

By late August, some players were questioning his tactics, and Casey took exception to that. "A lot of them are making a living because they're playing my way," he said. "There are always ball players who will complain, but I haven't heard yet of any of them complaining about taking home that World Series money."

Stengel always said, "The secret of managing is to keep the five guys who hate you away from the guys who are undecided."

When Casey offered wisdom on the secrets of managing, one listener might well have been the team's new first-base coach, Ralph Houk. Houk had moved up to replace Charlie Keller after a stellar performance as manager of Denver, and almost at once, sportswriters speculated that in Houk might be a Stengel successor one day.

THERE WAS A BIT of midseason humor after the Yankees picked up forty-one-year-old Virgil Trucks. Trucks and Kucks were warming up in the bullpen and Casey called for Trucks. His directive was misheard; Kucks came in, and pitched the Yankees out of a jam.

SCHEDULE MAKERS HAD THE Yankees in Kansas City again for Casey's sixty-eighth birthday, and 250 admirers gathered at the Hotel Bellerive on Armour Boulevard for another Casey birthday celebration in K.C. Casey, when he rose to speak, said: "The greatest thing of my life has been what you might call fortunate that I'm sort of a WPA manager that gets fired and rehired. . . . There's my wife, Edna. I want to get her name in. When the team has had a bad day or you might say the manager had had a bad day, she's very good with the players' wives and the players, speaking kindly to them as they leave the clubhouse because she says, 'Why not, I might as well because I'll get it from him when we get home.'"

Despite the big lead, the season did not play out especially well for the Yankees. There was a complacency, as might be expected. There was a fear that the lackluster play might carry into the World Series, and if that was the case, the manager would be held accountable. The Yanks were only 27-28 in the final two months.

The Yankees clinched the pennant—Casey's ninth—by winning the first game of a doubleheader on September 14 in Kansas City. There was a sedate celebration in the clubhouse, followed by dinner at the Muehlebach, and then a continued celebration on the Wabash Cannonball train to Detroit, where a six-game losing streak would begin.

On the train, where too much drinking ensued, Duren pushed a cigar into Houk's face. Houk had been his manager at Denver; they had a history, and Duren was often inebriated. (When his career was finished, he would write two books about his alcoholism.) Houk struck back with a hand, or a fist, to Duren's face, and Ryne got a gash over his eye, a cut on his hand, and some bruises on his neck.

The traveling beat reporters would likely have ignored the story, as was the style of the day. But not Len Shecter of the *New York Post* (who eleven years later would collaborate with Jim Bouton on the book *Ball Four*), who reported it all to his readers and forced the other writers to play catch-up. The story certainly must have looked bad to Topping and Weiss back home.

THE BRAVES REPEATED AS National League champions.

Whether the Wabash Cannonball incident or the previous year's "busher" incident en route to Milwaukee factored in, this time the Yankees chose to fly to Milwaukee. Their traveling secretary, McCorry, hated to fly; he even took the team across the Great Lakes by boat one year to avoid it. But the days of train travel were winding down in baseball, especially since there were now teams on the West Coast.

Spahn and Ford met in Game One, but it was Duren who gave up a tenth-inning single to Billy Bruton to give the Braves the opener on October 1. Then, in Game Two, the nemesis of the year before, Burdette, stopped the Yankees 13–5; Turley was knocked out in the first inning. Things did not look good for the Yankees as they flew home to New York, down 2–0.

Larsen won the third game, but it was Spahn over Ford in Game Four, aided in part by the left fielder Norm Siebern, a Stengel favorite, who butchered two fly balls in the tough October sun. These events certainly hurt Siebern's standing with fans (and he didn't play again in the series), but Casey stood behind his decision to play him over Howard or Slaughter. "Casey stuck by me when I needed him," said Siebern, "He had every right to jump me, but he didn't."

The Yanks were now down 3–1. Few teams had ever come back

from such a deficit, considering they had to win three straight from a championship-caliber team. Only the 1925 Pirates had come back from 3–1 to beat Washington, thirty-three years before.

But the Yankees took it one game at a time. And Turley, who had bombed out in Game Two, proved to be the Man. In Game Five, he hurled a 7–0 complete game, a five-hit shutout, as the Yankees finally beat Burdette.

Two days later, back in Milwaukee, Casey called on Turley to relieve Duren in the tenth inning, with the Yankees leading 4–3, but with Hank Aaron on third and Felix Mantilla, pinch runner for Joe Adcock, on first. If they could score, the Braves would win the series. Turley was facing a pinch hitter, Frank Torre, Joe's older brother. He got him to line out to McDougald at second, and the Yankees won. There would be a seventh game.

Burdette, on two days' rest, got the ball for the Braves. Casey went with Larsen, who was well rested and had won Game Three.

The Yankees held a 2–1 lead in the third inning when the Braves threatened. With one out, Casey went to the mound and again called on Turley. And Bullet Bob, appearing in his third straight game, got out of the jam, and proceeded to pitch six and two-thirds innings, allowing just one run and two hits. The one run did tie the score in the sixth, but then he hurled three shutout innings, allowing only a leadoff walk in the ninth. The Yankees meanwhile scored four runs in the eighth, largely on a three-run homer by Skowron. The game ended with a third straight Yankee victory, a second Turley win to go with his save, and another world championship for the Yankees.

It would be Casey Stengel's last one.

For those on the team or in the front office, the 1958 comeback victory would be the most satisfying of the Stengel era. Those who accumulated a lot of World Series wins in that time period tended to wear the 1958 ring ahead of all others. When the PR director, Bob Fishel, turned sixty-five in 1979, he was given a '58 ring as a gift—front-office people did not receive rings in those days.

The flight home to New York was one of the happiest trips a Yankee team had ever taken. Joy reigned. Ford, taking the ash from a cigar, painted dollar signs on Casey's cheeks. Three days after the Series ended, the Yankees held a World Series triumph party for some 250 guests at the Crystal Room of the Savoy-Plaza Hotel, across the street from the

Yankees' Fifth Avenue offices.* The same week, the press was summoned to the same room, where Casey was rewarded with his sixth two-year contract. He would again receive seventy-five thousand a year.

With that, it was home to California for the Stengels, and the usual banquet of honor at the Verdugo Club, with Del Webb in attendance. Then came a banquet at the Beverly Hilton Hotel at which he received the Manager of the Year award from *The Sporting News*. Ty Cobb and Wahoo Sam Crawford were there for that one.

Sometime during that period, a reporter got Casey to name the top three players of his tenure. And Casey named DiMaggio, Berra . . . and Hank Bauer, who had just hit four home runs in the World Series.

He did not name Mantle, who had already won a Triple Crown and two MVP Awards. "He's not one, two or three at this time," said Stengel. "He has a tremendous potential. He's only 26, strong, and now he's in great shape." Weiss had notified Mantle that his pay was to be cut. Defending this, Casey said, "This outfielder holds the triple crown, has led in three big points [home runs, walks, and runs scored]. He should lead in all points."

At an event in Modesto, California, just before he left for spring training, Casey added: "That Mantle could be the greatest player that ever lived. Some days he is—and then there are other days. He constantly fights himself. Mickey actually gets discouraged when he can't hit a certain pitcher since he hardly believes that it is possible for anyone to strike him out. He's got everything, but he also is his own worst enemy. Sure he has a great handicap and must play with his legs taped. Still he has broken every distance record in every park he has played in. If he makes up his mind to put in the time that it will take to overcome his weaknesses, he can do things that will make other players look silly. Among other things, he must try to eliminate strikeouts and not go after bad balls."

There was no Stengelese in these comments. Casey was indeed tough to please, and Mantle's inability to be even better than he was—perhaps as good as Ruth—was never far from Casey's thoughts.

---

* Today it is the site of the General Motors building and an Apple Store. It was renamed the Savoy Hilton after 1958.

32

THIRD-PLACE
YANKEES?

CASEY REFLECTED ON HIS long career in baseball as 1959 spring training began. Speaking with Dan Daniel, he was, in a sense, marveling over the changes in athletes:

You know what made so many players very familiar with alcohol? They couldn't make a decent living out of baseball so they had to get off-season jobs.

What were they fit for? They had no skills off the field and they had to leave come spring. So they became bartenders, and from tending bar to sampling the wet goods wasn't much of a jump. So when you gathered the players for spring training, you saw pot bellies, rum blossom noses and other evidence of the free and easy life.

In them days, the training season was supposed to be mainly for melting the lard off the fatties and getting the boozers ready to run 90 feet without being winded.

Nowadays, the players report down to weight, there ain't no bartenders which they have to belong to a union, anyways, and you will be surprised of the number of Yankees now under-weight they showed during the 1958 World Series.

Baseball today is serious business. You don't tolerate heavy drinkers. No man is so good, so important, that you have to take a lot of nonsense from him and shut your eyes to his wanderings and rule fractures.

The ball player of today is a serious, hard-working, ambitious man eager to get every dime there is in the game for himself and his family. Then, today he must stay around at least ten years to qualify for his full pension, and you don't stay in your booze. That pension gimmick is a wonderful thing for the managers.

Some called Casey "old-school" and "set in his ways," but he had clear vision when it came to "today's players." He often did not get enough credit for the adjustments in thought and observation that he did embrace.

THE 1959 YANKEES, WITH only three new faces on the roster (Clete Boyer, Johnny Blanchard, and Jim Coates), got off to a horrible start—or a continuation of their bad regular-season finish of 1958.

Tempers were quicker. Stengel feuded with Joe King of the *World-Telegram & Sun* over a story mentioning that Ford had brushed off a photographer. Houk tossed a helmet onto the field to shoo away a television cameraman in Baltimore, where photographers were allowed on the field. Casey even criticized his pitching coach, Jim Turner, in the press after a Washington Senators pinch hitter, Julio Becquer, got a single. "He's beaten our brains out by hitting the inside ball, and I told Turner to have the pitchers brush him back, then throw outside."

A week after celebrating his thousandth victory as Yankee manager, he was thrown out of a game while protesting a check swing call. He was now nearly sixty-nine years of age, the oldest man in uniform (six years older than the Cubs' coach Rogers Hornsby, two years older than the Red Sox coach Del Baker), and some felt it was inappropriate for him to get so worked up on the field.

Newsweek, whose sports editor was Roger Kahn, wrote that a "Yankee executive" felt the Yankees could still win if Stengel were to retire, "but he won't do it."

On May 26, the Yankees lost a 12–2 decision to Boston at Yankee Stadium—and fell into last place. The headline writers had a ball: YANKS HIT CELLAR. It was unthinkable. But it was true—they were now 14-22 and would remain in last place for six days, until seven wins in nine games lifted them to sixth. They hovered at the borderline of the first and second divisions for much of the summer. This was very unfamiliar territory, and the usual joy of going to the ballpark abated for the high-payroll team.

It went practically unnoticed that, from Memorial Day to season's end, the Yankees were 65-55, which enabled them to finish third. That would be called a "respectable third" for any other team, but not this one.

It hurt that the teams above them—Chicago (the pennant winner) and Cleveland—included people who had gloatingly criticized Stengel for most of the season. Frank Lane, the Indians' general manager, continued to carry on his long-standing public feud with Casey. The White Sox's owner, Bill Veeck (Casey's old absentee boss from his 1944 managerial turn in Milwaukee), and general manager, Hank Greenberg, were frequent critics who seemed to enjoy beating Stengel as much as they did winning the pennant. Above the fray was Casey's old pal and business partner Al Lopez, who had guided the '54 Indians and now the '59 White Sox to pennants when the Yankees didn't make it.

Richardson, playing every day for the first time, hit .301. Duren had a 1.88 ERA. But most of the stars had "off-years," especially Turley. Though he had won the Cy Young in 1958, in '59 his game went south. He was 8-11 with a 4.32 ERA. Except for perhaps Bob Grim, no starting pitcher had ever fallen as sharply as Turley did during the Stengel years. Many fingers were pointed at Stengel. Mantle hit a pedestrian .285 with only seventy-five RBIs and thirty-one homers; had Stengel's criticisms affected him adversely instead of giving him a boost? Bauer, now thirty-seven, fell to .238. Ford reached double digits in losses for the first time in his career.

Still, on Old-Timers' Day in August, Casey's ovation was the loudest, even louder than DiMaggio's. It was part admiration, part rally of support: Yankee fans refused to give up hope. At the after-party for the guests, where Joe McCarthy, Dizzy Dean, and Charlie Grimm sang, where talks were delivered by Paul Waner, Bill Dickey, and Zack Wheat, and where Mrs. Babe Ruth, Mrs. Lou Gehrig, and Mrs. John McGraw were honored guests—Casey was the hit of the evening with his predictably colorful speech at the end of the evening. And then Casey and Edna danced to "The Band Played On."

On September 8, the Yankees were eliminated from the pennant race. The White Sox were going to win it, and Casey sent Al Lopez a telegram wishing him "the best of luck in the World Series" as soon as they clinched.

So he had finished third, just as Bucky Harris had done before getting fired in 1948. Was this an omen? It was no secret that Houk, the first-base coach, was considered Stengel's successor, even though a line drive to the head by Larsen had put him in the hospital during the season. (Charlie Keller filled in.)

Casey had another year left on his contract. His bosses all stood strongly behind him. The players, who may have joked among themselves about Casey's zaniness, respected his record of success and supported him publicly. Even Madison Avenue still banked on him: Skippy Peanut Butter hired him for print ads in national magazines. At the end of the season, Yankee management took the step of announcing, unnecessarily because of his contract, that Casey would be back in 1960.

And Stengel took his share of blame, by bringing up one of his favorite characters. "Now I had been around quite a few years. I wasn't Little Ned out of the Fourth Reader. Yet I allowed my elation over the 1958 world championship to give me a distorted picture of 1959. I should have known better. That was my first mistake. As for the other errors, I ain't gonna make them mistakes again."

But the Yankees also announced that Jim Turner would be retiring as pitching coach. This was not presented as a major announcement, but Turner was not retiring, he was absolutely being pushed overboard, most certainly as a scapegoat for the pitching staff's failures—notably Turley's.

"The Colonel," also known as "the Milkman," Turner had been with Casey from the start, through all those triumphs. Now he was out, and, as with Billy Martin, Casey was not defending him or lurching into the fray to keep him. Ed Lopat would replace him. (And Dickey would return to the team as batting coach). Turner went home to Nashville and came "out of retirement" to manage his hometown minor-league team. He said nothing in his departure—it was not his style. In fact, Turner long maintained that he was not really "fired": you are not fired if your contract is expired.

Turner had run the pitching, no doubt. Who's pitching Sunday? Ask Turner. Who is warmed up and ready to come in? Ask Turner. Casey had relied on him and won nine pennants with him. He was thought to be the best pitching coach in the business, and would resurface with pennant-winning Cincinnati in 1961. From 1966 to 1973, Houk would even bring him back to the Yankees for another tour as pitching coach. But for now, "Certain disgruntled pitchers who had miserable seasons revolted against Turner and greased the skids under him," *The Sporting News* reported.

Instead of a World Series share for Casey in 1959, he got fifteen thousand dollars to cover the series for *Life* magazine—more than anyone on either team got.*

---

* The Dodgers' winning share was $11,231. The third-place money for each Yankee was $1,229. All first division teams received World Series money before division play was instituted in baseball.

Was he an able reporter for *Life*? "I'm much too popular," he said. "Every time I want to say something, somebody gets in my ear and I forgot to write down my observations."

Casey's friends in California did not forget him. After the season, there was the now annual salute to Casey at the Verdugo.

Of course, back in the Yankee offices at 745 Fifth Avenue, the feelings could not have been good. Casey was getting fifteen thousand dollars while the team was losing out on its annual expected World Series revenues. It would be natural to expect that certain front-office people—including the owners—were not thinking "Good for ol' Case." Even though he had one more year to go on his contract, at this moment the wheels were perhaps beginning to turn.

LATE IN THE SEASON, when the Yankees were playing Kansas City, their manager, Harry Craft, sidled up to Casey during batting practice. Craft was an old veteran of the baseball wars, and had managed in the Yankees organization. He had a pretty good sense that he was going to be fired by the A's.

He had a friendly piece of advice for Stengel: "My outfielder, [Roger] Maris—he would be a heckuva pickup for the Yankees. He is one terrific player. You should see him on a daily basis." And, on December 11, the Yankees got Maris, their latest acquisition from Kansas City, along with two other players, for Bauer, Larsen, Siebern, and Throneberry.

"Of course Casey didn't say good-bye," said Bauer. "No manager ever does. That's the way baseball is. But I always did like Casey and thought he was a good guy and a wonderful manager. He handled me fine. He could make me see red—especially when he took me out for a pinch-hitter. I never talked back to him. But then, I never talked back to my dad, either. He was fair. When we won fifteen in a row, he kept us on the ball by reading the riot act after every game. But when we were down and out, he'd leave us alone."

Bauer would become a player-manager for the Athletics the following year. With his departure from the Yankees, only Berra was left from Casey's first team. Casey rated Bauer highly—ahead of Mantle, even—but here was a chance to get the twenty-five-year-old Maris for thirty-seven-year-old Bauer, who was nearing the end of a fine playing career.

It was the kind of trade a smart organization makes.

33

A PEBBLE AT
SHORTSTOP

THE YEAR 1960 MARKED the fiftieth anniversary of Casey Stengel's entry into professional baseball, and, including 1937, the year when Brooklyn paid him to stay home, he had been employed in every one of those years.

It was a remarkable achievement, but he had been honored so often by so many over his Yankee years, there was little left to do to pay him tribute.

Of course, the Yankees could win him a tenth pennant; that would be nice. And it is probably what he would have asked for if given the opportunity.

Maris was a nice gift. Casey first thought of him as his left fielder, with Héctor Lopez to play right, and that is what happened during spring training, but by the opening of the season, he felt Maris's strong arm made him the better choice in right. The unsteady Lopez would play left, and, of course, Mantle would be in center.

Maris would come through with thirty-nine home runs for Casey and win himself an MVP Award, edging Mantle by a very narrow margin. As usual, the trade worked out well, the Athletics looked bad, and Maris's performance would in fact play a big part in another big season. So impressed was Casey by Maris that when he named his personal All-Yankee team from 1949 to 1960, he put Maris in the outfield with DiMaggio and Mantle, over Bauer. (He also put Coleman at second over Billy Martin. And at least Mantle had surpassed Bauer by now.)

The Yankees played just .500 ball until early June, and there was frequent talk of Casey's retiring. Of course, that had been going on almost since he arrived in New York in 1949. Even he had told Edna that the Yankees would just be for a year . . . or two. Speculation continued that Houk would be the successor, and that was bolstered when Casey was hospitalized for ten days (May 29–June 7) with what was variously described as a bladder infection/virus/flu. Signs of illness, as he approached seventy, were quickly translated into "Maybe it's time."

During the ten-day stretch, Houk ran the club.

"I'll tell you something," said Casey when he rejoined the team. "They examined all my organs. Some of them are quite remarkable, and others are not so good. A lot of museums are bidding for them."

His support team was in transition, too. The traveling secretary, Bill McCorry, and the trainer, Gus Mauch, both had heart attacks. McCorry's led to his retirement, and Bruce Henry moved up from business manager at Richmond to take his place; Mauch returned in August but now had an assistant, Joe Soares, to work with. George Weiss, who was sixty-seven, was hospitalized with ulcers during the season, and his workload was taken up by his assistant, Roy Hamey, until he returned.

IN 1960, BILL VEECK, feeling flush from having hosted a World Series, installed an exploding scoreboard in Comiskey Park. It was set to send off fireworks every time a White Sox player hit a home run (a rare event).

Bob Fishel, who had once worked for Veeck with the St. Louis Browns, came up with a countermeasure that Casey loved. On a visit to Chicago on June 17, Fishel delivered sparklers to the Yankee dugout, to be lit when a Yankee homered. With July 4 approaching, sparklers were readily available. It was a playful idea, and they got to work it twice that day, first on a Clete Boyer home run, and later on one by Mantle. Casey was among those who held sparklers, which was perfectly fitting for the man who had spent a lifetime of having fun with the game.

THE YANKEES WERE HOME, playing Kansas City, to celebrate Casey's seventieth birthday. The assistant general manager, Roy Hamey, presented him with a silver tray (which went on display at Casey's bank in Glendale); the players presented him with a desk set; and the team's sponsor, Ballantine Beer, presented him with a color television set, to be shipped off to Glendale.

None of those gifts could compare to a purchase ten days earlier, when the Yankees obtained the relief pitcher Luis Arroyo from the Reds' Jersey City farm team. The team had been transferred there from Havana on July 15 after U.S.-Cuban relations turned bad. The cigar-smoking Arroyo, who had pitched earlier in his career for the Cardinals, Pirates, and Reds, made twenty-nine appearances for Casey down the stretch, winning five, saving seven, and being a genuinely well-liked guy in the clubhouse.

"Who'd have ever thought a guy like that would be laying around dead somewhere?" wondered Casey, marveling at Arroyo's screwball as well as at other clubs' lack of interest in him. Duren had been generally ineffective, and Bobby Shantz had stepped up in a relief role in fine style, but the luxury of having a second man to go to proved to be of enormous benefit.

Arroyo took a spot that might have been occupied by a left-hander named Hal Stowe, a Clemson University product with good stuff. "It's true that Hal Stowe pitched pretty good this spring," said Casey when the roster cuts were made. "But I noticed that he never ran in the outfield, that he never did all the things he was supposed to do. He never really hustled and he never really worked at it. That's why he didn't make the squad cut. He could bullshit everybody but the manager."

Art Ditmar emerged as the team's leading winner with a 15-9 mark; Ford only 12-9. Turley made twenty-four starts and won nine, and Ralph Terry, who had come over with Lopez from the Athletics the year before, won ten. Jim Coates was 13-3, a better record than Ford's.

Another splendid pickup was the first baseman Dale Long, purchased on August 21. Long was a throwback—Casey had discovered him playing sandlot ball when he was managing Milwaukee for Veeck in 1944. He signed Long and farmed him out to the Ohio State League. Now, in 1960, after a journeyman career, Long was back with Stengel for a pennant run, and he hit .366 in twenty-six games—an acquisition reminiscent of the Yankees' picking up Johnny Mize in the summer of '49.

Although Mantle finished second in MVP voting, he still was falling short in Casey's eyes. It seemed as though he could never please the skipper. He hit forty home runs to lead the league, but he batted only .275, and he struck out 125 times. In August, he failed to run out a ground ball in a game against Washington, thinking that a force play was the third out, and Casey took him out of the game and sent him to the clubhouse after the sixth inning. A punishment.

It turned out the game went fifteen innings—it was the second game of a doubleheader, no less—and the Yankees lost it. A lot of players grumbled privately that removing Mantle on what had been a mental error cost them the game, but the press was supportive. "That single bit of managerial strategy may have won a pennant," wrote one.

Indeed, the Yankees showed signs of better baseball down the stretch, in what turned out to be a tight race. The Baltimore Orioles—no one saw them coming—were the "Baby Birds," with terrific young pitching, and they nearly pulled off a shocking pennant under Paul Richards. When they beat the Yankees three straight in Baltimore just before Labor Day—behind Milt Pappas, Jack Fisher, and Chuck Estrada, they moved ahead of New York and into first.

The Yankees regained first place on September 10 and held it the rest of the way, winning their final fifteen games of the season, including a four-game sweep of Baltimore September 16, 17, and 18, the last two a doubleheader. Over 150,000 came out for those three dates, as Ford, Coates, Ditmar, and Terry won to build the lead to four games. The Yanks wound up eight games ahead, which belied how close the race really was.

Casey's tenth pennant in twelve years only increased the talk of his retirement. "A good way to go out," some speculated. Asked about Casey's future—and George Weiss's—before the World Series began, Dan Topping said, "I have not talked retirement with either man, and they have not broached the subject to me." This pennant tied him with McGraw for most, and put him one ahead of McCarthy and Connie Mack. McGraw, though, won only three World Series.

The National League pennant winners were the Pittsburgh Pirates, who had not been to the World Series since the Murderers' Row Yankees of 1927 had swept them.

The series opened in Pittsburgh on October 5. Casey had played there as a Pirates outfielder in 1918 and 1919.

Casey had to make a decision on his opening-game pitcher. Ford, long his ace, had started the final game of the season, and pitched just two innings, presumably a move to tune him up for the series. That outing, which was unnecessary, meant he would have just two days off, although he had faced only nine batters on October 2. Ditmar, who had pitched four innings on September 30, would have had four days off. Casey also considered the rookie Bill Stafford, who had come up in mid-August and gone 3-1 with a 2.25 ERA. He had thrown three innings on October 1 and would have three days' rest.

Casey, conferring with his pitching coach, Lopat, chose to go with

Ditmar. If Ford was hurting at all, it was certainly not in evidence. Some in the press raised their eyebrows over the decision, but Ditmar, after all, had been the team's leading winner.

The choice did not work out. That's baseball. Casey bet on Ditmar, and started him in Game One (one-third of an inning, three runs) and again in Game Five (one and a third innings, three runs), and the Yankees lost both of those games.

Game One also featured a tough Casey moment, when he called back Clete Boyer in the second inning for a pinch hitter. "When Casey called me back," said Boyer, "I thought he was going to talk to me—maybe tell me how he wanted me to swing. But when he told me that Long was going to hit for me, I was ready to crawl all the way home. I was never so shocked in my life."

Meanwhile, his longtime ace, Ford, had a fabulous series, winning Game Three 10–0, and a potential elimination game, Game Six, 12–0, making the Ditmar call look exceptionally bad. Ford would not be available for Game Seven.

The Yankees also took Game Two behind Turley by a 16–3 score, and for the series they would outscore Pittsburgh 55–27, outhit them .338 to .256, out-homer them 10–4, and had a lower ERA, 3.54 to 7.11. Bobby Richardson, who hit one homer and drove in twenty-six runs during the regular season, hit a grand slam, had a record six RBIs in one game and a record twelve for the series. Mantle hit three homers and drove in eleven. By almost every measure that statistics could churn, the Yankees were the better team on the field.

On the eve of Game Six, with the Yankees on the brink of elimination and with so many rumors swirling about Casey's future, a group of thirty-seven sportswriters signed a petition to retain him—an unimaginable act for supposedly neutral reporters. But Ford's inability to take the ball for Game Seven continued the second-guessing about Stengel's strategy.

It all came down to Game Seven in Pittsburgh, on October 13. This game included nineteen runs and twenty-four hits, but not a single strikeout—a rarity that still stands alone in World Series history.

And, given the swirling of retirement rumors, it might also be the last game managed by one Charles Dillon Stengel.

Ford, unavailable after winning Game Six, could only sit and watch as a procession of Yankee hurlers tried to seal the deal for New York. Turley lasted only an inning, and was followed by Stafford, Shantz, Coates, and Terry. Shantz was the one who shone brightest, giving the Yanks five solid innings, making a neat fielding play, and even delivering a hit.

The Pirates jumped out to a 4–0 lead after two, with Rocky Nelson hitting a two-run homer in the first. But Skowron hit a solo home run in the fifth, Berra hit a three-run homer in the sixth, and suddenly the Yankees were rising and took a 5–4 lead. In the eighth, they added two more; it was now 7–4 New York, and the home crowd was silenced.

Now came the fateful last of the eighth. With the leadoff runner on first, Virdon, the old Yankee farmhand who had been traded for Slaughter, hit what should have been a double-play grounder to Kubek at short.

Forbes Field had opened in 1909. Somehow, in this fifty-second season, the ball found a pebble in front of Kubek. How the pebble had survived fifty-one years of infield maintenance was a wonder. The ball struck the pebble and bad-hopped itself into Kubek's throat. Everyone was safe, and Kubek was down. Stengel went out to short for the medical emergency—Kubek would spend the night in the hospital—and called on Joe DeMaestri to take over.

But now, instead of having the bases empty with two out—Kubek to Richardson to Skowron had seemed like a sure double play—now it was two on, none out, and Dick Groat up. He singled past Boyer at third, as Gino Cimoli scored, making it 7–5.

Casey went to the mound to remove Shantz, and called on Jim Coates.

Bob Skinner sacrificed and Nelson flied out. Up came Roberto Clemente, who hit a slow chopper between first and second, but close enough toward second that Coates's instinct told him to field the ball. Realizing he couldn't, he raced to cover first—and was late. It was a single, a run scored, and it was 7–6.

For years after, the Yankee players blamed Coates for extending the inning by not covering first. A lot of them said it publicly over the years. But fifty years later, in 2010, a kinescope of the game was discovered in the archives of the singer Bing Crosby, who was a part-owner of the Pirates. Kinescopes were essentially films made by pointing a movie camera at a TV screen before videotape was invented. The Coates play was not included in the official World Series film produced by Major League Baseball, and thus was never seen or analyzed until the Crosby discovery.

"We had it wrong," said Richardson, during a screening on the MLB Network. "We've blamed Coates all these years. But the ball was hit into a no-man's-land—he was right to break towards the ball, and it was just bad luck that it was hit there. Anyone would have played it as he did."

So be it. Hal Smith, who had taken over as catcher in the top of the inning, came up. He was another one of those Yankee farmhands traded off to find a major-league career elsewhere, part of the contingent sent to Baltimore in the Larsen-Turley trade.

And he hit a three-run homer off Coates, to put the Pirates ahead 9–7. On that one, the players could rightfully blame Coates.

What a blow. And what a game this was.

Casey went to the mound to remove Coates and bring in Terry. Don Hoak flied out, and the game went to the ninth inning.

The Yankees needed two to tie—and got them. They scratched and clawed for them, with a grounder to first by Berra scoring McDougald with the tying run, as Mantle, the runner at first, dove back to avoid a double play after Nelson had stepped on the base to remove the force-out.

Now it was the last of the ninth, Game Seven, a 9–9 score.

On Terry's second pitch to Bill Mazeroski, at 3:36 p.m., the Pirates' second baseman delivered the biggest single sports moment in the city's history—a drive over Berra's head in left, over the scoreboard, and out of the park.

Bedlam! The Pirates won it 10–9 and were world champions for the first time in thirty-five years.

They may have been outplayed over the eight days of the Fall Classic, but when it counted, Maz came through, and the Yankees walked off the field, losers.

As several players, including Mantle, wept in the silence of the visiting clubhouse, Terry went to see Casey in his office "He was great," said Terry later. "He asked me what I was trying to do on Maz, and I told him I thought I had him set up for a slider. 'Well,' said Casey, 'you were working on him. If you told me you had given him a high fastball that would be another thing.' He sensed I felt guilty as hell and he was enough of a pro not to make it worse."

Still feeling the second-guessing over his use of Ditmar, Casey acknowledged "You could say I picked the wrong starter for the first and fifth game. Since [Ditmar] was still my top winner and had pitched only 17 balls in the opener, I had to call him back for the fifth game."

The team flew back to New York in silence.

34

FIRED!

NOBODY COULD READ THE tea leaves of baseball like Casey. After a half-century in the game, he knew all the signs. Nothing could surprise him.

A few days after the series, he got a call to visit with Topping and Webb at Del Webb's suite in the Waldorf Astoria. Casey took a cab from the Essex House, and as soon as he walked in and saw that there was no contract on the table waiting to be signed, he knew it was over.

That had always been the procedure, and he'd seen this coming. As Casey wrote in his autobiography:

> The last month and a half of the 1960 season I could tell I was through. . . . The attitude of people in the office that I knew and liked was different. They knew that things were going to change.
>
> I said to Mr. Weiss near the end of the season, "You're not running this club the way you were before."
>
> And he dropped his head and said, "I'm afraid you're right."

Topping and Webb explained their new retirement plan, including the rule that no one in the organization work beyond the age of sixty-five, and there was really nothing Casey could say. They weren't looking for a discussion; the decision was made. This must have been particularly difficult for Webb, who genuinely liked Casey and could always be counted on to fly to any testimonial affair honoring him. Their relationship went back long before Casey's Yankee days.

Topping brought up a "generous" parting gift for Casey, a $158,747.25 check he would be receiving. Casey was a banker; he knew this was nonsense. It was due him from the team's profit-sharing plan, in which he and all full-time employees except the players were enrolled. It was no gift at all. There was no talk of making him a senior adviser or consultant—something they would offer George Weiss, who was also getting a pink slip (he was sixty-six), but would stay on the payroll.

Casey had but one request, which was granted. He wanted the announcement to be made at a press conference, so that he could be among his writers, his greatest loyalists. This was agreed upon, difficult though it may have been for the owners to partake in such an event. Webb, in fact, found an excuse not to be there: he had business in Los Angeles.

And so, on Tuesday, October 18, 1960, Bob Fishel and his first-year assistant, Bill Guilfoile, began dialing the phones, summoning the New York press corps to Le Salon Bleu in the Savoy Hilton (the former Savoy-Plaza). The corps included reporters, photographers, and columnists from the New York newspapers and wire services, and reporters and producers from the TV, newsreel, and radio stations. There were enough "extra bodies" to swell the attendance to nearly 150.

The hotel was next door to the team offices, across the street from the Plaza Hotel. It was a two-block walk for Casey from the Essex House, where he had more or less holed up since the team got home. He took a cab; he was in no condition to chat with fans on the way over. When he arrived, at seven minutes past twelve, and saw the packed room, he may have felt empowered by their presence, knowing how pro-Casey they tended to be.

At the front of the room was a microphone, with no head table or podium. Topping went to the mike, as Casey more or less blended in with the reporters in the front row.

Reading from a prepared text, Topping noted that Casey "has been—deservedly—the highest-paid manager in baseball history, and a great manager, he was to be rewarded with $160,000 to do with as he pleases."

He never said the word "fired," or even "not coming back."

A reporter shouted, "Do you mean he's through? Has he resigned?"

Topping never answered the question. Casey went to the mike.

Speaking somewhat hesitantly, with his hands in his pockets, he said, "Mr. Webb and Mr. Topping have started a program for the Yankees. They needed a solution as to when to discharge a man on account of age. My services are not desired any longer by this club. I told them if this was their idea not to worry about me."

He began talking about changes he might have made if he were coming back in 1961, saying, "I've always handed in my own lineups, with none of the office people telling me what to do."

This wasn't what the writers were looking for.

"Casey, were you fired?" shouted a voice.

"No, I wasn't fired," he answered. "I was paid up in full."

There was some awkward laughter.

He smiled. "Quit, fired, whatever you please, I don't care."

A seventy-nine-year-old fan who had wandered into the room had the audacity to walk up to Casey and shake his hand. The reporters screamed, "Go away, go away!"

Another voice was heard. "Casey, an Associated Press bulletin says you're fired. What do you think about that?"

The AP's Joe Reichler had spotted a pay phone—he always had his dime ready—and was calling in the story.

"What do I care what the AP says," said Casey. "Anyway, what about the UP?" The UP, which stood for United Press, had two years earlier become United Press International.

And it was over. The press conference and the reign of Casey Stengel, winner of seven World Series and ten pennants in twelve years, and the man who may have done more for baseball through the force of his personality than anyone except Babe Ruth.

Casey had a couple of drinks at the portable bar set up in the room, and he did a few more radio interviews. He even sat on a couch with Topping and did a joint interview, awkward though it must have been.

"I'm just sorry Casey isn't 50 years old," said Topping, "but all business comes to a point when it's best for the future to make a change." He insisted this decision would have been made even if the Yankees had won the World Series.

Interviewed in Los Angeles, Webb said: "It's always been common knowledge that Topping runs the baseball club. He's president of the club and we each own 50 percent. Topping is the baseball man. I'm in the construction business but I'm co-owner of the club. Casey had a sick spell last season and at his age he might find the strain of managing the club too much for him. We felt we couldn't afford to allow ourselves to get into a position of losing our manager through illness in the middle of the season."

BY TWO-THIRTY, IT WAS all winding down. Someone from the front office stopped by to ask about his plans. Casey said, "I'm taking a jet home, and I'm charging it to the club. A man gets his transportation home even if they don't want him anymore."

A waitress came by and said, "I got to kiss you," and did.

"Thank you very much," said Casey.

He headed for the door and out into the brisk October weather. This time, he would walk back to his hotel, along Central Park South. If people wanted to shake his hand and wish him well, that was fine with him. He told the front desk "no calls," but that led to a deluge of telegrams from the baseball world, since most people in the baseball world knew where he lived.

Reaction was swift. "Gigantic organizations such as General Motors and United States Steel have retirement deadlines, but they have sense enough to use them with flexibility," wrote Arthur Daley in the *Times,* in a column titled "A Sad Day for Baseball." "However, a puny organization like the Yankees blindly adheres to the letter of its own law. It's a new law, too. It could have waited for implementation until Casey had decided to quit on his own."

"I'll never make the mistake of being 70 again," said Casey.

"MY WRITERS" THREW A party for Casey the very next night, at the Starlight Roof of the Waldorf. Even with such short notice, Commissioner Ford Frick, American League President Joe Cronin, Branch Rickey (working on the possibility of a new league, the Continental), the power lawyer Bill Shea, the West Point football coach Red Blaik, the football Giants owner Jack Mara, the New York Knicks president, Ned Irish, and former Postmaster General Jim Farley all attended, as did Skowron, Howard, McDougald, Weiss, Hamey, Lopat (to be bitterly dismissed as pitching coach the next day), and, yes, Dan Topping.

Said Topping, "I feel like Khrushchev talking into the United Nations," which had happened just a week earlier, when he infamously banged his shoe on his desk.

"I don't want to put ridicule on Mr. Topping, who has the nerve and guts to come here tonight," noted Casey; in a rare sentimental moment, he added, "It's the first time I was ever near tears. I was never shocked so much in my life."

On Pittsburgh Hilton stationery, the petition signed at the World Series by thirty-seven writers was delivered to the Yankees, urging them to keep Casey.

He stayed in New York a few extra days, but he told Edna there was no need for her to come east. Before he left for California, he taped a *Perry Como's Kraft Music Hall* show, (it aired in November), in which he kiddingly said of Kubek, "He's a player without a weakness, except that he can't catch a bad hop." He was very polished on the show, which had him reading cue cards. Perry said, "You have so many trophies for your mantle," and Casey responded "I don't even have a Mantle anymore." Roy Face and Hal Smith, in Pirates uniforms, came out and serenaded Casey with guitars.

Sure enough, the Yankees named Ralph Houk as their new manager on October 20 at the Savoy Hilton. It was not nearly as well attended. Part of the reason for releasing Casey was that they did not want to lose Houk, who was getting offers from other teams, particularly Detroit. And they knew Boston had eyes on him as well. (Houk wound up managing both of them after his Yankee career ended.)

Houk was an impressive guy. He was smart, he was a war hero, the writers liked him, and the owners liked him. Combining that with Casey's age (in an era free of age discrimination suits), and with what some saw as "blowing the World Series" by not starting Ford in Game One, it all added up.

On November 2, Weiss, the team's last link to the Ruppert-Barrow years, bowed out as general manager at a press conference. "I wasn't fired. I am still here. I am under contract for the next five years as a consultant. I feel fine." Roy Hamey was promoted to fill his position the next day.

Casey flew to Los Angeles, where he was met at International Airport by a helicopter, which flew him to Glendale. He had tears in his eyes when he stepped out of the helicopter and into a parade through downtown Glendale, followed by a reception at Stengel Field, and a gathering at the Verdugo Club. When he got home, a children's neighborhood band, which had been welcoming him home since 1949, awaited. Some of the singers were now adults, but they returned for this quaint ritual one more time.

Another testimonial by the Los Angeles Baseball Writers' Association chapter was held at the historic Biltmore Hotel on November 22. "Right now," said Casey, "Edna should be able to get a job as a secretary for some ball club. She has a good system answering those letters, too. Any letters that mention jobs or money get a quick answer. Any which say I shoulda started Ford in the seventh game of the World Series, she puts aside for the time being."

To a whole generation of new baseball fans—the baby boomers' generation, born in the years following World War II—this was a shock to the system. Many had become Yankee fans because of Mickey Mantle, or because they liked winners, but Casey was the father figure, the guy who would somehow figure things out. He was the only manager they ever knew. This was like the loss of La Guardia as mayor of New York, or Roosevelt as president, or Joe Louis as heavyweight champion. Some things seemed like they would always be there. This one was not.

THERE WAS NO NEED to weep for Casey's lot in life. On December 14, it was announced that *The Saturday Evening Post* would be paying him $150,000 to write his life story. His old traveling secretary, Frank Scott, now a prominent player agent, negotiated the deal. Casey later said *Life* had offered thirty thousand more, but he didn't want to create a bidding contest out of it.

35

SUMMER IN GLENDALE

I N 1961, FOR THE first time since 1937, Casey Stengel had the "summer off."

"You could say this is the first time I was unemployed in baseball for many years," he reported. "There was one year in Brooklyn when I was unemployed but I got paid and there was another quarter of a year when I was traded to the Phils and I didn't report."

He was three thousand miles removed from the center of the baseball universe, which was the Mantle-Maris home-run race back in New York. He followed it all—he never missed *The Sporting News* (the publisher, Taylor Spink, had put him on the comp list), and told people that he thought both Mantle and Maris would break Ruth's home-run record.

As offers poured in—a very serious one to manage Detroit; a meeting with the new Angels general manager, Fred Haney, and owner, Gene Autry, about managing that club; conversations with Horace Stoneham about taking over the San Francisco Giants—he demurred. The Detroit offer advanced to the point where he considered hiring Leo Durocher and the just-retired Ted Williams as coaches. "I sit down with my wife and we talk," he said. "We figure why don't I rest a year and see how it feels. It sounded like a good idea. So I tell the Tigers that I'm sorry but I'm going to sit this one out."

Anyway, he was anxious to tell his story to Harry J. Paxton to fulfill his *Saturday Evening Post* obligation.

Veeck, of all people, said he would find a job for Casey in the White Sox organization. The Oakland Raiders of the new American Football League wanted him for some undefined role, remembering how popular he had been with the Oakland Oaks baseball team.

ABC Television asked him to come aboard as a color commentator for their Game of the Week (blacked out in major-league markets), with Jack Buck.

"I can make a living with my face," Casey liked to tell people.

Paxton was *The Saturday Evening Post*'s sports editor, so he assigned himself to the task, and during the year, a deal for a twenty-five-thousand-dollar advance would be struck with Bennett Cerf, publisher of Random House, to move the serialized magazine articles to book form for April 1962 publication. This was on top of a hefty magazine payment. The Stengels appeared to have "no hard feelings" with Paxton, who had earlier turned down Edna's memoir for publication—or, rather, refused to meet her asking price.

"A hundred and fifty thousand dollars was a lot of money," observed the sportswriter Ray Robinson, a veteran magazine editor. "But it was spread over a number of installments. Still, we know that *Saturday Evening Post* eventually went out of business [its days as a weekly ended in 1963], and this was probably a reason why."

Paxton wasn't one of "Casey's writers," so at least there were no hard feelings about his choosing one over another. Paxton did not have much in his background as a sports book author—he did a 1950 book on the Philadelphia Whiz Kids, and a biography of Babe Didrickson Zaharias in 1955—and some felt that the eventual work product fell short of the sly and ironic humor Casey was known for.

In May 1958, Paxton had had the sad duty of informing Edna that the hundred thousand dollars she was seeking for "My Life with Casey" in *The Saturday Evening Post* "is so far removed" from what they were prepared to offer "that we hesitate even to mention it." He explained in a letter that their normal fee to baseball personalities for signed stories was one thousand dollars. This, of course, puts into even sharper relief how far the magazine extended their policy for Casey himself.

The first installment came out in the September 18, 1961, issue, and future installments ran into spring training of 1962.

In the meantime, other publications were rushing out long Casey features to beat *The Saturday Evening Post*. Tom Meany, who was one of Casey's writers (and who would soon be the first public-relations director of the Mets), did a long story for *Look* magazine, which came out in their June 6 issue. The magazine *This Week* did a multi-part feature prepared by Leslie Lieber, who was not at all connected to the baseball world.

Walker and Company published *Casey Stengel's Secret,* a profusely illustrated softcover book by Clay Felker. Featuring a haunting cover of

Casey staring at a baseball as though it were a crystal ball (a UPI picture), it cost only $1.95; some remarkable photos of Casey's career were collected in it, largely from *The Sporting News*.

Just after New Year's, Casey slipped while walking in his home and was hospitalized at Glendale Memorial for a sore back complicated by a virus. When he returned home, wearing a corset, he continued dictating his story to Paxton. "I spent all last week in bed making money," he said, "which is something I never was able to do in baseball." (Well, after he was run over in Boston in 1943, he did just that.)

He went to his office on the second floor of Valley National Bank (owned by Edna's family, with Del Webb and Randy Moore among the stockholders) on North Brand Boulevard, or would greet customers in the main hall of the bank and sign autographs. The bank had season tickets to Dodger Stadium, and he could be generous with them.

When the *New York World-Telegram & Sun* sportswriter Joe King visited to do a Casey feature, Stengel showed him the bank vault, though he said, "I'm only a vice president; I'm not empowered to pass out samples."

The sportswriter Jack Lang's son Craig moved to Los Angeles after serving in Vietnam, and Jack arranged for him to meet Casey at the bank, perhaps to gain some career guidance. "Casey was not like I remembered him, and I went back to 1958 with him," recalls Craig. "He was in a banker's suit and tie, with no Stengelese, no funny faces. It was all banker talk. He asked about my war experience and expressed happiness that my injuries were slight. He asked me what my ambitions were, but concluded that I was still 'sowing oats.'"

Casey entered into a partnership on a golf driving range—Casey Stengel's Golf Center, on a one-acre site in Burbank. This was an interesting venture for a man who had never been seen holding a golf club. He owned just under 17 percent of it.

He threw out the first pitch at the All-Star Game at Candlestick Park on July 10, the one in which Stu Miller was famously "blown off the mound" by Candlestick winds.

By then, the New York Mets had been created, and were rapidly filling positions, signing a lot of former Yankee employees for the front office. There was suddenly a lot of talk about the possibility of Casey's going to the Mets, especially since George Weiss had been named general manager on March 14. But he wasn't ready to commit. Weiss talked to him at the All-Star Game and called him a few times to feel him out. There was no pressure, and the calls weren't too frequent—Casey would remember just two. But Weiss was obviously thinking it would be great to have him with the new team, which would begin play at the Polo Grounds in 1962.

No one ever considered Weiss a marketing genius. "Do you think I want every kid in this town walking around in a Yankees cap?" he said, for instance, when presented with the possibility of a "Cap Day" at Yankee Stadium. But if he was truly thinking of Casey as the Mets' manager, he had to be thinking that (1) the team would be awful under the expected draft rules (other team's discards), and (2) Casey could divert attention away from the bad players and make the Mets press-worthy and fun. Taking attention away from the Yankees would be a bonus.

Casey turned down the Yankees Old-Timers' Day invitation. Bob Fishel knew the invitation met the definition of "chutzpah," but opted to reach out anyway. He was not surprised when it was declined.

RALPH HOUK WON PENNANTS in his first three seasons as Casey's Yankee successor, the first two producing world championships, and no one doubted that he would be successful. Casey never included Houk in his small list of Yankee personnel who had somehow done him wrong. And Ralph always paid homage to Casey. "Casey didn't manage for the crowd," he said. "He managed for the players and made the most of their abilities. He also taught me how to handle writers. More managers are probably fired by the press than any other way. He knew which ones to get on and which ones to leave alone. I always remember one thing Casey said. 'If a decision goes wrong, never admit it to the press. There's always a reason why you did it. 'Be sure to give them the reason.' I did and it was helpful."

THE NEW YORK METROPOLITAN Baseball Club—the Mets—was born to begin play in 1962 as the National League's response to American League expansion: the AL had added the Los Angeles and Minneapolis markets in 1961, so the NL would add Houston and New York. The New York franchise would come four years after the Dodgers and Giants had moved to California. There was still a large fan base in New York—an angry and disappointed one, of course, and a base that did not rush to become Yankees fans. Having one team instead of two, it was believed, would allow the Mets to capture the "National League fans" and be a success.

Bill Shea, a New York power broker and attorney, spearheaded the effort, and the rights to the franchise were secured by Mrs. Joan Whitney Payson and M. Donald Grant, who had been on the Giants' Board of Directors. Everything about the team was an attempt to give a home to the disenfranchised fans of the Dodgers and Giants—from the logo to the team colors.

A new stadium would be built in Flushing, and the hope was that the Mets would have to spend no more than one season at the antiquated Polo Grounds, which had lain fallow since the Giants' last game in 1957. It was the same Polo Grounds in which Casey had played for McGraw in the early 1920s. The same Polo Grounds where he first met Edna Lawson.

Although there was newspaper speculation about Casey's managing the Mets, by September 1961 it did not appear he would give up his life in California for a move back to what promised to be a pretty bad team, perhaps wiping out the legacy he had left behind with the mighty Yankees. Why would he take such a job at seventy-one? If he really wanted to manage again, why not the Angels, which would allow him to commute from Glendale, work for Autry (whom everyone in baseball loved), and, not secondarily, please Edna.

The newspaper speculation moved to Gil Hodges, still an active player, but perhaps one who could be a player-manager as the Mets started life. However, Jimmy Cannon, who was still a powerful voice in sports journalism at the time, wrote an "open letter" to Joan Payson advocating Casey: "I am not asking you to engage Casey for sentimental reasons. Most of your players will be obscure kids or used-up old timers. Casey's the most famous man in baseball. He's the only box office manager in the game."

The Yankees, meanwhile, were coasting to another pennant under their rookie manager, Houk. Maris was now within striking distance of Ruth's record of sixty home runs, though a lot of enthusiasm had been drained from the chase when Commissioner Frick ruled that the feat had to be accomplished in the first 154 games or it would get a separate listing. Maris hit his sixtieth on Tuesday, September 26—the 159th game of the season. Then, at 7:00 a.m. on Friday, September 29, just before the Stengels were preparing to fly to New York to attend the World Series, Edna heard Casey on the phone.

"I heard Casey say to George Weiss, 'All right, all right, I'll do it, I'll take it,'" said Edna. "He hung up the phone and turned sheepishly to me. I said, 'Casey how could you? You've nothing to gain and everything to lose!' He set his jaw and replied, 'I just TOOK it, that's all! I couldn't let George down. And we're gonna do okay.'"

Conversations he'd had in previous days with Mrs. Payson and Grant had apparently sealed the deal for Casey. "They're high-class people," he said.

Casey told people that Weiss had brought up a four- or five-year contract, but that he insisted on just one year. He would receive sixty-five thousand dollars, a figure that stayed locked in with each of his subsequent Mets contracts.

Later that day, when he met a few West Coast reporters at his bank office, he appeared in perfect health, posing with a black baseball bat in his hand. He accidentally called his new team the "Knickerbockers," and he pronounced their ballpark as the "Polar Grounds."

So, instead of merely flying east to attend the series, Casey would now be attending a press conference on Monday, October 2—the day after Maris hit his sixty-first. The press conference was held at the Savoy Hilton—the "scene of the execution"—which had to feel good to Casey.

At the press conference were two coaches Casey was introducing that very day—Cookie Lavagetto and Solly Hemus—both of whom had managed (and been fired) in 1961, Minnesota and St. Louis, respectively. Hemus would run the clubhouse meetings that preceded each series as the season played out. The former Yankee great Red Ruffing was already aboard as a pitching coach; Red's "closer" from his days with the Yanks, Johnny Murphy, was the Mets' scouting director. Ruffing would operate from the bullpen; there was no pitching coach in the dugout. That would be a departure for Casey, who was used to having Jim Turner at his side in the dugout as pitching coach.

The plan would be to draft veteran players, familiar names, to break onto the big stage that was New York City. Having a seasoned manager would be wise under those circumstances. Having one who had proved to be a master at public relations was the added bonus. No one in uniform could "sell" a team the way Casey could. The idea of his deflecting criticism away from the players and instead drawing attention to himself was not on people's minds at the time: no one thought the Mets would be *that* awful.

The World Series opened at Yankee Stadium two days after the press conference. Casey was there, and, of course, a center of attention. He was on the field before the game and talked casually with his old players. It was his first time back.

"Stick around," said Yogi. "When I get through here I'll come over and give you a lift."

Casey responded, "You'll be here until they retire you at 65."

The second game of the series was the only one that Cincinnati won. A 2–2 tie was broken in the fifth, when the Reds' Venezuelan infielder, Elio Chacon, hustled home from third on a passed ball. Casey made note of the kid; and he was the second Met selected five days later when the expansion draft was held.

George Vecsey, a young reporter with *Newsday,* was sitting in the main press box when he heard a commotion below him, in the seats behind home plate. Casey and Edna were departing a little early, and were walking below them in the aisle separating the box seats from the reserves.

"I saw that red hair," said Vecsey. "Milton Gross [*New York Post* columnist] used to call him Bixby—a brand of shoe polish—for that hair. It was really the color between his younger blonde and his aging white. And the people were all rising and cheering and shouting his name and applauding. And he was loving every moment of it. The two of them walked towards the exit ramp even with first base, where you could go out to the street. He had it all that day—adulation, redemption, love. If a man could define 'the best day'—that could have been it. It was a thing of beauty to see."

There was much work to be done. Casey was now happy to talk about his Mets to everyone. The Mets had a float in the Macy's Thanksgiving Day Parade in New York, and there was Casey in all his glory, up on the float with ex-Dodgers Hodges and Billy Loes, and ex-Giant Monte Irvin, who worked for Rheingold beer, by then the Mets' principal sponsor. "It was a splendid experience," he said. "Most of the kids musta thought I was Santa Claus."

"You could tell from the people in the street that day," said Irvin in 2015, "that the town was about to fall in love with the Mets, and Casey was going to lead them there."

PART THREE

36

SELLING THE
AMAZIN' METS

ONE MIGHT SAY THAT Casey Stengel reinvented the selling of professional baseball with the 1962 Mets.

Sure, he expected better results on the field. He did not know that his team would go 40-120, the worst record of the twentieth century. Or that they would be last in team batting, last in ERA, and last in fielding. Given that, it was hard to point a finger at anything specific that went wrong. But he had something special brewing—something he could not have anticipated. He created the only expansion team ever to be considered "lovable losers," and did it in a city that was known for accepting only winners. No expansion team that followed was able to mirror this formula. It wasn't as though anyone figured, "Hey, let's be the worst team ever and people will love us."*

The newspapers did not focus on that, however. In fact, they championed the Mets' accomplishments and forgave their sins with understanding smiles. And, in many ways, this was due to Casey: he was as quotable as ever, as lovable as ever, and the writers bought it. He made them feel "we are all in this together." The writers, then, became part of the team's effort to sell the club to New York, and when the Mets won the World Series seven years later, they awarded those same writers with World Series rings—something that had never been done before in baseball. Among "my writers" who got rings were Maury Allen, Jack Lang, Dick Young, and Barney Kremenko, all still on the scene in '69.

Whitey Herzog—a Yankee prospect in the 1950s and a Mets executive later in the 1960s, and later a successful manager—said, "Casey

---

* Eventually, the means for stocking expansion teams improved, largely because of what happened to the Mets.

taught me how to handle reporters. He said, "Be very nice to them. You feed them. You drink them and you put them to bed at 4 a.m.—too late for them to remember the score."

The Mets were perfect fodder for a new breed of sportswriters who called themselves "the Chipmunks." They were perpetually curious writers who had a measure of disdain for the perfection that was the Yankees, and the Mets' arrival fell right into their hands—a team of very human failures, at a perfect time.

"The new young baseball writers were writing who the players were as people—with a special consideration for sense of humor," recalls one of them, *Newsday*'s Steve Jacobson. "The old school guys called us Chipmunks and we liked that. Dick Young had been doing the same thing without the humor, but he rejected identifying with us. The Mets, with [Richie] Ashburn's wit and Stengel, fit just right. Jimmy Cannon refused to write about the Mets without a sneer as if they were less than human. There is no question that if Stengel had been a writer, he would have been a Chipmunk. He was all Chipmunk."

CASEY DID NOT PARTICIPATE much in the October 10 expansion draft. While Houston, the other 1962 NL expansion team, drafted young, the Mets drafted old and went for known names to populate their roster. Each of the eight National League teams left an unprotected list of what amounted to unwanted players. Weiss, assisted by the coaches Lavagetto and Hemus, took Hobie Landrith as their first pick, because, as Casey would later tell the announcer Lindsey Nelson, "You gotta start with a catcher 'cause if you don't you'll have all passed balls."

The other fifteen players the Mets picked that day had some familiarity to fans—Gus Bell, Roger Craig, Gil Hodges, Don Zimmer—or would become well known over time, such as Jay Hook, Craig Anderson, Jim Hickman, Choo-Choo Coleman, Al Jackson, Felix Mantilla, Elio Chacon, and Joe Christopher.

"They really gave it to us," Casey later reflected. "They sold us all the disabled players they had."

The Mets tried seven catchers in 1962. "I've got one that can throw, but can't catch, and one that can catch but can't throw; and one who can hit but can't do either," Casey reflected at one point.

On November 28, 1961, they acquired three-time All-Star outfielder Frank Thomas, who would lead the team with thirty-four home runs and ninety-four RBIs; on December 8, they bought four-time All-Star Richie Ashburn from the Cubs. Thomas would give them genuine power in the middle of the lineup, and Ashburn would give them a .306 season. But more than that, the erudite Ashburn became an immediate friend to the press corps, a counterbalance to Stengelese. The writers loved his insight, loved his leadership, loved his intelligence, and loved how he could speak the truth without compromising the magic that was going on amidst the losing.

Casey had reversed all the "clown" talk and memories of his failed Brooklyn and Boston assignments with his Yankee success. He was often asked whether he was concerned that this new assignment would tarnish his great reputation as a manager. "How big is baseball and how big is a record?" asked Stengel. "Well, I'll tell ya—baseball is far bigger than any record, including my own. I'm here to help baseball by helping Weiss rebuild this new club in a hurry."

Leonard Koppett, the scholarly reporter with *The New York Times* (he considered himself a badger, not a Chipmunk) and *The Sporting News,* saw it like this: "It was a loyalty and obligation Stengel felt with deep sincerity—that he might be able, by his promotional flair and perhaps by his instruction on the field, to contribute something to the game-business-sport that had been his life and had made him wealthy. That he could indulge his ego while doing so was simply icing on the cake."

IN JANUARY, THE METS hired Rogers Hornsby as a hitting coach, to work both at the major- and minor-league levels. Hornsby was a heavy drinker and was always a difficult hire for teams. He was one of the great hitters in baseball history—.358 lifetime!—but a difficult man to work with, whether managing or coaching. The deal he made with the Mets was that he wouldn't have to make road trips. His own autobiography, the controversial *My War with Baseball,* was published that spring, and Casey agreed to write a foreword for it. In midseason, however, Hornsby was transferred to "special assignments" and more or less vanished from the scene. He died in January 1963.

Then they changed Red Ruffing's assignment from scouting to coaching, naming him pitching coach. Ruffing, the leading winner in Yankee history (at that time), had scouted in the Cleveland organization from 1948 to 1958. He and Casey had never worked together. Red Kress was also named as a minor-league pitching coach, with time assigned to the major-league club. He died of a heart attack in late November 1962, at age fifty-five.

This, along with Lavagetto and Hemus, would be Stengel's support staff, and much more involved in running the games than the coaches on the Yankees had been. Casey's age would slow him down, and he turned over much of the daily duties to his coaches. He also brought back his Yankee trainer, Gus Mauch, to train the Mets.

FLYING TO FLORIDA FROM the West Coast for his first spring camp, Casey had to show resiliency at seventy-one, and he did. Unable to land in Tampa because of fog, his plane was rerouted to Miami. Another plane took them on a short hop to Orlando. Casey told the airline people he needed another plane to go the ninety-five miles to Tampa to complete this long journey. But the airline couldn't provide one, and got him a bus for his party of five. And that's how Casey got to his first Mets camp.

The Mets were taking over the Yankees' St. Petersburg facilities, the Yankees having moved to Fort Lauderdale. Everything would be done in surroundings familiar to Casey, including the hotel, the Colonial Inn, which featured a lobby sign: STENGELESE SPOKEN HERE. It was Casey's first National League camp since 1943. He wore the familiar uniform number 37.

He was a delight in spring training, talking endlessly to fans, signing everything from pizza boxes to plaster casts, dancing the Twist for TV cameras, basking in the adulation of "my writers," who included Dick Young of the *Daily News*. Young, by now the most influential columnist in town, really took to the Mets, loved that Stengel had been hired as their manager, and took to calling their fans "the New Breed."

The fans took to chanting "Let's Go Mets," which remained part of the culture of being a Mets fan past the team's fiftieth anniversary.

Casey did interviews with anyone who had a tape recorder or a camera. He talked about the "Youth of America" growing up to play for the Mets. He talked about babies being born whose first words would be "Metsies, Metsies, Metsies." When fans started to bring banners to games with clever sayings (to be captured on TV), he said, "The placards are amazin'"—he liked saying the word "placards." (Nonsense like placards was banned in Yankee Stadium.)

He latched on to the word "amazin'" for everything Met. The fans were amazin'. His writers were amazin'. Choo-Choo Coleman (his catcher whose specialty was catching low pitches), was amazin'. He might latch on to an unknown prospect like Ken MacKenzie and call him an amazin' phenom.

"I pitched for Yale," said MacKenzie, who at 5-4 would have the only winning record on the '62 Mets, "and I'm not sure Casey admired that or not, but one day he came to the mound and told me to 'pretend you're pitching against the Harvards.' I think he actually knew that I was 6-0 against Harvard; I was the only Yale pitcher in history to beat them six times. He knew. He knew everything."

EVEN THOUGH THE WRITERS were enthusiastically supportive of the Mets' efforts to put a decent team on the field, it was becoming apparent that the band of over-the-hills they had assembled were not, in fact, going to challenge for much. Asked where he thought the Mets would finish, Casey responded, "Chicago."

Robert Lipsyte, a twenty-four-year-old reporter for *The New York Times,* was assigned that spring to do some stories on the Mets. He didn't have Casey the Yankee to fall back on, and he was observing the legend for the first time.

Thirteen years later, Lipsyte wrote in his book *SportsWorld* that Stengel "was treated as a clown and a breathing museum piece. He was neither. . . . He was unfailingly true to himself. He thought the Mets were 'horseshit' (a favorite baseball epithet for incompetence), and that 'Mrs. Payson and the attendance got robbed' every time they played. This was treated as a charming eccentricity by the press rather than honest appraisal, which they were not used to.

"He worked hard diverting the writers for the Mets, but he soon lost interest in the team itself. . . . He was capable of foul-mouthed nastiness, especially toward ballplayers who messed up or dogged it, and he could be incredibly kind."

Lipsyte told of Casey's patience with the handicapped, how he actually walked through the stands to greet someone in a wheelchair so the person wouldn't have the bumpy ride down the steps toward the field. There was also the story of an old fan in Houston who came down to meet Casey, with his embarrassed teenage son in tow, telling Casey they had played against each other at Kankakee in 1910. Casey had no idea who the guy was, but he went to great lengths to recall the fellow's skills so that the son would be impressed.

—

ON MARCH 22, THE Yankees returned to St. Pete for the first spring meeting between the New York teams, and Casey delighted in winning 4–3
against a lineup that included Mantle, Maris, Richardson, Howard, Skowron, Lopez, Boyer, Cerv, Stafford, and Terry. He happily posed for all sorts
of photos with his old charges—anything "my photographers" needed.

Optimism is always the hallmark of spring training—for everyone.
The New Yorker had Roger Angell on hand for the Yankees-Mets game;
he reported: "The Mets are an attractive team, full of echoes and over-
tones, and one must believe that George Weiss has designed their clean,
honest, but considerably frayed appearance with great care. Gus Bell,
Frank Thomas, Eddie Bouchee, and Richie Ashburn are former head-
liners whose mistakes will be forgiven and whose accomplishments will
win sentimental affection. . . . Finally, there is Casey himself, a walking
pantheon of evocations. His pinstripes are light blue now, and so is the
turtleneck sweatshirt protruding above his shirt, but the short pants, the
hobble, the muttering lips, and the comic, jerky gestures are unaltered,
and today he proved himself still capable of the winning move."

The Mets opened the regular season with a single game on the road
before coming home. It was an 11–4 loss in St. Louis, after a stuck hotel
elevator almost caused half the starting lineup to arrive late.

The next day, April 12, Bill Shea arranged for a ticker tape parade
up Broadway to welcome National League baseball back to town (just
a week after a similar parade for the astronaut John Glenn), followed
by a reception at City Hall. All the players sat outdoors behind the
podium, as Mayor Robert Wagner, relieved of the burden of having lost
the Dodgers and Giants, addressed the fans assembled in front. Then it
was Bill Shea's turn. After a less-than-rousing, almost apologetic speech,
he paused, looked at the crowd, leaned into the mike, and said, quite
dishearteningly, "And fans, all we're asking for is a little patience until
we get ourselves some real ballplayers." One can imagine how that went
over with Hodges, Zimmer, Craig, Ashburn, Bell, Thomas, and all the
other veterans sitting up there behind their new owner.

ATTENDANCE FOR THE HOME opener the next day was small—12,447
for a game played with the lights on, on a gray and murky afternoon.
Clearly, the Mets still had some work to do.

Casey's office in the Polo Grounds was not what had been the manager's office for McGraw, Terry, Ott, Durocher, or Bill Rigney. That area had been carved into quarters, with the traveling secretary Lou Niss, the PR director Tom Meany, and the statistician Joe McDonald each getting a piece. Casey had a round table rather than a desk—a place to entertain his writers. His office had a window onto the field, where he could watch batting practice with binoculars.

And then he accidentally locked himself out of the office on opening day, and a locksmith had to be found so he could retrieve his lineup card.

Casey loved having the presence of Zimmer at third. "Zimmer is going to give me a spark in that infield," he said. "You can put him down as the third baseman and forget about it." But Zimmer somehow knew better. "The first time he took BP at the Polo Grounds," says Roger Craig, "he said, 'I won't be here long—I can't pick up the ball out of the Rheingold sign in the scoreboard.'" (The Rheingold sign graced the bottom of the inning-by-inning scoreboard, and would light up with an illuminated "h" for "hit" and "e" for "error," which were plentiful.)

Zim went 4-for-52 in fourteen games, and was traded to Cincinnati on May 7.

As he recited his opening-day lineup on video for the announcer Lindsey Nelson, a classic Casey moment emerged. He listed his players and said a little about each one, but when he got to right field, he drew a blank.

Nelson said, "He paused for just a second or two, trying to remember Gus Bell's name. Then he resumed talking, saying, 'We got five or six fellas that's doing very good and the best played for Hornsby at Cincinnati, bats lefthanded and hit .300, done very good, delighted to have him, is married, has seven kids in the station wagon he drives down here from Cincinnati where he lives. . . .'

"Twelve minutes after I asked the original question, he said, 'Yes, sir, he comes down for spring training with his whole family and if he can hit for us like he hit for Hornsby, he'd ring the bell—and that's his name, Gus Bell!'"

THE METS LOST THE home opener 4-3 (they would go 19–39 in one-run games), and then they lost again, and again, and again—until the losing streak was nine. Finally, on April 23, Jay Hook beat the Pirates 9–1 at Forbes Field, and the Mets had a victory. But by then they were already eight and a half games out of first.

Few victories would follow as the season played on. And Casey was already a different manager from the one he had been in the Bronx. He relied on his coaches more. He didn't learn his players' names or always know who was available. These games were not pennant-contending, and he knew it.

"It seemed like a lot to ask for him to know all the pitchers he had on any given day," recalled MacKenzie. "They didn't write all the extra players on the lineup cards in those days. One afternoon the phone rang in the bullpen. [The bullpens at the Polo Grounds were in fair territory, out along the running track in the outfield.] Ruffing answered it and Casey said, 'Get someone up!' Ruffing said, 'Who do you want? Casey couldn't think of any names, so he just said, 'Better get two guys up,' and he hung up. Red got to choose."

The Mets would go 2-16 against Los Angeles, 4-14 against San Francisco, and an embarrassing 3-13 against Houston, the other expansion team that started the same day they did.

They were only 17-61 in the second half, when improvement might have been expected. They were 4-13 in extra-inning games. They led the league with 210 errors, and each loss seemed to feature a unique error that had everyone talking.

And laughing. Yes, the manner in which the Mets blew leads or got clobbered was indeed the stuff of water-cooler talk the next day.

"They commenced to hit the ball over the building," Casey would say, in describing what happened following a loss. And he wasn't talking about foul balls leaving the ballpark. They were all fair.

"It wasn't very good but at least it was long," he would say after another loss on a hot summer's day.

Humorists were catching on. Johnny Carson took over *The Tonight Show* the day after the season ended, and, since the show originated in New York, he quickly worked Mets humor into his monologues.

The only one who didn't seem to "get it" was Howard Cosell, who was doing pre- and post-game radio shows with Ralph Branca. Cosell pretty much reverted to calling Casey a clown, and regularly berated the team for its lack of progress. "We would watch the game on TV at WABC on Seventy-seventh Street," said Branca later. "Or sometimes at [Cosell's] home in Pound Ridge. I'd let him have his say; I didn't really agree or disagree. Howard definitely didn't like Casey, but off mike, he never said anything critical about him. He saved it all for the live reports on air."

Casey took defeat as hard as ever—he still needed to walk off the games around Central Park South at night—though he tried to point out positives. If he was upset with a veteran player's mistakes, he let him know it. He encouraged Weiss to make trades—he counted on them! But they never seemed to materialize in a big way.

The victories, of course, were special events. When the Mets beat the Phillies April 28 in the Polo Grounds—only their second win of the month!—he trotted all the way to the clubhouse in center field, stopping a few times along the way to bow to the fans.

CASEY AND EDNA LOVED the players' families. The first "Met baby" was a son born on February 23, 1962, to the catcher Chris Cannizzaro (whom Casey always called Chris "Canzonari"). As Cannizzaro recalled:

> He was born in California, so I didn't get to see him until we went to San Francisco for the first time. Except I wasn't going to San Francisco; I was being sent to Buffalo! So our equipment man, Herb Norman tells me, "Casey wants to see you." And Casey said, "I'll bring you back in thirty days," which he did. By then, my wife came to New York, so I finally got to see him there.
>
> Edna was great with little Chris, would hold him and take pictures. The two of them were great with kids, they loved Family Day, and Casey always knew which kids belonged to which players.
>
> If Casey had a pet player that would have been Rod Kanehl. He knew him as a Yankee farmhand, same as Marv Throneberry, but Kanehl never got called up to the Yanks like Marv did. Now Casey thought he could be a breakthrough player.

Kanehl, a minor leaguer since 1954, scored the tying or winning run seven times, six as a pinch runner, and that was enough for Casey to consider him a lucky charm.

"I think Casey saw Kanehl as his Mets version of Billy Martin," says Joe McDonald, the team's original statistician, who years later became their general manager. "He saw Rod as the dirty-uniform type who would do anything to win a game. He liked that."

"Casey called Kanehl 'My little scavenger,'" says the sportswriter

Steve Jacobson. "This was a big advance from being a 'road apple,' which is a term he used for bad players. 'Road apple' was a euphemism for 'horse manure.'"

Marvin Eugene Throneberry (check out those initials) became a media darling, and hence a fan favorite. There was a fan club, whose members wore T-shirts that said "VRAM" ("Marv" backward). He made base-running errors and fielding errors and missed bases while running. His history really wasn't that bad! He had played first for Houk at Denver and done very well!

On June 17, he hit a triple against the Cubs. But he was called out when the umpire ruled that he'd missed second base. When Casey came out to argue, the umpire Dusty Boggess reportedly said, "Don't bother arguing, Casey, he missed first base, too."

Charlie Neal, a former Dodger playing second for the Mets, homered the next day, and Casey popped out of the dugout and pointed to each base so Neal wouldn't miss any."

One day, the roof was leaking in the Mets clubhouse—right on Throneberry. And Marv said, "Fine, I deserve it.'"

"I was in awe of Casey when I met him for the first time in 1960 with the Yankees," Jacobson remembers. But you could talk to him—he was seldom hostile. He could get riled up talking about the Yankees when he managed them, but with the Mets he was far more explanative. "And funny. When I introduced him to my new wife, he took her by the elbow and said, 'I don't even know you and you could be my number-three catcher."

CASEY KEPT SELLING HIS team. On April 15, he appeared as the "Mystery Challenger" on *What's My Line?*, whose panelists included Bennett Cerf, the head of the Random House publishing company. Cerf had just published Stengel's book, *Casey at the Bat*. Casey signed his name on the blackboard as he entered to a wild ovation from the audience—enough to make the blindfolded panelists think it was a beautiful film star. But they quickly guessed his identity and treated him with awe, praising him for giving New Yorkers the underdog team they needed.

He posed for billboard advertisements with Miss Rheingold, holding a bat in a bunt position with the beauty queen behind him in the posture of a catcher. There was no beer in the photo, but Casey was fined five hundred dollars by Commissioner Ford Frick for violating the ban on uniformed personnel appearing in alcoholic beverage advertising.

In June, the Mets picked up the aging outfielder Gene Woodling, who had been a member of Casey's five straight world-champion Yankees. "One day, we're dropping throws, wild pitching, getting clobbered and Casey catches my eye while I'm sitting in the dugout," said Woodling. "He winks at me and whispers, 'Ain't like the old days, is it?' "

IT WAS JUST AFTER a big Memorial Day in New York when the Los Angeles Dodgers came "home" to play the Mets. The Mets had just lost six straight in California to the two former New York teams. A total of 55,704 turned out—mostly Dodgers fans, of course—to see the Mets lose a doubleheader, the first game to Sandy Koufax. The Giants came next, with Willie Mays returning to the Polo Grounds, and they also swept the Mets. Before this was all over, the Mets had rolled up a seventeen-game losing streak.

In fairness, a huge part of the Mets' first-season box-office success (they set an attendance record for a last-place team with 922,530) was due to New York's longing for the Dodgers and Giants. And when the relocated Los Angeles Dodgers and San Francisco Giants returned to New York for the first time in five years, those fifteen games accounted for 51 percent of the total attendance. The remaining fifty home dates averaged only 9,009 paying customers apiece.

ON JUNE 30, IN Los Angeles, Koufax no-hit the Mets, striking out their first three batters on nine pitches. Unfortunately, it was for that game that the City of Glendale had bought twelve hundred tickets. "I thought it was just dandy, until I found out they had sold a lot of 'em to my own bank!" said Stengel.

Casey, of course, was one of the few people in baseball who could watch Koufax and compare him with long-departed legends. When asked if he thought Koufax might be the best pitcher he'd ever seen, Casey responded, "I would have to say that [Grover Cleveland] Alexander was the most amazing pitcher in the National League," he said. "He had to pitch in the Philadelphia ball park, with that big tin fence in right field, and he pitched shutouts, which must mean he could do it. He had a fastball, a curve, a change of pace and perfect control. He was the best I batted against in the National League."

It was true that Casey hadn't seen everyone, of course—not quite. Cy Young was retired for four years before Casey broke into the majors.

On July 3, Casey went to the Stockton, California, home of the amateur pitching prospect Bob Garibaldi to persuade him to sign with the Mets. The next day, Garibaldi signed a $150,000 bonus contract with the Giants. For a twenty-year-old raised in California, perhaps there was little connection and little big-league glamour associated with the Ol' Perfessor.

THE CINCINNATI MANAGER, FRED HUTCHINSON, managing the National League all-star team, picked Casey as his first-base coach for the game in Washington, D.C., in July. This was the first time Casey had coached at first since he had managed the Boston Bees. (He coached third a few weeks later, when Solly Hemus was ejected from a game.)

President Kennedy was in attendance, and word was received that he would like to meet with Stan Musial, Warren Spahn, and Casey. Musial and Spahn arrived promptly; Casey was a little late and didn't stay long.

"Mr. President," he said, "I am delighted to meet you but I am not my own boss today and I have to work for another union."

Hutchinson was one of Casey's special people. "He loved him," recalled Steve Jacobson. A few years later, Hutch was dying of cancer; everyone knew it. The Mets were leaving town and Casey was upset with himself. He had neglected to say goodbye to Hutch in the Reds' clubhouse. The Mets were on the bus when he said out loud, but to himself, "Oh, maybe I better not."

Closer to home, on July 23, Casey's older brother, Grant, who had been in bad health, died of pulmonary tuberculosis in Kansas City at age seventy-four. He had been hospitalized for a week. Casey always said Grant was a good player, maybe the better of the two, but that freak accident that injured his foot when he was a boy killed off any hope of Grant Stengel's turning pro. Instead, he became a taxi driver in Prairie Village, just south of Kansas City. That left their sister, Louise, who was unmarried and still lived in the old family house, as Casey's surviving sibling. Casey left the team to go to the funeral.

A week later, he received the customary birthday cake at home plate—for birthday number seventy-two—before a game in St. Louis.

37

WORST TEAM
IN HISTORY

EVEN THOUGH THE '62 Mets were by any measure an embarrassment, they came to take on cult status as time passed. Anyone on that roster that year was "an original Met," which meant autograph shows, anniversary revisits, and a special place in the hearts of baseball fans—just as though they had been world champions. As Ken MacKenzie would remember:

> My first real contact with Casey came the first day of the full squad reporting, when he walked us around the bases and explained the perils and opportunities at each one. He'd been doing this for years. It was mostly double talk, and I saw smiles on Craig, Hodges, Neal, and Zimmer as he did it.
>
> He used the newspapers to make points about the players. A lot of guys didn't like that. If he thought someone was any good, he'd say, "He could make a living."
>
> After that first season, when I was 5-4, I was sent the same contract, ten thousand dollars. I didn't sign it and I thought Casey had said he'd go to bat for me. But he didn't, I had to fight myself for the $13,750 that I got from Weiss. He told me I was lucky to win any games.

Roger Craig was clearly the staff leader, both in wins (ten) and in stature (he had seventeen "quality starts" by today's standards). One day, Casey went to pull him, and Roger lost his temper. " 'You're gonna lose another one, you old goat,' " said Craig, according to MacKenzie.

And he stormed off. Then, in the dugout, he felt badly. Casey put his hand on Roger's knee and said, "You know, you've lost a few yourself." After Craig apologized, Casey said, "Ah, forget it, I know you want to win. So do I."

Once, almost in desperation, he said he'd give fifty dollars to anyone who got hit by a pitch. Kanehl got hit! I drew a dollar sign on his bruise, and sure enough Casey took out his wallet and gave him the fifty.

Howard Clothes had a billboard at the Polo Grounds, and the guy who hit the sign the most would win a boat. Casey didn't like that contest at all, and he grumbled, "If you want a boat, join the navy." [Throneberry, from landlocked Tennessee, won the boat.]

When I got traded to St. Louis, I went to Casey in his office to say thank you. And he said, "Good luck to you; I know you tried your best."

HE WAS GREAT WITH the players' kids, recalled Jay Hook, forever to be remembered as the first pitcher to win a game in the team's history. Hook was brainy—he had a master's degree in thermodynamics from Northwestern, and wrote a paper proving that a baseball can curve. Casey sometimes called him "the professor," not to be confused with his own tag as "the Ol' Perfessor." Hook would later recall:

We had two little kids and lived in a rental house. Sometimes we'd bring them to dinner at the Colonial Inn. We'd dress the kids up nicely, and Casey and Edna really liked them. When I eventually got traded, Casey said, "Edna's gonna be really upset with me for moving those kids."

He showed me something with Al Jackson. Jackson arrived at the Colonial Inn for spring training, and the cab driver told him he would have to take him around to the back entrance. Al said, "I'm not paying you if you do that." He went to his room and got a call from hotel management, telling him he could not use the pool or eat in the dining room. Casey went to bat for him, and told the hotel, "If you want to treat our players that way, we'll move to another hotel." They let Al use the facilities.

After my first win, the reporters took a lot of time with me, and there was no hot water left in the showers. Casey said, "Take as much time as you want, we'll hold the plane."

CASEY CALLED ROGER CRAIG "Mr. Craig"; to him, Ashburn, Zimmer, Bell, Hodges, and Craig were the adults on the team. He looked to them for leadership.

"We all looked up to Roger Craig," said Craig Anderson. "He was mature—he was our leader."

Roger remembered:

He [Casey] told me if I got a contract that I didn't think was enough, I should call him and he'd help me. And, of course, I got one, I called him, and he did help. I admired that. When my pitching record was bad, with all those losses, he'd tell me, "You're pitching good, don't worry about it," and it did make me feel better.

Gus Mauch, with all his training equipment that he'd travel with, also carried a case of booze for Casey on the road. It was one of his responsibilities. Casey could hold his liquor, everyone knew that.

He would occasionally fall asleep in the dugout, especially on a doubleheader day. One year we played twenty-one doubleheaders! If he'd nod off, Lavagetto would cover for him, or he might prod him and say, "You might want to send so-and-so up to pinch-hit." But he didn't really manage that much; he'd do the lineup card, and he'd let his veterans play the whole game. Hemus and Lavagetto would help with small moves during the game.

Craig Anderson agreed. "He slept on the bench. Once we played in St. Louis on a Sunday, and all commercial airlines had been grounded. We had to take an overnight train to Pittsburgh and played two the next day. I saw him nodding off that day—who could blame him—he was seventy-three then—but he'd wake up and start flashing signals to make you think he was paying attention."

"I was pitching one day and all of a sudden I kinda lost my control," added Roger Craig. "Casey walked to the mound and says, 'Mr. Craig, what seems to be the trouble?' And I said, 'The balls feel real slippery.' He reaches down, and he says, 'Well, there's one ton of dirt below your feet. You might want to reach down and rub the blasted ball up.' And with that, he waddled off.

"Casey always let the starting pitcher go over the other team's lineup, so the defensive guys would know where to play. I'm going over the Giants one day, and I get to McCovey. I said, 'He's a low-ball hitter and a dead pull hitter. Play him to pull.' And Casey interrupts me and says, 'Mr. Craig, do you want the right fielder to play in the upper deck or the lower deck?' "

Late in the season, Craig stayed home with an injury as the Mets began a road trip. "I left my pitching staff back home," Casey told his writers. It was a high compliment for Roger.

Craig Anderson had first met Casey when he was in high school in the Washington, D.C., area. A Yankee scout took him to Griffith Stadium to see Stengel, who said, "Oh, I've heard a lot about you." "Of course," recalls Anderson, "he'd never heard of me at all. But that was Casey; the gift of gab. He never had one-on-one moments with players. It was always the press in his office with him. No one just popped in and said, 'How ya' doin', Casey?' "

Early in that first season, we were behind 5–0 in the fourth inning when Casey lifted our starter and brought in Herb Moford. Moford was to lead off our half of the inning. The coaches said to Casey, "Who you wanna pinch-hit?" They sort of pushed him, but he wouldn't go along with it. He went to Moford and said, "Are you a good hitter?" Naturally, Moford said yes—no pitcher ever wants to come out. The coaches were mad, shaking their heads. And Moford singles to left. That would be a funny enough conclusion, except Casey then sent in a pinch runner. You could never figure him out, you could never read his mind.

He always rode the team bus; he never took taxis. But, oh boy, he could be tough on Lou Niss, our traveling secretary. He wanted everything just so, and anything that wasn't, he'd let Niss have it. This was sad, because all the players liked Lou. We felt sad seeing that.

"He'd imitate Niss's walk, which was a little prissy, smoking a cigarette and walking behind him," Jacobson remembered, laughing.

Once, Niss overpaid everyone by ten dollars on their meal money, and had to ask for it back. Casey stood up and said, "Take it out of my check, Lou." That was about three hundred dollars—another reason Casey wasn't crazy about Niss.

"We were in Norfolk, Virginia, once to play an exhibition game with the Orioles," recalled Craig Anderson. "At a fund-raising breakfast, Casey was called upon to introduce his team. He completely skipped the outfielders. When he was asked about it, he said, 'We have big trades pending, and I didn't want to mention any names.' It made no sense."

ON AUGUST 16, THE city of St. Petersburg decided to rename Miller Huggins Field to Huggins-Stengel Field. There was considerable opposition by locals and old-time baseball writers (Huggins and his family actually lived in St. Petersburg, and his brother was still living there), but the vote passed; two plaques are now side by side outside the old ballpark.

In the last week of the season, the Mets announced that Casey would return to manage again in 1963, when it was expected that the team would move into the new Shea Stadium. The idea of having Casey on hand to open the ballpark was appealing, but, alas, it would not be ready, and a second year at the Polo Grounds was necessary.

"Around this time, the Mets got Joe Pignatano, the former Dodger—he was like the tenth catcher of the season," recalled Matt Winick, a long-time Mets publicist. "He got to New York early and sat in the dugout with Casey for a long time, just the two of them. Around four-thirty the writers arrived, and one of them says, 'Who's catching tonight?' And Casey said, 'This Italian fellow, if he ever shows up.' He somehow missed Piggy's greeting and never knew that was him."

The inaugural season ended with a thud. The next-to-last game was a victory, the team's fortieth. Somehow thirty-nine would have sounded a lot worse than forty, but 40-120, sixty games out of first, was easy to remember. (Two rained-out games were not made up.)

Fittingly, in the eighth inning of the last game, Pignatano popped up to second (in short right field), and the Cubs turned it into a 4-3-6 triple play. It was, in a sense, a perfect ending.

The Mets had used forty-five players and 124 different lineups. They never could find the right mix, because there wasn't enough talent to mix anything. The regular starters had embarrassing marks of 10-24 (Roger Craig), 3-17 (Craig Anderson), 8-20 (Al Jackson), and 8-19 (Jay Hook). Casey called the right-hander Bob Miller, 1-12, "Nelson," for reasons

Miller never knew. The Mets also had a left-handed Bob Miller, who had a 7.08 ERA.

The season was memorable and defined in a number of ways, but the popular columnist Jimmy Breslin struck the right chord by writing the book on the Mets, *Can't Anybody Here Play This Game?,* which was published in 1963.

He took the title from a supposed quote of Casey's, which he may or may not have said: "You look up and down the bench and you have to say to yourself, 'Can't anybody here play this game?'" (Some felt it was "Can't anybody play this here game?")

There were other books to come in ensuing years. The book agent Bill Adler compiled *Love Letters to the Mets* from real letters the PR department received. George Vecsey wrote *Joy in Mudville*. Leonard Shecter wrote *Once Upon a Time*. Leonard Koppett wrote *The New York Mets*. Lindsey Nelson wrote *Backstage at the Mets*. Jerry Mitchell wrote *The Amazing Mets*. All focused on Casey, which was what the Mets wanted. That's a lot of books about a last-place team, although later ones ran up to the team's 1969 championship from such humble beginnings.

An unpublished diary of the second season, "Let's Go Mets," written by two teenage fans in suburban New York, was discovered. Maury Allen, who would come to prominence with the *New York Post* in the sixties, made a side living doing Mets books and Casey books.

One thing was certain. Casey Stengel had more than earned his salary in 1962. The New York Mets were on the national consciousness, and on the heels of genuinely competing for attention with the Yankees.

38

CLOSING THE
POLO GROUNDS

THE 1963 SEASON, WHEN it came to inept play, was similar to 1962, but without the beauty of being shocking.

True, the Mets lost only their first eight this time around, not their first nine, but they did manage to put up a twenty-two-game road losing streak, which was the longest in baseball since 1890—the year Casey was born. (The streak ended with a win at Dodger Stadium on Casey's seventy-third birthday.)

Ordinarily, an eleven-game improvement from one year to the next would be notable, but the Mets' 51-111 record was still awfully bad, and, in fact, awful in so many other ways.

It became obvious that Shea Stadium—not yet officially named—would not be ready for opening day of 1963. When the Mets made that announcement, they still intended to move there sometime during the season, but that never happened. For the second year in a row, Casey would walk off to the clubhouse in center field to the strains of "Auld Lang Syne," marking the last game ever played at the Polo Grounds. Again.

Ed Kranepool, just eighteen, had a "cup of coffee" with the Mets in '62, which meant he could forever be called an "original Met." Casey knew that Ed wasn't going to be his next Mickey Mantle, but he later told listeners, "You've got this phenom, Ed Kranepool, and in ten years, he might be on his way to the Hall of Fame. And you've got this other phenom, Greg Goossen, and in ten years, he'll be 30."

Kranepool came out of James Monroe High School in the Bronx, where he had broken Hank Greenberg's home run records. Local boy, good fodder for the New York press. At eighteen, he hit only .209 with two homers in eighty-six games in 1963, but Casey did see potential in him, and he would go on to play more games than any Met in history.

The Mets obtained the Brooklyn Dodgers icon Duke Snider on April 1, and one day soon after, Duke stood near the cage as Kranepool hit.

Casey had told Kranepool, "If I see you hitting the ball to right, I'm gonna send you to the minors."

But Snider, observing the strapping lad going the other way, said, "What the hell are you doing—pull the ball!"

Kranepool, literally half Snider's age, said, "Mind your own business; you're not doing so good yourself." Kranepool later said:

> I apologized the next day; that was wrong on my part, and he didn't deserve that. But some writers heard it and wrote about it, and suddenly Casey had a generation-gap fracas to deal with. Casey was good to me. In those days there was a thing called a progressive bonus, and I needed ninety days in the Majors for a fifteen-thousand-dollar bonus off my signing contract to kick in. The Mets were going to send me out on the eighty-seventh day, just as the All-Star Game was approaching. There would be three off days that made the difference. Casey knew when a player was getting screwed, and he spoke up for me and saw to it that I was sent out on Thursday—the ninetieth day—and that I got my bonus.
>
> He really liked working with young players. He was a teacher at heart. He took me out to right field one day and said, "I want you to hit the cutoff man," and he decided to demonstrate. Remember, he's about seventy-three years old. And his throw—well, he hit himself in the foot with it. The ball sort of stuck in his hand. "That's the way I keep it low, keep the ball down," he laughed.
>
> In clubhouse meetings, he would get right to the point—there was no Stengelese there. He was bright and articulate; always a little bit disheveled, not at all a Wall Street sort of guy despite being rich and being a banker. And he always rode the team bus with us.
>
> I'll tell you the truth, I was in awe of him, and he was great with me. He'd critique things he'd see on the field, never to embarrass a player, but to teach. He would call me over to sit with him in the dugout.

Snider, meanwhile, was playing out the final acts of his fine career. According to his old Brooklyn teammate Carl Erskine, one day, with the

Mets down 6–1 to Cincinnati, Stengel said, "Hey, Duke, you manage a few innings and maybe you can get something started!"

As the story went, Casey proceeded to move to the far corner of the dugout to take a nap. After a few innings, Snider woke him up to say it was now 9–1. "I didn't do any good," he told Casey.

"Duke, don't feel bad, look at that Cincinnati bench. All mahogany. Now look at our bench . . . all driftwood."

JIMMY PIERSALL, OBTAINED FROM Washington in a trade for Gil Hodges, was thirty-three and had been in the majors since 1950. Casey had always admired him from a distance, always said nice things about him to the press, and sort of liked his zaniness. His arrival on the Mets team marked his first time in the National League. On June 23, in the first game of a doubleheader at the Polo Grounds, Piersall hit his first home run for the Mets. It was the hundredth of his career, and he decided to run the bases backward—not in reverse order, but with his back turned.

Casey was not above on-field pranks—remember the bird flying out of his cap?—but this really rubbed him the wrong way. This wasn't how you respected the game. Piersall played in fourteen more games for the Mets, with six hits, and he was gone, he and his .194 average. The Mets released him on July 27.

A genuine star the Mets added in 1963 was the second baseman Ron Hunt. Hunt, twenty-two, hit .272 and played a gritty brand of baseball on an everyday basis, finishing second to Pete Rose in Rookie of the Year voting. The following year, he hit .303 and made the All-Star team, and he is best remembered today for having been hit by a pitch 243 times, a record at the time he retired, eleven years later.

Fans were showing small signs of losing patience. On July 15, Casey started four second-string players in the second game of a doubleheader—Joe Hicks, Larry Burright, Norm Sherry, and Kanehl. Only sixty-five hundred fans were in attendance that day, and the Mets were losing 8–0 to Houston when Casey went out to change pitchers and bring in Grover Powell. And the fans booed Casey. This had never happened before. It was a one-day occurrence, not the start of a trend, but it was noteworthy.

Sherry was a respected receiver who had helped Sandy Koufax mature into a superstar during his time with the Dodgers, and later became a manager himself. "I remember sitting next to Hodges on the first day of spring training, as Casey addressed the team," says Sherry. "I turned to

Gil and I whispered, 'I have no idea what he's talking about. And Gil said, 'I know, I got lost, too.' " *

Sherry added:

His expressions were unique. "Run, sheep, run," was one that I never really figured out. "Butcher boy, butcher boy," he might yell if he wanted you to chop the ball into the ground and try to get a big bounce and beat it out. One day he yelled it to Kanehl, who missed the ball, and our guy gets thrown out at home. Casey muttered, "That should have been a walk across the river."

One day, when we were playing in Pittsburgh, Gus Mauch came and told me Casey wanted to see me. I assumed he was sending me out or I was getting traded. He was sitting there in his Yankee underwear—I couldn't believe how disfigured his right leg was— but all he said was "How did you pitch Clendenon when you were in L.A.?" That was all.

In September we were playing in Los Angeles, where I lived. He said to me, "You don't have to go to Houston [where the Mets finished the season], you can call it a season and stay here." We had three games left. And I said, "Oh no, I'm getting paid to be with you." So Casey said, "If you had said okay I would have made you go. But since you said what you did, you can stay home, it's okay."

Matt Winick, the assistant PR director, was there for one of Casey's better-remembered quotes. "There was a young reporter in Philadelphia who was assigned to interview Casey, and frankly he was pretty frightened. We all knew he was scared. He finally said something like 'Mr. Stengel, what do people your age think of the modern player?' And Casey said, 'How the hell should I know, most people my age are dead at the present time!' "

Grover Powell, just twenty-two, pitched twenty games for the Mets that year, his only season in the majors. He was an Ivy League product— University of Pennsylvania—and the writers found him interesting and were drawn to him. The day of his only major-league win, a 4–0 shutout

---

* One guy in spring training who probably understood all—or at least most—of what Stengel "was talking about" was Bill Dickey. Casey brought him to St. Pete for ten days to work with the catchers, as he had for so many years in Yankee camps on the same turf. He returned the following year, too. Alas, there were no Berras and no Howards to be found.

in Philadelphia, sort of imitating their interest, Casey wiggled through the pack of writers surrounding him after the game and, with a pencil and a notepad in hand, said, "Wuz you born in Poland?" It was satire, it was clever, it was probably a little bit of a Polish joke, but it was a much-repeated Casey line, since so many writers were standing there when he did it.

THE WHOLE 1963 SEASON could be characterized by an August 27 game at Pittsburgh, in which the Mets had a 1–0 lead going into the ninth. Galen Cisco was pitching for the Mets, and with one out, he walked Dick Schofield, and then allowed a single to center by Manny Mota. As Mets fans were now accustomed to seeing, the center fielder, Duke Carmel, let the ball go past him. (Carmel was known to his teammates for ridiculing Casey's mannerisms behind his back.) The right fielder, Joe Christopher, recovered the ball as Schofield scored the tying run. Mota was racing around the bases—all of them. Christopher threw home, off-line, and it sailed to the backstop. Cisco chased it down as Mota headed for home. Cisco fired to Jesse Gonder, the defensively challenged Mets catcher, who might have been able to make a tag had he not been two feet from the sliding runner. He never reached for the plate.

Pirates win it, 2–1. Stay tuned for a recap after this word from fine cold Rheingold.

What can you say about a season in which the high point was an exhibition victory—the Mayor's Trophy Game on June 20 at Yankee Stadium? A rainout of the original date caused the Yankees to have to play a regular-season day game against Washington, and then the exhibition in the evening.

This was Casey's first competitive visit to the old place, but, in true John McGraw fashion (circa 1923), he had the Mets dress at the Polo Grounds and take a bus to Yankee Stadium.

Mets fans arrived with their handmade placards and bedsheets, only to find them confiscated by Yankee Stadium ushers. Such behavior was unacceptable there: the Yankees explained (not incorrectly) that the banners blocked the view of other fans. At the Polo Grounds, that was often a good thing. But not at Yankee Stadium.

Casey started Jay Hook and all his regulars and played to win. The Yankees, a little less so, in front of over fifty thousand fans. And the Mets won it 6–2 behind a five-run third inning.

"There was no heartbreak for baseball's most passionate fans this time . . . only glory," wrote Leonard Koppett in the *Times*. His colleague Bob Lipsyte, covering the placard controversy, wrote:

"The establishment began the evening with a sneer. The Stadium has always been a cold and haughty place, and early yesterday evening it was hostile to Met fans as well. Their placards and their signs and their bugles were taken away at the gate.

"'Whaddya think this is,' asked the ushers and guards, 'the Polo Grounds?'"

The Mets won both on and off the field that night, and the contrast between Casey's former club and current club was now obvious even to those who weren't paying attention.

CASEY MET THE GIANTS coach Wes Westrum for the first time in a bar at the All-Star Game in Cleveland. The next morning, Casey said, "Say, that fellow really knows his baseball. He's a pretty shrewd guy." After the season, Westrum was added to Casey's coaching staff, sort of a trade for Lavagetto, who went to coach San Francisco. Westrum would eventually succeed Casey as the Mets' manager.

Casey covered the World Series for AP News Features, dictating twelve stories to Frank Eck, who said, "His knowledge of the game and of the participating Dodgers and Yankees made this writer's task the easiest spot assignment ever." It was understood that Casey would return to manage the Mets in '64—this time, at last, in the new ballpark in Flushing.

39

SHEA STADIUM

THE MOVE TO THE newly named Shea Stadium made Casey the only man to have "worked" in five New York ballparks—Washington Park, Ebbets Field, the Polo Grounds, Yankee Stadium, and now Shea.

The modern conveniences made it a jewel among ballparks, and it opened to wonderful reviews, save for the sound of jets taking off and landing at nearby LaGuardia Airport. Casey knew all the particulars. At a winter sports dinner, when someone asked him about Shea, he said, "It has 57 bathrooms, and I need one now."

By the time Shea closed in 2008, as the third-oldest park in the league, its new shine had faded and it was hardly beloved. But the excitement in its opening year was high, especially since it was parked next to the thrilling World's Fair in Flushing Meadow, which Casey suggested would be helped more by the presence of the Mets than vice versa. (Casey went several times, and loved the "It's a Small World" ride.)

TO THE FANS, HE reported, "Yes sir, the most tremendous stadium in the world. There are 29 escalators. No more heart attacks walking to your seat. You sit down and watch the game with air conditioning and with leather-backed seats. If you don't like what's going on, you can take a nap. Or you can go see the World's Fair."

THE NEW BALLPARK, FACTORED in with the continued promotion by Casey (and certainly not for an improving team), helped the Mets outdraw the Yankees by more than four hundred thousand in 1964.

The Yankees, meanwhile, hired Yogi Berra to succeed Houk as manager, Houk having been named general manager. Managers as far back as Al Lopez had played for Casey, but Yogi was one who had spent the bulk of his playing career under Stengel. The two understood each other, and had real warmth for each other, even if they could both be challenged when it came to showing emotion. Casey was genuinely proud to see his reliable old catcher elevated, though many questioned whether Berra, a former teammate of the players he would now manage, would succeed.

Just after the new year, Bob Lipsyte of *The New York Times* initiated a three-way call between Stengel, in Glendale, Berra, in Montclair, New Jersey, and himself. It was a chance for fans to eavesdrop on the two legends in casual conversation, talking about Edna, talking about Carmen, talking about Yogi's boys, and talking a little pre–spring training baseball. The baseball talk was really "inside baseball," a treat for readers who were overhearing a genuine conversation between these two now legendary figures.

Yogi thought that Choo Choo Coleman pulled the ball too much, and Casey agreed, saying that he had killed two spectators the previous year (an obvious exaggeration), but noting that Yogi used to hit a lot of balls foul too. Yogi thought maybe Coleman needed a heavier bat.

"I never go to sleep when I'm sittin' on the bench," said Casey. "He'll pull it clear into our bench."

The story occupied six columns on the front page of the Sunday sports section.

It was a clever idea by Lipsyte, and there was no indication that the two baseball legends were "playing for the camera." This was a rare insight into a genuine conversation between these two legends, old friends and colleagues, famous for their use of the English language; something readers could never imagine eavesdropping on.

THE METS DECIDED TO re-create Casey's early-spring instructional school before spring training opened, with Casey, of course, leading it. It opened on February 7, in St. Petersburg, and the students included Bud Harrelson, Cleon Jones, and Ron Swoboda, three players who would ultimately see action in a World Series for the Mets. This was the first time Casey would have his fingerprints on the origins of a championship team, aside from Kranepool, whom he had tutored since the first year. Swoboda, all of nineteen, really impressed him—plus, he liked saying his name, "Saboda." He wanted Swoboda to go north with the team, but others overruled him, and it would be another year before the slugger from Baltimore made the club, and belted nineteen home runs in his rookie season.

Just before leaving for camp, Casey went to New York for the Baseball Writers' Dinner, where he entertained the audience with tales of his 1949–53 champions, and then the Long Island Mets Boosters gathering at the Garden City Hotel.

"He was exhausted," recalled Matt Winick, the team's assistant PR director. "But he was a good soldier and understood the importance of being with the Long Island fans. He was supposed to speak for ten minutes and wrap up at 10 p.m. So he stood up at 9:50, walked to the lectern, spoke continuously in one sentence without pausing for a punctuation mark, had everyone laughing at the Stengelese, and then, without a peek at his watch or a clock on the wall, concluded—in mid-sentence—at exactly 10:00. Not 9:59. It was a masterful performance."

"This year we're going to have a new scoreboard costing a million and a half dollars and our television will be in color," Casey told the gathering. "You can build a building in any city for $1.5 million. To make the scoreboard worthwhile and to look good in color, I'm sure the boys will rise to the occasion and score more."

Winick loved watching Casey in action. "It was an unwritten rule: never leave him alone in the hotel bar," he said. "He needed someone to talk to, someone who might look after him should he drink too much. In St. Louis, the handsome singer Robert Goulet was entertaining in our hotel. He greeted Casey during his performance. Casey said, 'I'm like this here fellow,' pointing to Goulet. 'I have effeminate appeal.'"

Winick also marveled at Casey's mastery of the press. "He knew everything about their jobs. He kept up on who the writers were. He was doing interviews in the front of a plane one day, and Leonard Shecter came up, notebook in hand, to join in. Casey said, 'I'm taking care of the morning guys now; I'll give different stuff later for your afternoon paper.'"

During spring training, the Mets made a weekend trip to Mexico City, where huge crowds came to their games, and no one was cheered more loudly than Casey.

When the Mets went to Fort Lauderdale to play the Yankees, Casey took the cap off Yogi's head and said, "Gee, no Beatle haircut, someone told me you had one."

Shea Stadium had its formal dedication on April 16, and Casey delivered the "benediction." The move to Shea did not change Casey's living habits—he retained his suite at the Essex House—but Edna fretted. "It's a $6 cab ride now," she told him. "Maybe you should take the subway."

Well, that wasn't going to happen. Casey continued to cab it.

(His annual cost for staying at the Essex House, out of his own pocket, was about forty-five hundred dollars.)

This time, the Mets' opening-week losing streak was only four, but they quickly fell to 1-8, and were in last place on April 29, doomed to spend another season there.

On May 4, a Monday-night game in Milwaukee, the Mets got into a fight with the Braves, and Casey, at seventy-three, got into the action. The old fight was still in him. He grabbed Denis Menke, the Braves' shortstop, from behind, and Menke, trying to shrug his shoulders and remove the body, dumped Casey onto the ground.

"The first body I stepped over was Casey's," said Tracy Stallard. "Oh my God."

"I didn't know whether to offer him a hand or just laugh," said Menke.

On May 10, the Mets farmed out Kranepool to Buffalo, and signed Tom Sturdivant, who had been a reliable starter for Casey in the mid-1950s with the Yankees. He made 16 appearances. The Mets would sign almost anyone with a pulse at this point. Frank Lary, thirty-four, the old Yankee-killer from the Detroit Tigers, got a contract and made eight starts.

They certainly needed bodies on May 31, when the Mets played a Sunday doubleheader with the Giants that began 1:08 p.m. and ended at 11:25 p.m. The Giants won both games, the second one lasting twenty-three innings and taking seven hours and twenty-three minutes. There were 57,037 at Shea that day, although most had departed by the time the evening came to a close. Casey (or his coaches) used twenty-one players in the second game, with a number of them—Roy McMillan, Thomas, Christopher, Kranepool (already back from the minors), Hickman, Charley Smith, and poor Cannizzaro getting ten plate appearances apiece. (McMillan, Christopher, Kranepool, and Smith also played the complete first game.)

It was just like old times for Casey: he'd actually managed a twenty-three-inning tie game in 1939 with the Bees.

On June 21—Father's Day—the Phillies' Jim Bunning made baseball history, hurling a perfect game against the Mets, the first one thrown in the National League in the twentieth century. It was only the thirty-first home game the Mets had played at Shea Stadium. Casey was right about the amazin' things fans might see there.

BILL WAKEFIELD WAS AN effective reliever for Stengel in 1964, pitching in sixty-two games with a 3.61 ERA. It was his only big-league season, but he made a lot of friends among the writers and was an insightful observer of Casey Stengel in action.

"Jerry Hinsley was with us," he said, "and he told Casey that his parents were coming to Los Angeles from New Mexico on May 20. Casey said, 'Okay, you're gonna pitch,' and he did, true to his word. A clubhouse meeting wouldn't include criticism of anyone, but he might tell a long story and look around the room, and everyone thought he was talking about them. He was always 'on.' 'You know, guys,' he'd say, 'this isn't a honeymoon trip, we're not here to entertain girlfriends, we're here to win some ballgames.' He liked to be a little vague, to get your mind going, get you thinking."

When Old-Timers Day came around, Casey was in his glory. He knew everyone, and, with a few drinks, could regale the guests with endless stories. At the dinner at Toots Shor's, he spoke for sixty-seven minutes, paused to drink some water, then went on for another twenty-eight. At least, that is what Leonard Lyons reported in the New York Post.

In mid-August, when Casey and Edna were celebrating their fortieth wedding anniversary, the Mets had a bit of a hot streak, winning nine out of eleven. Though they were buried deep in last place and only picked up two games in the standings during the streak, this was new ground for them—they were not used to good streaks at all—and there was the predictable talk about their "turning a corner." But it was not to be. They returned to their losing ways, lost eleven of twelve in late September, and wound up only two games better than the year before.

Even some of Casey's more supportive writers began to question when the Mets might "move to the next step," which implied getting a manager who was more about winning games and less about winning fans. Casey had, they felt, fulfilled his purpose—drawn attention to the franchise, put them ahead of the Yankees in attendance, opened the new stadium, and charmed the media. But maybe it was time to move on. They certainly didn't want ever to have to fire him and earn the bad will the Yankees had reaped when he departed.

Critics were heard from, and not just Cosell. Jackie Robinson, still no fan of Casey's, said he was "too critical of his players and falls asleep on the bench." Two of his departing players, Piersall and Tim Harkness, also accused him of sleeping on the bench. Snider had left bitterly at the end of spring training, sold to the Giants for thirty thousand dollars. He had no desire to play for a last-place club; at the very least, he wanted more money to serve as a player/coach.

"Maybe he'll be more content on the coast and will help that club," said Casey. "But for us you've got to ask: How many games can he play? Can you cut young pitchers to make room for him when he'd rather be nearer home, and then maybe he plays only part-time? What we need are young fellows who can play maybe eight or nine years."

The Mets called a press conference for September 29 at the New York Hilton, to announce that Casey had signed another one-year contract, to return for 1965. Weiss told the press that Casey's authority to veto trades had been removed, and that the front office now took full responsibility for the roster. Meanwhile, Casey received what he called a "splendid raise."

The "Ol' Perfessor" was delighted to carry on.

40

A SLIP AND A FALL

JUST AFTER LOSING GAME Seven of the World Series of 1964, the Yankees fired their manager, Berra, in a move reminiscent of the firing of Casey four years earlier. It was even done in the same hotel and produced the same public-relations backlash.

Yogi reached out to Casey to inquire how his coaching staff looked for '65, and the Mets hired Yogi, reuniting the two. Yogi had to pay two tolls to get from New Jersey to Flushing, but he was glad to stay in uniform and to be working with Stengel again. The Mets also signed Warren Spahn as a pitcher and coach.

So it was off to St. Pete for spring training with the can't-miss photo opportunity of Casey and Yogi together, and even the ironic photo of Casey with Spahn—who had played for him at the very start of his pitching career, "before [Casey] was a genius," with the Boston Braves.

YOGI DID NOT MAKE too many bad decisions in his career, but he made one in late April, when he agreed to be activated and do some catching for the Mets at age forty. Beginning on April 27, he appeared in four games, two of them complete games behind the plate, both as Al Jackson's batterymate. (The Mets were 1-1 in those games.) Yogi had two singles in nine at-bats and retired again, this time for good. He came to regret the foolishness of his decision to play, because it took him off the rarified air list of men who had played for only one team over lengthy careers. "I don't know what I was thinking," he said.

Spahn lasted until July 14, when Casey just told him it was time for the team to go with younger players. He'd gone 4-12 in nineteen starts.

—

A MILESTONE OF SORTS was reached on May 8, when Jack Fisher
hurled a 4–2 victory over Milwaukee and someone calculated that it was
the three thousandth victory of Casey's managing career, minors and
majors included. The victory lifted the Mets out of the cellar into ninth
place, and they would stay at that "lofty" point until May 28, when they
returned to their accustomed position.

Ron Swoboda, still just twenty, was a delight to Casey early that season. The rookie slugger from Baltimore hit .333 in April with four home
runs, and represented what Casey had always hoped for—the "youth of
America" coming to play ball for the Mets. "He can hit the ball out of the
building," bragged Casey, secretly hoping for his next Mickey Mantle.
Swoboda would remember:

> On opening day, we're playing the Dodgers, and suddenly I hear
> "Sa-boda—grab a bat." He sends me up to pinch-hit—and to bat
> against Don Drysdale. I "hear" a fastball go by me for strike one,
> and I foul off strike two. Finally, I hit a liner to second—I had
> survived. The next game, he started me and I hit a homer off Turk
> Farrell. And I was his guy that month.
>
> But in mid-May, I had a bad moment. I forget my sunglasses
> and screw up a fly ball in Busch Stadium; it gets by me for a triple
> in the ninth inning. I wanted to dig a hole and climb in. The Car-
> dinals tie the game.
>
> I was due to bat in the tenth and I wanted to make up for this in
> the worst way. But I pop out, and when I get back to the dugout, I
> throw my helmet down. There it sits. No one moves it or says any-
> thing. We don't score and I have to go back in the field. Before I do
> it, I decided to stomp on the helmet, give it one good shot. And I
> cracked it. Team equipment, and I cracked it.
>
> That was enough to Casey. He bounces up the stairs before I
> could go to my position and he says, quite sternly, like a father might,
> "Goddamn it, kid, when you screwed up that play in right field, did I
> run into the clubhouse and throw your watch on the floor?"
>
> And he was right, of course. He yanked me out of the game, and
> I went into the clubhouse and cried. But he put me back out there
> the next day, which was his way of saying, "I hope you learned
> your lesson."

I was a right fielder and Casey was a right fielder. I felt privileged to play for him. I was enthralled.

He had his own way of explaining things. When he was teaching me about hitting the cutoff man, he told me to throw like I was picking up grass—to follow through like that. One day in St. Pete, I was throwing with Carlton Willey, and my throw sailed over his head and broke the middle panel of the three windows in Casey's office. I could see his silhouette peering through the hole—and I know I'm in his bull's-eye.

Swoboda liked talking to the "old man." A conversationalist at heart, he once engaged Casey in nonbaseball talk at a writers' dinner: " 'Would you be having this much fun if you were a dentist?' " he asked? "And Casey said, 'If I was a dentist, I'd be an orthodontist. People will pay to have things done for their kids before they pay for themselves.' Very smart observation.

"He had a face right off Mount Rushmore, those incredible blue eyes, the gimp in his walk—what a wonderful character."

The game when Swoboda threw his helmet was on May 23. Swoboda remembered that Casey's arm was in a cast. On May 10, an off-day on the regular schedule, the Mets took a bus up to West Point to play an exhibition game against Army. These exhibitions had been going on for years against the New York teams, and Casey himself had even played in one in 1922, while with the Giants. That long-ago game summary in *The New York Times* noted that the Giants were "aided and abetted by Casey Stengel, whose comedy amused the cadets in the stands."

As he had done when the Yankees went up to West Point in the 1950s, Casey read the Orders of the Day in the cadets' mess hall before the game, and had a good time with that. But, leaving the gym where the team changed, and walking in his spikes to the bus (which would take the team to the playing field), Casey slipped on the concrete walk. He had asked the clubhouse boy to put shoes without spikes in his bag, but the shoes he found in there had spikes. His right wrist was fractured. It was set at the West Point hospital, and he rode back to New York with a cast on his right arm.

"It was my fault," he said. "I should have been early, and then I wouldn't have been rushed to move fast on the concrete with my spikes."

It wasn't enough to sideline him, of course. The season moved ahead.

THE JULY 31 ISSUE of *The Saturday Evening Post* came out on July 24 and featured a story by Ed Linn titled "The Last Angry Old Man." It was fairly unflattering.

Linn had collaborated with Bill Veeck on his best-selling memoir (*Veeck—As in Wreck*) and was no doubt influenced by Veeck's rather dubious overview of Stengel.

"Casey Stengel has two faces," wrote Linn. "There is the face the public has come to know and laugh at, the gimpy, dog-eared old man winking, grimacing and babbling on in what is taken, on faith, to be profound—if not always decipherable—wisdom.

Veeck acknowledged that Casey was a "wonderfully funny and engaging man" and cited his loyalty too, but criticized him for being more loyal to his writers than to his players. He also raised suspicion that his coach, Solly Hemus, had been fired for attracting too much attention away from Casey (something that would have come as a surprise to Mets followers).

After the story circulated, Hemus was moved to respond. "I know Casey had nothing to do with my leaving the Mets, and the story is unjust to Stengel. I got along with Casey and it was a pleasure to work with him. He would be the first to tell a man if he couldn't use him any longer; if he had fired me, there would have been no secret about it."

The dustup over the magazine piece came and went, and it was back to business.

Casey's seventy-fifth birthday was coming up, on July 30. Three-quarters of a century. Fifty-five years in baseball. The fortieth anniversary of his first managing job.

On July 22, Mayor Wagner presented him with a scroll in honor of his milestone birthday and all he had meant to New York baseball over the years. Casey graciously accepted and said a few words in Stengelese. (He paid Lindsey Nelson two dollars to write him a speech, and Lindsey wrote, "Thank you very much." Casey expanded a bit.) The next day, Friday, July 23, was proclaimed "Casey Stengel Day" in New York City.

Saturday, July 24, was Old-Timers' Day at Shea Stadium, and Casey participated in the festivities by wearing a Brooklyn Dodgers uniform. Then he filled out a lineup card for the regular game against Bunning and the Phillies.

He had Chuck Hiller at second, Roy McMillan at short, Ed Kranepool at first, Charlie Smith at third, Johnny Lewis in right, Ron Swoboda in left, Gary Kolb in center, Chris Cannizzaro catching and Tom Parsons pitching. Bunning went the distance to beat the Mets 5–1, in a two-hitter. The Mets fell to 31-64, still in tenth place, twenty-four games out of first.

After the game, all the Old-Timers' Day participants, the writers, and the Mets officials headed for Toots Shor's on West Fifty-second Street in Manhattan for a party. "He heard someone speak about the continuing glories of the game," wrote Leonard Lyons in the *Post,* "by quoting Branch Rickey at 82: 'My greatest thrill? I haven't had it yet.'" When Dan Daniel said, "If he hasn't had it at 82, then he'll never have it," Casey applauded.

The party went late into the night, and Joe DeGregorio, the Mets' comptroller, suggested that Casey spend the night at his house, since he would have to be at Shea early the next day; they had a doubleheader, and Casey would be honored for his birthday again, between games. DeGregorio lived in Whitestone, eight minutes from the ballpark. It sounded like a good plan, even though the Essex House was just seven blocks from Shor's.

Like most people at the party, Casey had been drinking. He slipped and fell sometime in the next hour. There is some uncertainty about where the fall happened. If it was at Shor's, there would have been many witnesses, so that seems unlikely, although Joe Durso thought the fall took place in the men's room. It was either at Shor's or at DeGregorio's home, early in the morning hours of July 25. He could even have had a fall at both places. For history's sake, it was like the punch from Ali that knocked out Liston in Lewiston, Maine: nobody really saw it.

DeGregorio got him into the house and into bed. But Casey woke up at 8:00 a.m. in great pain. DeGregorio called the trainer, Gus Mauch, to come over. By 11:00 a.m., Casey was in an ambulance on his way to Roosevelt Hospital in Manhattan. He had suffered a displaced fracture in his left hip. There would be no Casey at the ballpark that day. Wes Westrum would run the team.

Two days later, July 27, the Mets' team physician Dr. Peter Lamotte operated on him, inserting a ball made of a cobalt-chromium alloy, vitallium, called a Moore hip prosthesis. Casey would require at least three weeks in the hospital. There was, at once, a growing belief that he would not manage again.

Yogi Berra was among the first to visit him, and observed, "He's got more flowers in his room than there is in a garden." Edna had been home in Glendale all season, nursing a bad back and wearing a brace. But, despite her own back pain, which had her in bed most of the day, she managed to fly east on July 26 to be at Casey's side.

By August 6, Casey was starting to get around with a walker, and was in his usual gregarious form. The Mets scheduled a press conference at the hospital, in which Casey entertained everyone for forty-five minutes, sitting up in a yellow kimono. He popped up to show his mobility, and answered every question. As for the big one, "Will you be back?," he could only say, "I couldn't tell you."

On August 8, the Mets held their annual Banner Day at Shea, with many of the "placards" sending love and good wishes to Casey.

He was discharged from the hospital on August 13 and returned to the Essex House, a few blocks away. He wanted to stay in New York, because if he went home to Glendale, he would be out of TV and radio touch with his team. In New York, he could at least follow the games.

Coincidentally, his sister, Louise, who was now seventy-eight and lived alone in the old family house in Kansas City, took a fall at home around this same time and fractured her hip. She was alone when it happened, and she lay on the floor for more than a day until a neighbor heard her cries for help.

On August 30, Harold Weissman and Matt Winick, the Mets' PR men, called around to alert the media to a press conference at the Essex House that day. Casey entered the room with the help of a black metallic crooked cane, and went to sit with Weiss and Joan Payson at a head table.

"After much consideration," he said, "I have decided to retire as manager of the Mets at the close of the 1965 season. This is due to my wish to be relieved of the arduous duties of active management and on medical advice following my injury. I am delighted to be remaining with the Mets organization in an executive capacity."

A long question-and-answer session followed. "I'll probably be the highest-paid scout you ever saw," he said, and he described his new activities and his salary. (He would receive $50,000 in 1966, $25,000 in 1967, and $12,500 in 1968, but no pension. He would continue with the Mets organization after 1968 because of "all the club did for me.")

"You don't expect me to go onto the mound and take a pitcher out by putting this around his neck, do you?" he laughed, holding up the cane. "If I can't run out to the mound, I don't wanna finish out my service."

It was time. The Mets made him a vice president.

"I had hoped to do better, but it didn't work out that way," he said.

"However, I can see some good coming out of it. We have eight or nine players who could become big."

He wasn't far off. The '65 Mets had Kranepool, Swoboda, Cleon Jones, Bud Harrelson, and Tug McGraw—five players who would be on the roster of the world-champion Mets four years later. Larry Bearnarth, Ron Hunt, and Jim Hickman were also developing into good players.

His coach, Wes Westrum, the opposite of Casey in personality, would succeed him as manager.

On September 2, Casey returned to Shea to say goodbye to his players, and to hobble to the mound with his cane before an empty ballpark, holding a folded number-37 Mets uniform. "I don't know if they're going to burn it. If they don't put this old uniform away, I hope 37 gets a good prospect in it some day."

But the Mets were retiring his number that very day, the first time this had happened in the franchise's short history. "I hope they don't put ME under glass," he said.

He was next on his way home to Glendale, but first came a stopover in Kansas City to visit Louise. In Glendale, he was greeted by kids from Hoover High School holding WELCOME HOME CASEY signs.

Casey did not go to the first Mickey Mantle Day at Yankee Stadium, on September 18, 1965—celebrating his having played in two thousand games—but he was invited, and he did send a handwritten postcard:

To: Mickey Mantle; c/o Yankee Stadium.

Regardless of being the greatest distance hitter. Regardless of winning pennants for the Yankees and Casey Stengel, the two thousand games will be known as your greatest day.

Casey Stengel.

Casey might really have wished to say "You hit amazing home runs for me, but I always wanted more." His postcard was a bow to public relations, knowing it would be read on the field.

Invited to throw out the first pitch at Game Three of the World Series at Dodger Stadium, he cast away his cane, stepped out of the dugout-level boxes, and threw a nifty pitch to the Dodger catcher, John Roseboro.

It was time to figure out what retirement would mean.

—

THERE WAS NO DOUBT that, by taking on the Mets job, he hurt his reputation as a manager. Once again, it was clear that with good players he was a good manager, and with bad players, not. Still, his Yankee years had put him so high on the list of games won, championships won, etc., that he will always be included in conversations about the greatest managers.

The Mets job gave him fame in mainstream America and made him one of the nation's most beloved citizens—even among people who cared little about baseball. He was a living American folk hero. On balance, it was a good tradeoff.

PART FOUR

41

COOPERSTOWN

EDITORIAL WRITERS AND COLUMNISTS, led by Dick Young, quickly encouraged Casey's induction into the Hall of Fame. "At 75, a man shouldn't have to wait five years," wrote Young. On December 2, 1965, the Baseball Writers' Association, feeling Casey merited special consideration, voted unanimously to "recommend to the Hall of Fame Veterans Committee that it act immediately and favorably on the candidacy of Casey Stengel as a member of the Hall of Fame."

And there the story sat for three months.

It was almost time for Casey to go to St. Petersburg for spring training, in his new role as Mets vice president, generally described as "heading West Coast scouting." Before leaving, Casey went to the Baseball Writers' Dinners in both New York and Los Angeles, and presided over a press conference at the Essex House, intended simply to catch "my writers" up on what Casey was up to.

On March 8, 1966, on the pretense of being needed to present a plaque to George Weiss, Casey and Edna were driven to St. Petersburg's Huggins-Stengel Field.

There, former Commissioner Ford Frick, head of the Baseball Hall of Fame's Veterans Committee, spoke to the assembled press and club officials. "Ladies and gentlemen, I'm supposed to be through with baseball, but as chairman of the old-timers committee I have a very happy honor. I'm pleased to tell you that Mr. Charles Dillon Stengel has been elected to baseball's Hall of Fame."

He was the 104th inductee into the Hall, and he had probably played with or against or managed more of the other 103 than had anyone else.

Casey, in a brown suit and gold necktie, dropped his cane and seemed genuinely caught by surprise. He had suspected there was more to the day than a plaque for Weiss, but thought it might be a big trade announcement by the Mets—maybe even getting Willie Mays. The Mets were always trying to do that.

He moved next to Frick, and the new commissioner, Spike Eckert. Beginning to tear up, he said:

Thank you, I appreciate it. I guess I should say a thousand thank yous.

This is amazin' to me because there are so many guys who I think belong there ahead of me who are not in there yet. I go in with that other great man, Ted Williams, next July 25 at Cooperstown. I will save my acceptance speech if Ted Williams will be kind enough to allow me five minutes when I am inducted at Cooperstown.

I want to thank everyone, especially the baseball writers, who I feel are responsible for my election while I still can enjoy it. I guess there are a thousand other things I ought to say so I just want to say thank you to everyone.

"Casey, is this the greatest moment of your life?" shouted a reporter.

"Well now, I've lived a long time," he answered with a wink.

Edna kissed him, and then kissed him again at the photographers' request.

The vote was unanimous, and Casey became the fifth man for whom the five-year waiting period was waived, the others being Connie Mack, Lou Gehrig, Judge Landis, and Joe DiMaggio, who was elected in his fourth year of retirement, although he had fallen short the previous year. (In voting based strictly on his playing career, Casey received a smattering of votes in nine different elections, with a high of sixty-one in his final year of consideration, 1953. His managerial success was surely a factor in that total, given that his vote total between 1938 and 1951 never reached double figures.)

At a breakfast in St. Pete a few days later, a telegram from President Lyndon Johnson was read: "It is most fitting that Stengel should be enshrined in the Hall of Fame, as he already is enshrined in the hearts of millions of his countrymen."

—

ON APRIL 19, CASEY was back home to help the Angels dedicate the hundred-million-dollar Anaheim Stadium, where he threw out the first pitch. Casey had been Gene Autry's first choice to manage the Angels, and Del Webb Construction had built the park, so there were close ties. The park was thirty-five miles south of Glendale.

Bobby Case, now twenty, had been a visiting-clubhouse attendant for the Angels while they shared Dodger Stadium with the Dodgers. In the mid-1950s, he had been a batboy for the Brooklyn Dodgers Rookies, who trained at Stengel Field in Glendale. (Yes, Brooklyn did already have a presence in Los Angeles in the mid-1950s.) Casey got to know Bobby then. Now Bobby was offered a job to move with the Angels down the I-5 to their new location, where he could commute and continue to work in their clubhouse.

"Why would you want to do that?" asked Casey, as the two met in Casey's den. "Come work for me."

"It was the greatest break of my life," says Case. "He became my mentor, my tutor, my father, and I would serve him as 'business manager,' taking care of whatever needed care."

Case worked for Casey for the rest of Casey's life.

ON APRIL 27, THE Stengels left for a two-week trip to Hawaii, courtesy of Mutual of Omaha, for whom Casey was doing advertising and promotion. There are a lot of Mutual of Omaha signed Stengel baseballs in American homes, created for his personal appearances.

Edna did all the planning, as usual. She also wrote all the household checks, cashed one when Casey needed money, and reminded him to deposit checks that had been sitting around for months. She oversaw the upkeep on their fourteen-room house, the swimming pool, the tennis court, and the sunhouse, plus the formal gardens and the orchard with fruit-bearing trees. He was still a director of her family's bank and had an office there; interestingly, she was not. She or Bobby Case answered his fan mail.

After his Hall of Fame induction, many of the requests for autographs were Hall-issued plaque postcards, which he would sign in his large handwriting. "The surface of the postal cards is too slick to write on with a ball-point pen," he observed. "But did you know that if you take some cigarette ash and rub it on, you can then write on it okay? But cigarette butts are hard to find these days, so I've got this felt-tip pen that doesn't smudge and works fine."

Casey's duties as a West Coast scout had him watching and talking with Steve Chilcott, a seventeen-year-old catcher who had been Player of the Year in his seven-team league while at Antelope Valley High School. In this, the second year of the amateur draft (then called the "free agent draft"), the Mets had the very first pick in the nation, having finished last in 1965.

"One look is enough for me," said Casey. "This boy has all the tools to become a major league hitter." The Mets selected Chilcott.

The Kansas City Athletics, picking second, chose Reggie Jackson. Chilcott never played a major-league game. In fairness, Casey was never sent to scout Jackson in Arizona.

TED WILLIAMS AND STENGEL were named honorary coaches of the All-Star teams for the July 12 game in St. Louis. Wearing his Mets uniform, Casey remarked that the newly built Busch Memorial Stadium "holds the heat real well." It was 105 degrees at game time, probably even hotter on the field. Casey managed to reinjure his leg at the game—not seriously, but enough so he required special assistance to depart.

Before they headed to Cooperstown, a party was held at Stengel Field in Glendale. Casey's onetime infielder Jerry Coleman, now a Yankee broadcaster, was master of ceremonies, and Casey was given a home plate from Shea Stadium autographed by more than a hundred New York writers, broadcasters, photographers, and baseball people during the recent Mayor's Trophy Game.

About ten thousand people filled Cooper Park in Cooperstown for the July 25 induction ceremony. It was the largest gathering since the Hall's 1939 dedication ceremonies, fueled largely by Ted Williams's popularity with New England fans and Casey's with New York fans, both markets being within driving distance. Only four Hall of Famers were there—Bill Terry, Bill Dickey, Joe McCarthy, and Joe Cronin, who was then president of the American League. These were the days before the Hall of Famers themselves—led largely by Tom Seaver and Johnny Bench—began actively rounding up as many living members as they could and turning the weekend into a much larger event.

Bob Fishel represented the Yankees, present to receive a trophy for their winning the Hall of Fame game the year before. No Topping, no Webb—they had sold 80 percent of the team to CBS a year and a half before. That would be considered a disappointing turnout from the team that made him a Hall of Famer. Still, Fishel was the logical representative, someone who had worked closely with Casey. And they really liked each other.

George Weiss and Johnny Murphy were there from the Mets' front office. Weiss, Stan Musial, Warren Giles, and Tom Yawkey were future Hall of Famers in the crowd. (If one includes players in the annual Hall of Fame game which followed, the list grows, to include Red Schoendienst, Lou Brock, Orlando Cepeda, Steve Carlton, Bob Gibson, and Harmon Killebrew.)

Commissioner Eckert, in his first visit to Cooperstown, introduced Williams first, and Ted made news by saying, "I hope some day Satchel Paige and Josh Gibson can be added here in some way as a symbol of great Negro players. They are not here only because they didn't get a chance." Then he said, "I'll lose a good friend if I don't stop talking. I'm eating into his time and Casey Stengel will never forgive me."

The Hall of Fame secretary, Ed Stack, fondly remembered that Williams was very protective of Stengel and looked after him all weekend.

The sunny afternoon—baseball weather for sure—was perfect. Up hobbled seventy-six-year-old Casey Stengel, in a dark suit and light tie against a white dress shirt, his credential ribbon pinned to his right lapel. This was his moment. It would be the highest honor afforded him in the game to which he had given years of his life. It had been exactly a year since his career-ending fall.

He had written and rehearsed a speech, but completely ignored it when his time came. Instead, he thanked a number of people, including Edna, and thanked the two league presidents for "not taking more of my money when I was obnoxious and they respected my age." He mentioned Bill Terry, Joe McCarthy, and John McGraw for teaching him "the art of managing"; Terry was an odd choice, but, after all, he was present; Casey was being kind.

He spoke in his rapid style for twenty minutes, starting, appropriately, at the beginning, and saying in part:

> I played my first year and was transferred to Kentucky, and that was fine with me, because I knew that's where they kept the gold in this country.
>
> I worked for Mr. Ebbets and got $2100 a year and lived at 47th and Broadway.
>
> Since I've been in baseball from the year 1910 to 1966, I want

to thank everybody, including Worcester, Mass., which is the first team I managed and where I was fortunate enough to meet Mr. George Weiss who had the New Haven club, because whenever I was discharged, Mr. Weiss found it out and would reemploy me.

When I first played the game, they couldn't play on the Sabbath because that was the preachers' day to collect. I still remember my first game against Babe Ruth and that day he hit two over my head and then I knew who Babe Ruth was. I moved back after the first one and yelled to Hi Myers, "Is this far enough?" And he answered yes, and Ruth hit another one over my head.

I'm thankful I had baseball knuckles and couldn't become a dentist.

The toughest competition we ever had when I was managing the Yankees was from the Boston Red Sox. Between my English and the Bostonese English, we had a little difficulty understanding each other.

Now I don't want to take any more of your time or the game may not start. And keep going to see the Mets.

His plaque showed him in a Yankees uniform, looking quite serious. For someone famous for funny faces when he posed—winking an eye, playfully teasing the photographer—it didn't tell the real story. But the likeness was good. It said:

CHARLES DILLON STENGEL
"CASEY"

MANAGED NEW YORK YANKEES 1949–1960.
WON 10 PENNANTS AND 7 WORLD SERIES WITH
NEW YORK YANKEES. ONLY MANAGER TO WIN
5 CONSECUTIVE WORLD SERIES 1949–1953.
PLAYED OUTFIELD 1912–1925 WITH BROOKLYN,
PITTSBURGH, PHILADELPHIA, NEW YORK AND
BOSTON N.L. TEAMS. MANAGED BROOKLYN
1934–1936, BOSTON BRAVES 1938–1943,
NEW YORK METS 1962–1965.

It was true: the five-year-old, hapless New York Mets were on a Hall of Fame plaque.

Then it was off to watch the Hall of Fame game at Doubleday Field, followed by a retreat for cocktails to the back porch of the stately Otesaga Hotel overlooking Lake Otsego, and the conclusion of a splendid day in Casey Stengel's life.

AFTER THE HALL OF FAME ceremony, Casey went back to Shea for Old-Timers' Day, suiting up again in his Mets uniform for a day whose theme was the 1950 All-Star Game, in which he managed the American League. When he was presented with his usual late-July birthday cake, and said, "Since I was in the Hall of Fame I think that the players that were introduced here were possibly the greatest ones of all time. I have one more message for the wonderful fans who have paid their way into this here stadium. You got a manager here who is doing an accomplished job. There are three or four or eight or nine players who will go into the Mets Hall of Fame."

There probably weren't. And there wasn't yet a Mets Hall of Fame, but when they created one in 1981, Casey and Joan Payson were the first people selected.

42

AN ACTIVE
RETIREMENT

WITH THE EXCITEMENT OF his Hall of Fame year behind him, Casey's life settled into a post-baseball routine that would last for his remaining years.

The beautiful home on Grandview would become sort of a post–White House retreat such as presidents enjoyed. Rod Dedeaux and Babe Herman were his closest baseball neighbors, living just a block away and dropping in often. But so, too, would other old friends, perhaps paying their respects to this grand old man.

Oh, there might be a younger visitor now and then. Rod Kanehl was known to stop by, drunk, at, say, two in the morning. And sometimes that was all right: Casey welcomed him, until Rod went overboard, teasing him at an Old-Timers' Day by calling him a geezer and saying his old man made money watering down whiskey in Kansas City; at that point, Casey cut off the friendship. This recalls Casey's elevator meeting with Mickey McDermott in the mid-1950s; supposedly, when the door opened, Casey saw his inebriated pitcher and said, "Drunk again?," to which McDermott allegedly replied, "Me, too."

An evening cocktail with a smoke was *de rigueur* at the Stengels'. Crown Royal was his favorite, either straight or with a little Coca-Cola. Edna did not smoke, but she would join him for the drink.

When people gathered to talk about Casey, his drinking prowess would take on near-legendary tones. Some of it was exaggerated in the storytelling, but this was still a time when the ability to hold one's whiskey was thought to be a manly act, even admirable. It was true—Casey seldom appeared drunk, and seemed to be just as fine after six or seven drinks as after one. (On at least one occasion, however, the Mets players Roger Craig and Norm Sherry found him passed out in the hallway of the team hotel. They got a night manager to help put him in his bed.) The capacity was spoken of in awe.

"We were never much at drinking," confided Edna, perhaps naïvely. "But we did like to sit around at the end of a day with a double shot of rum and sweet lime drink."

Their home was quite welcoming to visitors. His phone number was listed: 241-4041. On Halloween, the doorbell never stopped ringing—he gave out dollar bills and candy. Kids who wanted autographs might get "I'm gonna send a Mets scout to see you," or "You're gonna be a Met someday." Even adults, if they were touring the neighborhood and aware of his address, might ring the bell. He'd invite them in and show off his den with all his bats and balls and trophies, even the den's "secret door," which opened to reveal more treasures. And the school bell and bricks from his elementary school, presented at long-ago celebrations.

The parents of Darrell Evans, the Atlanta Braves slugger, showed up one day, and Casey entertained them for eight hours. He might stuff four or five kids from the neighborhood into his car and take everyone to the El-Vaq for ice cream, which was across the street from Stengel Field.

In October 1970, when *The New York Times* had just initiated an op-ed page, with guest columns, they asked Casey if he wanted to write one. It was called "They've All Got Automobiles," and went on about players with long hair being fine as long as they followed club rules, and about how the high salaries in the game allowed players the independence to own cars and drive wherever they want. It was in pure Stengelese, as the *Times* editors had probably hoped it would be, and woe to anyone who tried to edit it.

He was a good correspondent. He wrote letters and postcards to people of all ranks, in and out of baseball. Dutch Zwilling was his closest friend among old players—Casey had actually once dated Zwilling's future wife—with Babe Herman a close second. Other visitors over the years included Chief Meyers, Wilbur Cooper, Johnny Rawlings, Del Webb, High Pockets Kelly, and Charlie Deal, who had played for the "Miracle Braves" of 1914. There were regular calls from Al Lopez, Rosy Ryan, Max Carey, and many others. Seldom did he call his Yankee players, such as Mantle, Ford, and Berra, the ones most identified with his era. Of the three, Berra, the oldest, his "assistant manager," was the most likely to keep in contact.

Of course, Casey would reunite with them at many of the Old-Timers' Days that he attended at parks other than Yankee Stadium. A few years after his retirement, a uniform and a cap were made for him for such appearances, bearing the logos of all of his major-league teams—as a player and as a manager. It was fun, and he would return the fun by making grand entrances, taking deep bows, or hiking his trousers and dancing a little jig out of the dugout. Eventually, he was able to abandon his cane.

Edna, who still enjoyed designer clothes, both cut his hair and dyed it. They liked to sit in the original Polo Grounds seats, next to the swimming pool, but Casey seldom ventured to New York, even to get out of the summer heat of southern California. Sometimes he would pick avocados from the orchard behind the Stengels' fenced-in tennis court and give a bunch to Bobby Case to take home.

Classical music could be heard on the old phonograph in the house. There were reproductions of Norman Rockwell's baseball paintings, which Casey loved. He would not watch much TV, but he would watch Walter Cronkite deliver the news at seven, and through the night his radio could be heard upstairs, in the bedroom, as he listened to the early days of talk radio, and shouted at it, "Ahhh, you're full of shit and I'll tell you why." This was another of his favorite expressions.

He liked Richard Nixon, who named him the greatest manager of the 1925–70 era in 1972, when Nixon was developing lists with the help of his son-in-law David Eisenhower. "Well, for heaven's sake, I'm very glad," Casey said. "And he picked it himself, you say? Well, it's very nice the President is so well versed in sports with so many things he has to do in his sojourn as President."

But Casey also liked the Kennedys, and Edna displayed a signed picture from Robert Kennedy that said, "From one of the many Kennedy fans of the Stengels."

He liked hippies, and he defended long hair. He would watch the evolving culture on TV reports and find them interesting. He seemed to know that there was a growing movement in there somewhere, and he embraced it. He always liked hell raisers more than goody-two-shoes people, and even though the hippies were hardly hell raisers, he appreciated their nonconformity.

Casey watched a lot of baseball and was quick to spot everything wrong. "Goddam it, you put your left foot first," he'd shout. And he'd laugh about Marv Throneberry and the early Mets when he'd see a play that reminded him of them. He was clearly a Mets fan, and was still bitter about the Yankees, despite wearing Yankee underwear—it was just more comfortable.

He became a fan of USC sports, partly because of his friendship with their coach, Rod Dedeaux, and partly because Tom Seaver, the star of the Mets, had played for Dedeaux.

He was good at keeping doctor's appointments—Dedeaux would select the doctors—but he remained in excellent health. The occasional flu bug would come and go, but for an old man, he was in excellent shape. He took no medications.

"Casey would love to go out with my dad," said Justin Dedeaux, Rod's son—especially if some members of Edna's family were visiting. "And they both loved sports themed restaurants—Paul's Duck Press, the House of Murphy. He was happy to get out. Dad, of course, didn't like the way Casey drove, so he'd always pick him up."

He took care of old players, writing checks if they needed money, without any expectation of being repaid—three hundred, five hundred dollars, whatever came into his head. It caused him anguish to see that Ernie Lombardi was washing windshields at a service station during the 1973 World Series in Oakland, which Casey attended because the Mets were playing. He paid the funeral expenses for as many as ten former players with whom he'd had friendships. He sent money home to his sister, Louise, regularly, as he had long done for their mother.

"It was funny," recalls Bob Case. "He was so generous. He would pick up a dinner tab for eight people like it was nothing. But the next day might have me phone eight places to get the best price on a car battery. If we found one where he saved ten dollars, he was happy."

Sometimes he would attend church. His bank secretary, Margaret Mollett, was Catholic, and he liked and admired nuns, and the traditions and order of the church teachings, although he respected all religions. "I was with him almost daily all those years," says Bob Case. "Even in the privacy of his home, you'd never hear him cut down a race or a religion. He respected everyone."

He loved baseball people, of course, and the community of baseball people extended a wide net. Fans who seemed to have nothing else in their lives but collecting autographs at airports—well, they were part of the community. They loved the game just as he did. He never put them down. And if someone sent a request for an autograph without a self-addressed stamped envelope for its return, Casey would reach into his desk and get his own envelope and his own stamp and ready it for mailing.

He respected every player who had made it into *The Baseball Encyclopedia*. "If your name's in there," he'd say, "you were a great player."

He drove his big dented black 1960 Cadillac into his eighties—dangerously, on occasion. "He drove like he talked," recalled his Mets publicist Matt Winick.

On December 11, 1968, he suffered minor injuries in a traffic accident in Glendale, when his Cadillac collided with a car driven by a twenty-seven-year-old woman. He spent three days in the hospital, treated for cuts and bruises, and was fined $302 for drunken driving and charged with leaving the scene of an accident. The charge was dismissed, however. Eventually, they took away his license, but before DUI was taken seriously, the Glendale police would give him an escort home if he was wavering from lane to lane.

Casey liked big steaks and he liked a lot of butter on his rolls, and he would snack on cookies, pretzels, and potato chips. Sometimes he would go to the Oakmont Country Club for a big breakfast, or the Robin Hood Inn. He loved going to Winchell's Donuts for a sweet treat. If he was recognized, that was all the better. He loved holding court and enchanting his audience with humor. He didn't suffer fools—he could walk into a room and immediately separate the phonies from the real people. And he never "big leagued" anyone, never acted superior.

Trips to Stengel Field to see whoever was playing were a welcome break. Even a sloppy youth-league game could hold his attention; he'd sit there signing autographs and remarking on how "splendid" the pitcher looked.

Casey kept old baseball gloves in his car. "Sometimes he'd just feel like pulling over and having a catch," said Case. "Even in his seventies, he could keep a catch going for an hour. He had these old left-handed gloves with no strings through the fingers. I don't know if they were from his playing days, but they were old."

Case also remembered, "And he'd spell things out. If he was talking about some old Brooklyn teammate and he knew I'd never heard of him, he'd say something like 'Ragan! R-A-G-A-N!'" (Don Carlos Patrick Ragan, also from Missouri, was among the eleven teammates of Casey's who played in Cuba in the 1913 post-season series.) Meanwhile, Case drove him around or did whatever nonhousekeeping chores needed attention. "Be at Stengel Field at four," Casey might tell him on the phone, without bothering to say hello.

Case didn't mind at all. He reported for work each day, thrilled to be in the old man's company.

Each December, the Stengels always had a Christmas tree, and sometimes Casey would don a Santa hat to greet people at the door. Edna did the Christmas cards, including a card for everyone who sent one, even fans.

He was still in demand for advertisers. For instance, RCA ran ads for its new color TVs showing Casey and Edna posing in front of one in their Glendale den.

Clarice Lennon was his housekeeper in the first years of his retirement. About five or six months before Casey's death, a woman named June Bowlin took charge of the house. She had begun communicating with Casey from her home in Kentucky, and sent him scrapbooks she had kept on him. That was the way to get into Casey's good graces; he loved fans like that. He hired her after a fuss was made over the disrepair the house was falling into. He was reluctant to acknowledge Edna's inability to take care of the house any longer. June was hired when Casey learned she had taken care of Jesse Haines, a Hall of Fame pitcher with the Cardinals. June Bowlin was a take-charge presence. When Edna's niece Lynn Rossi inquired as to how Casey was doing, June finished her reply with "Thank you for your interest," as though she had become the ultimate gatekeeper.

At Casey's age, death came often to people whom he loved. "There was an obit a week, for sure," says Case. "But I only saw him cry three times over news of a passing—George Weiss in 1972, Frankie Frisch in 1973, and Edna's niece Margaret Mollett, his bank secretary, in 1975. She was the one in the Lawson family he liked the most, trusted the most. She and Mae Hunter, Edna's sister." As for the rest of the Lawsons, Casey called them "my relations" in a somewhat negative way. He began stashing away cash at his home rather than the bank.

Casey's Old-Timers' Day routine centered on the Mets, and they usually held theirs around the time of his birthday. So a trip to New York with Edna for a birthday and the old-timers gathering always marked the center of the summer, as did a trip to Cooperstown for the annual induction ceremony. And there was still spring training every year in St. Petersburg, and the annual Baseball Writers' Association Dinner in New

York. He would occasionally take the stage at the writers' dinner to perform a little song written for him.

Those were the "givens."

The 1967 Mets Old-Timers' Day featured his 1960 Yankees and his 1962 Mets—quite a contrast between good and bad—and he had a ball mingling with both. There were Throneberry, Kanehl, Neal, Chacon, Hook, Zimmer, Mizell, Moford, Ashburn, Chiti, and Coleman, along with Richardson, McDougald, Shantz, Turley, Duren, Lopat, Berra, and Ford, who had just retired. Ruffing, Henrich, and DiMaggio were also there. He still got a great kick out of that first Mets team, despite their 40-120 record. He knew there was something special, something historic about them. As for the '60 Yankees, they represented his last pennant winner, but also the team that "got me fired" after they lost the World Series.

He went to the All-Star Game in Anaheim that year, the one that lasted fifteen innings, and celebrated his birthday at Dodger Stadium. Maury Allen, seeing him without his cane, said, "Casey, you said you couldn't manage so long as you couldn't go to the mound without a cane to remove a pitcher. Any chance of a comeback?" He laughed. But he probably thought he could do it.

Joe Durso's biography of Casey came out in 1967, a book that was most noteworthy for a long and loving portrayal of Edna as a woman of great warmth and a lot of class. Casey liked the book because of that section, even if it exposed an occasional tiff between them that was visible to Durso and the traveling party. If Edna caused a team bus or team flight to be delayed, Casey could silently fume. Like most marriages, it was not without complications.

Gil Hodges became manager of the Mets in 1968, and Casey was there in St. Petersburg, talking to everyone about what a splendid manager he would be. Among his Old-Timers' Days in 1968 was one in Oakland, where his champion 1948 Oaks regrouped to play an abbreviated game against the '48 San Francisco Seals. Billy Martin, now managing Denver at the start of his managing career, played second for the Oaks. All three baseball-playing DiMaggio brothers were there that day to play in the same outfield.

Casey always thought Joe DiMaggio lived with a sense of "entitlement," but the two never said publicly anything negative about each other, and greeted each other warmly at Old-Timers' Days or in Cooperstown. DiMaggio had to accept that the man who was once a "clown" had become a legend himself, and as famous as he was.

Privately, when reminded how angry DiMaggio was about playing first base one day, Casey would just say, "I'm managing the team." He could discuss the old days, but he never lost sight of who was boss.

ON JANUARY 10, 1969, he had surgery for a perforated peptic ulcer at Glendale Memorial Hospital. The surgery was performed the very day he complained of pain, and his recovery was relatively swift. He was able to go to the Mets training camp as usual, but he didn't speak at the annual dinner in Bradenton, which featured sixteen Hall of Famers. For Casey, choosing not to speak was a story in itself.

There were twenty-three Hall of Famers at the Mets' Old-Timers' Day in June, and then, in July, came baseball's gala centennial celebration in Washington, with events built around the All-Star Game. (It was the centennial of professional baseball, as defined by the birth of the Cincinnati Red Stockings.) In a national poll, Casey was voted the game's Greatest Living Manager ("I want to thank all my players for giving me the honor of being what I was," he said). At a memorable White House reception line on the eve of the game, President Nixon asked Casey about his banking interests. As a baseball fan and as a Californian, Nixon knew all about Casey and his bank.

He kept on the move. A few weeks later, he went to an Old-Timers' Game in St. Louis, where he danced a polka at the post-game party. No one knew he could polka.

By late August and early September, his Amazin' Mets were still in the race for their first Eastern Division title, and people were beginning to pay attention to the job Hodges was doing.

"They're not playing today with the green peas I had," said Casey when he was asked to comment. "And they aren't Snider and Hodges and other well-known men around New York that Mr. Weiss asked me to take in '62 and '63."

It was one of the great moments in American sports when the Mets won it all in '69. Casey threw out the first ball for Game Three of the World Series at Shea Stadium, and covered the whole series for the New York *Daily News* by dictating his thoughts after each game. Of the sensational catches made by Swoboda and Agee (two, in Agee's case), moments that defined the miraculous nature of the triumph, Casey said, "Watch those catches. You'll see how amazing those men are, and you say, 'How can you teach it?' Well, you look at how they do it and you can see they are one-handed, so don't be afraid of calling it showboat and tell them to catch it two-handed—because you can catch it two-handed only you don't catch it."

In the commotion of the Mets' clubhouse after the final game victory, Casey slipped into the crowd. He talked to anybody and everybody. "Now if I throw strikes, are you going to hit them? No. The center fielder, [Agee] he's wonderful. We never had a center fielder. And what's wrong with [Cleon] Jones? They're like roommates. They run into each other, but they don't knock each other down.

"But you'll have to excuse me. I have to go to Europe. My newspapers over there are waiting. There is a good eight hours difference and I have to get my sleep. Goodbye, everybody."

And off he went into the night, back to the familiarity of the Essex House, having lived long enough to see a world championship won by his Mets. There was no European trip.

FALL TURNED TO WINTER, and early in 1970, there was Casey, pondering the Yankees' invitation to their Old-Timers' Day, when they planned to retire his number. It was an invitation to end his exile and return to Yankee Stadium. Ownership had changed, and the people who had dismissed him were no longer running things.

All the years he had managed the Mets, it had been unthinkable: he wouldn't leave his team for this. From 1966 to 1969, he could have attended and chose not to, not even for Mantle Day in '69.

But Casey appreciated the culture of the game, and knew that to have a number retired—as the Mets had done—was a very big deal. With the retirement of Mantle's number 7 the year before, only four Yankee numbers had been retired: Ruth's, Gehrig's, DiMaggio's, and Mantle's. This was still a very elite society. Casey got it. He knew it was big. Edna encouraged him to go. And the invitation included that personal note from Bob Fishel. So he accepted.

A week after his eightieth birthday, the day arrived. The old-timer guests all stayed at the Americana on Seventh Avenue, but Casey and Edna got the okay to stay at the Essex House. A car would be sent for them at the appointed hour. The Yankees paid for Edna's travel, too—a break from club policy for Old-Timers' Days.

In anticipation of the day, a poster was made for all fans in attendance, announcing the appearance of Casey Stengel's All-Time Yankee

Team, and before the ceremonies, all the players on the poster (except Crosetti and Kubek, who were not present) signed the poster. Casey went last, affixing his large signature over his photo at the top.

He would share Ralph Houk's office—the one that used to be his. He'd always liked Houk; he never considered him part of some conspiracy to oust him in 1960. Ralph insisted he sit in the large, comfortable plush desk chair. Casey changed into his Yankee uniform in there—the first time he had worn one since Mazeroski's home run a decade before.

He had never agreed to the team's holding a Casey Stengel Day during his twelve seasons as manager. This would, in essence, be it.

He was the last guest introduced, and he did a little jig on his way onto the field. Fishel motioned for Ford and Berra to come forward, with a folded number 37 in hand. And the longtime "Voice of the Yankees," Mel Allen, who, like Casey, had been harshly dismissed years before, announced that on this day the Yankees would retire Casey's number. The crowd roared its approval.

Casey was clearly moved. Proudly holding it high, he said, "I want to thank these players and you fans for putting me in this uniform. Now that I've finally got one [a retired jersey], I think I'll die in it." Everyone cheered as the old man hobbled back to the Yankee dugout and carefully down the steps.

That night, at a private party at Toots Shor's, he regaled everyone with stories, even remembering specific plays involving the old-time Yankees who were present. The players were like fans, eager to get a moment with Casey.

As was the style of the times, the women had dinner in a separate dining room, lest they hear the foul language that accompanied the men's stories. At a certain hour late into the evening, the women were allowed to join the men, and Edna led the small group (Mrs. Ruth, Mrs. Gehrig, Mrs. Weiss, and a few others) into the "men's dining room," to the music of the Bunny Hop.

The Stengels departed the next day. About a week later, a postcard arrived at the stadium and was delivered to the PR office. It was simply addressed "New York Yankees, Yankee Stadium, Bronx, NY 10451." On the back, in the familiar large handwriting, it said, "Mrs. Stengel and I had a marvelous time and it was nice to see old friends. Will send my expense receipts separately. And thank you for my prize. Casey Stengel."

Ah, the prize. Each old-timer received a gift—an engraved clock radio, valued at about sixty dollars. To Casey, this was the "prize" he was referring to. It hardly merited a thank-you, but he had old-school grace and sent the postcard.

Retired numbers were not yet displayed at Yankee Stadium, other than in the reception area to the street-level Stadium Club restaurant. Casey's 37 joined the other four in individual frames next to the elevator: Ruth 3, Gehrig 4, DiMaggio 5, Mantle 7, Stengel 37. Lofty company.

He displayed a framed 37 in his den. Eventually, as the number of honorees grew and as the display area extended in new and refurbished stadiums, there would be the 37 on the wall behind the bleachers, in Monument Park, and at the Yankees spring-training site in Tampa. It was easy to forget that number 37 was only the fifth that the team retired. In fact, at the time he retired as Mets manager, only twelve uniform numbers had been retired in all of baseball, including his.

LIFE MAY HAVE BEEN idyllic for the Stengels at their fabulous home in Glendale, but trouble was coming.

In 1971, Edna Stengel began to show forgetfulness and signs of what was then called senility. She was no longer handling her check-writing chores properly. The early stages of her oncoming Alzheimer's disease were taking hold. She would continue to live at Grandview.

"Clarice Lennon told me he was up at the Brand Park Field near the house," said Bob Case. "Edna had just been diagnosed. I found him in his big black Cadillac, watching a Little League game, but mostly staring into space. I asked what was wrong, and he said, 'She's batty.'"

Although his expressions seemed to make light of the situation, his heart was breaking. He cared for her as best he could, even giving her baths and dressing her. They continued to sleep in the same double bed in the upstairs master bedroom.

Eventually, it was time for this elegant woman to enter a care facility, the Glenoaks Convalescent Hospital on Glenoaks Boulevard, two miles away. Unless he was out of town, Casey would visit her every day; when his driver's license was finally "retired," he would walk. He'd bring flowers, or her favorite See's candy. Though he would wheel her around, she was no longer able to recognize him.

Edna had always written all the household checks; now Casey had to do it himself. He could no longer sleep soundly at night; he and Edna had shared the same bed for some forty years. He paced. He chain-smoked Kents. He turned down Thanksgiving invitations at his grandniece Toni

Mollett's home, because he couldn't bear to go without his wife. He'd pace the supermarket aisles by himself, something he'd never done before.

The home at 1663 Grandview was not what it had been—no longer a joyous receiving ground for his friends and neighbors. Calls from friends were fewer. There was sadness in every room.

43

SAYING GOODBYE

THE ROUTINE OF HIS annual baseball appearances meant a lot to Casey. He went to spring training with the Mets in 1971, went to Old-Timers' Days in Cincinnati, Los Angeles, Pittsburgh, two in New York, the Hall of Fame induction, and an event in Kansas City in appreciation of Satchel Paige, who was elected to the Hall of Fame that year—one more chance to "go home."

In November, the *New York Post*'s Maury Allen, the writer among "my writers" who most admired Casey, announced that the New York chapter of the Baseball Writers' Association would change the name of its "Retroactive Award" to a "Casey Stengel You-Could-Look-It-Up Award" each year, with Casey being the first winner in 1970 (for his 1923 World Series performance with the New York Giants). It would honor some special achievement in the game that had been forgotten and never sufficiently recognized. Mostly, it would honor Casey, by using one of his pet phrases, one that Allen would use as the title of his 1979 Stengel biography. None of the modern group of "my writers" loved Casey more than Allen did, so it was not surprising that he led the charge to create this award.

"I always remember the first names of the writers, never the ballplayers," said Casey at an Old–Timers' event. It was another secret of his success.

IN 1972, THAT SPECIAL uniform with all the team logos was unveiled, and Casey came to home plate at Old-Timers' Day at Shea in a horse and buggy, wearing it proudly. There was also a Salute to Casey Stengel Day at Dodger Stadium in June, which featured the return of Jackie Robinson to a Dodgers event. Like Casey with the Yankees, Jackie had gone through a long estrangement.

While cutting back on his travel to help attend to Edna, Casey did make it to Yankee Stadium in 1973 for the final Old-Timers' Day before the ballpark was gutted and renovated.

At the end of that season, he went to the World Series to see his Mets play Oakland.

"I went to the World Series at Oakland when the Mets were there," he said at a rare banquet appearance after the season, talking about a flu bug that hit him. "That's when I got it. I had a stomach thing but I also had, which is a bad place to get the flu. I have what is called, something that has kept me from, I can go out walking but I can't go every place they have an old timers game. But at my age, I have been very fortunate to see the country and work there. I worked in New York, which was very good to me, and I worked in New England, where I broke my leg, and I was born in Kansas City and now I am living in the West but I am having trouble in the West because I don't know Spanish too well. And thank you very much."

He was not a man for all seasons; he was a man for baseball season. But, culturally, he came to represent all the regions of the United States—not just those in which the baseball season took place—thanks to his half-century of spring training in the South, and, of course, those oil fields in Texas.

IN MAY 1974, CASEY acknowledged publicly that Edna had been transferred to a nursing home. Now he was able, even as his eighty-fourth birthday approached, to keep up a pace of appearances around the country, encouraged by friends who thought it would do him good. His admission of Edna's illness brought with it a certain freedom. Now he could talk about it. To old friends who asked, "How's Edna?" he might even point to his neck and say, "From here up . . . nothing." Dark humor. There would be no gala fiftieth wedding-anniversary party on August 18. It could have been a grand event.

In June, at the request of his old third baseman Dr. Bobby Brown, he attended an Old-Timers' Day held by the Texas Rangers. Dr. Brown had retired from his Fort Worth cardiology practice and been named interim president of the Rangers. (He would later be president of the American League.)

Since the theme of the event was old Yankees, and current Yankees were the opponent, and since Billy Martin was managing the Rangers, a Yankee publicist was present. The Yankees Old-Timers' Day was in two weeks, but Casey had not yet responded to his invitation, though he had attended the last four. The publicist decided to ask him in person.

"Now, goddamn it, I told you I'd tell you when I knew," he gruffly responded, sending the humbled publicist (me) on his way. The short-tempered outburst was unusual; perhaps it reflected the stress Casey was feeling, unable to visit Edna, and his generally depressed spirits.

He did attend the Yankees' Old-Timers' Day, which was held at Shea Stadium while Yankee Stadium was undergoing renovations. He wore his multi-team cap with his Yankee uniform.

A few weeks later, looking very southern California (checkered pants, white shoes), he returned to Cooperstown for the annual induction day. This time, Mantle and Ford were being installed, and Casey seemed to be in a great mood, happily posing with his two stars for hundreds of photos. It was reported that, aside from the celebrants Mantle and Ford, Stengel, Musial, Spahn, and Campanella got the biggest response from the fans.

If Mickey or Whitey thought this might be the last time they would see him, the day did not give way to any emotional confessions or memories between them. They were now just three old soldiers of the baseball wars, bound together for posterity in the Hall of Fame.

CASEY WENT TO LOS ANGELES to tape a thirty-minute program for PBS, hosted by Curt Gowdy, discussing the 1956 World Series. The Yankees were also represented by Mel Allen, Mickey Mantle, and Don Larsen; Duke Snider, Sal Maglie, and Clem Labine represented the Dodgers. The program was called *The Way It Was,* and Casey was paid four hundred dollars for his participation. Its premiere, on September 25, 1975, would mark his last appearance on television. In it, he was uncharacteristically laconic.

CASEY STRUGGLED WITH THE flu during the winter of 1974–75, and it made him cranky. When the phone did ring, he'd sometimes answer by saying, "I ain't dead yet." But it was debilitating. Whereas he used to go to the supermarket, after Edna was hospitalized, he now sent

June Bowlin or Bobby Case on errands. Said Case, "He missed the supermarket—he loved being recognized and chatting with fans."

He missed his first New York Baseball Writers' Dinner in about twenty-five years, and then missed the Mets' spring-training camp in St. Petersburg. People worried about him, and talked about how it wasn't spring training without him. Indeed, Casey and spring training had gone together since 1910—except for 1937, when he was paid not to manage, and 1961, when he was out of the game.

"He had the flu, and he certainly felt lousy," said Bob Case. "But even at eighty-four, there were no signs that he might be dying."

But there were signs.

Though he had recovered enough to go to the Mets' Old-Timers' Day on June 28, he expressed regrets at not being able to attend an Old-Timers' Game in Denver, even after his friend A. Ray Smith, who owned the minor-league Tulsa Oilers, offered to fly to California to accompany him there. "My belly hurts," he told people.

The Yankees' Old-Timers' Day was August 2, 1975, and what a day that turned out to be. Billy Martin was named Yankees manager. The prodigal son was coming home, ending an eighteen-year exile that went back to his 1957 trade to Kansas City. "Casey's Boy" (as his eventual plaque in Monument Park would read) was replacing Bill Virdon. George Steinbrenner, the team's owner since 1973, couldn't resist the opportunity to bring home the Yankees legend.

Martin had written to Casey on Texas Rangers stationery earlier in the year, looking to make peace with the old man. Casey responded politely, but to him, there never was a lack of "peace" in their relationship. "He always took it too personally," Stengel told Bob Case. "Getting traded is part of baseball. It's the industry you're in. It wasn't the big deal he always made of it."

It would have been a photographer's feast to have Casey present the day Martin became manager, but he couldn't make it. Too ill to travel now, he instead recorded a five-minute tape wishing everyone well, concluding, "I appreciate the amazin' ability that they accomplished under my management."

The quality of the tape wasn't strong enough to play over the Shea Stadium PA system, so it was instead played at the Old-Timers' party in the Diamond Club, where it was well received by the guests, who then shared many Casey stories.

This was a better audience than Casey himself had enjoyed in years. It had come to a point where he would be at a dinner, and as he walked to the mike, the audience members—all too familiar with hearing ten minutes of Stengelese at such events—would roll their eyes or head for the restroom. At least, that's what those who had been through it for years would do. For newcomers, it was a treat.

On July 30, Casey turned eighty-five. He had a quiet day at home—no celebratory birthday cake at home plate, with thousands singing "Happy Birthday."

Edna had suffered a stroke earlier in the year, and now she was not only mentally disabled, but physically. Still, Casey went to see her almost daily.

He did a long interview on the phone with Dave Anderson of *The New York Times,* which ran on August 5. He expressed regrets about his inability to travel as much as he had done before and told Anderson that he visited Edna every day. He complained about his driver's license being taken away and about the effects on his body from time zone shifts when he went back east and returned home.

"This time I got to stay here too because my wife is in a home," he said.

He seemed to sigh as he evaluated his lot in life.

"I promised everyone in New York [that he'd attend Old-Timers' Day], but I can't make that. I can't make every one because I am handicapped. I have a terrible cold and I have lost my voice."

"The Ol' Perfessor" was winding down.

He didn't travel to Cooperstown for Induction Day on August 18 (the Mets' announcer, Ralph Kiner, was among those honored), but he had one public appearance left. He accepted an invitation to the Dodgers Old-Timers' Day on August 24, which honored members of the 1955 world-championship team. Red Patterson, his original Yankees publicist (who had run the Dodgers' PR since 1954), called to invite him. His housekeeper, June Bowlin, and her son Greg drove him there. He appeared quite thin and frail.

Casey's knee was hurting him, and he asked the Dodgers' executive Fred Claire if a doctor might take a look at it. Claire summoned Dr. Robert Woods, who said, "When did this first start bothering you?"

Casey responded, "Oh, I think it was about 1938 or '39, when I was managing the Boston Bees."

Dr. Woods smiled and told him not to stand on it for too long.

The '55 team was the one that had beaten Stengel's Yankees to win their only Brooklyn title. Surrounding Casey on this occasion were players he had later managed at the Mets—Craig, Snider, Zimmer, and, briefly Clem Labine, along with great names like Campanella, Newcombe, Reese, Gilliam, Koufax, and Drysdale. Gil Hodges and Jackie Robinson had both died three years earlier. Yet, despite being surrounded by baseball people, he was out of sorts. He looked very frail in his multilogo uniform and cap. And, make no mistake, it was tiring for an eighty-five-year-old man to put on that uniform one more time. But he got the greatest ovation of the day.

After the field ceremony, he changed into street clothes and sat for only a few innings behind home plate, seated with Rod Dedeaux and the actor Cary Grant, and then said he wasn't feeling well and wanted to go home. He didn't smile much; he was uncomfortable.

ON MONDAY, SEPTEMBER 15, after a rather uncomfortable weekend, Casey left his home for a "general checkup" at Glendale Memorial Hospital. He would never return home. June Bowlin drove him to the hospital, and he fought against being helped out of the car. "He had somewhat of a bump on his abdomen," said Bob Case. "We thought it might be a hernia."

A decision was made to conduct exploratory surgery on Casey, who continued to complain of a bellyache.

"The doctors opened him up, saw cancer, and closed him up," said Case. "Surgery and treatment would be too much for him at eighty-five."

During his hospital stay, he did what he always did—he followed baseball. On Saturday, September 27, he watched the NBC Game of the Week, Pittsburgh at St. Louis, with Joe Garagiola and his old shortstop Tony Kubek announcing. The Pirates had clinched the National League East and were getting ready to face the great Cincinnati Reds—the Big Red Machine—in the National League Championship Series.

In those days, the playing of the national anthem was part of the telecast—unlike today, when it's generally done before the game goes on air. Knowing the ritual well, Casey decided to rise from his bed and stand for the anthem. "I might as well do this one last time," he said, as he stood barefooted in a hospital gown (open at the back), with his hand over his heart.

"One last time." Obviously, he had a sense that the end was near. And if he did indeed think he was dying, surely the absence of Edna at this moment must have been on his mind.

The regular season ended the next day. Bob Case visited him that day and read *The Sporting News* to him. "I really didn't think he was dying," said Case.

On Monday, September 29, his friend and neighbor, coach Rod Dedeaux, now acting as de facto Stengel spokesman, publicly revealed the illness. It was a malignant sarcoma, a cancer of the lymph glands, centered in his abdomen.

HE DIED THAT NIGHT, at 10:58 p.m. Edna's niece Lynn Rossi was the only one with him at the time. He was comatose by then; she didn't think he heard her at all or knew she was there, even as she patted his hair. She watched him take two long-drawn-out breaths. A third one never came. She went into the hall to find a nurse and said softly, "I think he just said goodbye."

With his brother and sister having predeceased him, and since none of the three had had children, he was the last of the Stengel line.

CASEY'S DYING SO LATE at night turned out to benefit his afternoon writers back east, since it was too late for the East Coast morning papers to report it. So it was a "gift" to Maury Allen, who loved him the most and who could write the first column about him as he got ready to cover the playoffs.

"He is gone and I am supposed to cry, but I laugh. Every time I saw the man, every time I heard his voice, every time his name was mentioned, the creases in my mouth would give way and a smile would come to my face."

"He was the happiest man I've ever seen," said Richie Ashburn.

The wake, funeral, and cemetery arrangements were made by Edna's brother John and by June Bowlin, with assistance from Rod Dedeaux.

The funeral would be held on Monday, October 6, the off-day before the third game of the American League Championship Series, in Oakland. The scheduling of the funeral was an accommodation to "baseball people" who might be able to attend, with the post-season having swung to the West Coast.

The night after the all-day viewing at Scovern Mortuary in Glendale, there was a wake at Casey's home. Given Casey's age and the joyous life he had led, it was not a sad occasion, and, not surprisingly, a lot of drinking took place. There were a lot of bottles in the house, which might as well be consumed.

In the kitchen, a group of men gathered to tell Casey stories. When Billy Martin, the only representative of the current Yankees organization, entered, Joe Stephenson, a former catcher and current scout, greeted him with an exaggerated "Oh, it's the great Billy Martin!" or something to that effect. And Billy, true to form, responded with something like "Yeah, what about it?" And the next thing those assembled knew, the two of them were in the backyard, near the swimming pool, fighting like schoolkids in the playground—except that Stephenson was fifty-four, Martin forty-seven. It was quickly broken up.

The weather was rainy on the 6th, the day of the funeral, which was held at the Church of the Recessional at Forest Lawn. A Methodist minister, Dr. Kenneth A. Carlson, presided. There was an overflow gathering of several hundred, everyone from baseball scouts to neighbors to teenage boys. But it did not, unfortunately, include Edna Stengel, whose condition made her attendance impossible. She was disabled physically and mentally and would not have known what was going on.

The honorary pallbearers were Emmett Ashford, Buzzie Bavasi, Peter Bavasi, Bobby Case, Jerry Coleman, Jocko Conlan, Bob Fishel, Whitey Ford, M. Donald Grant, Fred Haney, Babe Herman, George Kelly, Tom Lasorda, Joe McDonald, Lee MacPhail, Billy Martin, Harry Minor, Tom Morgan, Irv Noren, Red Patterson, Bob Scheffing, Ken Smith, A. Ray Smith, Chuck Stevens, Horace Stoneham, Maury Wills, and Dutch Zwilling. Zwilling, two years older than Casey, went back the furthest with him.[*]

The Mets contingent was a little smaller than expected because of the passing of the team owner Mrs. Joan Payson, who had died on Octo-

---

[*] Of those not previously identified in this book, Buzzie Bavasi, longtime Dodgers general manager, was president of the San Diego Padres; his son Peter was general manager of the Padres; Minor was a longtime Mets scout who lived in Long Beach; Scheffing was a Mets scout who had been replaced by McDonald as general manager in 1975; Ken Smith was a longtime New York sportswriter who became PR director of the Hall of Fame in 1976; Chuck Stevens headed the Association of Professional Baseball Players of America, which Casey served as a director; Wills was an NBC broadcaster following his 1972 retirement as a player; and Ashford, the first black umpire in the Major Leagues, was working for the Office of the Commissioner.

ber 4, the day before Casey's wake. Her memorial service would be the day after Casey's.

THE COFFIN INCLUDED FOLDED Yankee and Met uniforms.

Rod Dedeaux and Baseball Commissioner Bowie Kuhn gave eulogies. Kuhn said: "No one has a greater debt to Casey Stengel than baseball. When you think of all the things he could have been, and been outstanding at, to have him 100 percent in baseball was a wonderful thing for us. He helped us not to take ourselves too seriously. He made more fans for baseball than any other man who ever lived." Dedeaux, quoted the *Los Angeles Times*'s Jim Murray: "Well, God is certainly getting an earful tonight."

There was much laughter during the ceremony, although Billy Martin was seen crying. The night before the funeral, June Bowlin gave Billy permission to sleep in Casey's bed.

When the service concluded, Casey was buried in Forest Lawn's "Court of Freedom," with a spot reserved next to him for Edna.

ED STACK, THE SECRETARY (and future president) of the Baseball Hall of Fame, had been simultaneously contacted by Arthur Richman, the former sportswriter who was then public-relations director of the Mets, and by representatives of the Stengel family, who expressed interest in having Casey buried in Cooperstown. Richman was sure that was the place for Stengel. "We did not have any burial plots," said Stack, "and so I went out and bought four plots in the local cemetery, thinking this might happen. But the family finally decided on Glendale, feeling no one would visit the grave in Cooperstown, and we eventually used those plots for Ken Smith and his wife, and for Emmett Ashford's ashes. Afterwards, I was invited out to tour the house and claim what I wanted for the Hall. We already had some great Casey material, which he donated at the time of his induction. I put yellow stickers on everything in the house, basement to attic, and then we did the same in the pool house and the garage. There was his big black Cadillac, full of dents, as though it had been through a Demolition Derby. We arranged for a Casey exhibit and I asked the family for twenty-five thousand dollars to help ship everything to Cooperstown and to arrange for a display, which they accommodated."

The Old-Timers' Day uniform with all the team logos was among the items retrieved.

On November 4, a memorial service was held at St. Patrick's Cathedral in New York; three hundred people turned out for a forty-minute service conducted by Terence Cardinal Cooke. Kuhn read from the Book of Wisdom, Grant delivered a eulogy and Robert Merrill sang the Lord's Prayer. Mel Allen and a number of active baseball executives were present. Yogi Berra, soon to return to the Yankees as a coach after being fired by the Mets as manager during the 1975 season, was the only player in attendance.

Casey's burial place has a simple marker for him and for Edna. On the adjacent wall is a more elaborate plaque, featuring his image in a Yankee cap and jersey with crossed bats, and the inscription:

CHARLES DILLON STENGEL
'CASEY'
FOR OVER SIXTY YEARS ONE OF AMERICA'S
FOLK HEROES WHO CONTRIBUTED IMMENSELY
TO THE LORE AND LANGUAGE OF OUR
COUNTRY'S NATIONAL PASTIME, BASEBALL.
SON OF LOUIS E. AND JENNIE STENGEL
BORN KANSAS CITY, MISSOURI JULY 30, 1890
MARRIED EDNA LAWSON AUGUST 18, 1924
INDUCTED NATIONAL BASEBALL HALL OF FAME JULY 25, 1966
DIED GLENDALE, CALIFORNIA SEPTEMBER 29, 1975
"THERE COMES A TIME IN EVERY MAN'S LIFE
AND I'VE HAD PLENTY OF THEM"
CASEY STENGEL

44

LEGACY

BILLY MARTIN WAS THE only Yankee who wore a black armband in the pennant-winning season of 1976, in the newly renovated Yankee Stadium, to honor Casey.

On July 30, his birthday, the Yankees unveiled a plaque in the Monument Park section of their ballpark (one for Joe McCarthy, ordered at the same time, had been installed on April 21), which read:

CHARLES DILLON

"CASEY" STENGEL

1890–1975

BRIGHTENED BASEBALL FOR OVER 50 YEARS

WITH SPIRIT OF ETERNAL YOUTH

YANKEE MANAGER 1949–1960 WINNING

10 PENNANTS AND 7 WORLD CHAMPIONSHIPS

INCLUDING A RECORD 5 CONSECUTIVE

1949–1953

ERECTED BY

NEW YORK YANKEES

JULY 30, 1976

EDNA DIED ON FEBRUARY 3, 1978, some five years after her paralyzing stroke, and some seven years after the first signs of what was likely Alzheimer's. She was eighty-three. The conservator of her estate was her brother, John M. "Jack" Lawson.

June Bowlin, who lived with her family in the Stengel home until

Edna's death (at which point the house was sold), made the formal announcement of Edna's death. In 1981, she would marry Jack, whose first wife, Helen, had died after being burned in a fire in 1980. Jack was still chairman of Valley National Bank, But, ill with brain cancer, he died soon after his marriage to June. While he was dying in August 1981, he expressed surprise to learn that he was married. After his death, the Stengel Estate Trust was entrusted to John M. Lawson II, his son. From time to time, John was asked to donate items for charitable auctions, which he did.

Edna's surviving sister, Mae Hunter, the oldest of the four Lawson children, died in 1982.

Casey's will, drawn in 1933, had left everything to Edna.

One document in Casey's files showed a net worth of $1.3 million in 1965. But he was still making lots of money. In 1975, his final year, his tax return showed $162,678 income (equivalent to approximately $714,000 in 2016 dollars), largely from interest ($66,272), dividends ($34,485), and "other than wages" ($49,021), on top of $12,500 from the Mets, who were still paying him annually despite an earlier report of "no more."

THE DISTRIBUTION OF CASEY'S wealth passed to Edna, then to her heirs, but it made no one wealthy. It sort of got "watered down."

The furnishings were distributed throughout the family; items of unknown worth were auctioned in Los Angeles and purchased by family members.

From 1978 to 1981, the baseball memorabilia that the family then possessed was kept at the home of Jack Lawson. Upon his death in '81, it was moved to a storage facility and a safe-deposit box. (In the 1970s, few gave much thought to the possible cash value of memorabilia.) In 1996, John M. Lawson II entrusted what was left of the estate to Toni Mollett Harsh, grandniece of Casey and Edna. All business activities and memorabilia were transferred to Reno, Nevada, where she resided and served as a city councilwoman. Everything was carefully stored in a secured, temperature-controlled space.

Casey had kept a lot of cash in his home, estimated by the family at sixty thousand dollars, and he had given Mets equipment man Herb Norman (whom he called "Logan," after his old Giants equipment man, Pop Logan, circa 1921) a sack of cash (about thirty-five thousand dollars) to hold for him, but in the fog of disorder that followed his death, it was June Bowlin who got most of his memorabilia. June's stepdaughter, Sandra Waltrip, consigned the treasure chest of baseball memorabilia to Heritage Sports Collectibles for an October 2005 auction. The catalogue introduction to "The Casey Stengel Collection," ninety-five lots over twenty-seven pages of its catalogue, read: "The massive archive of material that comprises the Casey Stengel Collection comes to us through the family of the woman who cared for the Hall of Fame manager in the final years of his life. Thankfully for baseball history, and for our Heritage bidders specifically, Stengel was a tremendous 'pack rat' who seemed to throw away almost nothing, and certainly not anything with noteworthy baseball significance. . . . All pieces offered have been in the sole possession of the family of Stengel's caretaker since the passing of Casey in 1975, and are offered to the collecting public for the first time."

The auction showed that Casey did indeed save World Series programs (from as far back as 1913), the program from his 1924 European tour, old contracts, his baptismal certificate, letters sent to family members (meaning he had retrieved them at some point from their homes), a long letter from Ty Cobb, caps, Old-Timers' gifts, press pins, lineup cards (including Game Seven of the 1960 World Series), photos from dental school, and a ration coupon book from the Great War.

It was during a 2006 gathering that the heirs (descended from Edna's side of the family), first learned of the 2005 Heritage Sports Collectibles auction. At this time, there were eight beneficiaries who shared in licensing revenue and made estate decisions: John Lawson II's widow, Susie; Lynn Rossi; Toni Harsh and her brother Casey Mollett; and the four children of Ann Lawson Keller.* In 2006, three of the eight family members investigated auction houses, either to obtain an appraised value or to plan on auctioning the remaining items in Toni's possession. (Toni still uses Casey's desk from 1663 Grandview.) Sotheby's was selected to conduct an auction. Some items, including a number of cartoon art pieces, were purchased at the last minute by Toni, who decided they should be held by the family in the hopes of eventually creating a museum.

This auction took place in 2007. It included Casey's own copy of his Hall of Fame plaque (which, along with his Induction Day photos, went for $24,000), mementos from the 1955 Japan tour (including his kimono), his 1957 American League Championship gold cuff links ($72,000), a

---

* Casey Mollett, a race-car driver in the 1980s, whose real name was Charles, and Toni's son Casey Harsh, whose real name was in fact Casey, kept the name going in the family.

gold watch from Joe DiMaggio, his 1948 Pacific Coast League Championship ring, his twelve Louisville Slugger commemorative black bats from his twelve World Series ($27,000 for the lot), his Mets contracts from 1963 and 1964, his honorary 1969 Mets world-championship ring ($78,000), his 1951 Yankees World Series ring ($180,000), and a signed lineup card from the first game of the 1951 World Series, featuring Mantle and DiMaggio ($27,000).

Inspired by her visit east at the time of the auction, which included a visit to the Yogi Berra Museum in Little Falls, New Jersey, Toni created the Casey Stengel Baseball Center in 2007 "to serve as a sports based educator in team building, health and journalism."

A Board of Directors was elected, and the center proceeded to focus on educating the public on the life of Casey Stengel and his impact on baseball. A Web site, CaseyStengel.org, was created, along with a Facebook page, and the center works with the Stengel Field Foundation in seeking to restore Casey Stengel Field in Glendale.

CASEY'S POPULARITY REMAINED HIGH for a long time. Not a lot of his classic Stengelese moments lived into the YouTube age, but those that did still produced laughter.

Robert Creamer's 1984 biography of him, published nine years after his death, was very well received.

In 1996, along came Joe Torre to manage the Yankees. Like Casey, he had had mediocre results with bad National League teams, and then, suddenly, found himself rolling in the riches of talented players. His Yankee success—six American League pennants, four of them leading to world championships—thrust him into the Hall of Fame, just as it had Casey. But, whereas Casey had arrived as a "clown," Torre was greeted by a "Clueless Joe" tabloid headline. For both men, good players produced success, bad players did not. It wasn't rocket science.

Casey's work with the Mets, though, will be difficult to duplicate. Indeed, few expansion teams in any sport have tried the formula—a quotable, fan-popular man who would charm the press and deflect attention away from ineptness on the field. Today's expansion teams are better stocked with players and better able to improve their situations quickly. There may never again be a 1962 Mets.

For a long time, "You're full of shit and I'll tell you why," "Most people my age are dead at the present time," "You could look it up," "Tell 'em

I'm being embalmed," "Like Ned in the Third [or Fourth] reader," "splen-did" "commence," and other forms of Stengelese were regularly heard in press boxes. The players had their own pet expressions: "Hold the gun" was a call to hitters in the on-deck circle for whom he had decided to pinch-hit. The sportswriter Jack Lang continued to call Maury Allen and George Vecsey "Doctor" long after Casey died, since that was what he had called them. The generation that covered Casey departed those press boxes in the 1990s, leaving the younger ones to find other quotable figures.

His use of the word "amazin'" lived on with the team as a semi-official nickname. "The Amazins" was common for headline writers and still in use when the Mets won the 2015 National League pennant. Casey had helped birth the Mets by calling everything about them—the play-ers, the opponents, the new ballpark, the fans, the logo, the mascot, the writers—amazin'.

THE PROPERTY AT 1663 Grandview was sold in November 1978 to Dr. James C. Davis and his wife, Virginia, who passed it on to their daughter Cheryl. She sold it in 2012 to a Hollywood sitcom star and her husband for $1.9 million, and in 2014, the home was approved for the Glendale Register of Historic Resources as the Lawson/Stengel House.

Valley National Bank was sold to the Italian company that owned First Los Angeles Bank in 1987, and then to Wells Fargo Bank in 1989. The oil wells in Texas keep producing small annual checks for the eight family heirs. Casey's oil holdings produced $1,968 for him in 1965, and then it fell below a thousand dollars annually.

A youth league called the Casey Stengel League, for the age group just above Babe Ruth League baseball, flourished for a time. The New York chapter of the Society of American Baseball Research named itself the Casey Stengel Chapter. The Casey Stengel You-Could-Look-It-Up Award remained a staple of the New York Baseball Writers' Dinner.

A one-man play called *The Amazin' Casey Stengel or Can't Anybody Here Speak This Game?*—starring Paul Dooley—ran off-Broadway for thirteen performances in 1981, and a PBS special, *Casey Stengel*, starring Charles Durning, aired on May 6, 1981.

Stengel Field in Glendale, showing its age, was condemned and then demolished in July 2015, though a campaign was established to rebuild it. In its final years, it was home to Crescenta Valley High School and Glendale Community College teams, along with Little League and Babe Ruth League programs and high school graduations. The final game played at the facility was a local Babe Ruth League championship in May 2015.

THE CASEY STENGEL DEPOT, a transportation building near Shea Stadium, houses New York City buses. Shea Stadium was torn down and replaced by Citi Field in 2009, but Casey lives on there in the Mets Hall of Fame and with his retired number above the left-field seats. The area outside Gate E is called Casey Stengel Plaza. In 2014, the Mets celebrated Fan Appreciation Day by giving out Casey Stengel bobbleheads. Toni Harsh threw out the ceremonial first pitch. The demolition of Shea brought down the final regular-season ballpark that Casey had called home as a player or a manager.[*]

The noted American sculptor Rhoda Sherbell, created a forty-three-inch bronze of Casey, hands tucked into the back pockets of his Mets uniform, and castings are on display at the Smithsonian Institution's National Portrait Gallery, the Baseball Hall of Fame, the University Place Hotel at the Indiana University–Purdue University campus in Indianapolis, and the outdoor sculpture collection at Hofstra University. Casey posed for the artist (to much teasing from his players) in 1965, and he gave her a Mets uniform, complete with socks and shoes, to work from. The ones on display indoors include his Mets uniform, painted on; the ones displayed outdoors are bronze without the paint.

In Cooperstown, his plaque is among those most photographed by visitors.

PHIL JACKSON, THE GREAT NBA coach, grew up a Yankees fan in Montana.

> We got the Yankees on the radio, and my uncles and my father would crowd around the car radio to pull it in. That was around 1953, so, naturally, I became a Casey Stengel fan, too.
> He always got the media on his side. That was in my head. Sometimes I'd give an answer and I'd say to myself, "I think I said

---

[*] A portion of Braves Field in Boston exists as Nickerson Field, where Boston University plays its home football games.

that in Stengelese." And I've been accused of using the press to get a message to a player. I was probably channeling Casey when I did that.

He kept egos in check with a sense of humor, and I thought about the way he kept things light, kept things on an even keel.

YOGI BERRA DIED AT ninety in 2015, forty years after Casey, and the many tributes to him were, of necessity, largely tributes to Casey as well, and the roles they played in each other's lives. There would be no new Yogi-isms and no more Stengelese in the English language.

WHEN CASEY MANAGED, IT was said he was mentored by McGraw and, to some extent, Wilbert Robinson. When Billy Martin managed, it was said he was emulating Stengel. Today, there is no one who manages in the style of Stengel, because of the scientific use of situational statistics (Casey used them from instinct and memory), and the use of replays over disputed calls, which keeps managers in the dugout and prevents them from charging up their players with fiery arguments.

Platooning lives on, however, since it is based on the statistics that show who does best against whom; in fact, it is so widespread as to be no longer considered a Casey Stengel innovation or tool. And, of course, it wasn't his innovation; he just had the abundance of players to work with, and he made it popular.

IN 2009, THE MLB Network introduced a series called *Prime 9* in which they rated many areas of the game, such as best right fielder, rookie season, unbreakable records, and so forth. On the category they called "Characters of the Game," the third episode in the series, Casey Stengel finished first, beating out such people as Yogi Berra, Babe Ruth, Dizzy Dean, Leo Durocher, Satchel Paige . . . Well, he beat everyone in baseball history, some sixteen thousand people.

It was forty-four years since he had last worn a uniform, but it still rang true.

APPENDIX 1

CONGRESSIONAL RECORD
JULY 9, 1958

Casey Stengel, Mickey Mantle
Abridged

SENATOR KEFAUVER: Mr. Stengel, you are the manager of the New York Yankees. Will you give us very briefly your background and your views about this legislation?

MR. STENGEL: Well, I started in professional ball in 1910. I have been in professional ball, I would say, for forty-eight years. I have been employed by numerous ball clubs in the majors and in the minor leagues. I started in the minor leagues with Kansas City. I played as low as Class D ball, which was at Shelbyville, Kentucky, and also Class C ball and Class A ball, and I have advanced in baseball as a ball player. I had many years I was not so successful as a ball player, as it is a game of skill. And then I was no doubt discharged by baseball in which I had to go back to the minor leagues as a manager, and after being in the minor leagues as a manager, I became a major league manager in several cities and was discharged, we call it discharged because there was no question I had to leave. And I returned to the minor leagues at Milwaukee, Kansas City and Oakland, California, and then returned to the major leagues.

In the last ten years, naturally, in major-league baseball with the New York Yankees; the New York Yankees have had tremendous success, and while I am not a ballplayer who does the work, I have no doubt worked for a ball club that is very capable in the office. I have been up and down the ladder. I know there are some things in baseball thirty-five to fifty years ago that are better now than they were in those days.

In those days, my goodness, you could not transfer a ball club in the minor leagues, Class D, Class C ball, Class A ball. How could you transfer a ball club when you did not have a highway? How could you transfer a ball club when the railroad then would take you to a town, you got off and then you had to wait and sit up five hours to go to another ball club? How could you run baseball then without night ball? You had to have night ball to improve the proceeds, to pay larger salaries, and I went to work, the first year I received $135 a month. I thought that was amazing. I had to put away enough money to go to dental college. I found out it was not better in dentistry. I stayed in baseball. Any other question you would like to ask me?

SENATOR KEFAUVER: Mr. Stengel, are you prepared to answer particularly why baseball wants this bill passed?

MR. STENGEL: Well, I would have to say at the present time, I think that baseball has advanced in this respect for the player help. That is an amazing statement for me to make, because you can retire with an annuity at fifty and what organization in America allows you to retire at fifty and receive money? I want to further state that I am not a ballplayer, that is, put into that pension fund committee. At my age, and I have been in baseball, well, I will say I am possibly the oldest man who is working in baseball. I would say that when they start an annuity for the ballplayers to better their conditions, it should have been done, and I think it has been done. I think it should be the way they have done it, which is a very good thing.

The reason they possibly did not take the managers in at that time was because radio and television or the income to ball clubs was not large enough that you could have put in a pension plan. Now, I am not a member of the pension plan. You have young men here who are, who represent the ball clubs. They represent the players and since I am not a member and don't receive pension from a fund which you think, my goodness, he ought to be declared that, too, but I would say that is a great thing for the ballplayers. That is one thing I will say for ballplayers, they have an advanced pension fund. I should think it was gained by radio and television or you could not have enough money to pay anything of that type.

Now the second thing about baseball that I think is very interesting to the public or to all of us that it is the owner's own fault if he does not improve his club, along with the officials in the ball club and the players. Now what causes that? If I am going to go on the road and we are a traveling ball club and you know the cost of transportation now—we travel sometimes with three Pullman coaches, the New York Yankees and remember I am just a salaried man, and do not own stock in the New York Yankees. I found out that in traveling with the New York Yankees on the road and all, that is the best, and we have broken records in Washington this year, we have broken them in every city but New York and we have lost two clubs that have gone out of the city of New York. Of course, we have had some bad weather, I would say that they are mad at us in Chicago, we fill the parks. They have come out to see good material. I will say they are mad at us in Kansas City, but we broke their attendance record.

Now on the road we only get possibly 27 cents. I am not positive of these figures, as I am not an official. If you go back fifteen years or so if I owned stock in the club I would give them to you.

SENATOR KEFAUVER: Mr. Stengel, I am not sure that I made my question clear.

MR. STENGEL: Yes, sir. Well, that is all right. I am not sure if I am going to answer yours perfectly, either.

SENATOR O'MAHONEY: How many minor leagues were there in baseball when you began?

MR. STENGEL: Well, there were not so many at that time because of this fact: Anybody to go into baseball at that time with the educational schools that we had were small, while you were probably thoroughly educated at school, you had to be —we only had small cities that you could put a team in and they would go defunct.

Why, I remember the first year I was at Kankakee, Illinois and a bank offered me $550 if I would let them have a little notice. I left there and took a uniform because they owed me two weeks' pay. But I either had to quit but I did not have enough money to go to dental college so I had to go with the manager down to Kentucky. What happened there was if you got by July, that was the big date. You did not play night ball and you did not play Sundays in half of the cities on account of a Sunday observance, so in those days when things were tough, and all of it was, I mean to say, why they just closed up July 4 and there you were sitting in the depot. You could go to work someplace else, but that was it. So I got out of Kankakee, Illinois, and I just go there for a visit now.

SENATOR CARROLL: The question Senator Kefauver asked you was what, in your honest opinion, with your forty-eight years of experience, is the need for this legislation in view of the fact that baseball has not been subject to antitrust laws?

MR. STENGEL: No.

SENATOR LANGER: Mr. Chairman, my final question. This is the Anti-monopoly Committee that is sitting here.

MR. STENGEL: Yes, sir.

SENATOR LANGER: I want to know whether you intend to keep on monopolizing the world's championship in New York City.

MR. STENGEL: Well, I will tell you. I got a little concern yesterday in the first three innings when I saw the three players I had gotten rid of. I said when I lost nine what am I going to do and when I had a couple of my players I thought so great of that did not do so good up to the sixth inning I was more confused but I finally had to go and call on a young man in Baltimore that we don't own and the Yankees don't own him, and he is doing pretty good, and I would actually have to tell you that I think we are more the Greta Garbo type now from success.

We are being hated, I mean, from the ownership and all, we are being hated. Every sport that gets too great or one individual—but if we made 27 cents and it pays to have a winner at home, why would not you have a good winner in your own park if you were an owner? That is the result of baseball. An owner gets most of the money at home and it is up to him and his staff to do better or they ought to be discharged.

SENATOR KEFAUVER: Thank you very much, Mr. Stengel. We appreciate your presence here. Mr. Mickey Mantle, will you come around? . . . Mr. Mantle, do you have any observations with reference to the applicability of the antitrust laws to baseball?

MR. MANTLE: My views are about the same as Casey's.

APPENDIX 2

CAREER STATISTICS

Career Statistics as a Player

Year	Team	League	G	AB	R	H	2B	3B	HR	RBI	SB	BB	SO	AVG
1910	Kankakee	NORA	59	203		51	7	1	1					.251
1910	Shelbyville/ Maysville	BLGR	69	233		52	10	5	2					.237
1910	Kansas City	AA	4	11		3	1	0	0					.273
1911	Aurora	WIIL	121	420		148	23	6	4					.352
1912	Montgomery	SOU	136	479		139	20	13	1					.290
1912	Brooklyn	NL	17	57	9	18	1	0	1	13	5	15	9	.316
1913	Brooklyn	NL	124	438	60	119	16	8	7	43	10	56	58	.272
1914	Brooklyn	NL	126	412	55	130	13	10	4	60	19	56	55	.316
1915	Brooklyn	NL	132	459	52	109	20	12	3	50	5	34	46	.237
1916	Brooklyn	NL	127	462	66	129	27	8	8	53	11	33	51	.279
1917	Brooklyn	NL	150	549	69	141	23	12	6	73	18	60	62	.257
1918	Pittsburgh	NL	39	122	18	30	4	1	1	12	11	16	14	.246
1919	Pittsburgh	NL	89	321	38	94	10	10	4	43	12	35	35	.293
1920	Philadelphia	NL	129	445	53	130	25	6	0	50	7	38	35	.292
1921	Philadelphia	NL	24	59	7	18	3	1	0	4	1	6	7	.305
1921	New York	NL	18	22	4	5	1	0	0	2	0	1	5	.227
1922	New York	NL	84	250	48	92	8	10	7	48	4	21	17	.368
1923	New York	NL	75	218	39	74	11	5	5	43	6	20	18	.339
1924	Boston	NL	131	461	57	129	20	6	5	39	13	45	39	. 280
1925	Boston	NL	12	13	0	1	0	0	0	2	0	1	2	.077
1925	Worcester	EL	100	334		101	27	2	10					.302
1926	Toledo	AA	88	201		66	14	2	0					.328
1927	Toledo	AA	18	17		3	0	0	1					.176
1928	Toledo	AA	26	32	5	14	5	0	0		0			.438
1929	Toledo	AA	20	31		7	1	1	0					.226
1931	Toledo	AA	3	11		4	2	0	0					.364
	MLB Totals		1277	4288	575	1219	182	89	60	535	131	437	453	.284

Source: Baseball-Reference.com

Appendix 2

Career Statistics as a Manager

Year	Team	League	Position	Won	Lost	World Series
1925	Worcester	EL	3	70	55	
1926	Toledo	AA	4	87	77	
1927	Toledo	AA	1	101	67	def. Buffalo 5–1 (Little World Series)
1928	Toledo	AA	6	79	88	
1929	Toledo	AA	8	67	100	
1930	Toledo	AA	3	88	66	
1931	Toledo	AA	8	68	100	
1934	Brooklyn	NL	6	71	81	
1935	Brooklyn	NL	5	70	83	
1936	Brooklyn	NL	7	67	87	
1938	Boston	NL	5	77	75	
1939	Boston	NL	7	63	88	
1940	Boston	NL	7	65	87	
1941	Boston	NL	7	62	92	
1942	Boston	NL	7	59	89	
1943	Boston	NL	6	68	85	
1944	Milwaukee	AA	1	91	49	
1945	Kansas City	AA	7	65	86	
1946	Oakland	PCL	2	111	72	lost San Francisco 4–2 (Governor's Cup)
1947	Oakland	PCL	4	96	90	lost Los Angeles 4–1 (Governor's Cup)
1948	Oakland	PCL	1	114	74	def. Seattle 4–1 (Governor's Cup)
1949	New York	AL	1	97	57	def. Brooklyn 4–1
1950	New York	AL	1	98	56	def. Philadelphia 4–0
1951	New York	AL	1	98	56	def. New York 4–2
1952	New York	AL	1	95	59	def. Brooklyn 4–3
1953	New York	AL	1	99	52	def. Brooklyn 4–2
1954	New York	AL	2	103	51	
1955	New York	AL	1	96	58	lost Brooklyn 4–3
1956	New York	AL	1	97	57	def. Brooklyn 4–3
1957	New York	AL	1	98	56	lost Milwaukee 4–3
1958	New York	AL	1	92	62	def. Milwaukee 4–3
1959	New York	AL	3	79	75	
1960	New York	AL	1	97	57	lost Pittsburgh 4–3
1962	New York	NL	10	40	120	
1963	New York	NL	10	51	111	
1964	New York	NL	10	53	109	
1965	New York	NL	10	31	64	

Source: Baseball-Reference.com

ACKNOWLEDGMENTS

Toni Mollett Harsh made Edna Stengel's unpublished memoir, written in 1958, available and also spent countless time taking us through the Lawson and Stengel families. Bob Case, who worked for Casey in his retirement years, gave us many hours of reflection and recall. To those two, we are especially grateful for helping bring out the full Casey Stengel story.

Thanks as well to Michael McCoy for making available the unpublished memoir of Frank Crosetti, Casey's coach on the Yankees during his entire managerial career there.

From those who granted interviews, thank you to Janet Allen (for her memories of her husband Maury); Craig Anderson; Dave Anderson; Yogi Berra; Ann Branca; Ralph Branca; Dr. Bobby Brown; Chris Cannizzaro; Joe Carrieri; Fred Claire; Roger Craig; Justin Dedeaux (for his memories of his father, Ron); Art Ditmar; Whitey Ford; Hank and Liz Goldberg (for their memories of their father, Hy); Steve Greenberg (for memories of his father, Hank); Jane and Michael Gross (for memories of their father, Milton); Jay Hook; Arlene Howard (and for her memories of her husband, Elston); Monte Irvin; Phil Jackson; Steve Jacobson; Dave Kaplan; Ed Kranepool; Tony Kubek; Craig, Randy, and Victoria Lang (for memories of their father, Jack); Doug and Jeffrey Lyons (for memories of their father, Leonard); Ken MacKenzie; Joe McDonald; Irv Noren; Phil Pepe; Dan Reilly; Bobby Richardson; Martha Richman (for the memories of her husband, Arthur); Lynn Rossi; Bobby Shantz; Rhoda Sherbell; Norm Sherry; Charlie Silvera; Ron Swoboda; George Vecsey; Bill Virdon; Bill Wakefield; Matt Winick; and Bob Wolff.

For support or research assistance, appreciation goes to Dom Amore, Brian Appel, Deb Appel, Lourdes Appel, Norm Appel, Ron Bailey, Peter Bavasi, Darrell Berger, Ira Berkow, Hal Bock, Robert Brady,

Alana Pashon Case, Bob Chandler, Jim Charlton, Bill Chuck, Dennis D'Agostino, Jack Danzis, Joe Donnelly, Jerry Eskanazi, Steve Gietschier, Jane Hamilton, Chip Hider, Anne Gifford Jenkins, Dick Johnson, Lloyd Johnson, George Kalinsky, Lana Barcham Kaufman, Mark Langill, Jane Leavy, Marc Levine, Robert Lipsyte, Byron Magrane, Lauren Manning, David Margolick, Ryan McMahon, Fred McMane, Leigh Montville, Gene Morgan, Craig Muder, Kay Murcer, Ray Nemec, Ray Robinson, Jeff Roth, Matt Rothenberg, Frank Russo, Zach Sanzone, Al Silverman, Ed Stack, Andy Strasberg, John Thorn, Tom Tobar, Tom Villante, my agent Rob Wilson, and the team at Doubleday—Jason Kaufman, Rob Bloom, Bill Thomas, Maria Massey, Michael Goldsmith, and John Pitts.

I also wish to thank the sports writing community of 1910–75, for their reporting and collective contributions to the contents of this book, especially Fred Lieb, and the ballplayer Roger Peckinpaugh for audio interviews granted to me in the early 1970s.

BIBLIOGRAPHY

BOOKS

Adler, Bill, and George Price. *Love Letters to the Mets.* New York: Simon & Schuster, 1965.

Alexander, Charles. *Ty Cobb.* New York: Oxford University Press, 1984.

Allen, Lee. *The American League Story.* New York: Hill & Wang, 1962.

———. *The Hot Stove League.* New York: Barnes and Co., 1955.

———. *100 Years of Baseball.* New York: Bartholomew House, 1950.

———. *The World Series.* New York: Putnam's Sons, 1969.

Allen, Maury. *Now Wait a Minute, Casey!* Garden City, N.Y.: Doubleday, 1965.

———. *Roger Maris: A Man for All Seasons.* New York: Donald J. Fine, 1986.

———. *You Could Look It Up.* New York: Times Books, 1979.

Allen, Mel, and Ed Fitzgerald. *You Can't Beat the Hours.* New York: Harper & Row, 1964.

Anderson, Dave, Murray Chass, Robert Lipsyte, Buster Olney, and George Vecsey. *The New York Yankees Illustrated History.* New York: St. Martin's Press, 2002.

Antonucci, Thomas J., and Eric Caren. *Big League Baseball in the Big Apple: The New York Yankees.* Verplank, N.Y.: Historical Briefs, 1995.

Appel, Marty. *Baseball's Best: The Hall of Fame Gallery.* New York: McGraw-Hill, 1977.

———. *Joe DiMaggio.* New York: Chelsea House, 1990.

———. *Pinstripe Empire.* New York: Bloomsbury, 2012.

———. *Now Pitching for the Yankees: Spinning the News for Mickey, Billy and George.* Kingston, N.Y.: Total Sports, 2001.

———. *162-0.* Chicago: Triumph, 2010.

Appel, Marty, and Jeffrey Krebs. "Let's Go Mets." Unpublished manuscript, 1963.

Bak, Richard. *Casey Stengel: A Splendid Baseball Life.* Dallas: Taylor, 1997.

Barra, Allen. *Yogi Berra: Eternal Yankee.* New York: Norton, 2009.

Barzilai, Peter, Stephen Borelli, and Gabe Lacques. *Yankee Stadium.* McLean, Va.: USA Today Sports Weekly, 2008.

Berkow, Ira, and Jim Kaplan. *The Gospel According to Casey.* New York: St. Martin's Press, 1992.

Berra, Yogi, and Ed Fitzgerald. *Yogi: The Autobiography of a Professional Baseball Player.* Garden City, N.Y.: Doubleday, 1961.

Berra, Yogi, and Tom Horton. *Yogi: It Ain't Over.* New York: McGraw-Hill, 1989.

Berra, Yogi, and Dave Kaplan. *Ten Rings: My Championship Seasons.* New York: Morrow, 2003.

Bjarkman, Peter C. *Encyclopedia of Major League Baseball Team Histories: American League.* Westport, Conn.: Meckler, 1991.

Blauner, Andrew, ed. *Coach.* New York: Warner Books, 2005.

Borelli, Stephen. *How About That! The Life of Mel Allen.* Champaign, Ill.: Sports Publishing, 2005.

Breslin, Jimmy. *Can't Anybody Here Play This Game?* New York: Viking, 1963.

Brown, A. Theodore, and Lyle W. Dorsett. *K.C.: A History of Kansas City, Missouri.* Boulder, Colo.: Pruett Publishing Co., 1978.

Burns, Robert. *50 Golden Years of Sports.* St. Louis, Mo.: Rawlings, 1948.

Cannon, Jimmy. *Nobody Asked Me, But . . . : The World of Jimmy Cannon.* New York: Holt, Rinehart and Winston, 1978.

Cantaneo, David. *Casey Stengel: Baseball's "Old Professor."* Nashville, Tenn.: Cumberland House, 2003.

Carmichael, John P. *My Greatest Day in Baseball.* New York: Barnes & Co., 1945.

Carrieri, Joe, as told to Zander Hollander. *Yankee Batboy.* New York: Prentice Hall, 1955.

Castro, Tony. *Mickey Mantle: America's Prodigal Son.* Dulles, Va.: Potomac Books, 2002.

Chadwick Dean. *Those Damn Yankees: The Secret Life of America's Greatest Franchise.* New York: Verso, 1999.

Coates, Jim, with Douglas Williams. *Always a Yankee.* West Conshohocken, Pa.: Infinity Publishing, 2009.

Cramer, Richard Ben. *DiMaggio: The Hero's Life.* New York: Simon & Schuster, 2000.

Creamer, Robert W. *Babe: The Legend Comes to Life.* New York: Simon & Schuster, 1974.

————. *Baseball in '41*. New York: Penguin, 1991.

————. *Stengel: His Life and Times*. New York: Simon & Schuster, 1984.

Crosetti, Frank. Unpublished memoir, n.d.

Daley, Arthur. *Times at Bat*. New York: Random House, 1950.

Danzig, Allison, and Joe Reichler. *The History of Baseball*. Englewood Cliffs, N.J.: Prentice Hall, 1959.

DeVito, Carlo. *Scooter: The Biography of Phil Rizzuto*. Chicago: Triumph, 2010.

————. *Yogi. The Life & Times of an American Original*. Chicago: Triumph, 2008.

Dickson, Paul. *The Dickson Baseball Dictionary*. New York: Facts on File, 1989.

DiMaggio, Joe. *Lucky to Be a Yankee*. Revised edition. New York: Grosset & Dunlap, 1957.

Durant, John. *The Yankees: A Pictorial History of Baseball's Greatest Club*. New York: Hastings House, 1950.

Duren, Ryne. *The Comeback*. Dayton, Ohio: Lorenz Press, 1978.

Duren, Ryne, with Tom Sabellico. *I Can See Clearly Now*. Chula Vista, Calif.: Aventine Press, 2003.

Durocher, Leo, and Ed Linn. *Nice Guys Finish Last*. New York: Simon & Schuster, 1975.

Durso, Joseph. *Casey: The Life and Legend of Charles Dillon Stengel*. Englewood Cliffs, N.J.: Prentice Hall, 1967.

————. *Casey & Mr. McGraw*. St. Louis, Mo.: The Sporting News, 1989.

Epting, Chris. *The Early Polo Grounds*. Charleston, S.C.: Arcadia Publishing, 2009.

Eskenazi, Gerald. *The Lip: A Biography of Leo Durocher*. New York: Morrow, 1993.

Falkner, David. *The Last Yankee: The Turbulent Life of Billy Martin*. New York: Simon & Schuster, 1992.

Fischer, David. *A Yankee Stadium Scrapbook*. Philadelphia: Running Press, 2008.

Fitzgerald, Ed, ed. *The Book of Major League Baseball Clubs: The American League*. New York: Barnes & Co., 1952.

————. *The Book of Major League Baseball Clubs: The National League*. New York: Barnes & Co., 1952.

Fleitz, David. *Ghosts in the Gallery at Cooperstown*. Jefferson, N.C.: McFarland & Company, 2004.

Ford, Whitey, Mickey Mantle, and Joe Durso. *Whitey and Mickey: An Autobiography of the Yankee Years*. New York: Viking, 1977.

Ford, Whitey, with Phil Pepe. *Slick: My Life in and Around Baseball*. New York: Morrow, 1987.

Forker, Dom. *The Men of Autumn. An Oral History of the 1949–53 World Champion New York Yankees*. Dallas: Taylor Publishing, 1989.

———. *Sweet Seasons: Recollections of the 1955–64 New York Yankees*. Dallas: Taylor Publishing, 1990.

Frommer, Harvey. *A Yankee Century*. New York: Berkley, 2002.

———. *The New York Yankee Encyclopedia*. New York: Macmillan, 1997.

Fuchs, Robert S., and Wayne Soini. *Judge Fuchs and the Boston Braves*. Jefferson, N.C.: McFarland & Company, 1998.

Gallagher, Mark. *Day by Day in New York Yankees History*. New York: Leisure Press, 1983.

———. *Explosion! Mickey Mantle's Legendary Home Runs*. New York: Arbor House, 1987.

Gallagher, Mark, and Walter LeConte. *The Yankee Encyclopedia*. Fourth edition. Champaign, Ill.: Sports Publishing, 2000.

Gallo, Bill, with Phil Cornell. *Drawing a Crowd: Bill Gallo's Greatest Sports Moments*. Middle Village, N.Y.: Jonathan David Publishers, 2000.

Gentile, Derek. *The Complete New York Yankees: The Total Encyclopedia of the Team*. New York: Black Dog & Leventhal, 2001.

Gershman, Michael. *Diamond: The Evolution of the Ballpark*. New York: Houghton Mifflin, 1993.

Goldman, Steven. *Forging Genius: The Making of Casey Stengel*. Dulles, Va.: Potomac Books, 2005.

Golenbock, Peter. *Dynasty: New York Yankees 1949–1964*. Englewood Cliffs, N.J.: Prentice Hall, 1975.

Graham, Frank. *McGraw of the Giants*. New York: Putnam's Sons, 1944.

———. *The New York Giants*. New York: Putnam's Sons, 1952.

———. *The New York Yankees: An Informal History*. New York: Putnam's Sons, 1943.

Graham, Frank, Jr., *Casey Stengel: His Half-Century in Baseball*. New York: John P. Day Co., 1958.

———. *A Farewell to Heroes*. New York: Viking, 1981.

Grimm, Charlie, with Ed Prell. *Grimm's Baseball Tales*. Notre Dame, Ind.: Diamond Communications, 1983.

Halberstam, David. *Summer of '49*. New York: Morrow, 1989.

Henrich, Tommy, and Bill Gilbert. *Five o'Clock Lightning*. New York: Birch Lane, 1992.

Hermalyn, Gary, and Anthony C. Greene. *Yankee Stadium: 1923–2008.* Charleston, S.C.: Arcadia Publishing, 2009.

Holtzman, Jerome. *No Cheering in the Press Box.* Revised and expanded. New York: Henry Holt, 1995.

Honig, Donald. *The New York Yankees.* Revised edition. New York: Crown, 1987.

Howard, Arlene, with Ralph Wimbish. *Elston and Me: The Story of the First Black Yankee.* Columbia: University of Missouri Press, 2001.

Jackson, John. *New York Yankees: Unofficial Yearbooks.* New York: Jay Publishing, 1956–65.

James, Bill. *The New Bill James Historical Baseball Abstract.* Revised edition. New York: Free Press, 2001.

Johnson, Harold (Speed). *Who's Who in Major League Baseball.* Chicago: Buxton Publishing, 1933.

Kahn, Roger. *October Men.* New York: Harcourt, 2003.

Kavanagh, Jack, and Norman Macht. *Uncle Robbie.* Cleveland: Society for American Baseball Research, 1999.

Koppett, Leonard. *The New York Mets: The Whole Story.* New York: Macmillan, 1970.

Larsen, Don, and Mark Shaw. *The Perfect Yankee.* Champaign, Ill.: Sports Publishing, 1996.

Leavy, Jane. *The Last Boy.* New York: HarperCollins, 2010.

Lieb, Fred. *The Baseball Story.* New York: Putnam's Sons, 1950.

Lieb, Fred, with Bob Burnes, J. G. Taylor Spink, and Les Biederman. *Comedians and Pranksters of Baseball.* St. Louis, Mo.: Charles C. Spink & Son, 1958.

Light, Jonathan Fraser. *The Cultural Encyclopedia of Baseball.* Jefferson, N.C.: McFarland & Company, 1997.

———. *The Cultural Encyclopedia of Baseball.* Second edition. Jefferson, N.C.: McFarland & Company, 2005.

Lipsyte, Robert. *SportsWorld: An American Dreamland.* New York: Quadrangle, 1975.

Mack, Connie (Cornelius McGillicuddy). *My 66 Years in the Big Leagues.* Philadelphia. John C. Winston Co., 1950.

MacPhail, Lee, with Marty Appel. *My Nine Innings.* Westport, Conn.: Meckler, 1989.

Mann, Jack. *The Decline and Fall of the New York Yankees.* New York: Simon & Schuster, 1967.

Mantle, Merlyn, Mickey Mantle Jr., David Mantle, and Dan Mantle, with
    Mickey Herskowitz. *A Hero All His Life: A Memoir by the Mantle Family.*
    New York: HarperCollins, 1996.

Mantle, Mickey, with Herb Gluck. *The Mick.* New York: Doubleday, 1985.

Mantle, Mickey, with Mickey Herskowitz. *All My Octobers: My Memories of
    Twelve World Series When the Yankees Ruled Baseball.* New York: Har-
    perCollins, 1994.

Maris, Roger, and Jim Ogle. *Roger Maris at Bat.* New York: Meredith Press,
    1962.

Martin, Billy, with Phil Pepe. *Billyball.* New York: Doubleday, 1987.

Mayer, Ronald. *The 1923 New York Yankees.* Jefferson, N.C.: McFarland &
    Company, 2010.

McGraw, John J. *My Thirty Years in Baseball.* New York: Bovi & Liveright,
    1923.

McGraw, Mrs. John J. *The Real McGraw.* New York: David McKay, 1953.

McMane, Fred. *Quotable Casey.* Nashville, Tenn.: TowleHouse Publishing,
    2002.

Mead, William B., and Harold Rosenthal. *The 10 Worst Years of Baseball.* New
    York: Van Nostrand Reinhold, 1978.

Meany, Tom. *Babe Ruth.* New York: Barnes & Co., 1951.

———. *Baseball's Greatest Teams.* New York: Barnes and Co., 1949.

———. *The Magnificent Yankees.* Revised edition. New York: Barnes and Co.,
    1957.

———. *The Yankee Story.* New York: Dutton & Co., 1960.

Mitchell, Jerry. *The Amazing Mets.* New York: Grosset & Dunlap, 1964.

Montville, Leigh. *Ted Williams.* New York: Doubleday, 2004.

Nash, Bruce, and Allan Zullo. *The Baseball Hall of Shame 3.* New York: Pocket
    Books, 1987.

———. *The Baseball Hall of Shame 4.* New York: Pocket Books, 1990.

———. *The Baseball Hall of Shame's Warped Record Book.* New York: Col-
    lier, 1991.

Neft, David, and Richard Cohen. *The World Series.* New York: St. Martin's,
    1990.

Neft, David, Richard Cohen, and Michael Neft. *The Sports Encyclopedia:
    Baseball.* Twenty-third edition. New York: St. Martin's Griffin, 2003.

Nelson, Lindsey, with Al Hirshberg. *Backstage at the Mets.* New York: Viking,
    1966.

New York Yankees. *Play Ball with the Yankees.* Bronx, N.Y.: New York Yan-
    kees, 1952.

Nowlin, Bill, and Bob Brady. *Braves Field: Moments at Boston's Lost Diamond.* Phoenix, Ariz.: Society for American Baseball Research, Inc., 2015.

O'Neal, Bill. *The American Association, 1902–1991.* Austin, Texas: Eakin Press, 1991.

———. *The Pacific Coast League 1903–1988.* Austin, Texas: Eakin Press, 1990.

O'Toole, Andrew. *Strangers in the Bronx.* Chicago: Triumph, 2015.

Paper, Lew. *Perfect.* New York: New American Library, 2009.

Peary, Danny, ed. *Cult Baseball Players: The Greats, the Flakes, the Weird and the Wonderful.* New York: Fireside, 1990.

———. *Jackie Robinson in Quotes.* Salem, Mass.: Page Street, 2016.

Pennington, Bill. *Billy Martin: Baseball's Flawed Genius.* New York: Houghton Mifflin Harcourt, 2015.

Peterson, John E. *The Kansas City Athletics: A Baseball History, 1954–1967.* Jefferson, N.C.: McFarland & Company, 2003.

Pitoniak, Scott. *Memories of Yankee Stadium.* Chicago: Triumph, 2008.

Povich, Shirley. *The Washington Senators.* New York: Putnam's Sons, 1954.

Powers, Jimmy. *Baseball Personalities.* New York: Rudolph Field, 1949.

Prudenti, Frank. *Memories of a Yankee Batboy 1956–1961.* New York: Pru Publications, 2003.

Rice, Grantland. *The Tumult and the Shouting: My Life in Sport.* New York: Barnes & Co., 1954.

Richardson, Bobby. *The Bobby Richardson Story.* Westwood, N.J.: Fleming H. Revell, 1965.

Ritter, Lawrence. *The Glory of Their Times.* New York: Macmillan, 1966.

Rizzuto, Phil, and Al Silverman. *The "Miracle" New York Yankees.* New York: Coward-McCann, 1962.

Robinson, Ray, and Christopher Jennison. *Pennants and Pinstripes.* New York: Viking Studio, 2002.

———. *Yankee Stadium: 75 Years of Drama, Glamor, and Glory.* New York: Penguin Studio, 1998.

Rosenfeld, Harvey. *Roger Maris: A Title to Fame.* Fargo, N.D.: Prairie House, 1991.

Rosenthal, Harold. *Baseball Is Their Business.* New York: Random House, 1952.

———. *Baseball's Best Managers.* New York: Bartholemew House, 1961.

Salant, Nathan. *This Date in New York Yankees History.* Revised edition. New York: Stein & Day, 1983.

Schnakenberg, Robert. *The Underground Baseball Encyclopedia.* Chicago: Triumph, 2010.

Schoor, Gene. *Mickey Mantle of the Yankees.* New York: Putnam's Sons, 1958.

———. *The Thrilling Story of Joe DiMaggio.* New York: Frederick Fell, 1950.

Selter, Ronald M. *Ballparks of the Deadball Era.* Jefferson, N.C.: McFarland & Company, 2008.

Seymour, Harold, and Dorothy Mills Seymour. *Baseball: The Golden Age.* New York: Oxford, 1971.

Shapiro, Michael. *Bottom of the Ninth.* New York: Times Books, 2009.

Shapiro, Milton. *The Phil Rizzuto Story.* New York: Julian Messner, 1959.

Shatzkin, Mike, ed. *The Ballplayers.* New York: Morrow, 1990.

Siwoff, Seymour, ed. *The Book of Baseball Records.* New York: Elias Sports Bureau, 2015.

Slaughter, Enos, with Kevin Reid. *Country Hardball.* Greensboro, N.C.: Tudor Books, 1991.

Smith, Red. *Red Smith on Baseball: The Game's Greatest Writer on the Game's Greatest Years.* Chicago: Ivan R. Dee, 2000.

Smith, Robert. *Baseball.* New York: Simon & Schuster, 1947.

Spatz, Lyle. *New York Yankee Openers.* Jefferson, N.C.: McFarland & Company, 1997.

———. *Yankees Coming, Yankees Going.* Jefferson, N.C.: McFarland & Company, 2000.

Spatz, Lyle, and Steve Steinberg. *1921: The Yankees, the Giants, and the Battle for Baseball Supremacy in New York.* Lincoln: University of Nebraska Press, 2010.

Spink, J. G. Taylor. *Daguerreotypes.* St. Louis, Mo.: Charles C. Spink & Son, 1961.

Sporting News Editors. *Baseball: A Doubleheader Collection of Facts, Feats & Firsts.* New York: Galahad Books, 1992.

Stang, Mark, and Linda Harkness. *Baseball by the Numbers.* Lanham, Md.: Scarecrow Press, 1997.

Stengel, Casey, and Harry Paxton. *Casey at the Bat.* New York: Random House, 1962.

Stengel, Edna, with Jeane Hoffman. Unpublished memoir. 1958.

Stout, Glenn, ed. *Top of the Heap: A Yankees Collection.* Boston: Houghton Mifflin, 2003.

Stout, Glenn, and Richard A. Johnson. *Yankees Century.* New York: Houghton Mifflin, 2002.

Sugar, Bert Randolph. *The Baseball Maniac's Almanac.* Second edition. New York: Skyhorse, 2010.

Sullivan, George, and John Powers. *The Yankees: An Illustrated History*. Philadelphia: Temple University Press, 1997.

Swearingen, Randall. *A Great Teammate: The Legend of Mickey Mantle*. Champaign, Ill.: Sports Publishing, 2007.

Tan, Cecilia. *The 50 Greatest Yankee Games*. Hoboken, N.J.: John Wiley & Sons, 2005.

Tofel, Richard. *A Legend in the Making*. Chicago: Ivan R. Dee, 2002.

Trimble, Joe. *Yogi Berra*. New York: Barnes and Co., 1952.

Tullius, John. *I'd Rather Be a Yankee*. New York: Macmillan, 1986.

Turkin, Hy, S. C. Thompson, revisions by Pete Palmer. *Official Encyclopedia of Baseball*. Tenth revised edition. Cranbury, N.J.: A. S. Barnes, 1979.

Tygiel, Jules. *Baseball's Great Experiment*. New York: Oxford University Press, 1983.

Vancil, Mark, and Mark Mandrake. *One Hundred Years—New York Yankees: The Official Retrospective*. New York: Ballantine, 2002.

Vecsey, George. *Joy in Mudville*. New York: McCall, 1970.

Veeck, Bill. *The Hustler's Handbook*. New York: Putnam's Sons, 1965.

Veeck, Bill, with Ed Linn. *Veeck—As in Wreck*. New York: Putnam's Sons, 1962.

Waller, Spencer Weber, Neil B. Cohen, and Paul Finkelman. *Baseball and the American Legal Mind*. New York: Garland Publishing, 1995.

Ward, Ettie. *Courting the Yankees: Legal Essays on the Bronx Bombers*. Durham, N.C.: Carolina Academic Press, 2003.

Weinberger, Miro, and Dan Riley. *The Yankees Reader*. Boston: Houghton Mifflin, 1991.

Williams, Ted, and John Underwood. *My Turn at Bat*. New York: Simon & Schuster, 1969.

Wind, Herbert Warren. *The Gilded Age of Sport*. New York: Simon & Schuster, 1961.

ANNUAL REFERENCE GUIDES

New York Mets. Media Guides, Yearbooks, 1962–1965.

New York Yankees: Media Guides, Yearbooks, 1951–1960.

Reach's Official Base Ball Guide, 1911–40.

Society for American Baseball Research (SABR). *Baseball Research Journal*, various.

———. *The National Pastime*, various.

———. *The SABR Baseball List & Record Book*. New York: Scribner, 2007.

Spalding Official Baseball Guide. 1911–40.

Sporting News Guide. St. Louis, Mo.: Charles C. Spink & Son, various years.

Sporting News Record Book. St. Louis, Mo.: Charles C. Spink & Son, various years.

Sporting News Register. St. Louis, Mo.: Charles C. Spink & Son, various years.

WEB SITES

ballparksofbaseball.com, Baseball-almanac.com, Baseball-fever.com, Baseball hall.org, baseballlibrary.com, baseballprospectus.com, Baseball-reference.com, BioProj.SABR.org, HistoryoftheYankees.com, kansascitybaseballhistorical society.com, MLB.com, Newsday.com, NYDailynews.com, NYPost.com, NYTimes.com, Retrosheet.org, SI.com, sportsencyclopedia.com, Thebaseball page.com, Ultimateyankees.com, Wikipedia.com, Wirednewyork.com, Yankees .com.

ARCHIVAL NEWSPAPERS AND MAGAZINES

Abilene Reporter-News (Texas), *Alexandria Times-Tribune* (Elwood, Ind.), *The American* (New York), *Anderson Daily Bulletin* (Ind.), *Anniston Star* (Ala.), *Arizona Republic* (Phoenix), *Bakersfield Californian, Baseball Digest, Baseball Magazine, Baytown Sun* (Texas), *Berkshire Eagle* (Pittsfield, Mass.), *Bismarck Tribune* (N.D.), *Boston Daily Globe, Bourbon News* (Paris, Ky.), *Brandon Sun* (Manitoba), *Bridgeport Post* (Conn.), *Bridgeport Telegram* (Conn.), *Brooklyn Daily Eagle, Chicago Daily Tribune, Cincinnati Post & Times Star, Collier's, Coshocton Tribune* (Ohio), *Cumberland News* (Md.), *Daily Free Press* (Carbondale, Ill.), *Daily News* (Huntington, Pa.), *Daily News* (New York), *Daily Reporter* (Dover, Ohio), *Daily Review* (Kankakee, Ill.), *Daily Review* (Hayward, Calif.), *Daily Standard* (Sikeston, Mo.), *Daily Times* (Salisbury, Md.), *Des Plaines Herald* (Arlington Heights, Ill.), *Dixon Evening Telegraph* (Ill.), *Evening Independent* (Massillon, Ohio), *Evening Public Ledger* (Philadelphia), *Evening Review* (East Liverpool, Ohio), *Evening Tribune* (Hornell, N.Y.), *Fitchburg Sentinel* (Mass.), *Fresno Bee* (Calif.), *Hays Daily News* (Kans.), *The Herald* (New York), *Herald Tribune* (New York), *Independent Press-Telegram* (Long Beach, Calif.), *Inter Ocean* (Chicago), *Iola Register* (Kans.), *Ironwood Daily Globe* (Mich.), *The Journal* (New York), *Journal-American* (New York), *Journal News* (Hamilton, Ohio), *Kansas City Star, Kansas City Times, Lancaster Eagle-Gazette* (Ohio), *Lincoln Evening Journal* (Neb.), *Logan Daily News* (Ohio), *Los Angeles Times, Marion Star* (Ohio), *The Mirror* (New York), *Moberly Evening Democrat* (Mo.), *Moberly Monitor-Index* (Mo.), *Morning Herald* (Hagerstown, Md.), *Mount Carmel Item* (Pa.), *Mt. Sterling Advocate* (Ky.), *Mt. Vernon*

Register-News (Ill.), *Nevada State Journal* (Reno, Nev.), *New Castle Herald* (Pa.), *New York Post, The New York Times, The New Yorker, Newsday* (Long Island, N.Y.), *Odessa American* (Texas), *Ogden Standard-Examiner* (Utah), *Oshkosh Daily Northwestern* (Wis.), *The Pantograph* (Bloomington, Ill.), *Pasadena Independent* (Calif.), *Pittsburgh Post-Gazette, Portsmouth Daily Times* (Ohio), *Public Ledger* (Maysville, Ky.), *Reading Times* (Pa.), *Republican-Northwestern* (Belvidere, Ill.), *Rhinelander Daily News* (Wis.), *Salina Journal* (Kans.), *San Bernardino County Sun* (Calif.), *Sandusky Register* (Ohio), *San Francisco Examiner, Santa Cruz Sentinel* (Calif.), *The Saturday Evening Post, Sedalia Democrat* (Mo.), *Sport Magazine, SportFolio, Sports Collector's Digest, Sports Illustrated, Sporting Life, The Sporting News, The Sun* (New York), *The Telegraph* (New York), *The Telegram* (New York), *Times Herald* (Olean, N.Y.), *Times Recorder* (Zanesville, Ohio), *Traverse City Record-Eagle* (Mich.), *The Tribune* (New York), *USA Today Baseball Weekly, USA Today Sports Weekly, The World* (New York), *World Journal Tribune* (New York), *World-Telegram* and *The Sun* (New York)

AUCTION CATALOGUES
Lelands.com
Heritage
Sotheby's

NOTES
Notes of Leonard Lyons (provided by Jeffrey Lyons)

INDEX

Printed in the United States
by Baker & Taylor Publisher Services